FRANCIS T. LYNCH

EIGHTH EDITION

ACCURACY
IN FOOD
COSTING
AND
PURCH

THE
BOOK
OF YIELDS

JOHN WILEY & SONS, INC.

This book is printed on acid-free paper. ∞

Copyright © 2012, 2008, 2005 by John Wiley & Sons, Inc. All rights reserved

Published by John Wiley & Sons, Inc., Hoboken, New Jersey.
Published simultaneously in Canada.

No part of this publication may be reproduced, stored in a retrieval system, or transmitted in any form or by any means, electronic, mechanical, photocopying, recording, scanning, or otherwise, except as permitted under Section 107 or 108 of the 1976 United States Copyright Act, without either the prior written permission of the Publisher, or authorization through payment of the appropriate per-copy fee to the Copyright Clearance Center, Inc., 222 Rosewood Drive, Danvers, MA 01923, 978-750-8400, fax 978-646-8600, or on the Web at www.copyright.com. Requests to the Publisher for permission should be addressed to the Permissions Department, John Wiley & Sons, Inc., 111 River Street, Hoboken, NJ 07030, 201-748-6011, fax 201-748-6008, or online at http://www.wiley.com/go/permissions.

Limit of Liability/Disclaimer of Warranty: While the publisher and author have used their best efforts in preparing this book, they make no representations or warranties with respect to the accuracy or completeness of the contents of this book and specifically disclaim any implied warranties of merchantability or fitness for a particular purpose. No warranty may be created or extended by sales representatives or written sales materials. The advice and strategies contained herein may not be suitable for your situation. You should consult with a professional where appropriate. Neither the publisher nor author shall be liable for any loss of profit or any other commercial damages, including but not limited to special, incidental, consequential, or other damages.

Evaluation copies are provided to qualified academics and professionals for review purposes only, for use in their courses during the next academic year. These copies are licensed and may not be sold or transferred to a third party. Upon completion of the review period, please return the evaluation copy to Wiley. Return instructions and a free of charge return shipping label are available at www.wiley.com/go/returnlabel. Outside of the United States, please contact your local representative.

For general information on our other products and services, or technical support, please contact our Customer Care Department within the United States at 800-762-2974, outside the United States at 317-572-3993 or fax 317-572-4002.

Wiley also publishes its books in a variety of electronic formats. Some content that appears in print may not be available in electronic books.

For more information about Wiley products, visit our Web site at http://www.wiley.com.

Library of Congress Cataloging-in-Publication Data:

Lynch, Francis Talyn, 1943-
   The book of yields : accuracy in food costing and purchasing/Francis T. Lynch. — 8th ed.
      p. cm.
   ISBN 978-0-470-19749-3
1.   Food—Analysis—Tables. 2.   Food—Weights and measures—Tables.   I. Title.
   TX531.L9596 2010
   664'.07—dc22
                                                                    2009027775

Printed in the United States of America

SKY10047352_051223

DEDICATION

I dedicate this edition to my brother Dan Lynch and good friend Bill Cornick in appreciation for their constant friendship, helpful advice, and positive examples in living this wonderful life.

CONTENTS

ACKNOWLEDGMENTS

This edition was enhanced by a helpful group of professional and personal associates to whom I am very grateful. Certainly, my associates at John Wiley & Sons, Inc., namely, JoAnna Turtletaub, vice-president and publisher, James Metzger, editorial assistant, Richard DeLorenzo, senior production editor, Wendy Ashenberg, media editor, and Lydia Cheng, software consultant, have been key providers of guidance and encouragement.

Restaurateurs and chefs Eric Davis of the Diamondback Grill and Rob Bannwarth of Banny's Café in Sonora, California, have been particularly generous with their time and advice on day-to-day food costing and purchasing practices. Terry Renuio of Sysco Foods and Brian Johnson, also of Sysco, have provided me with additional information on current industry cost-management practices, as well as updating the wholesale prices of foods in Part II of the work.

Many food growers and producers, as well as key personnel in ethnic and organic markets in central and coastal California, provided me with information and instruction on the identification and handling of their products.

INTRODUCTION

The Book of Yields is a collection of food measurements you can use to help you cost recipes and figure out how much food to buy. Admittedly, this sort of knowledge isn't the most glamorous or exciting aspect of cookery, but knowing this information will help you be a more successful chef or food and beverage manager. Knowing yields and equivalents will help you write recipes that are fast and easy to follow, and that are accurately costed out. Why is this so important? A chef buys most food by weight (by the pound or kilogram), whereas most cooks prefer to use volume measures, such as tablespoons, cups, pints, quarts, and so on, in their recipes. It's just quicker and easier to measure a cup of sugar or a tablespoon of salt than it is to weigh everything. (That said, bakers generally do weigh most ingredients for extreme accuracy–but more on this later.)

Although it is easy to write or follow a recipe that uses volume measures, the tricky part is costing out a volume of food that you buy by weight. Why? Because a cup of one food does not weigh the same as a cup of another food. For instance, a cup of cracked pepper weighs 4 ounces, but a cup of honey weighs 12 ounces. So you have to know how many ounces of a food are in one cup in order to assign a cost to the cup of food in your recipe. *The Book of Yields* tells you what these weight-to-volume equivalents are.

To help you access this essential information easily, the chapters in Part I of *The Book of Yields* are organized according to food type; for instance, Dry Herbs and Spices and Fresh Herbs, Poultry, Meat, Seafood, Baking Products, and so on. In addition, you'll find tables for the various food categories that list food measurement facts:

- How much a volume of food weighs, such as a cup of sugar. This is called an *equivalent*.
- How much is left over after you have trimmed the food, for example, peeled carrots. This is called a *trim yield*.
- How much food was produced after cooking–boiled rice, for instance. This is called a *cooking yield*.

The Book of Yields lists the trim yields and the cooking yields for many foods. In many cases, it also tells you how much a volume of the trimmed or cooked food weighs and how many cups or pints of trimmed or cooked food you will end up with. This will enable you to cost a volume of trimmed or cooked food in recipes.

Just as important, *The Book of Yields* tells you how much food to buy! That will come in handy when you become responsible for ordering the food for your kitchen. You do not want to order too much or too little. *The Book of Yields* contains simple and easy-to-use formulas that tell you exactly how to use yields and equivalents to help you more accurately decide how much food to buy.

In Part II, the Workbook, you'll find food costing and food purchasing worksheets for all the different formulas for each type of food. They show you how to think through the process and how to do the math, step by step.

An **Instructor's Manual** (ISBN 978-0-470-25729-6) accompanies this book, and can be obtained by contacting your Wiley Sales Representative. If you don't know who your representative is, please visit www.wiley.com, click on Resources for Instructors, and click on Who's My Rep? The **Instructor's Manual** is composed of five parts:

1. Three quizzes based on *The Book of Yields* Introduction and General Measurements
2. A set of food costing exercises or quizzes for chapters 1–11
3. A section food purchasing exercises or quizzes for chapters 1–11
4. Additional information about chapters 12–15, including notes to Instructors and Additional Exercises
5. Two sets of recipe cards. One, which is partially filled in, is for use by students. The other, which is completely filled in, can be used by instructors.

A **Test Bank** for *The Book of Yields* has been specifically formatted for Respondus, an easy-to-use software for creating and managing exams that can be printed to paper or published directly to Blackboard, WebCT, Desire2Learn, eCollege, ANGEL, and other eLearning systems. Instructors who adopt *The Book of Yields* can download the **Test Bank** for free. Additional Wiley resources also can be uploaded into your LMS course at no charge. To view and access these resources and the **Test Bank,** visit www.wiley.com/college/lynch, click on the Resources for Instructors tab, then click on Instructor Companion site link.

Qualified instructors may also download an electronic version of the **Instructor's Manual** from the companion Website, at www.wiley.com/college/lynch.

NEW IN THIS EDITION

More than 200 new foods have been added to *The Book of Yields, Eighth Edition,* further expanding the scope and usefulness of this work and now including over 1,350 ingredients. Additions are particularly numerous in the lists of herbs and spices, produce, condiments, sweeteners, starches, dairy foods and beverages. These additions are more fully described as follows:

Chapter 1: Herbs and Spices. 24 new items have been added to these lists, including dried and fresh Stevia, a no-cal, herbal sweetener.

Chapter 2: Produce. 52 additional vegetable entries appear in this edition, including the juice yields enabling users to efficiently plan purchases and production of healthy drinks.

47 new foods have been added to the table of Fruits. Among these you will find more depth in the variety of general food types such as bananas, tangerines, and oranges. Candied fruits for holiday baking are now included plus the juice yields for many fruits are given, reflecting the growing trend of fresh beverage menu offerings.

Chapter 3: Starchy Foods. There are 23 new Pastas and 12 additional foods added to the list of Rice, Grains, and Cereals.

Chapter 4: Baking Items. 12 new items join the lists of foods related to baking and sweetening, such as flavored syrups for hot and cold beverages.

Additionally, 9 new foods are in the Special Baking Items Table, primarily related to chocolate.

Chapter 5: Fats, Oils and Condiments. Duck Fat, a very popular cooking medium and essential ingredient in the preparation of potted meats and confits, has been added.

16 new condiments appear in this edition making this table an even richer compilation of multi-cultural flavorings.

Chapter 7: Dairy. European-style yogurts now compliment this list of frequently used foods.

Chapter 8: Beverages. Reflecting the surging popularity of teas on modern menus, 14 new items appear in this table, including many non-caffeinated herbals.

Chapter 15: Standard Portion Sizes. New to this edition is a chapter on Standard Portion Sizes. This reference list will help with menu planning, recipes development, and costing as well as planning food purchases for special events.

Price Lists. Of course, the Wholesale Price Lists have been updated to reflect current market levels. The **Instructor's Manual** has numerous additional recipes to facilitate costing exercises.

Much of the text that introduces each chapter remains largely unchanged. The explanatory principles and math examples remain clear and simple. Rather than make the entire book over, it is felt that keeping this aspect of the text as it was will help instructors and students use this newly expanded edition most successfully.

KEY CONCEPTS

MEASURES

The Book of Yields deals with measurements of weights and volumes. The following paragraphs explain some very important things about weights and volumes, so please read them carefully.

OUNCES VERSUS FLUID OUNCES   In the United States, a pint equals 16 fluid ounces—of anything. Coincidentally, a pound equals 16 ounces. So it sounds like a pint is a pound—you've no doubt heard the familiar saying, "A pint's a pound the world around." Well, in fact, a pint is not a pound. Why not? Because a fluid ounce is not a weighed ounce.

Fluid ounces are measures of volume (see Figure I.1). A volume refers to a space, not a weight. When you are speaking of a volume, as in a tablespoon, a cup, or a gallon, the ounces they contain are fluid ounces and are always labeled as such. That tells you how big the space is. For instance, a cup equals 8 fluid ounces of space; a pint holds 16 fluid ounces of space; a quart, 32 fluid ounces; and a gallon, 128 fluid ounces, no matter what food is in the cup, pint, quart, or gallon.

The ounces that we measure by weight are simply called *ounces*. These ounces are properly known as *avoirdupois ounces*. *Avoirdupois* is a French term that means "goods of weight." The avoirdupois ounce and pound were assigned a particular value for use in general trade (commerce) and are different from the ounces and pounds used by professionals working in the jewelry and chemical (apothecary) fields. As just stated, when working with weighed ounces, simply use the word *ounce*. However, when working with volumes rather than weights, always use fluid ounce as the correct description.

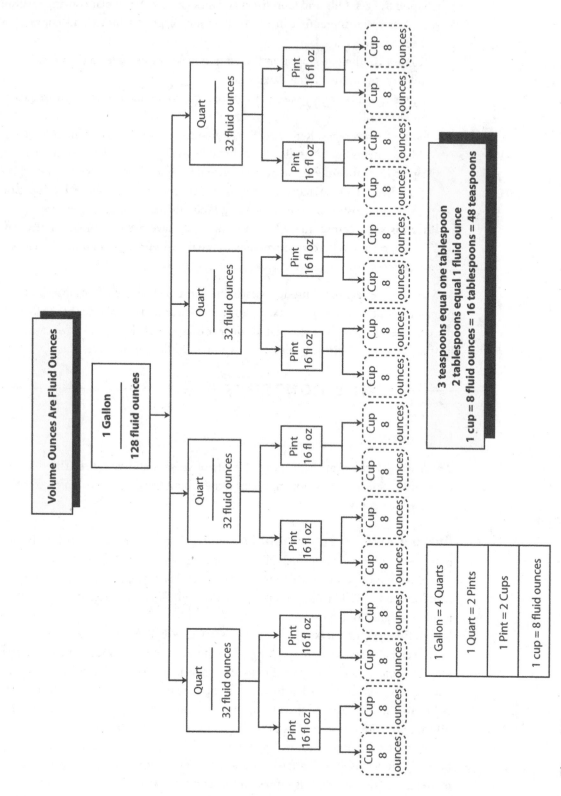

Figure I-1

NOTE

In the equations, for ease of use, ounce is abbreviated as oz., and pound as lb.; also gal. for gallon, fl. oz. for fluid ounce, and so on.

NOTE

In text, all these units of measure are spelled out; their abbreviations are used only in equations.

NOTE

One American fluid ounce equals 29.573 milliliters, another metric unit of measure, of volume. Interestingly, one milliliter of water *does* equal one gram (at 68 degrees Fahrenheit at sea level).

OUNCES AND POUNDS   *The Book of Yields* uses the standard American measures of weight (mass): ounces and pounds. One American pound equals 16 ounces; one American ounce equals 28.349 grams. A gram, by the way, is a unit of measure in another system of measurement used around the world, known as the metric system. Due to its logical and precise nature, it is used in the United States by engineers and the scientific community in general. The metric system weighs things in grams and kilograms, and volumes by the liter, which holds 1,000 milliliters. A liter is just a little bigger than a quart; 1 liter is defined as a cube whose sides are exactly one-tenth of a meter long. A meter is a measure of distance and is a little longer than a yard. The metric system measures volume, distance, and weight based on the meter (you'll learn more on this in Chapter 14). But fear not: We will be using the standard American measures in *The Book of Yields* because most people in the United States, including cooks and chefs, measure weight in ounces and pounds, rather than grams and kilograms.

VOLUME MEASURES   As noted previously, in the United States we measure volumes using containers that hold a certain number of fluid ounces. These containers or vessels are called the *cup, pint, quart,* and *gallon.* Small amounts are measured in *teaspoons* and *tablespoons.*

- 3 teaspoons make up 1 tablespoon.
- 2 tablespoons make up 1 fluid ounce.
- 1 cup contains 8 fluid ounces.
- 1 pint contains 2 cups (16 fluid ounces).
- 1 quart contains 2 pints (32 fluid ounces).
- 1 gallon contains 4 quarts (128 fluid ounces).

These measurements are typically abbreviated as follows:

- Teaspoons = tsp. (always lowercase)
- Tablespoon = tbsp. or Tbs.
- Cup = c., or cup
- Pint = pt.
- Quart = qt.
- Gallon = gal.
- Fluid ounce = fl. oz.

HOW THIS BOOK IS ORGANIZED

The Book of Yields is divided into two parts: the text and the Workbook.

PART I: THE TEXT

Most of the chapters are divided into two primary sections: Costing and Purchasing. The Costing sections explain how to carry out costing and conversion procedures; the Purchasing section provides purchasing formulas and examples to help you plan your food purchases accurately. In addition, as already noted, many of the chapters contain pertinent food lists, called tables. Chapter 2, Produce, for instance, contains four tables: Vegetables, Fruit, Canned Produce, and Canned Foods: Weight-to-Volume. The type of food in a table determines the measurement unit used in that table. A measure of tablespoons per ounce, for instance, is used in the Dry Herbs and Spices table because cooks often measure these foods by the tablespoon. Many other tables measure foods by the cup or pint because they are used in larger quantities. Tables for foods such as fresh produce or fresh meats show the trim yield percentages because it is important to know this factor when figuring out the true cost of a recipe ingredient that has been trimmed before using it in a recipe. Similarly, other food tables, such as for rices and grains, list the typical cooking yield percentages, as well as the weight of a cup or pint of these items so that they can be costed before or after cooking. Additional notes often follow a table, to give more information about the foods listed.

PART II: THE WORKBOOK

To make the formulas introduced in Part I easier to understand and use in recipe costing or food purchasing, you will turn to Part II of *The Book of Yields,* the Workbook, organized as follows:

+ Price lists
+ Costing worksheets
+ Purchasing worksheets

The Workbook begins with price lists of wholesale foods. (Note, food prices vary from region to region and change with the seasons of the year, so be aware that these prices are intended to give you a sense of how much foods cost; they should be used only to help you learn about food costing and purchasing, not in actual buying or costing situations.)

These price lists follow the sequence of the tables in the main section. Each food listed shows how it is typically packaged for the professional food service trade. Most foods come in relatively large quantities like 20-, 25-, 40-, or 50-pound bags or boxes— you won't be buying 2-pound boxes of sugar in the restaurant business. Canned or bottled foods are sold by the case rather than by the can. To cost these foods and to plan your purchases, you need to become familiar with these wholesale purchase units.

The next part of the Workbook contains costing worksheets, which demonstrate how to use the data presented in Part I to cost ingredients. Each worksheet takes you from a purchase unit to a recipe unit. For example, the Weight-to-Volume Worksheet will show you how to go from the price of a 50-pound sack of sugar to the cost of a cup, tablespoon, or teaspoon. Each worksheet also demonstrates how to do the math in each step, and where to plug in data from the tables in Part I to complete the formula. These worksheets make simple work of understanding the costing of recipes.

The final part of the Workbook contains purchasing worksheets, which illustrate how to plan food purchases. Each of the formulas is clearly laid out so that all you have to do is some simple math; even the multiplication and division symbols are supplied, directing you when and what to multiply or divide. This last part also contains forms you can use to take inventory and make out an actual order. They will help you learn to do your food buying in an organized way. This section is very useful for estimating your food costs for special banquets, as well as for day-to-day use.

TERMINOLOGY USED IN THE BOOK

Costing recipe ingredients, you will see, is a pretty straightforward process, as is purchasing the right amount of food. Both processes use similar words, phrases, and concepts, whose meanings are very important to understand. Here are the key words and

NOTE: EDIBLE PORTION VERSUS AS-SERVED

Edible portion (EP) is the amount you expect a guest to actually eat. For example, if you serve a 10-ounce steak, it has an as-served weight of 10 ounces. But, because some of the steak may be bone, fat, or gristle, the actual edible portion will be less; 7 ounces, for instance.

You should base your as-served amount decision on the edible portion amount that you want to prepare for your guest. For instance, the aforementioned 10-ounce steak is the AS amount, and the 7 ounces of trimmed, raw, and ready-to-cook steak is the edible portion. Once you have established your edible portion and as-served amounts, the as-served amount is all you'll usually need to make purchasing decisions.

In case you're wondering, the EP and the AS can be the same (the steak may be completely boneless and trimmed of all fat and gristle). However, they often are not. Therefore, you should use the AS amount when figuring out how much to buy. It is a clearer measure of what you need to know when deciding on your purchase amount, the AP amount.

And, remember, in *The Book of Yields* the as-served amount can also mean as-used—that is, the amount of a food that goes into a recipe, not just a trimmed portion of a meat or other item that goes directly onto a customer's plate.

NOTE

The AP and the AS amounts are usually very different, for the following reasons:

+ Trimming food makes it smaller, so it weighs less.
+ Fresh food tends to dry up or spoil the longer it is stored.
+ Some foods such as rice, pastas, and grains increase in weight and size when cooked.
+ Canned foods are often packed in water or syrup and may be drained before use.

phrases used throughout *The Book of Yields:*

+ As-served (abbreviated in equations as AS)
+ As-purchased (abbreviated in equations as AP)
+ Weight-to-volume equivalents
+ Yield percentages

Each is defined in turn in the following subsections.

AS-SERVED

As the term implies, *as-served* (AS) refers to the amount of food that is either served or used—put into a recipe—typically, after trimming or cooking. It can be a whole piece of food, such as a trimmed steak, or a cup of peeled and sliced carrots, and can be measured in many different ways: by a volume measure, a weight, or a piece count.

Pieces can be many things: a steak, a chicken breast, lettuce leaves, parsley sprigs, or apples. Pieces are usually measured in recipes by the "*each.*" For example, a recipe may call for two apples. The recipe would read: Apples, 2 each.

AS-PURCHASED

As a chef or food and beverage (F&B) manager, a very important part of your job will be to figure out how much food to buy. You will do this based on the amounts of food you expect to use or serve. The *as-purchased* (AP) value is the amount of food you buy, the amount of a food that comes in the door before you do anything to it. An AP amount can be measured in many ways: pounds, ounces, cans, bottles, sacks, cases, split cases, flats—the variety of packaging possibilities is enormous. Regardless of how the food comes in the door, however, certain events are going to change many of these foods in ways that make them shrink or grow as you (or just their environment) process them.

WEIGHT-TO-VOLUME EQUIVALENTS

When we say something is *equivalent* to something else, we are saying that those things are equal to each other in some way. In cooking, an equivalent defines how one type of measure equals a related measure, such as how a particular volume measure (like a cup) equals a weight of food (in the cup). For instance, a cup of dry dill weed weighs 1.68 ounces. When you say, for example, "1 cup of dill weed equals 1.68 ounces," you have just stated an equivalent.

These are known as weight-to-volume equivalents, and they are necessary to know in order to cost out recipe ingredients that are measured by volume, such as a cup of dill weed, because it is sold by weight, not by volume. To illustrate, assume a 5-ounce container of dill weed costs $12.28. One ounce would cost one-fifth of

$12.28. That calculates to $2.45 per ounce. Multiplying the 1.68 ounces of dill weed found in 1 cup gives you a cup cost of $4.12. Using volume measures is very helpful when writing recipes. Cooks can follow them quickly and accurately, and the chef can figure the recipe's cost just as quickly and accurately. All it takes is knowing your equivalents!

YIELD PERCENTAGES

Yield percentage is abbreviated in the equations in the book as Y%. In cooking, a yield percentage is the measure of the factor by which an item changes because of trimming, draining, and/or cooking. If you peel a medium carrot, for instance, you will end up with roughly 80% of its original weight. That 80% is the trim yield percentage. In another example, if you cook a pound of oatmeal, you will end up with nearly 7 pounds of cooked oatmeal. Its yield percentage is 697%.

The yield percentage is found by dividing the AS amount by the AP amount—that is, divide the amount you end up with after processing by the amount you started with. The yield percentage formula is:

AS ÷ AP = Y% (Amount served or used ÷ Amount purchased = Yield percentage)

Here is an example of how this formula works:

Given: You peel and trim 25 pounds of medium carrots, ending up with 20 pounds of usable carrots.

The 20 AS pounds divided by the 25 AP pounds equals .80, which is the same as 80%:

20 ÷ 25 = .80

Why are yield percentages important? Because we use them to calculate how much food to buy! Learn this next formula—the "how much to buy" formula—well. It is the most important one in the book, as it will save you money!

AS ÷ Y% = AP

It says that you divide the as-served or used amount by the food's yield percentage to see how much as-purchased food you need to cost out or buy.

Continuing with the carrot example, we already know that the trim yield percentage for medium carrots is 80%. Now do the following calculations:

1. Add up how much peeled and trimmed carrots you need (assume here that you want to serve 60 3-ounce portions of peeled and trimmed carrots):

60 × 3 oz. = 180 oz.

2. Divide the AS amount by the yield percentage:

180 oz. ÷ .80 = 225 oz.

The formula tells you to start with 225 ounces of raw carrots to have 180 trimmed ounces for use. Convert the 225 ounces to pounds, if you like, by dividing the number of ounces by 16. (There are 16 ounces in 1 pound, remember.)

225 ÷ 16 = 14.06 lb.

NOTE

Recall from your early arithmetic training that a decimal number can be written as a percentage number. Just move the decimal point two places to the right and place the % symbol at the right-hand side of the numbers. This is how .80 becomes 80%. In working with food service formulas, you will often be thinking in percentages but dealing with decimals as you do the math.

Thus, the formula tells you to start with (or buy) just over 14 pounds of as-purchased carrots in order to have 60 3-ounce portions of trimmed and peeled carrots ready to use or serve.

As you can see, this formula for calculating how much food to buy or cost out works perfectly for foods that get trimmed in their preparation. And here is more good news: This same formula works just as well for foods that increase in size and weight during preparation, such as rices, grains, cereals, and pastas!

OTHER PURCHASING FORMULAS

AP FORMULA FOR STATIC FOOD

NOTE

There are a number of variations to this basic formula of AS ÷ Y% = AP, and they reflect the differences in food types and how they are counted, used, and measured. None of these variations are hard to learn and use. Keep this book with you as you advance in your studies and move on in your career. It will save you countless hours and make you a smarter, more successful food service professional.

The term *static foods* refers to those that are used just as they are bought—foods like sugar, flour, rice, dry basil, honey, yeast, coffee grounds, and so on; they are used as is. These foods are usually purchased by weight but are often used in recipes by volume (tablespoons, cups, quarts, etc.).

Making purchasing decisions about these foods is pretty easy, if you know their weight-to-volume equivalents. Therefore, when a recipe lists these static foods in volume measurements, you'll need to convert the recipe's total AS volume back into an equivalent AP weight in order to calculate an appropriate amount to buy or cost out. (Remember: AS means as-served, as well as as-used, in recipes.)

The AP formula for static foods is:

AS number of measures × Weight per measure = AP

To explain how to use the formula to convert an AS volume back to an AP weight, assume a recipe calls for 6 cups of granulated sugar, and you need to make 18 recipes in one large batch. Take these steps:

1. Determine the total AS number of measures you need. In this example, calling for 18 recipes of 6 cups of sugar per recipe, you would multiply the 6 cups times 18 to get the AS number of measures:

18 recipes × 6 cups per recipe = 108 total AS cups

2. Determine the volume-to-weight equivalent for one measure. The Sweeteners table in Chapter 4 shows 1 cup of granulated sugar weighs 7.1 ounces.
3. Multiply the number of measures needed times the weight per measure to calculate the AS amount in ounces. In this case, you would multiply the 108 cups of sugar times the weight per cup of 7.1 ounces, like this:

108 × 7.1 = 766.8 oz.

4. To finish (and get the AP answer in pounds), divide the number of ounces by 16:

766.8 oz. ÷ 16 oz. = 47.9 lb.

In this example of granulated sugar, the formula looks like this:

108 cups × 7.1 oz. per cup = 766.8 oz.

The 108 cups is the number of AS measures, and the 7.1 ounces is the weight per measure.

Again, converting the ounces to pounds:

766.8 oz. ÷ 16 oz. = 47.9 lb.

Therefore, you need nearly an entire 50-pound sack of sugar to make this recipe batch.

PIECE-YIELD PURCHASING FORMULA

When you are going to use or serve an ingredient that is simply a *piece* from a larger item, you will use this formula. A piece, or a portion, can be many different things—for example, a slice of prime rib, an apple from a case of apples, or a tomato from a flat of tomatoes. The larger items are often the actual items you purchase, such as the whole prime rib, case of apples, or case of tomatoes. These larger items are called *purchase units*.

You need to know how many pieces or portions you expect to get from the purchase unit. A portion size, or portion count, is something you decide when you create your recipes and menu items.

The piece-yield formula tells you to divide the number of portions you need to serve your guests by the number of pieces you normally get from the purchase unit. This tells you how many purchase units to buy. Here is the formula:

Portion count needed ÷ Pieces per purchase unit = AP

As an example of how to use the piece-yield formula, let's determine how many whole prime ribs you would have to buy if you intend to serve prime rib portions to 75 guests, and you normally get 15 portions from each whole prime rib. Here, then, the portion count needed is 75 and the number of pieces per purchase unit is 15; therefore:

75 ÷ 15 = 5

So, you need to buy exactly five whole prime ribs.

NOTE

You'll notice that *The Book of Yields* often lists the purchase unit as a pound or an each, rather than a case or some other large unit. Why? A case can vary in size or weight, but a pound is always a pound.

USING YIELD FACTORS TO DETERMINE COSTS

FORMULA FOR THE COST PER PORTION BY COUNT

A yield count is simply the number of portions you typically get from a whole food item, such as the number of steaks you get from a loin. When you have a known yield count, you divide the purchase unit's AP cost by the count that you get from it.

AP cost ÷ Portion count = Cost per portion

For example, assume that a New York strip loin costs $45 and yields 18 cut-and-trimmed 8-ounce steaks. What is the cost per steak?

$45 ÷ 18 = $2.50

FORMULA FOR COST PER SERVABLE POUND (OR UNIT)

To determine the cost per servable pound or unit, you divide the cost per purchased pound (the AP cost per pound on your invoice) by the food's yield percentage; that is:

AP cost per lb. ÷ Yield % = Cost per servable pound

Assume that carrots cost 60 cents per pound and their trimmed yield is 80%, then:

$0.60 ÷ .80 = $0.75

Thus, the cost per servable pound of trimmed carrots is 75 cents.

When prices change, you can use the same formula: simply change the cost of the AP unit. For example, if the price of carrots drops from 60 cents to 40 cents per pound:

$0.40 ÷ .80 = $0.50

The new cost per pound of servable carrots is 50 cents. This works for any measure, not just pounds.

GETTING STARTED

Understanding the facts, principles, and concepts presented in this introductory section will set you up for success as you proceed with the following chapters. Each succeeding chapter contains formulas that are based on the fundamental information and the logic used in the formulas outlined on the preceding pages.

As you go forward with your food costing and purchasing activities, you will encounter new formulas that will enable you to master the skills needed for success in running a food service operation. These formulas are all somewhat similar in that they ask you to find the cost of a basic unit of measure such as an ounce, a fluid ounce, or a single piece and employ that in your calculations. I hope you'll find the formulas logical and easy to follow. Be sure to use the worksheets in Part II when you start doing the math. They are laid out in a way that leads you through each formula, step by step, showing you how to do the math.

You may find it helpful to buy some self-sticking page tabs that you can label with each chapter's food type. This will speed up your searches for foods.

To begin, the best approach is to look through the book in its entirety. You will learn how it is organized and start to become familiar with its content and scope. This book is not just a tool for learning how to cost foods and plan purchases. It is a tool you will keep by your side throughout your career as a chef or food service manager. It will save you time and help you become prosperous.

PART I

I

DRY HERBS AND SPICES AND FRESH HERBS

This chapter covers dry herbs and spices plus fresh herbs. Herbs and spices flavor other foods and are very important aspects of developing the character of a recipe. A few key herbs or spices distinguish many ethnic and national cuisines from others. Italian recipes, for instance, often have flat parsley, sweet basil, rosemary, and oregano, whereas Scandinavian recipes often call for dill weed, and French cuisine features tarragon, chives, and curly parsley. As important as they are in cookery, herbs and spices can be troublesome to cost out. Some texts on costing suggest that you simply add 5% to the cost of the recipe to account for the herbs and spices expense. This chapter will show you that it is quite simple (and far more accurate) to cost these items, whether they are fresh or dry. The same is true for planning purchases of these items.

COSTING DRY HERBS

The Dry Herbs and Spices table uses relatively small measures because these foods are often used in fairly small amounts. The key measures are:

✦ Number of tablespoons per ounce
✦ Number of ounces per tablespoon
✦ Number of ounces that a cup of the item weighs
✦ Count per ounce (such as whole bay leaves)
✦ Count per tablespoon (such as whole peppercorns)

IN THE WORKBOOK

Part II, the Workbook, has two worksheets to help you with costing dry herbs and spices and fresh herbs:

✦ Dry Herbs and Spices, Costing Worksheet 5
✦ Fresh Herbs, Costing Worksheet 6

If, for example, you need to cost a teaspoon of an item, simply divide the tablespoon-equivalent amount (the first column of numbers) by 3, because there are 3 teaspoons per tablespoon. All costing procedures begin by determining the cost per ounce of a food item. Once you know that amount, you look up the number of volume measures (tablespoons per ounce or ounces per tablespoon or cup) to cost out the volume measures in question.

Example
Given: A 22-ounce container of dry whole leaf basil costs $24.77.

To calculate the cost of 1 ounce:

1. Divide the cost of the container ($24.77) by the number of ounces in the container (22):

$24.77 ÷ 22 = $1.1259

Therefore, 1 ounce costs $1.126, rounded.

There are two steps in calculating the cost of 1 tablespoon:

1. Refer to the Dry Herbs and Spices table to learn the number of tablespoons per ounce of whole leaf basil. The table shows that there are 11.4 tablespoons of whole leaf basil per ounce.
2. Divide the cost of 1 ounce ($1.126) by the number of tablespoons in 1 ounce (11.4):

$1.126 ÷ 11.4 = $0.0988

That means that 1 tablespoon costs a little less than a dime.

To calculate the cost of 1 cup:

1. Look up the number of ounces that 1 cup weighs. The table shows this is 1.4 ounces.
2. Find the cost per cup by multiplying the cost per ounce ($1.126) by the number of ounces in 1 cup (1.4):

$1.126 × 1.4 = $1.5764

As you can see, 1 cup of whole dry leaf basil costs $1.58, rounded.

When it comes to calculating the cost of a single item, a few items, such as whole chilies or peppercorns, are used in recipes by the count, or *each*. Two types of these items are listed: *counts by the ounce* and *counts per tablespoon*.

To calculate the cost of a single item listed in the Number Each per Ounce column, take the following steps:

1. Again, calculate the cost of one ounce.
2. Divide the ounce cost by the count per ounce.

To calculate the cost of a single item listed in the Number Each per Tablespoon column, you'll need an additional step:

1. Calculate the cost per ounce.
2. Calculate the cost per tablespoon.
3. Divide the cost per tablespoon by the number found in 1 tablespoon.

This calculation comes in handy for recipes calling for 10 whole cloves or 25 peppercorns, for instance.

NOTE

The table also shows the number of ounces per tablespoon because some recipe-costing software programs ask for this value when entering a food into their databases. Having this data on hand will save you the trouble of doing the calculation yourself.

NOTE

When substituting dry herbs for fresh, substitute 1/3rd the volume of dry, *whole leaf* herb called for fresh. For instance, when 3 tablespoons of fresh chopped basil are called for, use 1 tablespoon, dry, whole leaf basil. If substituting dry, *ground* herb for fresh, chopped leaf, use 1/6th the volume of fresh herb to replace.

COSTING FRESH HERBS

Fresh herbs can be used as garnishes of whole leaves or whole leafy stems. They are also used whole in stocks and some roasting recipes. When stemmed and chopped, they find their way into recipes as flavorings and again as garnishes.

1 gal. = 4 qt. = 16 c. = 128 fl. oz. ✦ 1 qt. = 2 pt. = 4 c. = 32 fl. oz. ✦ 1 pt. = 2 c. = 16 fl. oz. ✦
1 c. = 8 fl. oz. = 16 tbsp. ✦ 1 fl. oz. = 2 tbsp. ✦ 1 tbsp. = 3 tsp. ✦ 1 lb. = 16 oz.

Fresh herbs are often sold by the bunch, but it is important to keep in mind that the size of the bunches will vary for one reason or another. One supplier may ship smaller bunches than another, and even if you only buy from one source, the size of a bunch can vary as seasons change. To help you in this regard, the Fresh Herbs table gives you yield information based both on a *bunch* and on an *as-purchased (AP) ounce.* (I recommend that you use the data based on the AP *ounce.*) To cost whole leaves or volumes of chopped leaves, you first determine the cost of the *as-purchased* (AP) ounce.

COSTING GARNISH LEAVES

NOTE

Over the course of time, it's a good idea to keep a record of the various weights of your fresh herb bunches. You can use the Food Weight Log in the Workbook section for this purpose.

Taking curly parsley as an example, assume that the average bunch weighs 3.4 ounces and costs $0.86 per bunch.

To calculate the cost per AP ounce:

1. Divide the cost per bunch by the number of ounces in 1 bunch:

   $0.86 ÷ 3.4 = $0.2529

   The cost per AP ounce is $0.25, rounded.

The Fresh Herbs table shows that, on average, you will obtain 22 lovely, large garnish leaves per purchased (AP) ounce.

To calculate the cost of 1 garnish leaf:

1. Divide the cost per ounce ($0.25) by the number of garnish leaves per AP ounce (22):

   $0.25 ÷ 22 = $0.0114

   As you can see, 1 usable curly parsley garnish leaf costs a little over 1 cent.

It's important to point out that this is a mathematical *ideal* cost, meaning that you have no spoilage and that you use every bit of parsley, which probably is not going to be the case. Therefore, you may want to "pad" the cost of your fresh herbs a bit to reflect the real conditions in your operation.

COSTING CHOPPED FRESH HERBS

Here, too, we'll use curly parsley as an example. Notice the column in the Fresh Herbs table labeled Yield of Tablespoons of Chopped Leaf per Purchased Ounce. This was calculated by measuring the number of cups of cleaned, stemmed, and chopped leaf obtained from one bunch. That number was then multiplied by 16 (there are 16 tablespoons in 1 cup), and dividing that result by the AP ounces in the bunch. For curly parsley, the number of chopped tablespoons obtained from 1 AP ounce is shown as 6.62.

To cost a tablespoon of chopped fresh parsley:

1. Divide the cost of 1 AP ounce ($0.25) by the number of chopped tablespoons obtained from 1 AP ounce (6.62):

   $0.25 ÷ 6.62 = $0.03776

Y% means yield percentage ♦ AS means as served (or used) ♦ AP means as purchased ♦ AS ÷ AP = Y% ♦
AS ÷ Y% = AP ♦ AP × Y% = AS ♦ Cost per AP unit ÷ Y% = Cost per servable unit

In this case, 1 tablespoon of chopped curly parsley costs $0.038, rounded.

To cost a cup of fresh chopped parsley:

1. Multiply the cost per tablespoon by 16:

   $0.038 × 16 = $0.608

   A cup of chopped curly parsley costs $0.61, rounded.

Or you can use this three-step alternate method for costing a cup:

1. Multiply the number of AP ounces in the bunch (3.4) by the number of tablespoons of chopped herb obtained from each AP ounce (6.62):

   3.4 × 6.62 = 22.508

   The entire bunch yielded 22.5 tablespoons of chopped parsley.

2. Divide the yield in tablespoons (22.5) by the number of tablespoons in 1 cup (16):

   22.5 × 16 = 1.406

   The 3.4-ounce bunch yielded 1.406 cups of chopped parsley.

3. Now divide the cost of the bunch ($0.86) by the number of cups yielded (1.406):

   $0.86 ÷ 1.406 = $0.61

PURCHASING DRY AND FRESH HERBS

IN THE WORKBOOK

Part II, the Workbook, has two worksheets to help you plan your purchases of dry herbs and spices and fresh herbs:

+ Dry Herbs and Spices, Purchasing Worksheet 1
+ Fresh Herbs, Purchasing Worksheet 2

Fresh produce (herbs, vegetables, and fruit) prices fluctuate widely as the seasons change, so be aware that you may well pay much more for the same item in the winter than you do in the summer or fall.

DRY HERBS

This section gives you four purchasing formulas for dry herbs, with an example of each.

FORMULA 1 The purchasing formula for dry herbs measured in tablespoons is as follows:

AS # of tablespoons ÷ # of tablespoons per ounce = AP in ounces

Example

Given: You need a total of 37 tablespoons of ground basil. To find out how many ounces you will need:

1 gal. = 4 qt. = 16 c. = 128 fl. oz. + 1 qt. = 2 pt. = 4 c. = 32 fl. oz. + 1 pt. = 2 c. = 16 fl. oz. + 1 c. = 8 fl. oz. = 16 tbsp. + 1 fl. oz. = 2 tbsp. + 1 tbsp. = 3 tsp. + 1 lb. = 16 oz.

NOTE

The # symbol stands for "number" or "the number of" in the formulas that follow here and in later chapters.

1. Divide the tablespoons needed by the number of tablespoons in 1 ounce. The Dry Herbs and Spices table shows there are 5.7 tablespoons of ground basil per ounce.

37 ÷ 5.7 = 6.49

Thus, you will need nearly 6.5 ounces of ground basil.

FORMULA 2   Next is the purchasing formula for dry herbs (volume-to-weight for cups):

AS # of cups × # ounces per cup = AP in ounces

Example
Given: You need 2 cups of ground basil. Find how many ounces you need.

1. Multiply the weight per cup times the number of cups needed. The Dry Herbs and Spices table shows that there are 2.81 ounces per cup for ground basil, so you get this result:

2 × 2.81 = 5.62

Therefore, you will need 5.62 ounces of ground basil.

FORMULA 3   The purchasing formula for dry herbs count to weight is as follows:

Count needed ÷ # each per ounce = AP in ounces

Example
Given: You need 12 dry Pasilla chile pods.

1. Divide the number of pods per ounce into the total pods needed. The Dry Herbs and Spices table shows that there are 2 Pasilla chile pods in 1 ounce:

12 ÷ 2 = 6

Thus, you will need 6 ounces of whole, dry Pasilla chile pods.

FORMULA 4   The last formula is for a dry spice-count-per-tablespoon to AP number of tablespoons:

AS count needed ÷ Count per tablespoon = AP tablespoons

Example
Given: You need 800 whole black peppercorns. The Dry Herbs and Spices table shows that there are 175 peppercorns per tablespoon:

1. Divide the number needed by the count per tablespoon. That means here you divide 800 by 175 to find the number of tablespoons needed:

800 ÷ 175 = 4.57 tablespoons

To convert to the number of ounces needed, just divide this answer by the value in the column headed Number of Tablespoons per Ounce in the table. For peppercorns, the table shows there are 4 tablespoons per ounce. So the calculation is as follows:

4.57 ÷ 4 = 1.14

Therefore, you need to order or cost 1.14 ounces of whole peppercorns.

FRESH HERBS

For fresh herbs there are three formulas; again, each formula is illustrated with an example.

FORMULA 1   The first formula is based on the number of garnish leaves needed:

# of leaves needed ÷ # of leaves per AP ounce = Ounces to buy

Example
You need 120 mint leaves, and the Fresh Herbs table shows that there are 24 garnish leaves of mint per AP ounce. Therefore, the equation is:

120 ÷ 24 = 5

which means you need to buy 5 ounces of fresh mint.

FORMULA 2   The second formula is based on the number of chopped tablespoons needed:

 # Chopped tablespoons needed ÷ # Chopped tablespoons per AP ounce = # Ounces to buy

Example
You need 16 tablespoons of chopped mint leaf, and the Fresh Herbs table shows that there are 3.88 tablespoons of chopped mint per AP ounce, so you use this equation:

16 ÷ 3.88 = 4.12

Therefore, you need to buy just over 4 ounces of fresh mint.

FORMULA 3   The last formula in this section is based on the number of cups of chopped leaf needed:

(# Chopped cups needed × 16) ÷ # Chopped tablespoons per AP ounce = # Ounces to buy

Example
You need 3 cups of chopped mint leaf. Here, too, the table shows there are 3.88 tablespoons of chopped mint per AP ounce. Follow this two-step process:

1 gal. = 4 qt. = 16 c. = 128 fl. oz. ✦ 1 qt. = 2 pt. = 4 c. = 32 fl. oz. ✦ 1 pt. = 2 c. = 16 fl. oz. ✦
1 c. = 8 fl. oz. = 16 tbsp. ✦ 1 fl. oz. = 2 tbsp. ✦ 1 tbsp. = 3 tsp. ✦ 1 lb. = 16 oz.

1. Multiply the number of cups needed by 16.

3 × 16 = 48

2. Divide that answer by the number of chopped tablespoons per AP ounce: 3.88.

48 ÷ 3.88 = 12.37

The result indicates that you need to buy 12.37 ounces of fresh mint.

Dry Herbs and Spices

Item Name	Number of Tablespoons per Ounce	Number of Ounces per Tablespoon	Number of Ounces per Cup	Number Each per Ounce	Number Each per Tablespoon
Achiote (Annato) Powder	3.08	0.325	5.20		
Allspice, ground	4.92	0.203	3.25		
Anise Seed, whole	5.00	0.200	3.20		
Anise, star				32	
Basil, ground	5.70	0.175	2.81		
Basil, whole leaf	11.40	0.088	1.40		
Bay Leaf, whole				130	
Bay Leaves, ground	4.21	0.238	3.80		
Bee Pollen	2.81	0.356	5.70		
Caraway Seed, whole	4.23	0.236	3.78		
Cardamom, ground	4.88	0.205	3.28		
Cayenne Pepper	5.30	0.189	3.02		
Celery Salt	1.95	0.513	8.21		
Celery Seed, whole	3.90	0.256	4.10		
Chervil, whole	13.00	0.077	1.23		
Chicory Root, ground as for coffee	4.00	0.250	4.00		
Chile Flakes, chipotle	5.00	0.20	3.20		
Chile Flakes, green	5.90	0.169	2.71		
Chile Flakes, red	5.90	0.169	2.71		
Chile Pods, Casabel				9	
Chile Pods, California and New Mexico				4	
Chile Pods, de Arbol				52	

Y% means yield percentage ✦ AS means as served (or used) ✦ AP means as purchased ✦ AS ÷ AP = Y% ✦
AS ÷ Y% = AP ✦ AP × Y% = AS ✦ Cost per AP unit ÷ Y% = Cost per servable unit

Dry Herbs and Spices (Continued)

Item Name	Number of Tablespoons per Ounce	Number of Ounces per Tablespoon	Number of Ounces per Cup	Number Each per Ounce	Number Each per Tablespoon
Chile Pods, Guajillo				5	
Chile Pods, Japones (Japanese)				81	
Chile Pods, Morita				9	
Chile Pods, Pasilla				2	
Chile Pods, Pequin				511	
Chile Powder	4.25	0.235	3.76		
Chile Powder (Ancho)	3.87	0.258	4.13		
Chile Powder (Chipotle)	3.35	0.298	4.77		
Chinese Five-Spice	4.25	0.235	3.76		
Chives, chopped	56.00	0.018	0.29		
Cilantro	36.00	0.028	0.44		
Cinnamon, ground	4.00	0.250	4.00		
Cinnamon, whole sticks, 5" long				3	
Cinnamon Chips (bark flakes)	3.33	0.300	4.80		
Cloves, ground	4.30	0.233	3.72		
Cloves, whole	5.33	0.188	3.00	266	50
Coriander Seed, ground	4.58	0.218	3.49		
Coriander Seed, whole	5.68	0.176	2.82		
Cream of Tartar	2.46	0.407	6.50		
Cumin Seed, whole	4.72	0.212	3.39		
Cumin, ground	4.80	0.208	3.33		
Curry Powder	4.50	0.222	3.56		
Dashi No Moto (no MSG)	2.32	0.431	6.90		
Dashi No Moto (with MSG)	2.50	0.400	6.40		
Dill Seed, whole	4.50	0.222	3.56		
Dill Weed	9.50	0.105	1.68		
Epazote	10.06	0.099	1.59		
Fennel Seed, whole	4.20	0.238	3.81		

1 gal. = 4 qt. = 16 c. = 128 fl. oz. ✦ 1 qt. = 2 pt. = 4 c. = 32 fl. oz. ✦ 1 pt. = 2 c. = 16 fl. oz. ✦
1 c. = 8 fl. oz. = 16 tbsp. ✦ 1 fl. oz. = 2 tbsp. ✦ 1 tbsp. = 3 tsp. ✦ 1 lb. = 16 oz.

Dry Herbs and Spices (Continued)

Item Name	Number of Tablespoons per Ounce	Number of Ounces per Tablespoon	Number of Ounces per Cup	Number Each per Ounce	Number Each per Tablespoon
Fenugreek Seed, whole	2.55	0.392	6.27		
Galangal Root, dry shredded	6.27	0.159	2.55		
Garlic Powder	4.32	0.231	3.70		
Garlic Salt	2.00	0.500	8.00		
Garlic, granulated	2.66	0.376	6.02		
Garum Masala	4.57	0.219	3.50		
Ginger, ground	4.20	0.238	3.81		
Gumbo File Powder	5.71	0.175	2.8		
Herbs de Provence	9.70	0.103	1.65		
Hibiscus Flowers, whole				40	
Juniper Berries, whole	5.33	0.188	3.00	331	62
Kelp Powder	3.20	0.313	5.00		
Lavender Flowers, broken	22.54	0.044	0.71		
Lemon Balm	17.78	0.056	0.90		
Lemon Grass, shredded	16.84	0.059	0.95		
Lemon Peel pieces (bits)	5.08	0.197	3.15		
Lemon Pepper, lightly salted	3.23	0.309	4.95		
Lemon Thyme	21.33	0.047	0.75		
Lemon Verbena	14.55	0.069	1.10		
Licorice Root, shredded	7.27	0.138	2.20		
Mace, ground	5.25	0.190	3.05		
Marjoram, ground	5.93	0.169	2.70		
Marjoram, whole leaf	10.60	0.094	1.51		
Mexican, Seasonings, Green	6.53	0.153	2.45		
Mint, whole leaf	34.00	0.029	0.47		
Monosodium Glutamate (MSG)	2.86	0.350	5.60		
Mustard Seed, whole	2.50	0.400	6.40		
Mustard, ground (powder)	5.16	0.194	3.10		

Y% means yield percentage ✦ AS means as served (or used) ✦ AP means as purchased ✦ AS ÷ AP = Y% ✦
AS ÷ Y% = AP ✦ AP × Y% = AS ✦ Cost per AP unit ÷ Y% = Cost per servable unit

Dry Herbs and Spices (Continued)

Item Name	Number of Tablespoons per Ounce	Number of Ounces per Tablespoon	Number of Ounces per Cup	Number Each per Ounce	Number Each per Tablespoon
Nori (Seaweed) sheets 8″ × 8.5″				10	
Nutmeg, ground	4.25	0.235	3.76		
Nutmeg, whole				6.50	
Onion Powder	4.32	0.231	3.70		
Orange Peel pieces (bits)	6.15	0.163	2.60		
Oregano, ground	5.70	0.175	2.81		
Oregano, whole leaf	10.00	0.100	1.60		
Paprika, ground	4.10	0.244	3.90		
Parsley Flakes, whole	22.00	0.045	0.73		
Pepper, Black, whole	4.00	0.250	4.00	700	175
Pepper, Black, coarse-cut	4.32	0.231	3.70		
Pepper, Black, cracked	4.00	0.250	4.00		
Pepper, Black, table grind	4.20	0.238	3.81		
Pepper, Red, crushed (flakes)	5.90	0.169	2.71		
Pepper, Szechuan, whole	8.27	0.121	1.93		
Pepper, White, ground	3.55	0.282	4.51		
Pepper, White, whole	3.08	0.325	5.20	590	192
Peppermint, flaked	15.24	0.066	1.05		
Poppy Seed, whole	3.20	0.313	5.00		
Poultry Seasoning	7.66	0.131	2.09		
Pumpkin Pie Seasoning Mix	5.06	0.198	3.16		
Rose Blossoms	24.24	0.041	0.66		
Rosemary, ground	5.70	0.175	2.81		
Rosemary, whole leaf	11.85	0.084	1.35		
Saffron, whole	13.50	0.074	1.19		
Sage, rubbed	11.00	0.091	1.45		
Salt, Hawaiian, white	1.79	0.559	8.95		
Salt: French, Sea: (Sel Gris, fine)	2.06	0.484	7.75		

1 gal. = 4 qt. = 16 c. = 128 fl. oz. ✦ 1 qt. = 2 pt. = 4 c. = 32 fl. oz. ✦ 1 pt. = 2 c. = 16 fl. oz. ✦
1 c. = 8 fl. oz. = 16 tbsp. ✦ 1 fl. oz. = 2 tbsp. ✦ 1 tbsp. = 3 tsp. ✦ 1 lb. = 16 oz.

Dry Herbs and Spices (Continued)

Item Name	Number of Tablespoons per Ounce	Number of Ounces per Tablespoon	Number of Ounces per Cup	Number Each per Ounce	Number Each per Tablespoon
Salt, kosher, (Diamond Crystal)	3.40	0.294	4.70		
Salt, kosher (Morton coarse)	1.87	0.534	8.55		
Salt, kosher flake	1.70	0.588	9.41		
Salt, Red Hawaiian, medium grain	1.77	0.566	9.05		
Salt, regular	1.55	0.645	10.32		
Salt, Seasoning	1.95	0.513	8.21		
Savory, ground	6.45	0.155	2.48		
Sesame Seed, whole	3.00	0.333	5.33		
Spearmint, flaked	17.78	0.056	0.9		
Stevia Leaf	12.31	0.081	1.3		
Stevia Leaf Powder	5.52	0.181	2.9		
Tarragon, ground	5.90	0.169	2.71		
Tarragon, whole leaf	13.00	0.077	1.23		
Thyme, ground	6.60	0.152	2.42		
Thyme, whole leaf	10.00	0.100	1.60		
Tulsi (Holy Basil)	9.41	0.106	1.70		
Turmeric, powder	3.75	0.267	4.27		
Wasabi, powder	5.90	0.169	2.71		

Y% means yield percentage ✦ AS means as served (or used) ✦ AP means as purchased ✦ AS ÷ AP = Y% ✦
AS ÷ Y% = AP ✦ AP × Y% = AS ✦ Cost per AP unit ÷ Y% = Cost per servable unit

Fresh Herbs

Item	Ounces per Bunch or AP Unit	Garnish Leaves or Sprigs per Bunch	Garnish Leaves or Sprigs per AP Ounce	Ounces of Stemless Leaf per Bunch	Weight Yield Percent: Stemless Leaf per Bunch	Ounce Weight of 1 Tablespoon Chopped	Yield: Tablespoons of Chopped Leaf per Purchased Ounce	Ounce Weight of 1 Cup, Chopped
Basil, Sweet	2.5	59	23.6	1.4	56.00%	0.088	6.40	1.408
Bay Leaves	0.6	68	113	0.48	80.00%	0.113	7.10	1.803
Chives, 6" lengths	1	115	115	0.95	95.00%	0.095	10	1.520
Cilantro	2.8	93	33	1.3	46.43%	0.093	5	1.486
Dill Weed	4.5	105	23	2	44.44%	0.112	41	1.785
Marjoram	1	38	38	0.76	76.00%	0.069	11	1.105
Mint	3.35	80	24	1.4	41.79%	0.108	3.88	1.724
Oregano	1	40	40	0.78	78.00%	0.065	12	1.040
Parsley, curly	3.4	75	22	1.8	52.94%	0.080	6.62	1.280
Parsley, Italian	5.7	91	16	2.3	40.35%	0.113	3.51	1.800
Rosemary	1	22	22	0.8	80.00%	0.150	5.33	2.400
Sage, green	1	68	68	0.6	60.00%	0.075	8	1.200
Stevia	2.6	90	34.6	1.1	42.31%	0.069	6.15	1.100
Tarragon	1	48	48	0.8	80.00%	0.114	7	1.828
Thyme	1	43	43	0.65	65.00%	0.100	6.50	1.600
Watercress	6.1	25	4.1	1.65	27.05%	0.092	2.95	1.470

Notes

1. Ginger yields 70% when peeled.
2. These measurements are based on herbs of normal commercial size and quality with respect to their size, maturity, freshness, moisture, and conformation.
3. Leaves for garnish are large and attractive.
4. Stemless leaf yield includes the garnish leaves plus remaining good leaves.
5. Leaves were stripped from stems before chopping.
6. Chopped leaves were cut *chiffonade,* then cross-cut and chopped a bit more.
7. Volume measures of chopped leaves were tapped down but not pressed down hard.
8. The Yield: Tablespoons of Chopped Leaf per Purchased Ounce column was obtained by physically measuring (in cups) the total yield of the purchased amount after stemming and chopping, then multiplying that amount by 16 and dividing the answer by the ounces purchased.

2 PRODUCE

Produce refers to fruit and vegetables. Vegetables are part of most recipes on the savory side of the kitchen, while fruit is a common ingredient on the baking and pastry side of the kitchen. This chapter addresses fresh produce as well as canned. Frozen vegetables and fruit are addressed briefly, but not in depth, because they are fairly easy to cost and buy correctly. There is little or no waste, and these products are sold by weight. Regarding fresh vegetables and fresh fruit, you will find the data in this chapter of significant help when costing ingredients and planning purchases. For instance, many recipes call for "2 cups of diced onion" or "1 pint of sliced strawberries." These volume measures of trimmed and cut produce are easy to cost out (and plan for purchases) when you follow the formulas and use the food tables in this chapter.

Be aware that wholesale prices for fresh produce vary widely over the course of a year. Quality, too, can fluctuate significantly due to the seasons and distances the food must travel from farm to market. This can affect your yields. Whenever possible, try to buy local fresh produce in season. Of course this is not going to happen in the dead of winter in colder climates. In those situations, try to modify your menu in a way that makes it less reliant on foods that have to travel from far away. If you cannot do this with all your produce needs (and it is probable that you cannot), you should perform your own winter yield tests on those produce items that come in the door showing signs of spoilage or shrinkage.

As you read through the chapter, you'll be referred to four tables:

1. Vegetables
2. Fruit
3. Canned Foods (in Number-10 cans)
4. Canned Foods Weight-to-Volume

Note that the Vegetables and Fruit tables are identical in layout. Each shows you the following:

+ An initial as-purchased (AP) unit (typically a pound)
+ The number of ounces, or *counts,* in the AP unit
+ The number of ounces left over after trimming
+ The percentage of the trimmed amount to the AP amount—that is, the yield percentage (Y%)
+ When applicable, the number of ounces a cup of the trimmed food weighs after further prepping, such as dicing or slicing
+ The number of cups obtained (i.e., yielded) of these processed foods from the AP unit

The last two items are shown in the two columns on the right. In particular, the yield percentages will be extremely helpful as you go about planning how much food to buy; more on that later, in the section on purchasing.

COSTING FRESH PRODUCE

IN THE WORKBOOK

Part II, the Workbook, has two worksheets to help you with costing fresh produce:

✦ Trimmed or Cooked Foods, Costing Worksheet 2
✦ Piece Counts, Costing Worksheet 3

NOTE: FROZEN VEGETABLES AND FRUIT

The vegetable and fruit tables in this chapter are devoted almost entirely to fresh produce. *Frozen* vegetables and fruit are packaged by weight. There is no trim or waste if the items are cooked or used when still frozen. When a recipe calls for a weight of a frozen item, the costing is simple.

Divide the cost of the wholesale unit (usually a case) by the number of pounds in the case. This gives you the cost per pound. Divide that by 16 to get the cost per AS ounce. Multiply that ounce cost by the ounces called for in the recipe. If the recipe calls for a volume measure, you will have to weigh the volume amount in order to cost it.

Steaming frozen vegetables will generally yield a weight of cooked product that is approximately 92 percent of the original frozen weight. The loss is due to the heat melting away any water glaze that may have been clinging to the frozen vegetables as well as some minor evaporation. Whole-kernel corn is an exception, yielding close to 100 percent of its weight.

If you let frozen produce, particularly fruit, thaw completely before using it, you will have a fair amount of weight loss due to the juices flowing out of the food. The longer the produce remains thawed before use, the greater the loss. Whenever possible, do not let frozen produce thaw completely before incorporating it in a recipe.

Fresh produce is typically trimmed for use in recipes. Therefore, to do cost breakdowns for fresh produce or produce items that are used after some trimming, use the Trimmed or Cooked Foods worksheet (Costing Worksheet 2). It will step you through the process of converting from a purchase unit cost to a cost per trimmed ounce or pound to a cost per volume measure of the trimmed and cut food.

For produce items that are used without trimming, you may find the Piece Counts worksheet (Costing Worksheet 3) helpful. It guides you through the process of finding the cost of a usable whole piece of fruit or a single vegetable from an entire purchase unit, such as a case or a pound.

COSTING TRIMMED FOODS

Here are the steps to follow for costing those produce items that are trimmed before use. For this exercise, we'll use a 25-pound bag of medium-size carrots that costs $9.45.

1. To determine how much an AP pound and ounce costs, divide the cost of the bag by the number of pounds in the bag to get the cost per pound:

$9.45 ÷ 25 = $0.378

So one pound costs $0.378.

2. Divide the cost of one pound by 16 to get the cost per AP ounce:

$0.378 ÷ 16 = $0.023625

Thus, the cost of one AP ounce of medium carrots is slightly less than 2.4 cents.

COSTING A TRIMMED WEIGHT

Now the yield percentage comes into play. If you divide the cost of an AP unit of measure (such as a pound or an ounce) by the food's trim yield percentage, you will get the cost of the pound or ounce after trimming. For example, the Vegetables table shows the trim yield percentage for medium carrots as 81.3 percent. (This

1 gal. = 4 qt. = 16 c. = 128 fl. oz. ✦ 1 qt. = 2 pt. = 4 c. = 32 fl. oz. ✦ 1 pt. = 2 c. = 16 fl. oz. ✦
1 c. = 8 fl. oz. = 16 tbsp. ✦ 1 fl. oz. = 2 tbsp. ✦ 1 tbsp. = 3 tsp. ✦ 1 lb. = 16 oz.

percentage means that if you start with 10 pounds of carrots, trim off their ends, and peel them, you will end up with 8.13 pounds of usable carrots.) Regardless of what the beginning cost amount is, you just divide that amount by the trim yield percentage to calculate the cost for the trimmed food.

To illustrate, the cost for the trimmed carrots in ounces is calculated as follows:

(AP cost per ounce) \$0.0236 ÷ 0.813 (0.813 is the trim Y% expressed as a decimal) = \$0.029

The cost of the trimmed carrots has risen from an AP cost per ounce of about 2.4 cents to a trimmed cost per ounce of 2.9 cents.

COSTING A TRIMMED VOLUME

The Vegetables table shows that a cup of diced carrots weighs 5 ounces. To assign a cost to 1 cup of diced carrots, you just multiply the number of ounces in 1 cup of diced carrots (5) by the cost of a trimmed ounce (\$0.029):

5 × \$0.029 = \$0.145

The cost of a cup of diced carrots is 14.5 cents.

On occasion, you may need to cost out an amount smaller than a cup. A recipe may, for example, call for 2 tablespoons of chopped garlic. In that case, you would divide the cup cost by 16 and multiply that answer by 2 (or just divide the cup cost by 8, if the math is obvious to you).

COSTING PRODUCE BY THE PIECE

When recipes call for a whole piece—say, a cherry tomato or two lemons—you will need to know how many pieces came in the AP unit or in a pound. If it is a count per case, you calculate the cost for one piece by dividing the AP unit cost by the number of pieces that came in the AP unit.

Example

Given: A 40-pound case of "165 count" lemons (165 lemons per case) costs \$24. The Fruit table shows that there are 4 lemons per AP pound. But 40 times 4 equals 160 lemons, not 165, so what about the other 5 lemons? They were deducted from the AP unit to account for discarded lemons due to spoilage. Use this two-step process to find the cost of one lemon:

1. To determine the cost of one piece (1 lemon) first calculate the cost of 1 pound:

\$24 ÷ 40 = \$0.60

Thus, 1 pound of lemons cost 60 cents.

2. Next, consult the Fruit table to find that there are 4 lemons per pound, so

\$0.60 ÷ 4 = \$0.15

One lemon costs 15 cents.

NOTE

Unless you deliberately pack or tamp down produce, it does not compact very much when placed in a slightly larger container, such as a pint or quart. That means, with simple multiplication, you can use the cup cost to calculate the price of these larger vessels. Just be aware that when you use even larger quantities, such as a half or whole gallon, there may be some settling or compacting of the food in the vessel and you may want to consider adding from 3 percent to a half-gallon measure and up to 7 percent to the calculated cost of a gallon to reflect possible compaction.

Y% means yield percentage ✦ AS means as served (or used) ✦ AP means as purchased ✦ AS ÷ AP = Y% ✦ AS ÷ Y% = AP ✦ AP × Y% = AS ✦ Cost per AP unit ÷ Y% = Cost per servable unit

NOTE

Discarded items called *culls* are common with fresh produce. The Piece Counts worksheet (Costing Worksheet 3) shows you how to adjust the cost per each after discarding your culled items.

(By the way, this is pretty inexpensive for lemons. As noted earlier, produce prices vary widely from season to season and from one region of the country to another.)

COSTING CANNED FOODS

Many canned foods are packed in water, juice, or syrup. Sometimes you will serve or use the food with the liquid in which it was canned; other times you will drain the liquid before use. A soup recipe, for instance, may call for using the liquid along with the solids in the can. It is, however, more common to use the solid contents after draining off the packing liquid, leaving what is called the *drained weight*. To address both possibilities, this section is divided into two subsections: "Costing Drained Canned Foods" and "Costing Undrained Canned Foods."

In food service, the typical-size can is the number-10 can. Number-10 cans are said to have a capacity of 13 cups, but in fact, they usually contain fewer than 13 cups of food—12 to 12.5 cups is the norm. Why? The canning process requires that some air-space be left in the container to allow for the expansion of food during the canning process. That said, when you empty the contents of a number-10 can into another container, you might find that they measure *more* than 13 cups. This is simply because, in the transfer, you have jumbled the contents and caused them to pack less densely than they were originally positioned in the can.

COSTING DRAINED CANNED FOODS

In the Canned Foods table you will find the minimum number of drained ounces allowed by the United States Department of Agriculture (USDA). You can use the USDA figures to calculate the cost of a drained ounce by dividing the cost of a can by the minimum number of drained ounces it must contain. This table is supplemented by the Canned Foods Weight-to-Volume table.

Generally, to comply with USDA practices, foods must be drained for two minutes over a screen. However, independent yield tests show that the minimum USDA weights are not always met; sometimes there is extra food in the can and sometimes there is less than the stated minimum. But be aware that in most kitchens, colanders, rather than screens are used for draining; moreover, foods in the independent test kitchen study were also given a final shake or two to simulate how most cooks drain canned items.

Take a look now at the USDA Recommended Drained Weight table and you'll see that a number-10 can of corn is supposed to yield 70 ounces of drained corn. Next, compare that to the Canned Foods Weight-to-Volume table, which lists the yield as 73 ounces. Probably, in this case, the canner simply put more than the minimum amount in the test can. The point is, it is a good idea to do your own can-cutting tests to determine what your actual yields are. In addition, rely on these two tables as a reference point.

1 gal. = 4 qt. = 16 c. = 128 fl. oz. ✦ 1 qt. = 2 pt. = 4 c. = 32 fl. oz. ✦ 1 pt. = 2 c. = 16 fl. oz. ✦
1 c. = 8 fl. oz. = 16 tbsp. ✦ 1 fl. oz. = 2 tbsp. ✦ 1 tbsp. = 3 tsp. ✦ 1 lb. = 16 oz.

For our purposes here, we'll go with the 73-ounce yield to proceed with the costing process. To begin, assume a six-can case of corn kernels costs $29.45, which means one can costs approximately $4.91:

$29.45 ÷ 6 cans = $4.91

Now divide the cost of the can ($4.91) by the drained ounces (73):

$4.91 ÷ 73 oz. = $0.067

Thus, 1 ounce of drained corn costs 6.7 cents.

As you no doubt noticed, the Canned Foods Weight-to-Volume table also lists various volume-to-weight equivalents, and these can be of help in costing cup, quart, and half-gallon measures of canned foods. Take note that most canned foods will become denser and, therefore, weigh more (per cubic inch) when placed in a quart or half-gallon container instead of in a single-cup container. Although a cup of corn kernels weighs 5.55 ounces, a quart weighs *more than four times* that, and a half gallon will weigh *more than eight times* the cup weight. This is caused by the compaction of the food and by relatively less interference with the walls of the larger containers. When costing quarts or half gallons, multiply the cost per drained ounce by the number of ounces held in either the quart or half gallon, as shown in the table.

To illustrate, say you want to cost a cup, quart, and half gallon of corn niblets (kernels). You already know that a drained ounce costs $0.067, and the table shows that a cup weighs 5.55 ounces, a quart weighs 23.7 ounces, and a half gallon weighs 48.4 ounces.

+ *To cost a cup,* multiply the drained ounce cost by 5.55 ounces:

  $0.067 × 5.55 oz. = $0.372

+ *To cost a quart,* multiply the drained ounce cost by 23.7 ounces:

  $0.067 × 23.7 oz. = $1.588

+ *To cost a half gallon,* multiply the ounce cost by 50.65 ounces:

  $0.067 × 48.4 oz. = $3.243

COSTING MISCELLANEOUS CANNED OR BOTTLED PRODUCE ITEMS

The produce tables also include some new items that are canned or bottled. There are often brined or marinated foods and are packed in containers other than number-10 cans. To cost these foods, use the following formulas.

FORMULA 1 The formula for costing a drained weight is really a variation of the drained weight formula for number-10 cans.

Cost per container ÷ Drained ounces per container = Cost per drained ounce

Y% means yield percentage ✦ AS means as served (or used) ✦ AP means as purchased ✦ AS ÷ AP = Y% ✦
AS ÷ Y% = AP ✦ AP × Y% = AS ✦ Cost per AP unit ÷ Y% = Cost per servable unit

NOTE: SERVING SIZES AND NUTRITION

The labels on canned foods show a "suggested" serving size that is stated as a volume (or a piece count), along with an equivalent weight in grams. These so-called serving-size weights almost always include the packing liquid. If you are not serving the liquid, but the suggested weight, drained, you will be overportioning the solid, drained foods. Be sure to do your nutritional analysis based on your *actual serving practices.*

Example

Given: A 60-ounce jar of marinated artichoke hearts costs $4.30. The Vegetables table shows the drained weight is 43 ounces. Do the math:

$4.30 ÷ 43 oz. = $0.10 per oz.

FORMULA 2 Costing canned produce by piece count is just like costing fresh produce by the piece. You divide the cost per container by the number of usable pieces it contains.

Example

Given: The table shows that there are 80 usable hearts per container. The cost per container is $4.30:

$4.30 ÷ 80 = $0.054

One artichoke heart piece costs 5.4 cents.

FORMULA 3 To cost a cup of drained food, use the formula for costing a trimmed volume:

 # Ounces per cup × Cost per ounce = Cost per drained cup

Example

Given: A 7-ounce jar of capers costs $5.20. The Vegetables table shows that this jar yields 4.7 ounces, drained.

First, calculate the cost per drained ounce by dividing the cost per container ($5.20) by the drained ounces per container (4.7).

$5.20 ÷ 4.7 oz. = $1.106

The table shows that a cup of drained capers also coincidentally weighs 4.7 ounces. So, multiply the cost per drained ounce $1.106 by 4.7.

$1.106 × 4.7 = $5.20

COSTING UNDRAINED CANNED FOODS

Certain canned items are not drained. Sauces, pastes, purees, soups, and stews are examples. To cost volumes of these items, you follow the drained food procedure just described, with one caveat: You *must* know how many ounces of food were in the entire can. You use that number to divide into the cost of the can to get the cost per ounce; then you use the cost per ounce times the number of ounces in your portion or recipe to cost the amount in question.

For instance, if a case of six number-10 cans of tomato puree costs $17.15, then one can costs $2.86. The Canned Food Weight-to-Volume table shows that the actual contents of a single number-10 can of tomato puree weighs 107 ounces. Therefore, to calculate the cost per weighed ounce, divide the cost of the can ($2.86) by the actual weighed ounces it holds (107):

$2.86 ÷ 107 oz. = $0.0267, or 2.67 cents

1 gal. = 4 qt. = 16 c. = 128 fl. oz. ✦ 1 qt. = 2 pt. = 4 c. = 32 fl. oz. ✦ 1 pt. = 2 c. = 16 fl. oz. ✦
1 c. = 8 fl. oz. = 16 tbsp. ✦ 1 fl. oz. = 2 tbsp. ✦ 1 tbsp. = 3 tsp. ✦ 1 lb. = 16 oz.

The table also shows that a cup of tomato puree weighs 8.9 ounces. To cost a cup, you multiply the cost per ounce ($.0267) by the 8.9 ounces in a cup:

$0.0267 × 8.9 oz. = $0.2376, or 24 cents (rounded)

Be aware that there can be some slight compaction of the food when measured in quart and half-gallon containers, so use the quart and half-gallon ounce weights to calculate the costs for those larger amounts. The Canned Foods Weight-to-Volume table provides this information:

+ A quart of tomato puree weighs 36.3 ounces:

$0.0267 × 36.3 oz. = $0.969, or 97 cents (rounded)

+ A half gallon weighs 72.9 ounces:

$0.0267 × 72.9 oz. = $1.946, or $1.95 (rounded)

——— PURCHASING FRESH PRODUCE AND CANNED FOODS ———

Miscellaneous Notes on Produce

+ A standard dinner salad (non-entrée) weight is 3 ounces of greens.
+ A standard portion weight of cooked vegetables on an entrée plate is 3.0 to 3.5 ounces.
+ Leafy vegetables such as spinach, kale, and chard lose 90 percent of their volume when cooked but actually gain a bit of weight because of water absorption. To cost portions of these leafy greens, count the cooked portions obtained from a known AP amount. Of course, this is true of all foods, but it is essential with leafy vegetables because their volume reduces so dramatically when cooked.
+ Root vegetables change little in weight or volume when cooked. Onions and mushrooms, by contrast, can shrink as much as 75 percent in volume when cooked to golden colors.

Before we get into the actual calculations, here are a few guidelines to help you better control your produce costs:

+ Keep your inventory levels low and rotating quickly on a first-in/first-out (FIFO) system.
+ Keep a close eye on the condition of your fresh produce, as some foods have very short shelf lives.
+ Produce is varied, and so are the ways it should be stored. Learn how to store all of your produce items correctly to retain their nutritional, textural, and flavor attributes as much as possible. Avoid overtrimming and overcooking produce, as either extreme can reduce servable yields appreciably.

PURCHASING FRESH VEGETABLES AND FRUIT

We cover four formulas in this section.

FORMULA 1   The amount to purchase formula for converting a trimmed weight to an AP weight is as follows:

**Amount needed in trimmed ounces ÷ Y%
= Amount to buy (AP)**

Example
Given: You need to serve 180 ounces of trimmed carrots. The yield percentage for medium carrots is 81.3 percent.

180 oz. ÷ 0.813 = 221.4 oz.

Therefore, you need to purchase 221.4 ounces of raw medium carrots.

Y% means yield percentage ✦ AS means as served (or used) ✦ AP means as purchased ✦ AS ÷ AP = Y% ✦
AS ÷ Y% = AP ✦ AP × Y% = AS ✦ Cost per AP unit ÷ Y% = Cost per servable unit

IN THE WORKBOOK

Part II, the Workbook, has one worksheet to help you make your calculations when going from a trimmed produce item, piece counts, or drained weights to a purchase unit:

♦ Produce, Purchasing, Worksheet 3

NOTE

When a formula involves a cup measure and you are dealing with large quantities such as a half gallon, add 3.5 percent to the half-gallon/8-cup weight equivalent and 7 percent to the gallon equivalent to account for compaction in these larger vessels. The worksheet reminds you to do this.

NOTE

A *base item* refers to the basic food used to produce the cut item. The base item in the following example would be the raw AP medium table carrots.

Compaction Factor

When cut vegetables are put into larger containers, such as a gallon, they will compact a little so it's a good idea to add to the calculated amount to account for this compaction. The actual amount of compaction depends on a number of factors. Large, irregular cuts such as a coarse *paysanne* cut compact less than small, uniform cuts such as a quarter-inch dice, *brunoise*, shredded, or grated foods. In general, add 2 percent to a quart, 3.5 percent to a half-gallon measure, and 7 percent to a gallon measure. For example, in the previous example, the 20 cups of grated carrots is 1.25 gallons, so you would add 7 percent to the 78 ounces:

78 oz. × 107% = 83.46 oz.

Then divide that by the trim yield percentage of 81.3 to get an answer that "builds in" the compaction factor:

83.46 oz. ÷ 81.3 = 102.7 oz.

FORMULA 2 The formula for converting as-served cups to an as-purchased weight using ounces is as follows:

**(Cups needed × Trimmed ounce weight per cup
= Trimmed ounces needed) ÷ Trim yield percentage
for the base item
= AP amount in ounces**

Example
Given: You need to serve 20 cups of grated carrots. The Vegetables table shows that 1 cup of grated carrots weighs 3.9 ounces; and 20 cups times 3.9 ounces equals 78 ounces. The percentage yield of the base item (medium table carrots) is 81.3 percent:

78 oz. ÷ 0.813 = 95.9 oz.

Therefore, you should buy 95.9 ounces of fresh, medium table carrots.

FORMULA 3 To convert AP ounces of carrots to AP pounds, you simply divide the AP ounces by 16.

Example (using the answer in the compaction factor note)
102.7 oz. ÷ 16 oz. = 6.42 lb.

You need to buy or cost 6.42 pounds of AP medium carrots. Another way to compute the amount to buy based on the number of cups yielded is to use the Number of Trimmed/Cleaned Cups per AP Unit column in the Vegetables table. This gives you an answer measured by purchase unit, which may be a pound or any other measure.

**(1 ÷ Trimmed cups per purchase unit)
× Cups needed = AP units to buy**

Example
Given: You need 15 cups of shredded Napa cabbage, and the purchase unit of Napa cabbage is 1 head, weighing 34 ounces. The Vegetables table shows that this head yields 12.105 cups of shredded cabbage. The formula application goes like this:

**1 ÷ 12.105 = 0.0826
0.0826 × 15 cups = 1.239 purchase units**

Therefore, you need 1.239 heads of cabbage (weighing 34 ounces per head).

FORMULA 4 Some produce items may be portioned by pieces, or parts, of a purchase unit. For example, red radishes may be portioned or called for in a recipe as a count of individual, whole radishes. Likewise, lettuce can be used by individual leaf counts. To determine how much to buy, first add up all the items (like radishes or lettuce leaves) you need to serve. Next go to that

1 gal. = 4 qt. = 16 c. = 128 fl. oz. ♦ 1 qt. = 2 pt. = 4 c. = 32 fl. oz. ♦ 1 pt. = 2 c. = 16 fl. oz. ♦
1 c. = 8 fl. oz. = 16 tbsp. ♦ 1 fl. oz. = 2 tbsp. ♦ 1 tbsp. = 3 tsp. ♦ 1 lb. = 16 oz.

food's listing in the appropriate table and see how many pieces are in the whole purchase unit. Then simply divide the number of pieces obtained from that purchase unit into the number of individual pieces you need to serve.

The formula for making purchases using piece, or individual item, counts is this:

AS # of leaves or pieces ÷ Trimmed and/or culled count = AP units to buy

Example
Given: You need 45 Bibb lettuce leaves for underliners. The Vegetables table tells you that Bibb lettuce type yields nine such leaves per head. So, divide 45 by 9 to compute how many heads you will need to buy:

45 ÷ 9 = 5

You need to buy or use five heads of Bibb lettuce to serve 45 Bibb lettuce leaves.

PURCHASING FORMULAS FOR CANNED FOODS

This section on canned foods contains three formulas, based on the contents of food sold in number-10 cans.

FORMULA 1 The formula for computing the quantity of number-10 cans needed based on USDA minimum *drained weights* is as follows:

AS weight in drained ounces ÷ USDA drained weight per #10 can = AP #10 cans

Example
Given: You are serving 222 ounces of canned pimento pieces. The Canned Foods (in number-10 cans) table shows there are 74 ounces of drained pimento pieces per number-10 can.

1. Divide the AS amount of 222 ounces by the USDA drained weight per can (74 ounces):

222 ÷ 74 = 3

Clearly, then, you will need three whole number-10 cans of pimento pieces.

FORMULA 2 This formula is used to convert undrained ounces to the quantity of number-10 cans needed:

**AS undrained ounces needed ÷ Total net (actual) ounces per can
= AP # of cans**

Example
Given: You need 210 ounces of tomato sauce. The Canned Foods Weight-to-Volume table shows that a number-10 can of tomato sauce contains 104.9 ounces.

210 ÷ 104.9 = 2 (rounded)

Hence, you will need two number-10 cans of tomato sauce.

FORMULA 3 To convert a volume of drained or undrained canned food to number-10 cans, use this formula:

**(AS volumes needed × Ounces per volume)
÷ Net or drained ounces per number-10 can = AP number-10 cans**

Y% means yield percentage ✦ AS means as served (or used) ✦ AP means as purchased ✦ AS ÷ AP = Y% ✦
AS ÷ Y% = AP ✦ AP × Y% = AS ✦ Cost per AP unit ÷ Y% = Cost per servable unit

Use the Canned Foods Weight-to-Volume table for the data on the measurements.

Example

Given: You need two cups of diced beets. The table shows that a cup of drained diced beets weighs 5.3 ounces. Therefore, 2 cups at 5.3 ounces equals 10.6 ounces. The Canned Foods Weight-to-Volume table shows that the can of diced beets contains 72.4 ounces, drained:

10.6 ÷ 72.4 = 0.146

You need 14.6 percent of a number-10 can.

PURCHASING MISCELLANEOUS CANNED OR BOTTLED PRODUCE ITEMS

The Produce table includes some items that are canned or bottled. These are often brined or marinated foods and are packed in containers other than number-10 cans. To determine how much of these foods to buy (or use), use the following formulae.

FORMULA 1   You can use the drained weight method.

Ounces needed ÷ Drained ounces per AP container = AP containers

Example

Given: You need 108 ounces of drained, marinated artichoke hearts and you buy these in 60-ounce jars. The Produce table shows that a 60 ounce jar of artichoke hearts yields 43 ounces, drained. To calculate the number of AP jars to buy or use, divide the total ounces needed (108) by the drained ounces per jar.

108 oz. ÷ 43 = 2.51

You need two and a half jars.

FORMULA 2   Use the yield percentage method to determine the amount of jars to buy by dividing the number of ounces needed (108) by the Y%: (71.67%), and then divide that amount by the ounces per AP container (60).

(Ounces needed ÷ Y%) ÷ Ounces per AP container = AP containers

Example

108 oz. ÷ 0.7167 = 150.7 oz.

150.7 oz. ÷ 60 = 2.51

FORMULA 3   Count per Container method

Count needed ÷ Count per AP container = AP containers

Example

Given: You need 180 marinated artichoke hearts. The table shows that there are 60 pieces per container. Divide 180 by 60.

180 ÷ 60 = 3

Thus, you need three jars.

1 gal. = 4 qt. = 16 c. = 128 fl. oz. ✦ 1 qt. = 2 pt. = 4 c. = 32 fl. oz. ✦ 1 pt. = 2 c. = 16 fl. oz. ✦
1 c. = 8 fl. oz. = 16 tbsp. ✦ 1 fl. oz. = 2 tbsp. ✦ 1 tbsp. = 3 tsp. ✦ 1 lb. = 16 oz.

Vegetables

Item Name	AP Unit	Number of Measures per AP Unit	Measure per AP Units	Trimmed/ Cleaned Ounce Weight or Count	Yield Percent	Trimmed/ Cleaned Ounce Weight per Cup	Number of Trimmed/ Cleaned Cups per AP Unit
Alfalfa seeds, for sprouting	pound	16	ounce	16	100.00%	6.85	2.336
Alfalfa Sprouts	bag	16	ounce	15.25	95.3%	1.70	8.971
Artichokes #18 (1 lb. each)	case	18	each	17.5 each	97.2%		
Artichokes #36 (8 oz. each)	case	36	each	35 each	97.2%		
Artichokes, baby	pound	9	each	9 each			
Artichoke Hearts, marinated, drained	jar	60	ounce	43	71.67%		
Artichoke Hearts, marinated, drained	jar	60	ounce	80 each			
Arugula Sprouts	pound	16	ounce	15.35	95.94%	0.95	16.158
Arugula, young leaves, cleaned	bag	5.15	ounce	5	97.09%	0.6	8.333
Arugula, young leaves, cleaned, chopped	bag	5.15	ounce	5	97.09%	0.8	6.250
Asparagus, jumbo trimmed	pound	16	ounce	9.52	59.5%	4.50	2.110
Asparagus, jumbo whole	pound	9	each	8.5 each	94.4%		
Asparagus, standard trimmed	pound	16	ounce	9.13	57.1%	4.75	1.920
Asparagus, standard whole	pound	16	each	14.5 each	90.6%		
Asparagus, thin export trimmed	pound	16	ounce	9.02	56.4%	5.00	1.800
Asparagus, thin export whole	pound	38	each	34 each	89.5%		
Asparagus, white, 8 in. long	pound	16	ounce	16 each			
Asparagus, white, 8 in. long, peeled, cut to 5 in.	pound	16	ounce	10.75	67.19%		
Avocado, whole	each	7	ounce	5.5	78.6%		
Avocados, 1/2 in. dice	each	7	ounce	5.5	78.6%	5.40	1.019
Avocados, puree	each	7	ounce	5.5	78.6%	8.10	0.679
Bamboo Root, trimmed, sliced, cooked	each	25.9	ounce	13.9	53.67%	4.85	2.866
Bamboo Shoot, sliced from whole piece	pound	16	ounce	15.4	96.25%		
Bamboo Shoot, sliced from whole, cored	pound	16	ounce	11.55	72.19%	4.5	2.567
Basil Sprouts	pound	16	ounce	15.25	95.31%	0.95	16.053
Bean Sprouts (Mung)	pound	16	ounce	15.5	96.9%	3.20	4.844
Beans, green	pound	16	ounce	14.1	88.1%		
Beans, green, 1 in. cut	pound	16	ounce	14.1	88.1%	3.90	3.615

Y% means yield percentage ✦ AS means as served (or used) ✦ AP means as purchased ✦ AS ÷ AP = Y% ✦
AS ÷ Y% = AP ✦ AP × Y% = AS ✦ Cost per AP unit ÷ Y% = Cost per servable unit

Vegetables (Continued)

Item Name	AP Unit	Number of Measures per AP Unit	Measure per AP Units	Trimmed/ Cleaned Ounce Weight or Count	Yield Percent	Trimmed/ Cleaned Ounce Weight per Cup	Number of Trimmed/ Cleaned Cups per AP Unit
Beets, whole 2 in. diameter	pound	16	ounce	10.56	66.0%		
Belgian Endive	head	4	ounce	3.3	82.5%		
Belgian Endive, leaves	head	1	each	12 leaves			
Bitter Melon, sliced	each	15.15	ounce	12.25	80.86%	3.20	3.828
Bok Choy, baby	pound	12	each	11	91.7%		
Bok Choy, regular	head	24	ounce	21	87.5%		
Broccoli, bunch, whole	each	21.5	ounce	13.5	62.8%		
Broccoli, Chinese	bunch	13.7	ounce	12.8	93.43%	4.30	2.977
Broccoli, florets	each	21.5	ounce	13.5	62.8%	2.50	5.400
Broccoli, florets—chopped	each	21.5	ounce	13.5	62.8%	3.10	4.355
Broccoli seeds, for sprouting	pound	16	ounce	16	100.00%	6	2.667
Broccolini, Sweet baby broccoli	bunch	17.2	ounce	20 each			
Broccolini, Sweet baby broccoli, trimmed	bunch	17.2	ounce	16.79	97.59%		
Brussels Sprouts	pound	16	ounce	14.2	88.8%	3.20	4.438
Brussels Sprouts, medium, each	pound	20	each	20			
Cabbage, Coleslaw mix	bag	16	ounce	15.9	99.38%	1.99	8.000
Cabbage, green/red	head	40	ounce	32	80.0%		
Cabbage, green/red—chopped	head	40	ounce	32	80.0%	2.50	12.800
Cabbage, green/red—shredded	head	40	ounce	32	80.0%	3.30	9.697
Cabbage, Napa	head	34	ounce	29.9	87.9%		
Cabbage, Napa, shredded ~1/4″	head	34	ounce	29.9	87.9%	2.47	12.105
Cabbage, Savoy	head	36	ounce	29.8	82.8%		
Cabbage, Savoy, shredded ~1/4″	head	36	ounce	29.8	82.8%	2.50	11.920
Capers, nonpareil, drained	jar	7	ounce	4.7	67.14%	4.7	1.000
Cardoon, large	head	35	ounce	18	51.4%		
Carrots, baby, cut and peeled	pound	16	ounce	66 each			
Carrots, chopped	pound	16	ounce	13	81.3%	4.90	2.653
Carrots, diced 1/3 to 1/2 in.	pound	16	ounce	13	81.3%	5.00	2.600

1 gal. = 4 qt. = 16 c. = 128 fl. oz. ✦ 1 qt. = 2 pt. = 4 c. = 32 fl. oz. ✦ 1 pt. = 2 c. = 16 fl. oz. ✦
1 c. = 8 fl. oz. = 16 tbsp. ✦ 1 fl. oz. = 2 tbsp. ✦ 1 tbsp. = 3 tsp. ✦ 1 lb. = 16 oz.

Vegetables (Continued)

Item Name	AP Unit	Number of Measures per AP Unit	Measure per AP Units	Trimmed/ Cleaned Ounce Weight or Count	Yield Percent	Trimmed/ Cleaned Ounce Weight per Cup	Number of Trimmed/ Cleaned Cups per AP Unit
Carrots, grated	pound	16	ounce	13	81.3%	3.90	3.333
Carrots, ground	pound	16	ounce	13	81.3%	5.33	2.439
Carrots, petite, 6 in. long (slender), topped, scrubbed	pound	16	ounce	14.61	91.34%		
Carrots, petite, 6 in. long (slender), whole	pound	16	ounce	13.8 each			
Carrots, sliced about 1/4 in.	pound	16	ounce	13	81.3%	4.20	3.095
Carrots, table, medium	pound	16	ounce	13	81.3%		
Carrots, table, medium, juice yield of 1 lb.	pound	16	ounce	10.08	62.98%	8.60	1.172
Carrots, whole, baby	pound	16	ounce	35 each	99.0%	6.20	2.550
Carrots, whole, jumbo	each	5.5	ounce	4.6	83.6%		
Carrots, whole, medium	each	4.1	ounce	3.3	81.3%		
Cauliflower	head	30	ounce	18	60.0%		
Cauliflower, cut 1" florets	head	30	ounce	18	60.0%	4.70	3.830
Celeriac (Celery Root)	head	19	ounce	11.5	60.5%		
Celeriac, julienne	head	19	ounce	11.5	60.5%	3.00	3.833
Celery	bunch	32	ounce	22	68.8%		
Celery, diced 1/3 to 1/2 in.	bunch	32	ounce	22	68.8%	4.00	5.500
Celery, juice yield of 1 lb.	pound	16	ounce	10.55	65.94%	8.60	1.227
Celery, stalks per bunch	bunch	1	each	10 each			
Celery, tops per bunch	bunch	32	ounce	9 ounce top	28.0%		
Chard, Red Swiss, stemmed, chopped	bunch	15.5	ounce	10.20	65.81%	1.11	9.169
Chard, Swiss	bunch	14	ounce	12.75	91.1%		
Chard, Swiss, chopped	bunch	14	ounce	12.75	91.1%	2.30	5.543
Chicory (Curly Endive)	head	18.95	ounce	16.15	85.22%	1.01	16.006
Cilantro Sprouts	pound	16	ounce	15.25	95.31%	0.9	16.944
Cocktail Onions, large, drained	jar	16.9	ounce	9.6	56.80%	4.95	1.939
Cocktail Onions, large, drained, cup count	jar	16.9	ounce	24 each			
Cocktail Onions, large, drained, jar count	jar	16.9	ounce	48 each			
Collard Greens	bunch	12	ounce	7.8	65.0%		

Y% means yield percentage ✦ AS means as served (or used) ✦ AP means as purchased ✦ AS ÷ AP = Y% ✦
AS ÷ Y% = AP ✦ AP × Y% = AS ✦ Cost per AP unit ÷ Y% = Cost per servable unit

Vegetables (Continued)

Item Name	AP Unit	Number of Measures per AP Unit	Measure per AP Units	Trimmed/ Cleaned Ounce Weight or Count	Yield Percent	Trimmed/ Cleaned Ounce Weight per Cup	Number of Trimmed/ Cleaned Cups per AP Unit
Collard Greens, chopped	bunch	12	ounce	7.8	65.0%	1.90	4.105
Corn Cob, fresh niblets	whole	17.24	ounce	5	29.0%	5.75	0.870
Cranberry Beans in pods	pound	16	ounce	8.55	53.44%	5.05	1.693
Cucumber	each	10	ounce	9.5	95.0%		
Cucumber, sliced	each	10	ounce	9.5	95.0%	4.80	1.979
Cucumber, peeled, seeded, sliced	each	10	ounce	5.5	55.0%	4.40	2.159
Cucumber, peeled, seeded, diced	each	10	ounce	5.5	55.0%	5.30	1.792
Cucumber, whole, English	each	16	ounce	15.7	98.1%		
Cucumber, whole, English, sliced	each	16	ounce	15.7	98.1%	4.50	3.489
Dandelion Greens	bunch	12.75	ounce	6.05	47.45%		
Dandelion Greens, chopped 1/2 in.	bunch	12.75	ounce	6.05	47.45%	1.21	4.992
Edamame, hulled (fresh Soybeans)	carton	19.6	ounce	17.6	90.0%	6.33	2.78
Eggplant, Indian, cubed	pound	16	ounce	14.95	93.44%	3.7	4.041
Eggplant, Indian, whole	pound	16	ounce	9.3 each			
Eggplant, Japanese, sliced	bag	9.3	ounce	8.4	90.32%	2.68	3.140
Eggplant, peeled	each	19	ounce	16	84.2%		
Eggplant, peeled, cubed	each	19	ounce	16	84.2%	2.90	5.517
Eggplant, Thai, quartered	bag	7.45	ounce	9 each	90.60%	4.20	1.770
Escarole, chopped	head	19.05	ounce	11.6	60.89%	1.2	9.667
Fennel with 6 in. stem	head	14	ounce	13	92.9%		
Fennel, stemmed	head	14	ounce	7.8	55.7%		
Fennel, stemmed, sliced 1/4 in.	head	14	ounce	7.8	55.7%	3.90	2.000
Fiddlehead Ferns	pound	16	ounce	150 each			
Galangal, peeled, sliced	piece	11.05	ounce	8.1	73.30%	3.3	2.455
Garlic	head	2.1	ounce	1.85	83.0%		
Garlic, chopped, fresh	head	2.1	ounce	1.85	88.1%	4.80	0.402
Garlic, cloves per head	head	2.1	ounce	12	cloves		
Garlic Cloves, already peeled	jar	16	ounce	15.8	98.75%	5.15	3.068

1 gal. = 4 qt. = 16 c. = 128 fl. oz. ✦ 1 qt. = 2 pt. = 4 c. = 32 fl. oz. ✦ 1 pt. = 2 c. = 16 fl. oz. ✦
1 c. = 8 fl. oz. = 16 tbsp. ✦ 1 fl. oz. = 2 tbsp. ✦ 1 tbsp. = 3 tsp. ✦ 1 lb. = 16 oz.

Vegetables (Continued)

Item Name	AP Unit	Number of Measures per AP Unit	Measure per AP Units	Trimmed/ Cleaned Ounce Weight or Count	Yield Percent	Trimmed/ Cleaned Ounce Weight per Cup	Number of Trimmed/ Cleaned Cups per AP Unit
Garlic Cloves, peeled and roasted	jar	16	ounce	15.7	98.13%	6.05	2.595
Garlic, chopped, in oil	jar	16	ounce	15.6	97.50%	9.2	1.696
Garlic, Elephant	each	7.55	ounce	7.05	93.38%		
Grape Leaves, bottled	jar	8	ounce	42 each			
Haricots Verts	bag	14.4	ounce	13.05	90.63%		
Haricots Verts, 1 in. lengths	bag	14.4	ounce	13.05	90.63%	3.35	3.896
Haricots Verts, whole	pound	16	ounce	252 each			
Hojas (dry corn husks)	bag	8	ounce	64 each			
Horseradish Root, peeled	pound	16	ounce	11.6	72.50%		
Horseradish Root, peeled, shredded	pound	16	ounce	11.6	72.50%	2.5	4.640
Jerusalem Artichoke	pound	16	ounce	11	68.8%		
Jerusalem Artichoke, sliced	pound	16	ounce	11	68.8%	5.30	2.075
Jicama	pound	16	ounce	13	81.3%		
Kale, flowering, leaves	bunch	12	ounce	24 leaves			
Kale, green	bunch	20	ounce	12	60.0%		
Kale, green, chopped	bunch	20	ounce	12	60.0%	2.36	5.085
Kohlrabi, leaves on	pound	16	ounce	7.5	46.9%		
Kohlrabi, sliced	pound	16	ounce	7.5	46.9%	4.70	1.596
Leeks	pound	16	ounce	7	43.8%		
Leeks, cross-sliced 1/4 in.	pound	16	ounce	7	43.8%	3.10	2.258
Lemon Grass, minced	pound	16	ounce	10.4	65.00%	3.05	3.410
Lemon Grass, trimmed	pound	16	ounce	10.4	65.00%		
Lemon Grass, whole	pound	16	ounce	6 each	100.00%		
Lentil seeds, for sprouting	pound	16	ounce	16	100.00%	6.85	2.336
Lettuce, Bibb, leaves	head	6	ounce	9 leaves			
Lettuce, Butter/Bibb 5 in.	head	6	ounce	4.8	80.0%		
Lettuce, Butter/Bibb, chopped	head	6	ounce	4.8	80.0%	1.95	2.462
Lettuce, European Baby Greens, bagged	bag	5.8	ounce	5.7	98.28%	1.40	4.071

Y% means yield percentage ✦ AS means as served (or used) ✦ AP means as purchased ✦ AS ÷ AP = Y% ✦
AS ÷ Y% = AP ✦ AP × Y% = AS ✦ Cost per AP unit ÷ Y% = Cost per servable unit

Vegetables (Continued)

Item Name	AP Unit	Number of Measures per AP Unit	Measure per AP Units	Trimmed/ Cleaned Ounce Weight or Count	Yield Percent	Trimmed/ Cleaned Ounce Weight per Cup	Number of Trimmed/ Cleaned Cups per AP Unit
Lettuce, Greenleaf	head	16	ounce	13	81.3%		
Lettuce, Greenleaf, chopped	head	16	ounce	13	81.3%	1.95	6.667
Lettuce, Greenleaf, leaves	head	16	ounce	12 leaves			
Lettuce, Iceberg	head	26	ounce	19	73.1%		
Lettuce, Iceberg, carrot, red cabbage mix, bagged	bag	24.6	ounce	24	97.56%	1.50	16
Lettuce, Iceberg, chopped	head	26	ounce	19	73.1%	1.95	9.744
Lettuce, Mâche Blend: (Mâche, Frisee, Radicchio)	bag	5.4	ounce	5.35	99.07%	1.13	3.85
Lettuce, Redleaf	head	14	ounce	10.5	75.0%		
Lettuce, Redleaf, chopped	head	14	ounce	10.5	75.0%	1.95	5.385
Lettuce, Redleaf, leaves	head	14	ounce	12 leaves			
Lettuce, Romaine	head	24	ounce	18	75.0%		
Lettuce, Romaine, chopped	head	24	ounce	18	75.0%	2.00	9.000
Lettuce, Romaine, leaves	head	24	ounce	16 leaves			
Lotus Root	each	5	ounce	4	80.0%		
Malanga, peeled	pound	16	ounce	11.77	73.56%		
Malanga, peeled, thinly sliced	pound	16	ounce	11.77	73.56%	4.5	2.616
Mushrooms, Crimini, stemmed	pound	16	ounce	11.89	74.31%		
Mushrooms, Crimini, stems tipped	pound	16	ounce	14.3	89.38		
Mushrooms, Crimini, w/stems, sliced	pound	16	ounce	11.89	74.31%	2.2	5.405
Mushrooms, large, each	pound	16	ounce	12 each			
Mushrooms, Lion's Mane, sliced 1/2 in. pieces	pound	16	ounce	15.00	93.75%	2.6	5.769
Mushrooms, medium, each	pound	16	ounce	22 each			
Mushrooms, Morels, dry	bag	16	ounce	416 each		0.7	
Mushrooms, Morels, fresh	pound	16	ounce	72 each	85.00%	3.80	4.200
Mushrooms, Oyster, sliced	basket	5.8	ounce	5.5	94.83%	2.10	2.619
Mushrooms, Oyster, whole	basket	5.8	ounce	5.5	94.83%	1.90	2.895
Mushrooms, Porcini, dry	bag	7.5	ounce	7.4	98.67%	0.94	7.893
Mushrooms, Portobello 2 in.	pound	16	ounce	15 each			

1 gal. = 4 qt. = 16 c. = 128 fl. oz. ♦ 1 qt. = 2 pt. = 4 c. = 32 fl. oz. ♦ 1 pt. = 2 c. = 16 fl. oz. ♦
1 c. = 8 fl. oz. = 16 tbsp. ♦ 1 fl. oz. = 2 tbsp. ♦ 1 tbsp. = 3 tsp. ♦ 1 lb. = 16 oz.

Vegetables (Continued)

Item Name	AP Unit	Number of Measures per AP Unit	Measure per AP Units	Trimmed/ Cleaned Ounce Weight or Count	Yield Percent	Trimmed/ Cleaned Ounce Weight per Cup	Number of Trimmed/ Cleaned Cups per AP Unit
Mushrooms, Shiitake	pound	16	ounce	46 each			
Mushrooms, Shiitake, culled, stem trimmed	pound	16	ounce	12.86	80.38%		
Mushrooms, Shiitake, dried	package	2.6	ounce	2.5	96.15%	1.2	2.083
Mushrooms, Shiitake, dried	package	2.6	ounce	25 each			
Mushrooms, small, each	pound	16	ounce	45 each			
Mushrooms, white	pound	16	ounce	15 ounce	93.8%		
Mushrooms, white, sliced	pound	16	ounce	15 ounce	93.8%	2.50	6.000
Mushrooms, white, whole	pound	16	ounce	15 ounce	93.8%	3.40	4.412
Mustard Greens	bunch	12	ounce	9	75.0%		
Mustard Greens, chopped	bunch	12	ounce	9	75.0%	2.50	3.600
Nopales (Cactus leaves)	bag	22.1	ounce	19.85	89.82%		
Okra, trimmed	pound	16	ounce	13.5	84.38%		
Okra, trimmed, sliced 1/2 in.	pound	16	ounce	13.5	84.38%	3.5	3.857
Okra, whole	pound	16	ounce	46 each			
Olives, Kalamata, pitted	pound	16	ounce	184 each		5.4	2.963
Olives, Kalamata, with pits	pound	16	ounce	92 each			
Onions, boiling, peeled	pound	16	ounce	14.4	90.00%		
Onions, boiling, peeled	pound	16	ounce	10 each			
Onions, bulb	pound	16	ounce	14.5	90.6%		
Onions, bulb, 1/2 in. diced	pound	16	ounce	14.5	90.6%	3.90	3.718
Onions, bulb, 1/4 in. diced	pound	16	ounce	14.5	90.6%	4.45	3.750
Onions, bulb, sliced	pound	16	ounce	14.5	90.6%	3.00	4.833
Onions, Cipollini, peeled	pound	16	ounce	15.48	96.75%		
Onions, Cipollini, whole	pound	16	ounce	13 each			
Onions, dehydrated, chopped	pound	16	ounce	16	100.0%	3.00	5.330
Onions, each large	each	13.7	ounce	12.5	91.2%		
Onions, each small	each	7.8	ounce	6.9	88.5%		
Onions, Green	bunch	3.5	ounce	2.9	82.9%		

Y% means yield percentage ✦ AS means as served (or used) ✦ AP means as purchased ✦ AS ÷ AP = Y% ✦
AS ÷ Y% = AP ✦ AP × Y% = AS ✦ Cost per AP unit ÷ Y% = Cost per servable unit

Vegetables (Continued)

Item Name	AP Unit	Number of Measures per AP Unit	Measure per AP Units	Trimmed/ Cleaned Ounce Weight or Count	Yield Percent	Trimmed/ Cleaned Ounce Weight per Cup	Number of Trimmed/ Cleaned Cups per AP Unit
Onions, Green, chopped	bunch	3.5	ounce	2.9	82.9%	2.00	1.450
Onions, Green, each	bunch	3.5	ounce	7 each			
Onions, Pearl	basket	11	ounce	9.3	84.5%		
Parsnips	pound	16	ounce	13.5	84.4%		
Parsnips, sliced	pound	16	ounce	13.5	84.4%	4.70	2.872
Peas, Snap	pound	16	ounce	15	93.8%	2.20	6.818
Peas, Snap, chopped	pound	16	ounce	15	93.8%	3.50	4.286
Peas, Snap, whole, each	pound	16	ounce	90 each			
Peas, Snow, whole, each	pound	16	ounce	120 each			
Peppers, all, Brunoise	pound	16	ounce	8	50.0%	7.00	1.143
Peppers, Anaheim 7 in.	pound	16	ounce	8 each			
Peppers, Anaheim, seeded, diced	pound	16	ounce	13.85	86.56%	3.80	3.645
Peppers, Green Bells, 7 oz.	pound	16	ounce	13	81.3%		
Peppers, Green, chopped	pound	16	ounce	13	81.3%	5.20	2.500
Peppers, Green, sliced	pound	16	ounce	13	81.3%	3.20	4.063
Peppers, Habañero, 1/6 in. rings	pound	16	ounce	14.04	87.75%	2.10	6.686
Peppers, Habañero, chopped	pound	16	ounce	14.04	87.75%	3.85	3.647
Peppers, Habañero, stemmed	pound	16	ounce	14.04	87.75%		
Peppers, Habañero, whole	pound	16	ounce	52 each			
Peppers, Jalapeño Rings, canned, drained	can	12	ounce	6.618	55.15%	4.55	1.455
Peppers, Jalapeño Rings, canned undrained	can	12	ounce	12	100.00%	8.25	1.455
Peppers, Jalapeño, chopped w/seeds	pound	16	ounce	14.96	93.50%	3.75	3.989
Peppers, Jalapeño, chopped, seedless	pound	16	ounce	14.96	93.50%	3.9	3.836
Peppers, Jalapeño, sliced w/seeds	pound	16	ounce	14.96	93.50%	2.8	5.343
Peppers, Jalapeño, sliced, seedless	pound	16	ounce	14.96	93.50%	3.4	4.400
Peppers, Jalapeño, stemmed	pound	16	ounce	14.96	93.50%		
Peppers, Jalapeño, whole	pound	16	ounce	26 each			
Peppers, Pasilla, cored, seeded	pound	16	ounce	12.16	76.00%		

1 gal. = 4 qt. = 16 c. = 128 fl. oz. ♦ 1 qt. = 2 pt. = 4 c. = 32 fl. oz. ♦ 1 pt. = 2 c. = 16 fl. oz. ♦
1 c. = 8 fl. oz. = 16 tbsp. ♦ 1 fl. oz. = 2 tbsp. ♦ 1 tbsp. = 3 tsp. ♦ 1 lb. = 16 oz.

Vegetables (Continued)

Item Name	AP Unit	Number of Measures per AP Unit	Measure per AP Units	Trimmed/Cleaned Ounce Weight or Count	Yield Percent	Trimmed/Cleaned Ounce Weight per Cup	Number of Trimmed/Cleaned Cups per AP Unit
Peppers, Pasilla, diced	pound	16	ounce	12.16	76.00%	3.8	3.200
Peppers, Pasilla, whole	pound	16	ounce	5 each			
Peppers, Red Bells, 10 oz.	pound	16	ounce	13.5	84.4%		
Peppers, Red, chopped	pound	16	ounce	13.5	84.4%	4.50	3.000
Peppers, Red, julienne	pound	16	ounce	13.5	84.4%	3.60	3.750
Peppers, Red, sliced	pound	16	ounce	13.5	84.4%	3.30	4.091
Peppers, Serrano, chopped fine w/seeds	pound	16	ounce	13.88	86.75%	3.8	3.653
Peppers, Serrano, stemmed	pound	16	ounce	13.88	86.75%		
Peppers, Serrano, whole	pound	16	ounce	106 each			
Peppers, Yellow-Hot, whole	pound	16	ounce	32 each			
Potato, Baker-Russet	pound	16	ounce	12.5	78.1%		
Potato, peeled, diced	pound	16	ounce	12.5	78.1%	5.00	2.500
Potato, peeled, shredded	pound	16	ounce	12.5	78.1%	6.00	2.083
Potato, peeled, sliced	pound	16	ounce	12.5	78.1%	5.20	2.404
Potatoes, dehyd. flakes	pound	16	ounce	16	100.0%	3.20	5.000
Potatoes, dehyd. granules	pound	16	ounce	16	100.0%	7.10	2.250
Potatoes, fingerling, whole	pound	16	ounce	14 each			
Potatoes, new, White Rose, cubed into eighths	pound	16	ounce	15.60	97.50%	6.15	2.537
Potatoes, new, White Rose, whole	pound	16	ounce	2.77 each			
Potatoes, Red, size A, diced 3/8 in.	pound	16	ounce	15.87	99.17%	5.25	3.022
Potatoes, Red, size A, whole	pound	16	ounce	4 each			
Potatoes, Small Creamers	pound	16	ounce	11 each			
Pumpkins, miniature (6.8 oz. each)	pound	16	ounce	2.35 each			
Pumpkin, whole	each	96	ounce	60.5	63.0%		
Purslane	pound	16	ounce	12	75.0%	1.50	8.000
Purslane, stemmed	pound	16	ounce	8.87	55.44%	1.4	6.336
Radicchio	head	8.7	ounce	8	92.0%	3.00	2.667
Radish, Black, 2 to 2-3/4 in. diameter	pound	16	ounce	4 each			

Y% means yield percentage ✦ AS means as served (or used) ✦ AP means as purchased ✦ AS ÷ AP = Y% ✦
AS ÷ Y% = AP ✦ AP × Y% = AS ✦ Cost per AP unit ÷ Y% = Cost per servable unit

Vegetables (Continued)

Item Name	AP Unit	Number of Measures per AP Unit	Measure per AP Units	Trimmed/ Cleaned Ounce Weight or Count	Yield Percent	Trimmed/ Cleaned Ounce Weight per Cup	Number of Trimmed/ Cleaned Cups per AP Unit
Radish, Black, peeled, grated	pound	16	ounce	12.68	79.25%	3.45	3.675
Radish, Daikon	each	16	ounce	14	87.5%		
Radish, Easter Egg, quartered lengthwise	bunch	11.3	ounce	7.30	64.60%	4.2	1.738
Radish, Easter Egg, whole	bunch	11.3	ounce	17 each			
Radish, Red, large 1 3/8 in.	bunch			12 each			
Radish, Red, sliced—trimmed	bunch					4.10	1.000
Radish, Watermelon, 2 in. diameter	pound	16	ounce	8.6 each			
Radish, Watermelon, sliced	pound	16	ounce	12.00	75.00%	3.85	3.117
Ramps (Wild Leeks)	pound	16	ounce	45 each			
Rhubarb	pound	16	ounce	4 stalks	92.0%		
Rhubarb, cubed	pound	16	ounce	14.7	92.0%	3.80	3.868
Rutabaga	pound	16	ounce	13	81.3%		
Rutabaga, Brunoise	pound	16	ounce	13	81.3%	4.40	2.955
Rutabaga, diced 1/4 in.	pound	16	ounce	13	81.3%	4.50	2.889
Rutabaga, julienne	pound	16	ounce	13	81.3%	3.70	3.514
Salsify (Oyster Plant)	pound	16	ounce	14	87.5%		
Shallots, whole	pound	16	ounce	9.6 each			
Shallots, peeled, diced	pound	16	ounce	12.83	80.21%	4.9	2.619
Shallots, peeled, sliced crosswise	pound	16	ounce	12.83	80.21%	4.1	3.130
Sorrel leaves, stemmed	pound	16	ounce	10.096	63.10%		
Sorrel leaves, stemmed, chopped	pound	16	ounce	10.096	63.10%	1.1	9.178
Soy Bean Curd (Tofu), firm, 3/4 in. cubes	package	12	ounce	11.8	98.33%	5.5	2.145
Soybean Sprouts	pound	16	ounce	15.5	96.9%	2.50	6.200
Spinach	pound	16	ounce	10.5	65.6%		
Spinach, Stemmed, Baby, bagged	bag	9.6	ounce	9.5	98.96%	0.68	14.000
Squash, Acorn	pound	16	ounce	12.1	75.6%		
Squash, Acorn, cubed	pound	16	ounce	12.1	75.6%	4.60	2.630
Squash, Banana	each	116	ounce	88.77	76.00%		

1 gal. = 4 qt. = 16 c. = 128 fl. oz. ✦ 1 qt. = 2 pt. = 4 c. = 32 fl. oz. ✦ 1 pt. = 2 c. = 16 fl. oz. ✦
1 c. = 8 fl. oz. = 16 tbsp. ✦ 1 fl. oz. = 2 tbsp. ✦ 1 tbsp. = 3 tsp. ✦ 1 lb. = 16 oz.

Vegetables (Continued)

Item Name	AP Unit	Number of Measures per AP Unit	Measure per AP Units	Trimmed/ Cleaned Ounce Weight or Count	Yield Percent	Trimmed/ Cleaned Ounce Weight per Cup	Number of Trimmed/ Cleaned Cups per AP Unit
Squash, Butternut	pound	16	ounce	13.5	84.4%		
Squash, Butternut, cubed	pound	16	ounce	13.5	84.4%	4.60	2.935
Squash, Chayote, sliced	bag	24.8	ounce	19.75	79.64%	4.70	4.202
Squash, Crookneck	pound	16	ounce	15.6	97.5%		
Squash, Crookneck, sliced	pound	16	ounce	15.6	97.5%	3.90	4.000
Squash, Hubbard	pound	16	ounce	11.4	71.3%		
Squash, Hubbard, cubed	pound	16	ounce	11.4	71.3%	4.10	2.780
Squash, Kabocha, seeded	pound	16	ounce	14.7	91.88%		
Squash, Kabocha, seeded, peeled	pound	16	ounce	11.67	72.94%		
Squash, Patty Pan (Summer)	pound	16.4	ounce	15.5	94.51%		
Squash, Patty Pan sliced	pound	16.4	ounce	15.5	94.51%	2.95	5.254
Squash, Spaghetti	pound	16	ounce	11	68.8%		
Squash, Summer	pound	16	ounce	15.2	95.0%		
Squash, Summer, sliced	pound	16	ounce	15.2	95.0%	3.90	3.897
Squash, Zucchini	pound	16	ounce	15	93.8%		
Squash, Zucchini, chopped	pound	16	ounce	15	93.8%	3.95	3.797
Squash, Zucchini, sliced	pound	16	ounce	15	93.8%	3.80	3.947
Sweet Potato	pound	16	ounce	12	75.0%		
Sweet Potato, cubed	pound	16	ounce	12	75.0%	4.70	2.553
Taro Corm, Peeled, 1/2 in. sliced	pound	16	ounce	12.4	77.50%	5.1	2.431
Taro Corm, whole	pound	16	ounce	6 each			
Taro Root	each	22.25	ounce	19.05	85.62%		
Taro Root, 1 in. dice	each	22.25	ounce	19.05	85.62%	4.20	4.536
Taro Root, 1/4 in. dice	each	22.25	ounce	19.05	85.62%	3.90	4.885
Taro Root, shredded	each	22.25	ounce	19.05	85.62%	2.75	6.927
Tomatillos	pound	16	ounce	14	87.5%		
Tomatillos, each 1 1/2 in. diameter	pound	16	ounce	10 each			
Tomato, Cherry, large	pound	16	ounce	22 each	95.0%	5.00	

Y% means yield percentage ✦ AS means as served (or used) ✦ AP means as purchased ✦ AS ÷ AP = Y% ✦
AS ÷ Y% = AP ✦ AP × Y% = AS ✦ Cost per AP unit ÷ Y% = Cost per servable unit

Vegetables (Continued)

Item Name	AP Unit	Number of Measures per AP Unit	Measure per AP Units	Trimmed/ Cleaned Ounce Weight or Count	Yield Percent	Trimmed/ Cleaned Ounce Weight per Cup	Number of Trimmed/ Cleaned Cups per AP Unit
Tomato, Cherry, small	pound	16	ounce	66 each	95.0%	5.13	
Tomato, Grape	pint	11.2	ounce	82 each	98.00%	4.85	2.310
Tomato, Sun-dried—dry	pound	16	ounce	16	100.0%	2.00	8.000
Tomatoes, Sun-dried, julienne, drained	jar	16	ounce	12.327	77.04%	5.3	2.326
Tomatoes, Sun-dried, julienne, in oil	jar	16	ounce	16	100.00%	7.35	2.177
Tomatoes, (5×6) cored	pound	16	ounce	15.75	98.4%		
Tomatoes, 5×6, juice yield of 1 lb.	pound	16	ounce	6.80	42.48%	8.75	0.777
Tomatoes, (5×6) per pound	pound	16	ounce	3 each			
Tomatoes, cored and peeled	pound	16	ounce	14.76	92.3%		
Tomatoes, peeled, seeded, chopped	pound	16	ounce	12.55	78.4%	5.90	2.127
Tomatoes, Roma	pound	16	ounce	15	93.8%		
Tomatoes, Roma, diced	pound	16	ounce	15	93.8%	5.70	2.632
Tomatoes, Roma, sliced	pound	16	ounce	15	93.8%	4.20	3.571
Turnips	pound	16	ounce	13	81.3%		
Turnips, diced, 1/4 in.	pound	16	ounce	13	81.3%	4.50	2.889
Turnips, julienne	pound	16	ounce	13	81.3%	3.70	3.514
Wasabi Root, peeled, grated very fine	pound	16	ounce	11.73	73.31%	8.8	1.333
Water Chestnuts	pound	16	ounce	11.5	71.9%		
Water Chestnuts, sliced	pound	16	ounce	11.5	71.9%	4.40	2.614
Yam, Garnet, peeled, cut in 1 1/2 in. pieces	pound	16	ounce	14.00	87.50%	5.75	2.435
Yam, Garnet, whole	pound	16	ounce	1.9 each			
Yam, Garnet, whole, peeled	pound	16	ounce	14	87.5%		
Yuca, peeled	pound	16	ounce	12.53	78.31%		
Yuca, peeled, 1/3 in. dice	pound	16	ounce	12.53	78.31%	4.6	2.724

Notes

1. **Asparagus:** Whole asparagus items show the yield after *culling* (discarding unservable stalks) but before trimming off the stalk ends. Trimming the ends yields about 63% of the whole asparagus. So, trimmed asparagus item yields reflect both the culling and stalk-end trimming, whereas the "whole" asparagus item yields reflect just that amount remaining after culling, but not trimming.

2. **Beans, Green:** Green beans are the Blue Lake variety. There are 66 each 4–6 inch beans per pound, AP. Strings and trim: 12%.

3. **Carrots:** Breakdowns of carrots—diced, grated, and so on—are based on medium table-size carrots.

4. **Cucumber:** Ends are trimmed to obtain the yield percentage.

5. **Lettuce, Bibb, Leaves:** All lettuce leaf values are large leaves, exclusive of heart leaves.

6. **Onion, Pearl:** There are about 30 trimmed, peeled pearl onions per pint, and a pint of cleaned pearl onions weighs 9 ounces.

7. **Peppers: Brunoise:** Interior membrane of peppers has been sliced off as part of the cutting.

8. **Potato:** Russet, peeled and eyed.

9. **Tomatoes, Roma:** Trim is from removing the ends.

Fruit

Item Name	AP Unit	Number of Measures per AP Unit	Measure per AP Unit	Trimmed/Cleaned Avoirdupois Ounce Weight or Count per AP Unit	Yield Percent	Trimmed/Cleaned Avoirdupois Ounce Weight per Cup	Number of Trimmed/Cleaned Cups per AP Unit
Applesauce	#10 can	111	ounce	110	99.0%	8.6	12.80
Apples, Fiji, 88 count	pound	16	ounce	11.91	74.44%		
Apples, Fiji, 88 count, peeled, cored, diced	pound	16	ounce	11.91	74.44%	4.3	2.770
Apples, Fiji, 88 count, peeled, cored, sliced	pound	16	ounce	11.91	74.44%	4.1	2.905
Apples, Fuji, juice yield of 1 Lb.	pound	16	ounce	9.11	56.97%	8.75	1.042
Apples, Golden Delicious, 80 count	pound	16	ounce	14.85	92.81%		
Apples, Golden Delicious, 80 count, peeled, cored, diced	pound	16	ounce	14.85	92.81%	3.92	3.788
Apples, Golden Delicious, 80 count, peeled, cored, sliced	pound	16	ounce	14.85	92.81%	3.73	3.981
Apples, Granny Smith, 88 count	pound	16	ounce	11.82	73.88%		
Apples, Granny Smith, 88 count, peeled, cored, diced	pound	16	ounce	11.82	73.88%	3.88	3.046
Apples, Granny Smith, 88 count, peeled, cored, sliced	pound	16	ounce	11.82	73.88%	3.73	3.169
Apples, Macintosh, 88 count	pound	16	ounce	11.56	72.25%		
Apples, Macintosh, 88 count, peeled, cored, diced	pound	16	ounce	11.56	72.25%	4	2.890
Apples, Macintosh, 88 count, peeled, cored, sliced	pound	16	ounce	11.56	72.25%	3.88	2.979
Apples, Red Delicious, 80 count	pound	16	ounce	14.38	89.88%		
Apples, Red Delicious, 80 count, peeled, cored, diced	pound	16	ounce	14.38	89.88%	4.3	3.344
Apples, Red Delicious, 80 count, peeled, cored, sliced	pound	16	ounce	14.38	89.88%	4.2	3.424
Apricots	pound	16	ounce	14.7	91.9%		
Apricots, halves	pound	16	ounce	14.7	91.9%	5.46	2.69
Apricots, halves, dry	pound	16	ounce	16	100.0%	4.58	3.49
Banana, Chips, dry	pound	16	ounce	16	100.0%	2.3	6.96
Bananas	pound	16	ounce	10.6	66.3%		
Bananas, Burro, each	bunch	19.15	ounce	4 each			
Bananas, Burro, peeled, sliced	pound	16	ounce	9.98	62.38%	5.3	1.883
Bananas, Dwarf (finger)	bunch	15.2	ounce	11 each			
Bananas, Dwarf (finger), peeled	bunch	15.2	ounce	10.58	69.61%		
Bananas, Dwarf (finger), peeled, sliced	bunch	15.2	ounce	10.58	69.61%	4.55	2.325
Bananas, Red, 5 in. long	bunch	21.2	ounce	5 each			

1 gal. = 4 qt. = 16 c. = 128 fl. oz. ✦ 1 qt. = 2 pt. = 4 c. = 32 fl. oz. ✦ 1 pt. = 2 c. = 16 fl. oz. ✦
1 c. = 8 fl. oz. = 16 tbsp. ✦ 1 fl. oz. = 2 tbsp. ✦ 1 tbsp. = 3 tsp. ✦ 1 lb. = 16 oz.

Fruit (Continued)

Item Name	AP Unit	Number of Measures per AP Unit	Measure per AP Unit	Trimmed/Cleaned Avoirdupois Ounce Weight or Count per AP Unit	Yield Percent	Trimmed/Cleaned Avoirdupois Ounce Weight per Cup	Number of Trimmed/Cleaned Cups per AP Unit
Bananas, Red, 5 in. long, sliced	pound	16	ounce	11.28	70.52%	5.80	1.945
Bananas, sliced	pound	16	ounce	10.6	66.3%	5.29	2.00
Blackberries	pound	16	ounce	15.2	95.0%	5	3.04
Blackberries, frozen	pound	16	ounce	16	100.0%	5.3	3.02
Blackberries, juice yield of 1 lb.	pound	16	ounce	6.64	41.50%	7.73	0.859
Blueberries	pound	16	ounce	14.3	89.4%	5.1	2.80
Blueberries, dried	pound	16	ounce	16	100.0%	4.5	3.56
Blueberries, frozen	pound	16	ounce	16	100.0%	5.46	2.93
Blueberries, juice yield of 1 lb.	pound	16	ounce	6.47	40.44%	4.73	1.368
Boysenberries	pound	16	ounce	15.2	95.0%	5	3.20
Boysenberries, frozen	pound	16	ounce	16	100.0%	5.3	3.02
Breadfruit	pound	16	ounce	12.48	78.0%	7.75	1.61
Carambola (StarFruit)	pound	16	ounce	15	93.8%		
Cherimoya	pound	16	ounce	8.3	51.9%	7.3	1.14
Cherries, dried	pound	16	ounce	16	100.0%	5.2	3.08
Cherries, sweet	pound	16	ounce	14	87.5%	5.11	2.74
Citron, candied, diced	pound	16	ounce	15.9	99.38%	6.25	2.544
Coconut, fresh, grated	each	19.5	ounce	8.30	42.56%	3.5	2.371
Coconut, fresh, whole	each	19.5	ounce	8.30	42.56%		
Cranberries, dried	pound	16	ounce	16	100.0%	5	3.20
Cranberries, juice yield of 1 lb.	pound	16	ounce	4.47	27.91%	8.4	0.532
Cranberries, whole	pound	16	ounce	15.4	96.3%	3.35	4.60
Currants, Dry Zante	pound	16	ounce	16	100.0%	5.07	3.16
Currants, Red and White	pound	16	ounce	15.5	96.9%	3.95	3.92
Dates	pound	16	ounce	14.4	90.0%		
Dates, pitted, chopped	pound	16	ounce	14.4	90.0%	5.08	2.83
Dates, pitted, whole	pound	16	ounce	14.4	90.0%	4.4	3.27
Feijoa	pound	16	ounce	11.1	69.38		

Y% means yield percentage ✦ AS means as served (or used) ✦ AP means as purchased ✦ AS ÷ AP = Y% ✦
AS ÷ Y% = AP ✦ AP × Y% = AS ✦ Cost per AP unit ÷ Y% = Cost per servable unit

Fruit (Continued)

Item Name	AP Unit	Number of Measures per AP Unit	Measure per AP Unit	Trimmed/Cleaned Avoirdupois Ounce Weight or Count per AP Unit	Yield Percent	Trimmed/Cleaned Avoirdupois Ounce Weight per Cup	Number of Trimmed/ Cleaned Cups per AP Unit
Feijoa, by count	pound	16	ounce	9.796 each			
Feijoa, peeled and sliced	pound	16	ounce	11.1	69.38%	5.45	2.037
Figs	pound	16	ounce	15.8	98.8%		
Figs, dried	pound	16	ounce	16	100.0%	7.02	2.28
Fruit Cake mix, candied	pound	16	ounce	15.9	99.38%	6.65	2.391
Ginger, crystallized, chips	pound	16	ounce	15.9	99.38%	6	2.650
Grapefruit	each	13.3	ounce	7	52.6%	7.4	0.95
Grapes, Green, seedless	pound	16	ounce	15	93.8%	3.24	4.63
Grapes, Red, seedless	pound	16	ounce	14.3	89.4%	3.35	4.27
Grapes, Red, seedless, juice yield 1 lb.	pound	16	ounce	10.68	66.77%	9	1.187
Guava	pound	16	ounce	12.8	80.0%	5.8	2.21
Jackfruit	pound	16	ounce	5.5	34.4%		
Jackfruit, sliced	pound	16	ounce	5.5	34.4%	5.67	0.97
Key Lime, juice yield of 1 pound	pound	16	ounce	6.3	39.38%		
Key Limes	pound	16	ounce	15 each			
Kiwi Fruit	pound	16	ounce	13.5	84.4%		
Kiwi Fruit, sliced	pound	16	ounce	13.5	84.4%	6.2	2.18
Kumquats, by cup	cup	1	cup	16 each		5	
Kumquats, by pound	pound	16	ounce	15	93.8%		
Lemons, juice, yield 1 each	each	4	ounce	1.65	41.3%	8.3	0.20
Lemons, juice, yield 1 pound	pound	16	ounce	6.62	41.4%	8.3	0.80
Lemons, 165 count whole	pound	16	ounce	4 each			
Lemons, 165, flesh	each	4	ounce	1.96	49.0%		
Lemons, Meyer, juice yield of 1 lb.	pound	16	ounce	6.9	43.13%	8.40	0.821
Lemons, Meyer, whole	pound	16	ounce	4 each			
Limes, juice, yield of 1 each	each	3.4	ounce	1.44	42.4%	8.3	0.17
Limes, juice, yield of 1 pound	pound	16	ounce	6.76	42.3%	8.3	0.81
Limes, 2 in. diameter	pound	16	ounce	4.7 each			

1 gal. = 4 qt. = 16 c. = 128 fl. oz. ✦ 1 qt. = 2 pt. = 4 c. = 32 fl. oz. ✦ 1 pt. = 2 c. = 16 fl. oz. ✦
1 c. = 8 fl. oz. = 16 tbsp. ✦ 1 fl. oz. = 2 tbsp. ✦ 1 tbsp. = 3 tsp. ✦ 1 lb. = 16 oz.

Fruit (Continued)

Item Name	AP Unit	Number of Measures per AP Unit	Measure per AP Unit	Trimmed/Cleaned Avoirdupois Ounce Weight or Count per AP Unit	Yield Percent	Trimmed/Cleaned Avoirdupois Ounce Weight per Cup	Number of Trimmed/ Cleaned Cups per AP Unit
Litchi Nut	pound	16	ounce	9.6	60.0%		
Loquats	pound	16	ounce	10.4	65.0%		
Mango	pound	16	ounce	11	68.8%		
Mango, sliced	pound	16	ounce	11	68.8%	5.82	1.89
Melon, Cantaloupe	pound	16	ounce	9.3	58.1%		
Melon, Cantaloupe, ball	pound	16	ounce	6	37.5%	6.25	0.96
Melon, Cantaloupe, cubed	pound	16	ounce	9.3	58.1%	5.65	1.65
Melon, Cantaloupe, juice yield of 1 lb.	pound	16	ounce	6.94	43.39%	8.5	0.817
Melon, Cantaloupe, Sweet Tuscan 3/4 in. cubed	pound	16	ounce	10.16	63.50%	5.05	2.012
Melon, Casaba	pound	16	ounce	9.5	59.4%		
Melon, Casaba, cubed	pound	16	ounce	9.5	59.4%	6	1.58
Melon, Crenshaw	pound	16	ounce	10.6	66.3%		
Melon, Crenshaw, cubed	pound	16	ounce	10.6	66.3%	5.8	1.83
Melon, Honeydew	pound	16	ounce	9.2	57.5%		
Melon, Honeydew, cubed	pound	16	ounce	9.2	57.5%	5.9	1.56
Melon, Pepino, peeled, seeded, diced	pound	16	ounce	12.8	80.00%	5	2.560
Melon Pepino, whole	pound	16	ounce	3 each			
Melon, Watermelon	pound	16	ounce	7.9	49.4%		
Melon, Watermelon, cubed	pound	16	ounce	7.9	49.4%	5.36	1.47
Melon, Watermelon, seedless, cubed	each	90.3	ounce	62.50	69.21%	5.7	10.965
Melon, Watermelon, seedless, juice yield 1 lb.	pound	16	ounce	6.24	39.00%	8.8	0.709
Nectarines	pound	16	ounce	12	75.0%		
Nectarines, sliced	pound	16	ounce	12	75.0%	5.6	2.14
Oranges, juice yield 1# (pound) 72 count	pound	16	ounce	6.01	37.6%	8.3	0.72
Oranges, juice yield of 1, 72 count	each	8.5	ounce	3.2	37.6%	8.3	0.39
Orange Peel, candied, diced	pound	16	ounce	15.9	99.38%	6.2	2.565
Oranges, Blood, juice yield of 1 lb.	pound	16	ounce	9.23	57.69%	8.3	1.112
Oranges, Blood, peeled	pound	16	ounce	9.89	61.81%		

Y% means yield percentage ✦ AS means as served (or used) ✦ AP means as purchased ✦ AS ÷ AP = Y% ✦
AS ÷ Y% = AP ✦ AP × Y% = AS ✦ Cost per AP unit ÷ Y% = Cost per servable unit

Fruit (Continued)

Item Name	AP Unit	Number of Measures per AP Unit	Measure per AP Unit	Trimmed/Cleaned Avoirdupois Ounce Weight or Count per AP Unit	Yield Percent	Trimmed/Cleaned Avoirdupois Ounce Weight per Cup	Number of Trimmed/ Cleaned Cups per AP Unit
Oranges, Blood, whole	pound	16	ounce	3.3 each			
Oranges, Navel, 72 count	pound	16	ounce	10	62.5%		
Oranges, sections, no membrane	pound	16	ounce	5.5	34.4%	6.1	0.90
Oranges, Valencia, 72 count	pound	16	ounce	10.5	65.6%		
Oranges, Valencia, 72 count, juice yield of 1 Lb.	pound	16	ounce	6.8	42.50%	8.30	0.819
Oranges, Valencia, 72 count., whole	pound	16	ounce	1.815 each			
Papaya	pound	16	ounce	10.7	66.9%		
Papaya, cubed	pound	16	ounce	10.7	66.9%	5.3	2.02
Papaya, Mexican (large), cubed	pound	16	ounce	11.98	74.88%	5.47	2.190
Passion Fruit	pound	16	ounce	10.2	63.8%		
Paw Paw, peeled, seeded	pound	16	ounce	5.94	37.13%	8.46	0.702
Peaches, peeled, seeded	pound	16	ounce	12.5	78.1%		
Peaches, sliced	pound	16	ounce	12.5	78.1%	6	2.08
Peaches, slices—dry	pound	16	ounce	16	100.0%	4	4.00
Pears, Asian, 1/2 in. diced	pound	16	ounce	11.92	74.50%	4.75	2.509
Pears, Asian, 1/4 in. slices	pound	16	ounce	11.92	74.50%	4.55	2.620
Pears, Bosc, 100 count	pound	16	ounce	14.24	89.00%		
Pears, Bosc, 100 count, peeled, cored, diced	pound	16	ounce	14.24	89.00%	5.75	2.477
Pears, Bosc, 100 count, peeled, cored, sliced	pound	16	ounce	14.24	89.00%	4.98	2.859
Pears, Comice, 90 count	pound	16	ounce	12.61	78.81%		
Pears, Comice, 90 count, peeled, cored, diced	pound	16	ounce	12.61	78.81%	5.73	2.201
Pears, Comice, 90 count, peeled, cored, sliced	pound	16	ounce	12.61	78.81%	4.9	2.573
Pears, Comice, juice yield of 1 lb.	pound	16	ounce	5.44	34.00%	8.8	0.618
Pears, d'Anjou, 90 count	pound	16	ounce	13.05	81.56%		
Pears, d'Anjou, 90 count, peeled, cored, diced	pound	16	ounce	13.05	81.56%	5.1	2.559
Pears, d'Anjou, 90 count, peeled, cored, sliced	pound	16	ounce	13.05	81.56%	4.9	2.663
Persimmon, Fuyu	pound	16	ounce	2.96 each			
Persimmon, Fuyu	pound	16	ounce	14.96	93.52%		

1 gal. = 4 qt. = 16 c. = 128 fl. oz. ✦ 1 qt. = 2 pt. = 4 c. = 32 fl. oz. ✦ 1 pt. = 2 c. = 16 fl. oz. ✦
1 c. = 8 fl. oz. = 16 tbsp. ✦ 1 fl. oz. = 2 tbsp. ✦ 1 tbsp. = 3 tsp. ✦ 1 lb. = 16 oz.

Fruit (Continued)

Item Name	AP Unit	Number of Measures per AP Unit	Measure per AP Unit	Trimmed/Cleaned Avoirdupois Ounce Weight or Count per AP Unit	Yield Percent	Trimmed/Cleaned Avoirdupois Ounce Weight per Cup	Number of Trimmed/ Cleaned Cups per AP Unit
Persimmon, Hachiya	pound	16	ounce	13.1	81.9%		
Pineapple, juice yield of 1 lb.	pound	16	ounce	4.55	28.46%	8.55	0.533
Pineapple, peeled and cored, cubed	each	67.6	ounce	30.80	45.56%	5.45	5.651
Plantains	pound	16	ounce	11.5	71.9%		
Plums	pound	16	ounce	14.4	90.0%		
Plums, sliced	pound	16	ounce	14.4	90.0%	5.8	2.48
Pomegranates	each	16.55	ounce	9.25	55.89%	5.25	1.762
Pomelo, peeled, sectioned (membranes removed)	each	27.88	ounce	6.93	24.86%	8.4	0.825
Prickly Pear Fruit	pound	16	ounce	11	68.8%		
Prunes, pitted	pound	16	ounce	16	100.0%	4.5	3.56
Quince	pound	16	ounce	9.75	60.9%		
Raisins, not packed	pound	16	ounce	16	100.0%	5.1	3.14
Raisins, packed down	pound	16	ounce	16	100.0%	5.8	2.76
Raspberries	pound	16	ounce	15.3	95.6%	4.3	3.56
Raspberries, juice yield of 1 lb.	pound	16	ounce	3.99	24.94%	7.88	0.506
Red Cherries, Candied, whole	pound	16	ounce	15.9	99.38%	6.7	2.373
Red Cherries, Candied, whole, by count	pound	16	ounce	98 each			
Sapotes	pound	16	ounce	11.35	70.9%		
Soursop	pound	16	ounce	10.7	66.9%		
Strawberries	pound	16	ounce	14.7	91.9%		
Strawberries, halves	pound	16	ounce	14.7	91.9%	5.36	2.74
Strawberries, juice yield of 1 lb.	pound	16	ounce	10	62.50%	6.67	1.500
Strawberries, pureed	pound	16	ounce	14.7	91.9%	7.9	1.86
Strawberries, sliced	pound	16	ounce	14.7	91.9%	5.85	2.51
Strawberries, whole, medium	pound	16	ounce	24 whole			
Tamarillo, Red	pound	16	ounce	5.614 each			
Tamarillo, Red	pound	16	ounce	14.88	92.98%	7.55	1.970
Tamarind, fresh, peeled with seeds	pound	16	ounce	11.81	73.81%		

Y% means yield percentage ✦ AS means as served (or used) ✦ AP means as purchased ✦ AS ÷ AP = Y% ✦
AS ÷ Y% = AP ✦ AP × Y% = AS ✦ Cost per AP unit ÷ Y% = Cost per servable unit

Fruit (Continued)

Item Name	AP Unit	Number of Measures per AP Unit	Measure per AP Unit	Trimmed/Cleaned Avoirdupois Ounce Weight or Count per AP Unit	Yield Percent	Trimmed/Cleaned Avoirdupois Ounce Weight per Cup	Number of Trimmed/ Cleaned Cups per AP Unit
Tamarind, fresh, peeled, seedless	pound	16	ounce	5.66	35.38%		
Tamarind, paste with seeds	pound	16	ounce	15.8	98.75%	12.00	1.317
Tangelo, Mineola	pound	16	ounce	10.677	66.73%		
Tangelo, Mineola, count	pound	16	ounce	1.74 each			
Tangerine, Clementine variety, whole	pound	16	ounce	3.89 each			
Tangerine, Satsuma, whole	pound	16	ounce	3.5 each			
Tangerines, Satsuma, peeled, sectioned	pound	16	ounce	12.36	77.25%	5.5	2.247
Tangerines, Satsuma, sections each	pound	16	ounce	11 per each			

Notes

1. **Apricots:** These are pitted to obtain the yield.
2. **Coconuts:** Coconut water yield is approximately 20% of its AP weight.
2. **Lemons:** One pound of raw lemons yields 6.62 avoirdupois ounces juice (or 6.35 fluid ounces). There are usually 10 sections in a lemon.
3. **Limes:** One pound of limes yields 6.76 avoirdupois ounces juice (or 6.49 fluid ounces). There are usually 10 sections in a lime.
4. **Melon Balls:** Balling reduces melon yields from 55–60% to 35–40%. Use waste if possible. One cup equals 13 standard balls.
5. **Oranges:** There are 10 to 12 sections in an orange (10 of full size). One pound of 72-count oranges yields 6.01 avoirdupois ounces juice (or 5.76 fluid ounces).
6. **Citrus Juices—Purchasing Formulas:** The ounce measures shown are ounces by weight. Fluid ounces can be substituted, but remember that a weighed ounce is about 95% of a fluid ounce of juice. To convert a weight ounce (avoirdupois) to a fluid ounce, multiply the number of weighed ounces by 0.96 to arrive at its fluid-ounce equivalent. When working with fluid ounces, use the cups purchasing formula for more efficiency in determining how much raw citrus to buy for an as-served volume of juice.

Canned Foods (in Number-10 Cans)

Item	USDA Recommended Drained Weight Minimum in Ounces per #10 Can
Apples, sliced	96
Apricots, halves or slices in heavy syrup	62
Apricots, halves or slices, light syrup, juice, or water	64
Apricots, whole, peeled in heavy syrup	60.4
Apricots, whole, peeled in light syrup, juice, or water	62
Apricots, whole, unpeeled in heavy syrup	60
Apricots, whole, unpeeled in light syrup, juice, or water	61.5
Asparagus, center cuts and tips	60.2
Beans, Garbanzo	68
Beans, Green or Wax, 1.5 in. cut	60
Beans, Green or Wax, french cut	59
Beans, Green or Wax, mixed or short cut	63
Beans, Green or Wax, whole	57.5
Beans, Kidney	68
Beans, Lima, fresh	72
Beans, Pinto	68
Beets, diced, 3/8 in.	72
Beets, julienne	68
Beets, sliced medium, 1/4 in.	68
Beets, whole, size 1 to 3	69
Beets, whole, size 4 to 6	68
Blackberries, heavy pack in light syrup or water	74
Blackberries, regular pack in heavy syrup	62
Blueberries	55
Blueberries, heavy pack in light syrup or water	70
Boysenberry, regular pack in heavy syrup	55
Carrots, diced, 3/8 in.	72
Carrots, julienne	68

Y% means yield percentage ✦ AS means as served (or used) ✦ AP means as purchased ✦ AS ÷ AP = Y% ✦
AS ÷ Y% = AP ✦ AP × Y% = AS ✦ Cost per AP unit ÷ Y% = Cost per servable unit

Canned Foods (in Number-10 Cans) (Continued)

Item	USDA Recommended Drained Weight Minimum in Ounces per #10 Can
Carrots, sliced	68
Carrots, whole	68
Cherries, Red, Tart, pitted in syrup	70.2
Cherries, Red, Tart, pitted in water or juice	72
Cherries, Sweet, dark and light, pitted in heavy syrup	66.5
Cherries, Sweet, unpitted in light syrup, juice, or water	70
Corn, whole kernel, grade A	70
Corn, whole kernel, grades B and C	72
Figs, Kadota, 70 count or less	63
Figs, Kadota, 71 count or more	66
Fruit Cocktail (in all packing media)	71.15
Fruits for salad (in all media)	64.5
Grapes, light, seedless (in all packing media)	62
Hominy, whole, style I	72
Loganberry, regular pack in light syrup or water	60
Mushrooms, stems and pieces	61
Olives, ripe, chopped	90
Olives, ripe, pitted, jumbo, colossal, super-colossal	49
Olives, ripe, pitted, small, medium, large, extra-large	51
Olives, ripe, whole, jumbo, colossal, super-colossal	64
Olives, ripe, whole, small, medium, large, extra-large	66
Olives, sliced, wedges, quartered	55
Onions, whole, 100 to 199 count (small)	63
Onions, whole, 200 count (tiny)	64
Onions, whole, 80 to 99 count (medium)	60
Peaches, Clingstone, diced, all media	70
Peaches, Clingstone, halves, 23 count or less in heavy syrup	65
Peaches, Clingstone, halves, 23 count or less in light syrup, juice, or water	67

1 gal. = 4 qt. = 16 c. = 128 fl. oz. ✦ 1 qt. = 2 pt. = 4 c. = 32 fl. oz. ✦ 1 pt. = 2 c. = 16 fl. oz. ✦
1 c. = 8 fl. oz. = 16 tbsp. ✦ 1 fl. oz. = 2 tbsp. ✦ 1 tbsp. = 3 tsp. ✦ 1 lb. = 16 oz.

Canned Foods (in Number-10 Cans) (Continued)

Item	USDA Recommended Drained Weight Minimum in Ounces per #10 Can
Peaches, Clingstone, halves, 24 count or more in heavy syrup	66.5
Peaches, Clingstone, halves, 24 count in light syrup, juice, or water	68.5
Peaches, Clingstone, heavy pack, all media	76
Peaches, Clingstone, quarters, pieces (irregular) in heavy syrup	66.5
Peaches, Clingstone, quarters, pieces (irregular) in light syrup, juice, or water	68.5
Peaches, Clingstone, slices in heavy syrup	66.5
Peaches, Clingstone, slices in light syrup, juice, or water	68.5
Peaches, Clingstone, solid pack, unsweetened	92
Peaches, Freestone, halves, 23 count or less, heavy syrup, light syrup, juice, or water	61.5
Peaches, Freestone, halves, 24 count or more, heavy syrup, light syrup, juice, or water	62.5
Peaches, Freestone, quarters, mixed pieces of irregular shape in all media	64.5
Peaches, Freestone, slices in heavy syrup, light syrup, juice, or water	61
Pears, diced in all media	67
Pears, halves, 25 count or less in all media	62.7
Pears, halves, 25 count or more in all media	64.1
Pears, slices or quarters in all media	65.5
Peas and Carrots (diced carrots)	71
Peas and Carrots (sliced carrots)	70
Peas, Field and Blackeye Peas	72
Peas, grade A	70
Peas, grade B	72
Pimentos, diced, chopped	74
Pimentos, pieces	74
Pimentos, sliced	71.7
Pimentos, whole—halves	70.7
Pimentos, whole—pieces	72.2
Pineapple, chunks in all media	65.75
Pineapple, cubes in all media	71.25

Y% means yield percentage ✦ AS means as served (or used) ✦ AP means as purchased ✦ AS ÷ AP = Y% ✦
AS ÷ Y% = AP ✦ AP × Y% = AS ✦ Cost per AP unit ÷ Y% = Cost per servable unit

Canned Foods (in Number-10 Cans) (Continued)

Item	USDA Recommended Drained Weight Minimum in Ounces per #10 Can
Pineapple, tidbits in all media	65.75
Pineapple, crushed in syrup (minimum is 63% of weight by content)	69.3
Pineapple, crushed, solid pack (minimum is 78% of weight by content)	85.8
Pineapple, sliced, in all media	61.5
Plums, purple, halves in all media	60.2
Plums, purple, whole in all media	54.7
Potatoes, Sweet	73
Potatoes, White, diced	76
Potatoes, White, sliced	75
Potatoes, White, whole	74
Prunes, heavy pack in all media	110
Prunes, regular pack in all media	70
Raspberries, grade C in water	60
Raspberries, Red, grade A or B in syrup	53
Sauerkraut	80
Spinach	58.4
Tomatoes, whole, peeled, grade B	63.5
Tomatoes, whole, peeled, grade C	54.7

1 gal. = 4 qt. = 16 c. = 128 fl. oz. ✦ 1 qt. = 2 pt. = 4 c. = 32 fl. oz. ✦ 1 pt. = 2 c. = 16 fl. oz. ✦
1 c. = 8 fl. oz. = 16 tbsp. ✦ 1 fl. oz. = 2 tbsp. ✦ 1 tbsp. = 3 tsp. ✦ 1 lb. = 16 oz.

Canned Foods Weight-to-Volume

Product	Total Ounces per #10 Can	Net or Drained Weight in Ounces	Drained Weight Yield Percentage	Ounces per Single Cup	Ounces per Quart	Ounces per Half Gallon
Applesauce	111	110	99.10%	8.6	34.4	68.8
Apples, sliced, dry pack in juice	97	95.8	98.76%	5.65	24.6	53.25
Baked Beans, with brown sugar and bacon	112.7	112.7	100%*	9.15	37.75	76.4
Beets, diced (3/8 in.), in water	107.6	72.4	67.29%	5.3	21.8	48.25
Beets, sliced, in water	107.3	76.95	71.71%	5.85	22.55	50.95
Carrots, diced (3/8 in.), in water	108.25	69.1	63.83%	5.05	22.2	51.2
Cheese Sauce for Nachos	104	104	100%*	8.89	35.9	72
Cherries, Dark Sweet, pitted, heavy syrup	112.9	67.9	60.14%	5.9	25.9	54.05
Chili con Carne, with beans	106.75	106.75	100%*	8.9	36	72
Corn, whole yellow kernels, in water	108.6	73	67.22%	5.55	23.7	48.4
Garbanzo Beans, whole, in water	111.3	68.5	61.55%	5.65	23.05	48.4
Green Beans, Blue Lake, cut 1.5 in. in water (grade A)	107.6	62.5	58.09%	3.75	16.75	33.75
Green Beans, Blue Lake, cut 1.5 in. in water (grade B)	105.45	62.1	58.89%	3.9	18	37.15
Hominy, white	112.95	79.3	70.21%	5.8	24.1	50
Ketchup	111.95	111.95	100%*	9.6	39.2	76.9
Kidney Beans, dark red, in water	110.7	66.8	60.34%	5.45	23.15	47
Menudo	109.85	109.85	100.00%*	9.154	36.6	73.23
Mushrooms, sliced, in water	102.95	65.3	63.43%	5.2	23.15	47.8
Peaches, halves, 35 count, in heavy syrup	107.8	70.65	65.54%	6.35	27.3	56
Pears, sliced, in light syrup	108.85	63.95	58.75%	7.4	30.5	63.97
Pears, diced, in light syrup	108.8	61.4	56.43%	6.95	31.9	65
Peas, whole, green, sweet, in water	108.65	70.65	65.03%	5.65	26.95	54
Pineapple, crushed, solid pack, with juice	104.55	85.3	81.59%	7.7	32.85	69.25
Pineapple, tidbits, in juice	109.8	70.5	64.21%	5.9	24.7	51.75
Potatoes, whole, peeled, 90 to 110 count, in water	109.5	76.65	70%	5.9	22.35	47.1
Sauerkraut, in water	107.6	72.8	67.66%	4.8	21.6	46
Spinach, leaf, stemmed, in water	102	46.4	45.49%	7.1	30.6	76.35
Tomato Paste	111	111	100%*	9.3	38	76.35

Y% means yield percentage ✦ AS means as served (or used) ✦ AP means as purchased ✦ AS ÷ AP = Y% ✦
AS ÷ Y% = AP ✦ AP × Y% = AS ✦ Cost per AP unit ÷ Y% = Cost per servable unit

Canned Foods Weight-to-Volume (Continued)

Product	Total Ounces per #10 Can	Net or Drained Weight in Ounces	Drained Weight Yield Percentage	Ounces per Single Cup	Ounces per Quart	Ounces per Half-Gallon
Tomato Purée	107	107	100%*	8.9	36.3	72.9
Tomato Sauce	104.9	104.9	100%*	8.75	36.35	72.8
Tomatoes, chopped, in purée	104.25	104.25	100%*	8.45	35.2	79.1
Tomatoes, crushed, in own juice	101.55	101.55	100%*	8.58	35.15	70
Tomatoes, diced, in juice	108.5	67.05	61.8%	7.15	29.55	67.05
Wax Beans, Yellow, 1.5 in. pieces, in water	104.85	60.95	58.13%	4.35	17.5	36.1

*The last three columns list drained weights unless noted by an asterisk.

1 gal. = 4 qt. = 16 c. = 128 fl. oz. ✦ 1 qt. = 2 pt. = 4 c. = 32 fl. oz. ✦ 1 pt. = 2 c. = 16 fl. oz. ✦
1 c. = 8 fl. oz. = 16 tbsp. ✦ 1 fl. oz. = 2 tbsp. ✦ 1 tbsp. = 3 tsp. ✦ 1 lb. = 16 oz.

3

STARCHY FOOD

$\mathscr{A}$ll starchy foods—which include legumes (beans and peas), rice, grains, cereals, and pasta—expand when cooked. This happens because they absorb the liquid (water, wine, stock, milk, etc.) that they are cooked with. This makes their original weights and volumes increase considerably by the time they are fully prepared. In fact, some starchy foods can easily double and may even triple in size when cooked. Happily, these foods are both popular and inexpensive to purchase, and become even less expensive when cooked because of their increased cooking yield. (If, however, you use very expensive cooking liquids like a rich, highly reduced stock or premium wine in your recipe, the cost of the cooked item may not decrease much, if at all.)

A portion of cooked, starchy food will vary in size from region to region and will vary according to the type of cuisine, as well as its presentation. For instance, some Caribbean cuisines cover an entire plate with cooked rice and use that as an *underliner* for the rest of the dish! Similarly, a pasta entrée will utilize more pasta than a side dish; a bean salad may utilize an amount that is less or more than a portion of beans on an entrée plate. Regardless of how they are used, you will find it useful to know the cost of a cooked weight and a cooked volume of these foods—and that is the purpose of this chapter: to illustrate how to obtain that information.

As you read through this chapter you'll be referred to these three tables:

1. Dry Legumes
2. Rice, Grains, and Cereals
3. Pasta

These tables all have the same format. They show the following:

+ The raw (AP) ounce weight per cup
+ The number of AP cups that equal 1 pound
+ The number of ounces a cooked cup weighs
+ The number of cooked cups 1 AP cup yields
+ The number of cooked cups 1 AP pound yields
+ The number of cooked pounds one AP pound yields
+ The AP-to-cooked-weight increase percentage

— COSTING DRY LEGUMES, RICE, GRAINS, AND CEREALS —

IN THE WORKBOOK

Part II, the Workbook, has two worksheets to help you cost volumes of raw ingredients, as well as cooked yields, in both weight and volume:

✦ Weights to Volumes, Costing Worksheet 1
✦ Trimmed or Cooked Foods, Costing Worksheet 2

NOTE

There may be some compaction, of 3.5 percent at the half-gallon measure and 7 percent or so as you approach the gallon measure, so feel free to add these percentages to the calculated larger volume costs.

COSTING BY VOLUME OF A RAW STARCHY ITEM

To calculate the cost of a volume of a raw, AP starchy item, follow this process:

1. Calculate the cost of a raw AP pound. Do this by dividing the cost of the AP unit by the number of pounds it contains.
2. Divide the AP pound cost by 16 to determine the cost of 1 AP ounce.
3. Look up the number of AP (raw) ounces in 1 cup in the appropriate table.
4. Multiply the AP cost per ounce by the AP ounces in 1 cup.

Here are the various multiples:

✦ For a pint cost, multiply the cup cost by 2.
✦ For a quart, multiply by 4.
✦ For a gallon, multiply by 16.

Example
Given: A 20-pound box of small white beans costs $11.20. To find the AP pound cost, divide the 20-pound box cost by 20:

$11.20 ÷ 20 = $0.56

Thus, 1 AP pound costs $0.56.

To determine the AP ounce cost, divide the pound cost by 16 (the number of ounces in 1 pound):

$0.56 ÷ 16 = $0.035

So, 1 AP ounce costs $0.035.

The Dry Legumes table shows there are 7.58 ounces of small white beans in 1 AP cup. By multiplying the AP ounce cost ($0.035) by 7.58 ounces, you get $0.265; so:

✦ 1 cup costs $0.265
✦ 1 pint costs $0.53
✦ 1 quart costs $1.06
✦ 1 gallon costs $4.24

Don't forget, you may add 7 percent to the gallon cost to account for compaction, as shown here:

$4.24 ×.07 = $0.2968 (round this to $0.30)
$4.24 + $0.30 = $4.54 per gallon

COSTING BY COOKED OUNCE OR POUND

To calculate the cost of 1 cooked ounce or 1 cooked pound, follow this procedure:

1. Divide the AP pound or ounce cost by the cooked yield weight increase percentage.

1 gal. = 4 qt. = 16 c. = 128 fl. oz. ✦ 1 qt. = 2 pt. = 4 c. = 32 fl. oz. ✦ 1 pt. = 2 c. = 16 fl. oz. ✦
1 c. = 8 fl. oz. = 16 tbsp. ✦ 1 fl. oz. = 2 tbsp. ✦ 1 tbsp. = 3 tsp. ✦ 1 lb. = 16 oz.

2. Convert these percentages to decimals so you can use them in calculations. Remember to move the decimal point two places to the left, drop the percent symbol, and then do your division. For instance, the small white bean percentage increase number is 229%. To do the math, you put the decimal place after the first 2 (2.29)— and then do the division.

3. The cost per cooked pound is calculated this way:

$0.56 ÷ 2.29 = $0.2445

4. The cost per cooked ounce is calculated this way: Divide the cooked pound cost by 16.

$0.2445 ÷ 16 = $0.0153

COSTING BY VOLUME OF A COOKED STARCHY ITEM

To calculate the cost of a volume of a cooked starchy item, follow these guidelines:

- For 1 cup, multiply the number of ounces in one cooked cup by the cost per cooked ounce.
- For a pint, multiply the cup cost by 2.
- For a quart, multiply by 4.

Again, there may be some compaction of the cooked food when you measure a quart to a gallon or more. The amount of compaction depends on how the cook fills the larger vessel. If the cook shakes down the food, vigorously tamps the vessel after filling, or packs or presses the food into the container, then you will have to weigh the contents of the packed vessel and multiply that by the cost of 1 cooked pound.

NOTE

The yield values of the cooked cups in *The Book of Yields* were spoon-filled and then slightly tamped down.

Example
Given: You have cooked a quantity of small white beans. From previous calculations, you know that 1 ounce of cooked white beans costs $0.0153. The Dry Legumes table shows that 1 cup of cooked small white beans weighs 6.31 ounces. Follow this process to find the cost of 1 cup and the cost of 1 gallon of cooked small white beans:

1. Multiply the cost per cooked ounce of $0.0153 by the 6.31 cooked ounces in 1 cup.

$0.0153 × 6.31 = $0.0965

So, 1 cup of cooked small white beans costs 9.65 cents.

2. A gallon would cost 16 times as much, plus 7 percent for compaction, as these calculations demonstrate:

$0.0965 × 16 = $1.544
$1.544 × .07 = $0.108
$1.544 + $0.108 = $1.65

A gallon of cooked small white beans costs $1.65. (You could just multiply the $1.544 times 1.07 to get the same answer.)

NOTE

Adding extra liquid to rice and bean recipes can result in greater cooked yields and thus lower your costs on paper. However, this often results in a mushy product that may not be salable in the form intended. Fortunately, many overcooked legumes can be sold as soups or used as purées. Likewise, you can increase the yield on pastas just by cooking them a bit longer than called for. But this is never a good idea, as pasta is inexpensive to begin with and its enjoyment depends on it being properly cooked— which means not mushy and broken.

COSTING PASTA

Because pasta shapes are so varied, and they change as a result of softening while cooking, it is not possible to compare uncooked to cooked volumes. The dry volumes in the Pasta table do, however, enable you to cost AP volume amounts in your recipes more easily.

COSTING DRY PASTA

Follow this procedure for costing a volume of dry pasta:

1. Determine the cost of 1 pound, AP, by dividing the cost of the AP container of pasta by the number of pounds it contains.
2. Divide the AP cost per pound by 16 to get the cost per ounce.
3. Multiply the number of ounces per cup or quart (from the Pasta table) by the cost per AP ounce.

Example

Given: A 20-pound box of large elbow macaroni costs $18.50. To get the cost, use this process:

1. To get the cost per AP pound, divide the box cost of $18.50 by the number of pounds it contains, in this case, 20:

$18.50 ÷ 20 = $0.925

So, 1 AP pound of elbow macaroni costs 92.5 cents.

2. To calculate the cost per AP ounce, divide $0.925 by 16.

$0.925 ÷ 16 = $0.0578

3. To determine the cost of a particular volume, multiply the number of ounces in 1 cup or 1 quart (from the Pasta table) by the cost per AP ounce. For example, the Pasta table shows that 1 quart of large elbow macaroni weighs 13.75 ounces, so we can figure out the cost:

13.75 × $0.0578 = $0.795

The result is that 1 quart of large elbow macaroni costs 79.5 cents.

NOTE

Dry pasta manufacturers are not consistent in their product specifications. Two brands may both label their pasta product as large, but one may be larger or smaller than the other. We have seen weight-per-quart differences of as much as 30 percent between brands of the same type of pasta. Therefore, it is wise to do a volume-to-weight test of the actual pasta you are using, especially if you sell a lot of pasta and use volume measures in your recipes.

COSTING COOKED PASTA

Dry pasta cooked *al dente* will increase in weight between 2.5 and 3.3 times. Fresh pasta, because it already contains quite a bit of moisture, will usually double or just slightly more than double in weight when cooked to the al dente stage. It is up to you to choose which degree of doneness you prefer and determine the weight increase that fits your standards in taste and texture. For our purposes here, we will go with a weight increase factor of 2.5 for dry pasta and 2.0 for fresh pasta.

You calculate the weight increase percentage by dividing the weight of the cooked pasta by the weight of the uncooked

1 gal. = 4 qt. = 16 c. = 128 fl. oz. ✦ 1 qt. = 2 pt. = 4 c. = 32 fl. oz. ✦ 1 pt. = 2 c. = 16 fl. oz. ✦
1 c. = 8 fl. oz. = 16 tbsp. ✦ 1 fl. oz. = 2 tbsp. ✦ 1 tbsp. = 3 tsp. ✦ 1 lb. = 16 oz.

pasta. For example, if you start with 4 pounds of fresh pasta, and its cooked weight is 8 pounds, you have a cooking yield of 200 percent:

8 ÷ 4 = 2, or 200%

To cost a pound of cooked pasta, you divide the AP cost per pound by the cooking increase percentage. Assume, for example, that the AP cost per pound is $1.40:

$1.40 ÷ 2.00 = $0.70

The cooked pasta costs 70 cents per pound. An ounce costs one-sixteenth of the pound cost.

$0.70 ÷ 16 oz. = $0.04375 per ounce

An 8-ounce serving would cost $0.35:

$0.04375 × 8 = $0.35

PURCHASING STARCHY ITEMS

DRY LEGUMES, RICE, GRAINS, AND CEREALS

There are three formulas you'll use to help plan your purchases of dry legumes, rice, grains, and cereals.

IN THE WORKBOOK

Part II, the Workbook, has one worksheet to help you with purchasing starchy products:

✦ Starchy Items, Purchasing Worksheet 4

FORMULA 1   The first formula, for cooked weight yield to raw AP weight, is as follows:

Amount needed to serve in cooked pounds ÷ Cooked yield of 1 pound raw = AP weight

Example
Given: You need to serve 40 five-ounce portions of cooked lentils.

40 × 5 oz. = 200 oz.
200 ÷ 16 = 12.5 lb.

So you need 12.5 pounds of cooked lentils.

The Dry Legumes table shows 1 pound of AP lentils yields 3.1 pounds cooked:

12.5 ÷ 3.1 = 4.03

You'll need a bit over 4 pounds of raw lentils as your AP amount.

FORMULA 2   This formula is for determining cooked AS cups to raw AP weight:

AS # of cooked cups ÷ # of cups cooked yielded from 1 pound = AP weight

Example
Given: You are to serve 48 half-cup portions of cooked black-eyed peas. The table shows that 1 pound of raw black-eyed peas yields 7.1 cups cooked.

Y% means yield percentage ✦ AS means as served (or used) ✦ AP means as purchased ✦ AS ÷ AP = Y% ✦
AS ÷ Y% = AP ✦ AP × Y% = AS ✦ Cost per AP unit ÷ Y% = Cost per servable unit

1. Convert your half cups to whole cups by dividing 48 by 2. (You need 24 cups.) Then divide the serving size by 7.1 cups per pound.

24 cups ÷ 7.1 cooked cups per lb. = 3.38 lb. AP

Therefore, you need 3.38 pounds of raw black-eyed peas to serve 48 half cups, cooked.

FORMULA 3   This raw starch or cold cereal purchasing formula for converting AS cups to AP pounds is defined as follows:

AS raw starch or cold cereal in cups ÷ # of cups per pound = AP in pounds

Example
Given: You need to serve 72 cups of puffed rice. The Rice, Grains, and Cereals table shows that there are 32 cups of puffed rice per pound.

1. Divide 72 by 32 to determine how many pounds to buy:

72 ÷ 32 = 2.25

You need to buy 2.25 pounds of puffed rice to serve 72 cups.

PURCHASING PASTA

The two formulas defined here will come in handy for planning your pasta purchases.

FORMULA 1   This is the formula for converting a cooked pasta weight to a dry pasta weight:

Amount of cooked pasta ÷ 2.5 = Amount of dry pasta to buy (AP dry)

This formula shows how to calculate the weight of dry pasta to buy based on an as-served cooked weight. The 2.5 factor is the *conservative* multiplier representing how many times a weight of dry pasta increases in cooking.

Example
Given: You need to serve 18 pounds of cooked, dried rotini.

1. Divide the weight you need to serve by 2.5:

18 ÷ 2.5 = 7.2

You need to buy 7.2 pounds of dry rotini in order to serve 18 pounds cooked.

FORMULA 2   The second formula shows how to convert a cooked pasta weight to a fresh pasta weight:

AS cooked weight ÷ 2 = AP weight of fresh pasta

Here, you simply follow the format of the formula for dry pasta, but change the 2.5 to 2, because fresh pasta increases by two times (or slightly more) in weight when cooked. And remember, if you cook your pasta softer than al dente, you will get an increased yield, so, to reiterate, it's a good idea to do your own pasta yield tests to determine the exact amount of the raw-to-cooked weight increase that results from your own cooking method and desired texture outcome. Then use that weight-increase factor in your calculations.

1 gal. = 4 qt. = 16 c. = 128 fl. oz. ✦ 1 qt. = 2 pt. = 4 c. = 32 fl. oz. ✦ 1 pt. = 2 c. = 16 fl. oz. ✦
1 c. = 8 fl. oz. = 16 tbsp. ✦ 1 fl. oz. = 2 tbsp. ✦ 1 tbsp. = 3 tsp. ✦ 1 lb. = 16 oz.

Dry Legumes

Item Name	Raw: Number of Ounces per Cup	Raw: Number of Cups per Pound	Cooked: Number of Ounces per Cup	1 Cup Raw Yields This Number of Cups Cooked	1 Pound Raw Yields This Number of Cups Cooked	1 Pound Raw Yields This Number of Pounds Cooked	Raw to Cooked Weight Increase Percentage
Adzuki Beans	6.95	2.3	8.10	2.50	5.8	2.9	291%
Anasazi Beans	6.4	2.50	5.3	2.76	6.90	2.29	229%
Black Beans (Turtle)	6.49	2.5	6.52	3.00	7.4	3.0	301%
Black-Eyed Peas	5.89	2.7	6.03	2.60	7.1	2.7	266%
Butter Beans, Florida	6.65	2.41	5.7	2.46	5.92	2.11	211%
Canalini Beans	6.6	2.42	5.45	2	4.85	1.65	165%
Cranberry Beans	6.88	2.3	6.24	3.00	7.0	2.7	272%
Fava Beans, Broadbean	5.29	3.0	6.00	2.90	8.8	3.3	329%
Flageolets	6.55	2.44	5.7	2.56	6.25	2.23	223%
Garbanzo Beans	6.45	2.48	5.6	2.56	6.35	2.22	222%
Great Northern Beans	6.46	2.5	6.24	2.75	6.8	2.7	266%
Kidney Beans	6.49	2.5	6.24	2.75	6.8	2.6	264%
Lentils	6.77	2.4	6.98	3.00	7.1	3.1	309%
Lentils, Baby	7	2.29	5.5	3.05	6.97	2.40	240%
Lima Beans, Baby	7.13	2.2	6.42	3.00	6.7	2.7	270%
Lima Beans, large	6.28	2.5	6.63	3.00	7.6	3.2	317%
Mung Beans	7.12	2.2	7.30	3.00	6.7	3.1	308%
Mung Beans, peeled, split	6.9	2.32	5.5	2.9	6.72	2.31	231%
Navy Beans	7.33	2.18	6.42	2.75	6.0	2.4	241%
Peruano Beans	7.25	2.21	5.4	6.5	14.34	4.84	484%
Pink Beans	7.41	2.2	5.96	3.00	6.5	2.4	241%
Pinto Beans	6.81	2.3	6.03	3.20	7.5	2.8	283%
Red Beans, Thai	6.75	2.37	5.85	2.5	5.93	2.17	217%
Scarlet Runner Beans	5.15	3.11	5.35	2.45	7.61	2.55	255%
Small White Beans	7.58	2.1	6.31	2.75	5.8	2.3	229%
Soybeans	6.56	2.4	6.07	2.75	6.7	2.5	254%
Split Peas	6.95	2.3	6.95	2.00	4.6	2.0	200%
White Beans	7.13	2.2	6.31	2.75	6.2	2.4	243%

Y% means yield percentage ✦ AS means as served (or used) ✦ AP means as purchased ✦ AS ÷ AP = Y% ✦
AS ÷ Y% = AP ✦ AP × Y% = AS ✦ Cost per AP unit ÷ Y% = Cost per servable unit

Rice, Grains, and Cereals

Items Name	Raw: Number of Ounces per Cup	Raw: Number of Cups per Pound	Cooked: Number of Ounces per Cup	1 Cup Raw Yields This Number of Cups Cooked	1 Pound Raw Yields This Number of Cups Cooked	1 Pound Raw Yields This Number of Pounds Cooked	Raw to Cooked Weight Increase Percentage
All-Bran Cereal	3.00	5.33					
Amaranth	7	2.29	8.85	1.86	4.25	2.35	235%
Arborio Rice	6.70	2.39	6.75	2.60	6.2	2.62	262%
Barley, pearled	7.05	2.27	5.54	4.00	9.1	3.14	314%
Basmati Brown Rice	6.6	2.42	7.00	3.31	8.02	3.51	351%
Basmati Rice	6.40	2.50	6.20	3.00	7.5	2.91	291%
Bran Flakes, Kellogg's	1.33	12.03					
Bran Flakes, Post	1.50	10.67					
Brown Rice, long grain	6.35	2.52	6.88	3.50	8.8	3.79	379%
Brown Rice, medium grain	6.70	2.39	6.88	3.40	8.1	3.49	349%
Brown Rice, short grain	6.7	2.39	6.90	3.40	8.12	3.50	350%
Buckwheat Grain (Kasha)	5.78	2.77	6.98	2.00	5.5	2.42	242%
Buckwheat Groats, whole, raw	6.3	2.54	6.75	2.02	5.13	2.16	216%
Buckwheat Groats, whole, roasted	6.15	2.60	5.20	3.21	8.36	2.72	272%
Bulgur, cooked	4.94	3.24	6.42	3.00	9.7	3.90	390%
Bulgur, Wheat-soaked	4.94	3.24	6.42	2.50	8.1	3.25	325%
Calif. Aromatic, long grain rice	6.60	2.42	6.40	3.00	7.3	2.91	291%
Cheerios	0.80	20.00					
Corn Bran	1.50	10.67					
Corn Chex	1.00	16.00					
Cornflake Crumbs, fine	4.15	3.86					
Cornflake Crumbs, hand-crushed	2.15	7.44					
Cornflakes	1.00	16.00					
Cornmeal/Polenta	6.30	2.54	7.50	4.50	11.4	5.36	536%
Cous Cous	6.80	2.35	6.31	4.00	9.4	3.71	371%
Cream of Rice	6.00	2.67	8.35	4.00	10.7	5.57	557%
Cream of Wheat	6.55	2.44	8.50	4.82	11.78	6.26	626%
Hominy Grits	6.06	2.64	8.54	3.50	9.2	4.93	493%

1 gal. = 4 qt. = 16 c. = 128 fl. oz. ✦ 1 qt. = 2 pt. = 4 c. = 32 fl. oz. ✦ 1 pt. = 2 c. = 16 fl. oz. ✦
1 c. = 8 fl. oz. = 16 tbsp. ✦ 1 fl. oz. = 2 tbsp. ✦ 1 tbsp. = 3 tsp. ✦ 1 lb. = 16 oz.

Rice, Grains, and Cereals (Continued)

Items Name	Raw: Number of Ounces per Cup	Raw: Number of Cups per Pound	Cooked: Number of Ounces per Cup	1 Cup Raw Yields This Number of Cups Cooked	1 Pound Raw Yields This Number of Cups Cooked	1 Pound Raw Yields This Number of Pounds Cooked	Raw to Cooked Weight Increase Percentage
Instant Rice	2.90	5.52	5.80	2.10	11.6	4.20	420%
Jasmine Rice, long-grained, white	6.7	2.39	4.55	4.49	10.72	3.05	305%
Malt-o-Meal	6.55	2.44	8.55	4.80	11.73	6.27	627%
Millet	7.05	2.27	8.40	3.00	6.8	3.57	357%
Oat Groats, whole	6.4	2.50	6.45	2.38	5.95	2.40	240%
Oats, steel cut	5.5	2.91	8.45	1.10	3.20	1.69	169%
Oatmeal (Quick)	2.96	5.41	8.25	2.50	13.5	6.97	697%
Oatmeal, old-fashioned	3.1	5.16	8.25	1.52	7.82	4.03	403%
Puffed Rice or Wheat	0.50	32.00					
Quinoa	6.00	2.67	7.10	2.65	7.1	3.14	314%
Rice Crispies	1.00	16.00					
Spelt Berries	6.5	2.46	5.60	1.30	3.21	1.12	112%
Sushi rice	7.25	2.21	6.50	3.08	6.79	2.76	276%
Tapioca, Pearl	5.36	2.99	8.50	4.00	11.9	6.34	634%
Wheat Berries, Red, hard	6.6	2.42	5.35	2.12	5.14	1.72	172%
Wheat Germ	4.00	4.00					
White Rice, glutinous	6.52	2.45	8.50	2.70	6.6	3.52	352%
White Rice, long grain, parboiled	6.52	2.45	5.25	2.80	6.9	2.25	225%
White Rice, long grain	6.50	2.46	7.23	3.00	7.4	3.34	334%
White Rice, medium grain	6.88	2.33	6.96	3.00	7.0	3.03	303%
White Rice, short grain	7.05	2.27	7.23	2.80	6.4	2.87	287%
Wild and White Rice, long grain mix	6.30	2.54	6.00	3.25	8.3	3.10	310%
Wild Rice	6.10	2.62	5.08	3.22	8.4	2.68	268%

Notes

1. **Rice:** Raw weights get a bit lighter as rice ages. Cooked yields are for standard recipe ratios.
2. **Grains:** Individual grain yields do vary according to the recipe ratios and soaking/cooking times.

Y% means yield percentage ✦ AS means as served (or used) ✦ AP means as purchased ✦ AS ÷ AP = Y% ✦
AS ÷ Y% = AP ✦ AP × Y% = AS ✦ Cost per AP unit ÷ Y% = Cost per servable unit

Pasta

Item	Ounces per Cup	Ounces per Quart	Item	Ounces per Cup	Ounces per Quart
Bow Ties	1.85	8.50	Orecchiette	3.35	14.5
Campanelle	2.55	11.2	Orzo, Melon Seeds	5.8	24.36
Ditalini #45	4.75	20.2	Orzo, Rice shape #26	7.25	30.45
Elbow Macaroni, large	3.30	13.75	Pappardelle, egg noodle, (1.875 in. wide)	0.8	4.5
Elbow Macaroni, small	4.43	18.90	Penne, mini (1 × 0.1875 in.)	4	15.7
Elbow Macaroni, whole wheat, small	4.15	17.5	Penne Rigate	2.95	12.95
Farfalle #93 (1.625 × 1.25 in.)	2.25	10.3	Penne Rigate, whole wheat (1.5 × 0.375 in.)	3.4	15.55
Farfalle, mini (0.875 × 0.6875 in.)	3.15	13.45	Pipe Rigate	2.3	9.9
Farfalle, small (1.25 × 1 in.)	2.55	11.55	Rigatoni #24	2.1	9.65
Farfalle, whole wheat, (1.25 × 1 in.)	2.25	10.8	Rotini, spirals	2.60	11.60
Fideo, 0.75 in. long strands	4.4	18.5	Rotini, whole wheat	2.6	10.95
Fiori	3.1	12.62	Shells, large	1.50	6.70
Fregala (medium Cous Cous)	6.1	25.62	Shells, medium	2.50	11.20
Fusilli	2.00	8.56	Shells, small	3.30	14.45
Gemelli #90 (1.33 × .25 in.)	4.05	17.92	Stars, small	5.65	23.7
Letters, (alphabet) small	5.10	21.80	Strozzapreti	3.4	15.6
Letters, large (0.25 in. high)	5.85	24.5	Tortellini, dry, cheese-filled	3.6	15.48
Macaroni Elbow, salad style (short)	4.05	17	Tubini	3.95	16.05
Mezze Penne Rigate (1.5 × 0.1875 in.)	4.25	16.5	Vermicelli, 1 in., thick	4.9	20.1
Mostaccioli or Penne	2.53	11.30	Vermicelli, 1 in., thin	4.75	19.95
Noodles, 0.5 in. wide	1.40	6.30	Wheels	2.20	9.80
Noodles, egg, extra wide	1.45	6.8	Ziti (1.375 × 0.625 in.)	3	13

Notes

1. **Dry pastas:** Volume yields of pastas depend on the degree of doneness and pasta shape and are not given. Pasta recipes are typically based on weights. The Pasta conversion table lists a few that may be used by volume.

2. One pound of spaghetti yields approximately 10.7 cups, cooked. One pound of elbow macaroni yields approximately 8 cups, cooked. On average, a cup of cooked pasta weighs between 5 and 6 ounces.

3. By weight, one pound of dry pasta yields 2.5 to 3 pounds, cooked.

4. By weight, one pound of fresh pasta yields 2 to 2.5 pounds, cooked.

5. Dry pasta dries (as much as 50% less weight) with age in very dry conditions.

1 gal. = 4 qt. = 16 c. = 128 fl. oz. ✦ 1 qt. = 2 pt. = 4 c. = 32 fl. oz. ✦ 1 pt. = 2 c. = 16 fl. oz. ✦
1 c. = 8 fl. oz. = 16 tbsp. ✦ 1 fl. oz. = 2 tbsp. ✦ 1 tbsp. = 3 tsp. ✦ 1 lb. = 16 oz.

6. By weight, 1 pound of dry mung bean threads yields 4.4 pounds, cooked. One pound of dry wheat somen yields 3.4 pounds cooked. One pound of dry udon noodles yields 2.6 pounds cooked. One pound of dry buckwheat somen yields 2.7 pounds.

7. Dry, wheat-based, 6-inch, round spring roll wrappers: There are approximately 7 per ounce, or 112 per pound.

8. Dry, wheat-based, 8.5-inch, round egg roll wrappers: There are approximately 2.5 per ounce, or 40 per pound.

9. Dry, rice-based, 8.5-inch, square spring roll wrappers: There are approximately 2.3 per ounce, or 36 per pound.

10. Fresh, wheat, and egg-based, 6.5-inch, square egg roll wrappers: There are approximately 1.15 per ounce, or 18 per pound.

11. Fresh, wheat, and egg-based, 3.5-inch, round won ton wrappers: There are approximately 5 per ounce, or 80 per pound.

12. Fresh, wheat, and egg-based, 3-inch, square won ton wrappers: There are approximately 4.5 per ounce, or 72 per pound.

4

BAKING ITEMS

$\mathcal{A}$mong professionals, baking recipes are known as *formulas*, because unlike savory recipes such as soups, salads, entrées, and so on, baking formulas measure most ingredients by weight rather than by volume. The reason is that formulas for breads, cakes, and pastries are really chemical and physical events that must begin with precise ratios of ingredients to ensure a successful outcome. Weighing ingredients is simply more accurate than using cups, pints, and so forth.

All that said, some recipes that use ingredients commonly found in the bakery are executed on the savory side of the kitchen, and savory-side cooks prefer to use volume measures rather than weigh all their ingredients. For this reason, the tables show the weight-to-volume equivalents for ease of use for those cooks. Moreover, bakers also use volume measures for some ingredients, such as ground or chopped nuts, spices, and certain leaveners.

Why is it more accurate to weigh most baking items? Primarily because of the way a cook fills a measuring container such as a cup or a gallon container. If, for example, you use the measuring device as a scoop, you may create air pockets that result in less than a full amount; conversely, you can easily jam an excessive amount of the food into the container if you scoop too forcefully. Similarly, some cooks, after filling a container, will vigorously tamp or shake the ingredients down, then top off the measuring vessel with more food, thereby adding extra food to the container and throwing off the ratio. Light, airy products—sifted powdered sugar, for example—can be tamped down as much as 20 percent!

This chapter makes reference to four tables:

1. Nuts and Seeds
2. Flour, Meal, Bran, and Crumbs
3. Sweeteners
4. Special Baking Items

Each table lists the following:

+ The number of ounces contained in 1 cup
+ The number of cups equal to 1 pound
+ The number of ounces contained in 1 pint
+ The number of pints equal to 1 pound
+ The number of pounds equal to 1 pint

NOTE

The items described in this chapter were spooned into the containers and gently tapped to settle the ingredients, then scraped level. When presifted powdery foods such as flours and sugars are measured by volume, it is typical for the amount in a cup to weigh less. How much less depends on how many times the food was sifted. Sifting, in addition to breaking up lumps, incorporates air into the food, so it is not surprising that the sifted ingredients weigh less per cup.

If you are using larger vessels to measure the more powdery foods, there will be some compaction of the foods as you work with volumes, ranging from a quart to a gallon. In general, you can use the cup measures to mathematically figure the contents of a quart, half gallon, and gallon. To do so:

+ For a quart, multiply the cup weight by 4 and add 1.5 percent to the answer.
+ For a half gallon, multiply the cup weight by 8 and add 3.5 percent.
+ For a gallon, multiply the cup weight by 16 and add 7 percent.

COSTING BAKING ITEMS

IN THE WORKBOOK

Part II, the Workbook, has one worksheet to help you cost volumes of baking items:

+ Weights to Volumes, Costing Worksheet 1

As usual, it is first necessary to determine the cost of an ounce of the food in question, *as purchased*, thusly:

+ If the purchase unit is measured in pounds, such as a 50-pound sack of granulated sugar, you simply divide the cost of the bag by 50 to get the cost per AP pound, then divide that answer by 16 to get the cost per AP ounce.
+ If the purchase unit is measured in ounces—say, ground cinnamon—divide the cost of the container by the number of ounces it contains, as purchased.

For example, if a case of sliced almonds costs $30, and each case contains three bags holding 2 pounds of sliced almonds, the total pounds purchased is 6:

3 × 2 = 6

Now divide the cost of the case ($30) by the total pounds in the case (6):

$30 ÷ 6 = $5

The sliced almonds cost $5 per pound. The cost per ounce is found by dividing the cost per AP pound by 16.

$5 ÷ 16 = $0.3125

One ounce of AP sliced almonds costs 31.25 cents.

This, by the way, is an *ideal* cost. Ideal, because you may not be able to use all of the almonds. Some may be spilled, burned, or simply eaten by your staff—or by you! Accordingly, you may want to add a penny or two to the cost per AP ounce to account for these factors. Say you "bump up" the cost per AP ounce to 33 cents to account for snacking by you and/or your staff. Now you can use this $0.33 cost per AP ounce to cost out volume measures of the sliced almonds.

To calculate the cost of sliced almonds per cup, you multiply the number of ounces in 1 cup—in this case, 3.35 ounces, according to the Nuts and Seeds table—by the cost per AP ounce ($0.33).

3.35 oz. × $0.33 = $1.106

Thus, you can see that a cup of sliced almonds costs approximately $1.11. It follows, then, that:

NOTE

Small quantities may not be quite precise when measuring irregularly shaped foods like sliced almonds, but they do work well for costing small measures of ground or finely milled items.

Y% means yield percentage ✦ AS means as served (or used) ✦ AP means as purchased ✦ AS ÷ AP = Y% ✦
AS ÷ Y% = AP ✦ AP × Y% = AS ✦ Cost per AP unit ÷ Y% = Cost per servable unit

Heavy Liquids

Liquids commonly used in baking—including syrups, molasses, preserves, and honey—weigh a lot more than other liquid foods. Syrups are often sold by fluid ounces, whereas honey and preserves are often sold by weight. If an item is sold by fluid ounces, costing a fluid ounce is just a matter of dividing the cost of the purchase unit by the number of fluid ounces it contains. To cost a fluid ounce amount for a food sold by weight, you multiply the ounce cost by the number of ounces in your measuring container—without making any adjustments for compaction, because these liquids do not compact.

+ A pint cost would be double that: $2.22.
+ A quart would cost four times the cup cost, plus 1.5 percent to account for compaction:

  $4.44 + $0.0666 = $4.5066

+ A half gallon would cost eight times the cup cost, plus 3.5 percent:

  $8.88 + $0.3108 = $9.1908

+ A gallon would cost 16 times the cup cost, plus 7 percent:

  $17.76 + $1.2432 = $19.0032

To compute the cost of a tablespoon, you would divide the cup cost by 16, since there are 16 tablespoons in a cup. To cost a teaspoon, you would either divide the tablespoon cost by 3 (since there are 3 teaspoons in a tablespoon) or just divide the cup cost by 48 (since there are 48 teaspoons in a cup).

PURCHASING BAKING ITEMS

We're going to cover five formulas in this section for purchasing baking items.

FORMULA 1   First we'll address the formula for converting AS cups to AP pounds. It is used to calculate the number of pounds to buy based on the number of cups you need to serve or use.

(Number of AS cups × Ounces per cup) ÷ 16 = AP in pounds

Example
Given: You need 14 cups of whole, shelled pine nuts (pignoli nuts). The Nuts and Seeds table shows that 1 cup of these weighs 4.7 ounces.

1. Multiply 14 cups by 4.7 to find that you need 65.8 ounces.
2. Divide 65.8 by 16 to determine that you need to buy (or use) 4.1 pounds.

FORMULA 2   The formula for converting AS tablespoons to AP ounces is as follows:

(Ounce-weight per cup ÷ 16) × Tablespoons needed = AP in ounces

Example
Given: You need 22 tablespoons of honey. The Sweeteners table shows that honey weighs 12 ounces per cup.

1. Divide 12 by 16 to determine that 1 tablespoon of honey weighs 0.75 of an ounce. (Why divide by 16? Because there are 16 tablespoons in 1 cup.)
2. Multiply 22 tablespoons times 0.75, the weight of a tablespoon.

22 tbsp. × 0.75 oz. per tbsp. = 16.5 oz.

IN THE WORKBOOK

Part II, the Workbook, has one worksheet to help you purchase baking items:

+ Baking Items, Purchasing Worksheet 5

1 gal. = 4 qt. = 16 c. = 128 fl. oz. ✦ 1 qt. = 2 pt. = 4 c. = 32 fl. oz. ✦ 1 pt. = 2 c. = 16 fl. oz. ✦
1 c. = 8 fl. oz. = 16 tbsp. ✦ 1 fl. oz. = 2 tbsp. ✦ 1 tbsp. = 3 tsp. ✦ 1 lb. = 16 oz.

You'll need 16.5 ounces of honey.

Converting to pounds is a two-step process:

1. Divide by 16, because there are 16 tablespoons in a cup (the first part of this formula is a repeat of the preceding formula):

[(Ounce-weight per cup ÷ 16) × Tablespoons needed] ÷ 16 = AP in ounces

2. Divide once more by 16 to convert the AP ounces to AP pounds:

16.5 oz. ÷ 16 oz./lb. = 1.03 lb.

The result? You need just over 1 pound of honey.

FORMULA 3   The third formula is for converting AS pints to AP pounds:

AS pints × Pounds per pint = AP in pounds

To make this conversion, you multiply the number of pints needed by the number of pounds per pint (from the right-hand column in the Baking Items tables). Your answer is the number of pounds to buy or cost.

Example
Given: You need 13 pints of Japanese bread crumbs. The Flour, Meal, Bran, and Crumbs table shows there are 0.35 pounds per pint for this item. Determine how many pounds of crumbs you need.

Multiply 13 pints times 0.35. You will need 4.55 pounds of crumbs.

<table>
<tr><td>

NOTE

Formulas 4 and 5 include compaction factors of 1.5 percent for a quart and 7 percent for a gallon, respectively. Use the compaction factors when dealing with powdery, ground, or milled foods that do compact in larger containers. Do not use the compaction factors when dealing with liquids or dense foods such as packed brown sugar.

</td><td>

FORMULA 4   Converting AS quarts to AP pounds is our fourth formula:

[AS quarts × (2 × pounds per pint)] + 1.5% = AP in pounds

Example
Given: You need 9 quarts of cornmeal mix. The Flour, Meal, Bran, and Crumbs table shows there are 0.75 pounds per pint for this item. Here are the steps:

1. Multiply 0.75 by 2 to get a quart weight—because there are 2 pints per quart:

2 × 0.75 = 1.50 lb. per quart (mathematically)

2. Because there is about a 1.5% compaction (increase in weight per volume) when going to a quart measure, you need to multiply 0.015 by the computed quart weight and add it to your quart weight.

1.5 lb. × 0.015 = 0.0225 lb.

Therefore, the compacted quart weight is actually:

1.5 lb. + 0.0225 lb. = 1.5225 lb.

3. Now multiply 1.5225 times the 9 quarts you need:

1.5225 × 9 = 13.7025

You need to buy or use 13.7 pounds of cornmeal mix.

</td></tr>
</table>

FORMULA 5 The final formula in this section is for converting AS gallons to AP pounds (see the previous note regarding the compaction factor of 7 percent):

[AS gallons × (8 × Pounds per pint) + 7%] = AP in pounds

Example

Given: You need 3 gallons of graham cracker crumbs. The Flour, Meal, Bran, and Crumbs table shows there are 0.52 pounds per pint for this item. There are 8 pints in a gallon.

1. Multiply the weight per pint (.52 pounds) by 8.

0.52 × 8 = 4.16 lb.

2. Multiply 4.16 pounds by 3 to get the number of pounds that equals 3 gallons:

3 × 4.16 lb. = 12.48 lb.

Purchasing Shelled versus Unshelled Nuts

Notice at the end of the Nuts and Seeds table the statements on the shelled yields of various unshelled nuts.

To calculate the weight of raw, unshelled nuts to buy based on the amount of shelled nuts you need to use or serve, divide the yield-per-pound weights into the weight you need. For example, if you need 40 ounces of shelled almonds, divide the yield per pound of 5 ounces into 40.

40 ÷ 5 = 8

Thus, you need to buy 8 pounds of unshelled almonds to have 40 ounces shelled.

Thus, you need to buy or use 12.48 pounds of graham cracker crumbs.

But, you're not done yet. Because we are working with a food that *does* compact in a larger container (powdery, ground, or milled foods), you would add 7 percent to the 4.16 pounds that represents the mathematically computed gallon weight.

4.16 × 0.07 = .2912

So the compacted gallon weight is now calculated as:

4.16 + .2912 = 4.4512

The compacted gallon weight is 4.4512 pounds, and you need 3 gallons, so:

3 × 4.4512 lb. = 13.3536 lb.

So, due to compaction, you need 13.35 pounds, rather than the 12.48 pounds calculated above.

1 gal. = 4 qt. = 16 c. = 128 fl. oz. ✦ 1 qt. = 2 pt. = 4 c. = 32 fl. oz. ✦ 1 pt. = 2 c. = 16 fl. oz. ✦
1 c. = 8 fl. oz. = 16 tbsp. ✦ 1 fl. oz. = 2 tbsp. ✦ 1 tbsp. = 3 tsp. ✦ 1 lb. = 16 oz.

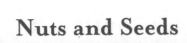

Nuts and Seeds

Item	Ounces per Cup	Cups per Pound	Ounces per Pint	Pints per Pound	Pounds per Pint
Almonds, ground	3.35	4.80	6.70	2.40	0.42
Almonds, sliced	3.35	4.80	6.70	2.40	0.42
Almonds, slivered	3.80	4.20	7.60	2.10	0.48
Almonds, whole, shelled	5.00	3.20	10.00	1.60	0.63
Brazil Nuts, whole, shelled	4.90	3.30	9.80	1.60	0.61
Cashews, halves and pieces	4.60	3.50	9.20	1.70	0.58
Cashews, whole, roasted	4.20	3.80	8.40	1.90	0.53
Chestnuts, European, peeled	3.70	4.30	7.00	2.29	0.44
Coconut, fresh, shredded	3.50	4.57	5.60	2.90	0.35
Coconut, packaged, shredded	2.50	6.40	5.00	3.20	0.31
Flax seed, brown	5.50	2.91	11.00	1.45	0.69
Flax seed, golden	5.55	2.88	11.10	1.44	0.69
Hazelnuts, chopped	4.00	4.00	8.00	2.00	0.50
Hazelnuts, ground	3.00	5.30	6.00	2.70	0.38
Hazelnuts, whole, shelled	4.75	3.40	9.50	1.70	0.59
Macadamia Nuts, whole and halves	4.70	3.40	9.40	1.70	0.59
Mixed Nuts, roasted, salted	5.00	3.20	10.00	1.60	0.63
Peanut Butter	8.47	1.90	16.90	0.90	1.06
Peanuts, chopped	5.00	3.20	10.00	1.60	0.63
Peanuts, whole, roasted, shelled	5.30	3.00	10.60	1.50	0.66
Peanuts, whole, roasted, unshelled	3.70	4.30	7.40	2.20	0.46
Pecans, chopped	4.20	3.80	8.40	1.90	0.53
Pecans, ground	3.00	5.30	6.00	2.70	0.38
Pecans, halves	3.50	4.60	7.00	2.30	0.44
Pine Nuts, whole, shelled	4.70	3.40	9.40	1.70	0.59
Pistachios, shelled, roasted	4.50	3.60	9.00	1.80	0.56
Pistachios, unshelled, roasted	4.00	4.00	8.00	2.00	0.50
Pumpkin seeds, raw, shelled	4.65	3.44	9.30	1.72	0.58

Y% means yield percentage ✦ AS means as served (or used) ✦ AP means as purchased ✦ AS ÷ AP = Y% ✦
AS ÷ Y% = AP ✦ AP × Y% = AS ✦ Cost per AP unit ÷ Y% = Cost per servable unit

Nuts and Seeds (Continued)

Item	Ounces per Cup	Cups per Pound	Ounces per Pint	Pints per Pound	Pounds per Pint
Pumpkin seeds, roasted, hulled	7.00	2.30	14.00	1.10	0.88
Sesame Seeds	5.33	3.00	10.70	1.60	0.67
Sesame Seeds, black, roasted	4.05	3.95	8.10	1.98	0.51
Sunflower Seeds, raw, hulled	5.00	3.20	10.00	1.60	0.63
Sesame Seeds, roasted, hulled	4.50	3.56	9	1.78	0.56
Sunflower Seeds, roasted, salted	4.60	3.50	9.20	1.70	0.58
Sesame Seeds, roasted, unhulled	5.15	3.11	10.30	1.55	0.64
Soy Nuts, roasted, lightly salted	3.60	4.44	7.20	2.22	0.45
Walnuts, shelled, chopped	4.30	3.70	8.60	1.90	0.54
Walnuts, shelled, ground	2.80	5.70	5.60	2.90	0.35
Walnuts, shelled, halved	3.40	4.70	6.80	2.40	0.43
Walnuts, shelled, pieces	4.20	3.80	8.40	1.90	0.53

Notes

1. **Almonds:** 1 pound whole almonds in the shell yields about 5 ounces, shelled.
2. **Chestnuts:** 1 pound whole chestnuts in the shell yields about 10 ounces, peeled—if you are careful!
3. **Coconuts:** Coconut yields about half its original weight after hulling and draining.
4. **Hazelnuts:** 1 pound whole hazelnuts (filberts) yields about 7.5 ounces, shelled.
5. **Macadamia nuts:** 1 pound whole macadamia nuts yields about 5 ounces, shelled.
6. **Pecans:** 1 pound whole pecans yields about 8 ounces, shelled.
7. **Peanuts:** 1 pound whole roasted peanuts yields about 11 ounces, shelled.
8. **Pistachios:** 1 pound whole roasted pistachios yields about 8 ounces, shelled.
9. **Walnuts, black:** 1 pound black walnuts yields about 4 ounces, shelled and cleaned.
10. **Walnuts, English:** 1 pound English walnuts yields about 9 ounces, shelled and cleaned.

1 gal. = 4 qt. = 16 c. = 128 fl. oz. ✦ 1 qt. = 2 pt. = 4 c. = 32 fl. oz. ✦ 1 pt. = 2 c. = 16 fl. oz. ✦
1 c. = 8 fl. oz. = 16 tbsp. ✦ 1 fl. oz. = 2 tbsp. ✦ 1 tbsp. = 3 tsp. ✦ 1 lb. = 16 oz.

Flour, Meal, Bran, and Crumbs

Item	Ounces per Cup	Cups per Pound	Ounces per Pint	Pints per Pound	Pounds per Pint
Barley, pressed, dry	4.70	3.4	9.40	1.7	0.59
Bisquick Mix	4.00	4.0	8.0	2.0	0.50
Bread Crumbs, dry	3.50	4.6	7.0	2.3	0.44
Bread Crumbs, Japanese	2.80	5.7	5.6	2.9	0.35
Cornflake Crumbs, fine	4.15	3.9	8.3	1.9	0.52
Cornflake Crumbs, hand crushed	2.15	7.4	4.3	3.7	0.27
Cornmeal Mix	6.00	2.7	12.0	1.3	0.75
Cornmeal, degermed, coarse	4.85	3.3	9.7	1.6	0.61
Cornmeal, fine	6.30	2.5	12.6	1.3	0.79
Cornmeal, whole grain, coarse	4.30	3.7	8.6	1.9	0.54
Cornstarch	4.70	3.4	9.4	1.7	0.59
Cracker Crumbs, saltine	3.20	5.0	6.4	2.5	0.40
Flour, all-purpose	4.60	3.48	9.2	1.74	0.57
Flour, Bread	4.80	3.3	9.6	1.7	0.60
Flour, Buckwheat, whole groat	4.25	3.8	8.5	1.9	0.53
Flour, Cake	3.90	4.1	7.8	2.1	0.49
Flour, high-gluten	5.00	3.2	10.0	1.6	0.63
Flour, Masa (Corn)	4.15	3.9	8.3	1.9	0.52
Flour, Pastry	4.25	3.8	8.5	1.9	0.53
Flour, Potato	6.35	2.5	12.7	1.3	0.79
Flour, Rice, brown	5.50	2.9	11.0	1.5	0.69
Flour, Rice, white	5.60	2.9	11.2	1.4	0.70
Flour, Rye, dark	4.50	3.6	9.0	1.8	0.56
Flour, Rye, light and medium	3.60	4.4	7.2	2.2	0.45
Flour, self-rising wheat, white	4.40	3.6	8.8	1.8	0.55
Flour, Soybean, defatted	3.50	4.6	7.0	2.3	0.44
Flour, Soybean, full-fat	3.00	5.3	6.0	2.7	0.38
Flour, Triticale, whole grain	4.60	3.5	9.2	1.7	0.58

Y% means yield percentage ✦ AS means as served (or used) ✦ AP means as purchased ✦ AS ÷ AP = Y% ✦
AS ÷ Y% = AP ✦ AP × Y% = AS ✦ Cost per AP unit ÷ Y% = Cost per servable unit

Flour, Meal, Bran, and Crumbs (Continued)

Item	Ounces per Cup	Cups per Pound	Ounces per Pint	Pints per Pound	Pounds per Pint
Flour, whole wheat	4.25	3.8	8.5	1.9	0.53
Graham Crackers, crumbs	4.15	3.9	8.3	1.9	0.52
Masa Harina, instant	4.50	3.56	9.0	1.78	0.56
Matzo Meal	4.00	4.00	8.0	2.0	0.50
Oat Bran	5.30	3.0	10.6	1.5	0.66
Oats, quick	3.30	4.8	6.6	2.4	0.41
Oats, rolled	3.00	5.3	6.0	2.7	0.38
Oyster Crackers	2.35	6.81	4.7	3.4	0.29
Pancake Mix	4.65	3.4	9.3	1.7	0.58
Potato Starch	5.75	2.78	11.5	1.39	0.72
Rice Bran, crude	4.16	3.8	8.3	1.9	0.52
Rice Bran, fine	1.80	8.89	3.6	4.44	0.23
Semolina	6.30	2.5	12.6	1.3	0.79
Soy Meal, defatted	4.30	3.7	8.6	1.9	0.54
Spelt Flour	4.65	3.44	9.3	1.72	0.58
Tapioca Starch	4.75	3.37	9.5	1.68	0.59
Wheat Bran	2.00	8.00	4.0	4.0	0.25
Wheat Germ	4.10	3.9	8.2	2.0	0.51
Wheat Grains, whole, hard	6.70	2.4	13.4	1.2	0.84
Wheat Grains, whole, soft	5.90	2.7	11.8	1.4	0.74
Wheat Starch Powder	3.95	4.05	7.9	2.03	0.49

Note

1. **Flour:** Volumes are *spooned,* not sifted. Sifting flours can reduce a volume's weight by 7%.

1 gal. = 4 qt. = 16 c. = 128 fl. oz. ✦ 1 qt. = 2 pt. = 4 c. = 32 fl. oz. ✦ 1 pt. = 2 c. = 16 fl. oz. ✦
1 c. = 8 fl. oz. = 16 tbsp. ✦ 1 fl. oz. = 2 tbsp. ✦ 1 tbsp. = 3 tsp. ✦ 1 lb. = 16 oz.

Sweeteners

Item	Ounces per Cup	Cups per Pound	Ounces per Pint	Pints per Pound	Pounds per Pint
Blue Agave Syrup, raw	10.80	1.48	21.60	0.74	10.80
Brown Sugar, packed	7.75	2.06	15.50	1.032	0.97
Brown Sugar, unpacked	5.10	3.14	10.20	1.569	0.64
Butterscotch Topping	11.30	1.42	22.60	0.708	1.41
Chocolate Fudge Topping	12.00	1.33	24.00	0.667	1.50
Chocolate Sprinkles	6.50	2.46	13.00	1.231	0.81
Corn Syrup, dark or light	11.50	1.39	23.00	0.696	1.44
Corn Syrup, High-Fructose	11.00	1.45	22.00	0.727	1.38
Fructose Powder	6.75	2.37	13.50	1.19	0.84
Granulated Sugar	7.10	2.25	14.20	1.127	0.89
Grenadine Syrup (Rose's)	10.6	1.51	21.20	0.75	10.60
Honey	12.00	1.33	24.00	0.667	1.50
Jam Preserves	11.30	1.42	22.60	0.708	1.41
Jelly Preserves	10.60	1.51	21.20	0.755	1.33
Lime Juice, Sweetened (Rose's)	9.6	1.67	19.20	0.83	9.60
Maple and Pancake Syrup	11.10	1.44	22.20	0.721	1.39
Maple Sugar, unpacked	5.10	3.14	10.20	1.569	0.64
Molasses	11.60	1.38	23.20	0.690	1.45
Nutrasweet, Equal	6.00	2.67	12.00	1.333	0.75
Pineapple Topping	11.00	1.45	22.00	0.727	1.38
Powdered Sugar, sifted	3.60	4.44	7.20	2.220	0.45
Powdered Sugar, unsifted	4.35	3.68	8.70	1.839	0.54
Rainbow Colors Sprinkles	6.25	2.56	12.50	1.280	0.78
Stevia Liquid Extract	9.2	1.74	18.40	0.87	9.20
Stevia Powder	2.96	5.41	5.91	2.71	2.96
Stevia Powder with Maltodextrin	3.7	4.32	7.40	2.16	3.70
Strawberry Topping	11.00	1.45	22.00	0.727	1.38
Sugar, Demerara	7.4	2.16	14.80	1.08	7.40

Y% means yield percentage ✦ AS means as served (or used) ✦ AP means as purchased ✦ AS ÷ AP = Y% ✦
AS ÷ Y% = AP ✦ AP × Y% = AS ✦ Cost per AP unit ÷ Y% = Cost per servable unit

Sweeteners (Continued)

Item	Ounces per Cup	Cups per Pound	Ounces per Pint	Pints per Pound	Pounds per Pint
Sugar, Turbinado	7.05	2.27	14.10	1.13	0.88
Sugar, Turbinado	7.35	2.18	14.70	1.09	7.35
Sugar, Ultrafine, Bakers'	6.95	2.30	13.90	1.15	0.87
Sugar Cane Syrup	11.3	1.42	22.60	0.71	11.30
Splenda	0.85	18.82	1.70	9.41	0.11
Syrups, Monin assorted flavors	11.1	1.44	22.20	0.72	11.10
Syrups, Toriani assorted flavors	10.4	1.54	20.80	0.77	10.40
Xylitol	7.7	2.08	15.40	1.04	7.70

Notes

1. Weights are avoirdupois (U.S.) ounces, not fluid ounces. Liquids are often sold by fluid ounces.

2. Piloncillo is an unrefined Mexican brown sugar produced in a rather hard cone. It is also known as Panela and Panocha. The size of the cone varies from .75 ounce to 9 ounces. A common size is 5.5 ounces. If you do not have a 5- or 6-ounce cone of Piloncillo, substitute an equal weight of dark brown sugar and two teaspoons of molasses.

1 gal. = 4 qt. = 16 c. = 128 fl. oz. ✦ 1 qt. = 2 pt. = 4 c. = 32 fl. oz. ✦ 1 pt. = 2 c. = 16 fl. oz. ✦
1 c. = 8 fl. oz. = 16 tbsp. ✦ 1 fl. oz. = 2 tbsp. ✦ 1 tbsp. = 3 tsp. ✦ 1 lb. = 16 oz.

Special Baking Items

Item	Ounces per Cup	Cups per Pound	Ounces per Pint	Pints per Pound	Pounds per Pint
Almond Paste, packed	8.10	2.0	16.2	0.99	1.01
Ammonium Bicarbonate	6.00	2.7	12.0	1.33	0.75
Apricot Glaze, firm gel	11.00	1.5	22.0	0.73	1.38
Arrowroot	4.50	3.6	9.0	1.78	0.56
Baking Powder	6.90	2.3	13.8	1.16	0.86
Baking Soda	8.40	1.9	16.8	0.95	1.05
Brewers Yeast	5.1	3.14	10.20	1.57	0.64
Cacoa Nibs	4.4	3.64	8.80	1.82	0.55
Carob Powder	4.8	3.33	9.60	1.67	0.60
Chocolate Chips, 1,000 count	5.35	3.0	10.7	1.50	0.67
Chocolate Chips, 4,000 count	5.65	2.8	11.3	1.42	0.71
Chocolate chips, dark, melted	10.5	1.52	21.00	0.76	1.31
Chocolate chips, dark, retail size	6.1	2.62	12.20	1.31	0.76
Chocolate chips, Milk	6.15	2.60	12.30	1.30	0.77
Chocolate chips, Milk, melted	10.4	1.54	20.80	0.77	1.30
Chocolate chips, White	5.85	2.74	11.70	1.37	0.73
Chocolate chips, White, melted	10.5	1.52	21.00	0.76	1.31
Cocoa, unsweetened, 22% sifted	2.90	5.5	5.8	2.76	0.36
Cocoa, unsweetened, 22% fat	3.35	4.8	6.7	2.39	0.42
Cream of Tartar	6.50	2.5	13.0	1.23	0.81
Egg White Powder	3.05	5.25	6.10	2.62	0.38
Gelatin, flavored, sweetened	7.30	2.19	14.6	1.10	0.91
Gelatin, unsweetened powder	5.08	3.15	10.16	1.57	0.64
Milk, Nonfat, powdered	5.45	2.9	10.9	1.47	0.68
Pectin, powdered	5.20	3.1	10.4	1.54	0.65
Salt, kosher, flake	9.41	1.7	18.8	0.85	1.18
Salt, table grind	10.32	1.6	20.6	0.78	1.29
Yeast, dry active	6.00	2.7	12.0	1.33	0.75

Y% means yield percentage ✦ AS means as served (or used) ✦ AP means as purchased ✦ AS ÷ AP = Y% ✦
AS ÷ Y% = AP ✦ AP × Y% = AS ✦ Cost per AP unit ÷ Y% = Cost per servable unit

Notes

1. **Fresh Yeast:** Use 2.4 times the weight called for dry.
2. **Gelatin:**
   + Gelatin Sheet: 1 = 3 grams. 1 ounce = 9.4 sheets.
   + 1 tablespoon of powdered gelatin weighs .317 ounces.
   + There are 3 tablespoons powdered gelatin per ounce.
   + 1 cup of powdered gelatin weighs 5.08 ounce. 1 pound of powdered gelatin = 3.15 cups.
3. **Sweetened Gelatin:**

   24 ounces of sweetened gelatin yields 1 gallon of finished gelatin.

   If you divide the 1 gallon (128 fluid ounces) by 24, you'll see that 1 ounce of sweetened gelatin powder yields 5.33333* fluid ounces of finished gelatin. (The asterisk after the last 3 signifies that this series of 3s is infinite.) To determine how much 1 pound of the powder yields in finished gelatin, simply multiply the number of ounces in 1 pound (16) times the yield of 1 ounce (5.33333*).

   $$16 \times 5.33333* = 85.333 \text{ fl. oz.}$$

   Convert the 85.333 fluid ounces to quarts by dividing it by 32, the number of fluid ounces in 1 quart.

   $$85.333 \div 32 = 2.666$$

   So, 1 pound of sweetened gelatin powder yields 2.66 quarts (or .66 gallons) of finished gelatin.
4. **Plain Gelatin—Unsweetened:**

   2.5 ounces of plain powdered gelatin yields 1 gallon plain gelatin. 1 ounce powder yields 51.2 fluid ounces.

   16 ounces (1 pound) ÷ 2.5 = 6.4.

   So, 1 pound of plain gelatin powder yields 6.4 gallons of plain gelatin.
5. **Tablespoons:**

   1 tablespoon baking soda weighs .525 ounces (1.9 tablespoons per ounce).

   1 tablespoon baking powder weighs .43 ounces (2.3 tablespoons per ounce).

   1 tablespoon cream of tartar weighs .4 ounces (2.5 tablespoons per ounce).

   1 tablespoon salt weighs .64 ounces (1.56 tablespoons per ounce).

   1 tablespoon dry yeast weighs .375 ounces (2.66 tablespoons per ounce).

   To calculate the weight needed based on a number of tablespoons you can either:
   1. Multiply the number of tablespoons needed by the weight per tablespoon.
   2. Divide the number of tablespoons needed by the number of tablespoons per ounce.

   Method 1:

   Given: You need 8 tablespoons of salt. Salt, as seen above, weighs .64 oz. per tablespoon.

   $$8 \times .64 = 5.12 \text{ oz.}$$

   You need 5.1 ounces of salt to equal 8 tablespoons.

   Method 2:

   Again, you need 8 tablespoons of salt. Above, it is seen that there are 1.56 tablespoons of salt per ounce.

   $$8 \div 1.56 = 5.1 \text{ oz.}$$

---

1 gal. = 4 qt. = 16 c. = 128 fl. oz. ✦ 1 qt. = 2 pt. = 4 c. = 32 fl. oz. ✦ 1 pt. = 2 c. = 16 fl. oz. ✦
1 c. = 8 fl. oz. = 16 tbsp. ✦ 1 fl. oz. = 2 tbsp. ✦ 1 tbsp. = 3 tsp. ✦ 1 lb. = 16 oz.

5 | FATS, OILS, AND CONDIMENTS

*F*ats such as shortening, butter, frying oil, and lard are sold in units measured by the pound. Many recipes—though not all—measure these ingredients using volumes such as tablespoons, cups, or quarts. Like liquids, these items do not pack down in larger measuring containers, so it is not necessary to add any compaction factors to quarts, half gallons, or gallons.

The discussion in this chapter makes reference to the following tables:

+ Fats and Oils
+ Condiments

The Fats and Oils table shows the following:

+ Ounce weight per cup
+ Cups per pound
+ Fluid ounces per cup, which is eight in all cases

Because many condiments are used sparingly (in quantities of teaspoons, tablespoons, or cups), the Condiments table lists the following measures:

+ Ounces per tablespoon
+ Tablespoons per ounce
+ Teaspoons per ounce
+ Ounces per cup

COSTING FATS, OILS, AND CONDIMENTS

This section addresses fats first, broken into two subsections—solid and liquid—followed by the Costing Condiments section.

COSTING SOLID FATS

To cost a volume of fat, follow this procedure:

1. Divide the number of pounds in the purchase unit into the cost of the purchase unit.
2. Divide that result by 16 (because there are 16 ounces in 1 pound) to get the cost per AP ounce.

IN THE WORKBOOK

Part II, the Workbook, has three worksheets to help you cost volumes of fats, oils, and condiments:

✦ Weights to Volumes, Costing Worksheet 1
✦ Volume (Fluid Ounce) Items, Costing Worksheet 4
✦ Rendered, Reduced, and Clarified Items, Costing Worksheet 14

NOTE

It is perfectly acceptable to round up slightly in order to account for the small bits of shortening that cling to containers and often go unused. Do not, however, round down. If you do, you will be understating your costs.

3. Look up the ounces contained in 1 cup from the Fats and Oils table.

4. Multiply the cost per AP ounce by the number of ounces in 1 cup. This is the cost per cup. For pints, multiply the cup cost by 2; for a quart, by 4; for a gallon, by 16. (As already noted, fats do not compact in larger vessels, so no compaction factor has to be added to these answers.) For tablespoons, divide the cup cost by 16. For teaspoons, divide the cup cost by 48, or the tablespoon cost by 3.

Example

Given: A 50-pound box of shortening costs $24.70:

1. Divide $24.70 by 50 to get the cost per pound.

$24.70 ÷ 50 = $0.494

So, 1 pound costs $0.494.

2. Divide the cost per AP pound by 16 to calculate the cost per AP ounce:

$0.494 ÷ 16 = $0.030875

One AP ounce costs 3.1 cents, rounded. The table states that there are 7.25 ounces in 1 cup of shortening:

7.25 oz. × $0.031 = $0.22475

So, 1 cup of shortening costs approximately 22.5 cents.

COSTING FLUID FATS

Some special oils, like walnut or olive, are sold by the pint, quart, or gallon, or they may be packaged in odd-sized containers such as an 18-ounce bottle. Costing Worksheet 4 will come in handy for costing a volume of these items.

Costing volume measures of these fats and oils is fairly straightforward. The fats are already sold by fluid ounces or by a volume measure that can be divided by the number of fluid ounces contained in the purchase unit. From there, it's simply a matter of following these four steps:

1. Determine the total fluid ounces purchased—just look on the container(s).
2. Divide the cost of the container(s) by the number of fluid ounces it (or they) contain(s). This is the cost per AP fluid ounce.
3. Multiply the cost per AP fluid ounce by 8 for 1 cup.
4. Follow the instructions already given for larger and smaller volumes.

Example

Given: A case of pure olive oil consists of three 1-gallon jugs and costs $56. There are 128 fluid ounces in 1 gallon. Do the math:

1. Multiply 128 by 3 to calculate the total number of fluid ounces purchased:

128 fl. oz. × 3 = 384 fl. oz.

2. Divide the cost of the case by the total number of fluid ounces it contained:

$56 ÷ 384 = $0.14583

1 gal. = 4 qt. = 16 c. = 128 fl. oz. ✦ 1 qt. = 2 pt. = 4 c. = 32 fl. oz. ✦ 1 pt. = 2 c. = 16 fl. oz. ✦
1 c. = 8 fl. oz. = 16 tbsp. ✦ 1 fl. oz. = 2 tbsp. ✦ 1 tbsp. = 3 tsp. ✦ 1 lb. = 16 oz.

One fluid ounce of pure olive oil costs 14.6 cents (after rounding up). Again, a cup's cost will be eight times the cost of 1 fluid ounce, and so forth.

Costing a Weight of Clarified Butter   Clarified butter is simply the pure butterfat rendered by heating whole butter to separate out the water and milk solids. (Whole butter is approximately 75 percent butterfat by weight. The other 25 percent is the water and milk solids.) The resulting butterfat is far less susceptible to scorching or smoking than hot, whole butter, and so it is called for in many sauté preparations, roux making, and some baking formulas.

To cost an ounce of clarified butter, take these two steps:

1. Divide the cost of an AP ounce of whole butter by 0.75. This tells you the cost of an ounce of clarified butter.
2. Multiply that by the number of ounces you need to complete costing the ingredient. For instance, say an ounce of whole butter costs 15 cents—$0.15 ÷ 0.75 = $0.20—and your recipe calls for a weight of 10 ounces of clarified butter:

   10 oz. × $0.20 = $2

The 10 ounces by weight will cost you $2.

Costing a Volume of Clarified Butter   Many recipes measure clarified butter in tablespoons, cups, or pints, but you cannot use the ounce weight cost already given to cost a fluid ounce, because a fluid ounce of clarified butter weighs less than an ounce.

The reason is that, although a pound of whole butter yields 12 ounces (75 percent of 16) of weighed clarified butter, the butterfat is relatively light, meaning that these 12 weighed ounces will occupy 12.857 fluid ounces of space; and 12.857 is approximately 80.4 percent of the original 16 ounces. Therefore, instead of using the factor of 75 percent for costing weighed ounces, costing fluid ounces uses a factor of 80.4 percent. Thus, the 15 cents AP cost per ounce of whole butter now becomes:

$0.15 ÷ 0.804 = $0.18657, or 18.7 cents, rounded

If your recipe calls for, say, 10 fluid ounces of clarified butter, the total cost will be $1.87. Yes, the 10 fluid ounces of clarified butter costs less than the 10 weighed ounces of clarified butter. This is logical, because you are using less butter. A fluid ounce of clarified butter weighs less than a weighed ounce—about 9.3 percent less.

COSTING CONDIMENTS

Condiments encompass a broad range of foods, from prepared sauces like ketchup and mustard to salad dressings or soup bases.

For condiments that are sold by weight but used by volume, you cost a volume measure by following these steps:

1. Calculate the cost per AP ounce (divide purchase unit cost by ounces in unit).
2. Multiply the ounces in 1 cup by the cost per AP ounce.
3. Divide the cup cost by 16 for a tablespoon cost.
4. Divide the tablespoon cost by 3 to get the cost of a teaspoon.

NOTE

Dressings are not listed in the Condiments table because they are both bought and used by volume. You won't find soup bases there, either, because they are bought by weight. However, their volume yields are printed on their containers, so costing them is simple math. Part II does address costing (Costing Worksheet 15) and purchasing (Purchasing Worksheet 13) flavor and stock bases.

Y% means yield percentage ♦ AS means as served (or used) ♦ AP means as purchased ♦ AS ÷ AP = Y% ♦
AS ÷ Y% = AP ♦ AP × Y% = AS ♦ Cost per AP unit ÷ Y% = Cost per servable unit

Example

Given: A case of ketchup consists of six number-10 cans and costs $27.95. Here's the breakdown:

✦ One can costs one-sixth of the case cost:

$27.95 ÷ 6 = $4.66

✦ One can contains 124 ounces:

$4.66 ÷ 124 = $0.0376

So, 1 ounce costs 3.8 cents (after rounding up).

The Condiments table shows there are 9.6 ounces of ketchup in 1 cup.

9.6 oz × $0.038 = $0.365

One cup costs 36.5 cents and one tablespoon costs one-sixteenth of a cup's cost:

$0.365 ÷ 16 = $0.0228

PURCHASING FATS, OILS, AND CONDIMENTS

IN THE WORKBOOK

Part II, the Workbook, has one worksheet to help you plan your purchases of fats, oils, and condiments:

✦ Fats, Oils, and Condiments, Purchasing Worksheet 6

As in the Costing section, this section, too, separates fats and oils from condiments for the purpose of illustrating purchasing formulas.

PURCHASING FATS AND OILS

There are three formulas you'll need to learn for purchasing fats and oils.

FORMULA 1   First is the formula for converting clarified butter weights to whole butter weights.

AS ounce weight of clarified butter × 0.75 = AP ounce weight, whole butter

Don't forget, whole butter yields 75 percent of its weight in clarified butter.

Example

Given: You need 48 weighed ounces of clarified butter. Find how many AP pounds you need to start with.

1. Divide 48 by 75 percent, or 0.75 (the raw-to-clarified weight yield percentage). This equals 64 ounces.
2. Since there are 16 ounces in 1 pound, divide 64 by 16. The answer is 4 pounds. Therefore, you need to begin with 4 pounds of whole butter to end up with 48 ounces (3 pounds) of clarified butter.

FORMULA 2   The second formula is used to convert a volume of clarified butter to a weight of whole butter.

AS fluid ounces of clarified butter ÷ 0.804 = AP ounce weight, whole butter

1 gal. = 4 qt. = 16 c. = 128 fl. oz. ✦ 1 qt. = 2 pt. = 4 c. = 32 fl. oz. ✦ 1 pt. = 2 c. = 16 fl. oz. ✦ 1 c. = 8 fl. oz. = 16 tbsp. ✦ 1 fl. oz. = 2 tbsp. ✦ 1 tbsp. = 3 tsp. ✦ 1 lb. = 16 oz.

Note that whole butter yields 80.4 percent of its original volume in clarified butter.

Example
Given: You need a gallon of clarified butter. How many pounds of raw butter should you start with, given that 1 gallon equals 128 fluid ounces?

1. Divide 128 by 0.804. The result is 159.2, so you need to start with 159.2 ounces of whole butter.
2. Divide 159.2 by 16 (the number of ounces in a pound). The answer is 9.95 pounds, meaning you will need nearly 10 pounds of whole butter to get 1 gallon of clarified butterfat.

FORMULA 3 The final formula is used to convert AS cups of fat to AP pounds of fat:

Cups needed ÷ Cups per pound = AP in pounds

Example
Given: You need to use 12 cups of lard. The Fats and Oils table shows that there are 2.21 cups of lard per pound. Do the math:

1. Divide 12 by 2.21 to determine how many pounds of lard to buy or use.

12 ÷ 2.21 = 5.43

You need to buy and/or use 5.43 pounds of lard.

PURCHASING CONDIMENTS

You'll find two formulas of use for planning your condiments purchases.

FORMULA 1 First, you'll want the formula for converting AS tablespoons to AP ounces.

AS tablespoons × Weight of 1 tablespoon = AP in ounces

Example
Given: You need to use 30 tablespoons of ketchup. The Condiments table shows that 1 tablespoon of ketchup weighs 0.6 ounces. Here's the calculation:

1. Multiply 30 tablespoons times .6 to determine the weight needed:

30 × .6 = 18

Therefore, you will buy or use 18 ounces of ketchup (by weight).

FORMULA 2 Next you'll need the formula for converting AS cups to AP ounces:

AS cups × Weight of 1 cup = AP ounces

Example
Given: You are going to use 3 cups of horseradish. The Condiments table shows that horseradish weighs 9.28 ounces per cup:

1. Multiply 3 cups by 9.28 to determine the weight needed.

3 × 9.28 = 27.84

Therefore, you need to buy and/or use nearly 28 ounces of horseradish.

Fats and Oils

Item	U.S. Avoirdupois Ounces per Cup	Cups per Pound	Fluid Ounces per Cup
Butter	8.00	2.00	8
Butter, whipped	5.30	3.02	8
Butter, worked (anhydrous)	7.25	2.21	8
Fat: Duck	7.60	2.11	8
Fat: Beef, Lamb, Chicken, Pork	7.25	2.21	8
Lard	7.25	2.21	8
Margarine	8.00	2.00	8
Oil, Vegetable	7.70	2.08	8
Roux, butter-based	9.40	1.70	8
Shortening	7.25	2.21	8

Notes

1. **Whole Butter:** 1 pound of whole butter yields 12 ounces (by weight) of clarified butter, a 75% yield; 1 pound of whole butter yields 12.864 fluid ounces of clarified butter, an 80.4% yield.
2. **Clarified Butter:** 1 cup of clarified butter weighs 7.5 ounces.
3. **Roux:** 1 cup of cooked, butter-based roux is based on making a "tight" roux, consisting of six parts clarified butter to seven parts flour, by weight.

Condiments

Item	Ounces per Tablespoon	Tablespoons per Ounce	Teaspoons per Ounce	Ounces per Cup
Adobo Paste	0.58	1.74	5.22	9.20
Aji-Mirin, sweet rice cooking wine	0.61	1.65	4.95	9.70
Barbeque Sauce	0.63	1.60	4.80	10.00
Belecan (dried shrimp paste)	0.60	1.66	4.97	9.65
Black Bean and Garlic Sauce	0.64	1.57	4.71	10.20
Chili Sauce	0.61	1.65	4.95	9.70
Chipotles in Adobo	0.55	1.83	5.49	8.75
Cocktail Sauce (ketchup plus horseradish)	0.61	1.63	4.90	9.80
Coconut Cream, canned	0.49	2.03	6.08	7.90
Coconut Milk, canned	0.52	1.94	5.82	8.25
Curry Paste	0.58	1.74	5.22	9.20
Curry Sauce, Lee Kum Kee	0.64	1.57	4.71	10.20
Fish Sauce	0.63	1.58	4.75	10.10
Ginger Purée	0.50	2.00	6.00	8.00
Hoisin Sauce	0.61	1.63	4.90	9.80
Horseradish Sauce	0.58	1.72	5.17	9.28
Kecap Manis	0.73	1.37	4.10	11.70
Kecap Sambal	0.65	1.54	4.62	10.40
Ketchup, 33% solids	0.60	1.67	5.00	9.60
Mayonnaise, whole egg	0.48	2.11	6.32	7.60
Miso Paste	0.62	1.62	4.85	9.90
Mustard, Dijon	0.54	1.89	5.66	8.48
Mustard Sauce	0.53	1.89	5.66	8.48
Nori Paste, various flavors	0.64	1.55	4.66	10.30
Oyster Sauce, ordinary	0.65	1.55	4.64	10.35
Oyster Sauce, premium	0.68	1.48	4.44	10.80
Pho (Vietnamese Beef) Base	0.68	1.47	4.41	10.88
Pickle Relish	0.50	2.00	6.00	8.00
Pico de Gallo	0.31	3.23	9.70	4.95

Y% means yield percentage ✦ AS means as served (or used) ✦ AP means as purchased ✦ AS ÷ AP = Y% ✦
AS ÷ Y% = AP ✦ AP × Y% = AS ✦ Cost per AP unit ÷ Y% = Cost per servable unit

Condiments (Continued)

Item	Ounces per Tablespoon	Tablespoons per Ounce	Teaspoons per Ounce	Ounces per Cup
Ponzu Flavored Vinegar	0.59	1.70	5.11	9.40
Plum Sauce	0.63	1.58	4.75	10.10
Sambal Goreng Udong, dried	0.17	5.82	17.45	2.75
Sambal Oelek	0.57	1.76	5.27	9.10
Sesame Tahini	0.55	1.81	5.42	8.85
Shoyu Sauce, Kikoman	0.59	1.68	5.05	9.50
Shrimp Paste	0.71	1.40	4.21	11.40
Shrimp, Bay, small, dried	0.24	4.10	12.31	3.90
Shrimp, medium, dried	0.18	5.61	16.84	2.85
Siracha Hot Sauce	0.60	1.67	5.00	9.60
Soy Sauce, Kikoman	0.59	1.70	5.11	9.40
Soy Sauce, Light Sodium	0.58	1.74	5.22	9.20
Soy Sauce, Ponzu flavored	0.57	1.75	5.25	9.15
Steak Sauce, A-1 or Heinz	0.58	1.71	5.13	9.35
Sweet and Sour Sauce	0.63	1.60	4.80	10.00
Tamari, low-sodium	0.60	1.67	5.00	9.60
Tapenade	0.56	1.78	5.33	9.00
Tabasco Sauce	0.50	2.00	6.00	8.00
Vinegar, Rice	0.52	1.92	5.75	8.35
Vinegar, White, 5%	0.52	1.93	5.78	8.30
Worcestershire Sauce	0.58	1.71	5.13	9.35

Note

1. Mustard, horseradish, and ginger are in standard prepared condiment forms, wet, not dry.

1 gal. = 4 qt. = 16 c. = 128 fl. oz. ✦ 1 qt. = 2 pt. = 4 c. = 32 fl. oz. ✦ 1 pt. = 2 c. = 16 fl. oz. ✦
1 c. = 8 fl. oz. = 16 tbsp. ✦ 1 fl. oz. = 2 tbsp. ✦ 1 tbsp. = 3 tsp. ✦ 1 lb. = 16 oz.

6 | LIQUIDS

$\mathcal{W}$ines and spirits (the latter of which includes hard liquor, liqueurs, and fortified wines) are sold by the liter or milliliter in the United States. Beer is sold by the fluid ounce or larger standard American volume measures. (Labels on other liquid beverages or liquid foods list the contents in both American and metric units of measure.)

The discussion in this chapter includes reference to one table:

+ Liquids, which lists the capacities of wine and spirits bottles in both fluid ounces and milliliters

COSTING LIQUIDS PACKAGED IN METRIC VOLUME MEASURES

IN THE WORKBOOK

Part II, the Workbook, has one worksheet to help you cost volumes of liquids:

+ Volume (Fluid Ounce) Items, Costing Worksheet 4

NOTE

A milliliter, one-thousandth of a liter, is abbreviated mL (with no ending period).

Let's start this discussion by assuming that you have a standard case of wine, which holds 12 bottles, and that each standard wine bottle contains 750 milliliters. You want to convert the milliliters to fluid ounces:

+ How: Divide the number of milliliters by 29.57353.
+ Why? There are 29.57353 milliliters in 1 fluid ounce. (You can round this to 29.574.)

Calculate how many fluid ounces are contained in a standard wine bottle:

1. Divide 750 by 29.574:

   750 ÷ 29.574 = 25.36

   Thus, a standard 750-mL wine bottle is also a 25.36-fluid-ounce bottle.

Determine the cost of 1 fluid ounce:

1. Divide the cost of a bottle by 25.36. For example, say a bottle of wine costs $7.60:

   $7.60 ÷ 25.36 = $0.29968, or $0.30, rounded

One fluid ounce of this wine costs 30 cents. A cup would cost 8 times that; a pint 16 times $0.30, and so on.

To speed up this process, use the Liquids table. It shows you how many fluid ounces are contained in standard bottles of wines and spirits. Just be aware that some spirits bottles are labeled as being common measures like pint, half pint, or half gallon, but they are not true half-pints, pints, or half gallons. To avoid confusion, use the table or simply read the label and divide the milliliters by 29.574 to convert to fluid ounces.

PURCHASING LIQUIDS PACKAGED IN METRIC VOLUME MEASURES

IN THE WORKBOOK

Part II, the Workbook, has one worksheet to help you plan your purchases of liquids:

✦ Bottled Liquids, Purchasing Worksheet 7

Planning your purchases of liquids is a two-step process:

1. Determine how many fluid ounces you plan to use or serve.
2. Divide that number by the number of fluid ounces in one bottle of the type you will be ordering. Your answer will be the number of bottles to buy or cost.

FORMULA 1   Here is the formula for converting U.S. fluid ounces to bottles:

U.S. fluid ounces needed ÷ Fluid ounces per bottle = # of AP bottles

Example
Given: A recipe calls for 76 fluid ounces of wine. You buy this wine in 750 mL bottles. The Liquids table shows that there are 25.36 fluid ounces in one 750 mL bottle:

76 ÷ 25.36 = 2.997

You will need to order, or cost, three full 750 mL bottles.

Liquids

Bottle Type	Bottle Size	U.S. Fluid Ounces	Milliliters
Wine Bottle	Champagne Split (Twentieth)	6.32	187
Wine Bottle	Double Magnum	101.44	3,000
Wine Bottle	Fifth (Regular Wine Bottle)	25.36	750
Wine Bottle	Half-Bottle (Tenth)	12.68	375
Wine Bottle	Liter	33.81	1,000
Wine Bottle	Magnum	50.72	1,500
Spirits Bottle (U.S.)	"Half Gallon," spirits	59.18	1,750
Spirits Bottle (U.S.)	"Half Pint," spirits	6.76	200
Spirits Bottle (U.S.)	"Pint," spirits	12.68	375
Spirits Bottle (U.S.)	Fifth, spirits	25.36	750
Spirits Bottle (U.S.)	Liter, spirits	33.81	1,000
Spirits Bottle (U.S.)	Miniature, spirits	1.69	50

Notes

(Refer to the Measurement Conversions page (page 141) for more data regarding liquid measures.)

1. In the United States there are 8 fluid ounces per cup, 16 per pint, 32 per quart, 128 per gallon. In the imperial (British) system there are 8 fluid ounces per cup, 20 per pint, 40 per quart, 160 per gallon. Thus, the British pint, quart, and gallon are all about 20% larger than their U.S. counterparts. The U.S. fluid ounce, however, is a bit larger than an imperial fluid ounce; and both the U.S. and imperial fluid ounces weigh more than the avoirdupois ounce.

2. 1 avoirdupois ounce equals 28.35 grams. A U.S. fluid ounce is 29.57; a British fluid ounce, 28.413. The avoirdupois ounce is the unit of measure used to state the ounce weight of goods like food. But fluid ounces measure liquid volume, not weight.
   - The U.S. fluid ounce of water equals 29.57 grams (29.57 milliliters). This equals 1.043 ounces, avoirdupois.
   - 1 imperial fluid ounce of water equals 28.413 grams and/or milliliters; two-tenths of 1% above avoirdupois.
   - 1 U.S. fluid cup of water weighs 236.588 grams (or 236.588 milliliters). This equals 8.346 ounces, avoirdupois.
   - 2 cups equal 1 pint. 2 × 8.346 ounces equals 16.692 ounces, avoirdupois.
   - 1 pound equals 16 ounces, avoirdupois—not 16.692 ounces!

   Thus, contrary to the old saying, a pint is not a pound the world around.

3. Always use units of liquid measure to express measurements pertaining to liquid capacities. These are fluid ounces, cups, pints, quarts, gallons, milliliters, and liters.

4. U.S. and Metric Volume Conversion Notes:
   - 1 liter equals 1.056688 U.S. quarts, or 33.8 fluid ounces. (A liter is about 5.6% bigger than a quart.)
   - 1 quart equals 0.946 liters.
   - 1 U.S. gallon (128 U.S. fluid ounces) equals 3.785 liters.

   To find quarts from liters, multiply the number of liters by 1.0568; for example, 4 liters × 1.0568 = 4.22 quarts. To find liters from U.S. quarts, multiply quarts by .946; for example, 4 quarts × 0.946 = 3.785 liters. Since there are 4 quarts in a gallon, there are 3.785 liters in 1 U.S. gallon. To find the U.S. fluid ounces in a bottle sold by milliliters, divide the number of milliliters by 29.57. For example, a wine bottle contains 750 mL; 750 milliliters ÷ 29.57 = 25.36. There are 25.36 U.S. fluid ounces in a standard 750 mL wine bottle.
   - 1 Cubic Foot of water equals 7.481 gallons. One gallon of water weighs 8.346 pounds, or, 133.536 ounces.

7

DAIRY

The dairy category includes a variety of products: milk, cream, eggs, cheeses, and yogurt. Liquid dairy products are typically sold in amounts measured by volume: half pints, pints, quarts, half gallons, or gallons, and most of the time these liquids are also measured in recipes by volume, making the costing and purchasing calculations rather simple. Baking recipes, however, often measure these (and other dairy products) by weight. The Dairy Products table lists the volume-to-weight relationships for liquids as well as cheese and egg products and will facilitate the costing and purchasing of dairy items, whether they are sold by volume or by weight. A few dairy items (butter pats and individual creamers, for instance) are sold by the count. While not listed in the table, the correct procedures for costing and purchasing count items is addressed in this chapter as well.

This chapter makes reference to one table:

+ Dairy Products

This table lists the following measures:

+ Ounces per cup
+ Cups per pound
+ Ounces per pint
+ Pints per pound
+ Pounds per pint

IN THE WORKBOOK

Part II, the Workbook, has two worksheets to help you cost volumes of dairy products:

+ Weights to Volumes, Costing Worksheet 1
+ Eggs, Costing Worksheet 9

COSTING DAIRY PRODUCTS

COSTING LIQUID DAIRY PRODUCTS

When you are dealing with liquid dairy products, like milk or cream, you first determine the cost of 1 fluid ounce. This is pretty simple because these foods are sold in volume measures based on the U.S. fluid ounce—half pints, pints, quarts, half gallons, and gallons—so it's a simple matter of dividing the cost of the container by the number of fluid ounces in the container. Say that a 4-gallon case of whole milk costs $11.12. Then 1 gallon will cost one-fourth of the case cost:

$11.12 ÷ 4 = $2.78

One gallon costs $2.78.

And because there are 128 fluid ounces in 1 gallon, you divide the gallon cost ($2.78) by 128 to get the cost per fluid ounce:

$2.78 ÷ 128 = $0.021718, or 2.17 cents, rounded

If your recipe calls for 40 fluid ounces of milk, you multiply the cost per fluid ounce times the number of fluid ounces needed:

$0.0217 × 40 = $0.868, or 87 cents, rounded

COSTING CHEESES

NOTE

The compaction factors for quarts, half gallons, and gallons apply to loose foods such as shredded or diced cheeses, but not to dense, almost-liquid foods like melted cheese, cream cheese, or cottage cheese, because they behave like liquids. They do not compact in larger vessels.

Dairy products like shredded or creamed cheese are sold by the pound but are measured in some recipes in cups, pints, or quarts. To cost a volume amount, make these calculations:

1. Determine the cost per ounce by dividing the cost of the purchase unit, a case, or block, for instance, by number of pounds in the purchase unit.
2. Divide the cost per pound by 16 to get the cost per ounce.
3. In the Dairy Products table, look up the number of ounces found in 1 cup or pint to determine the cost per cup or pint.
4. Multiply the cost per ounce by the number of ounces per cup or pint.
5. Multiply the cost per cup or pint by the number of cups or pints needed.

Example
Given: A case of crumbled bleu cheese costs $73.55 and contains four each 5-pound bags of crumbles. So there are 20 pounds in the case (four bags times 5 pounds per bag equals 20 pounds).

1. Divide the case cost of $73.55 by 20 pounds to get the cost per AP pound:

$73.55 ÷ 20 = $3.6775, or $3.68, rounded

2. One ounce costs one-sixteenth of the cost per pound:

$3.68 ÷ 16 = $0.23

3. The Dairy Products table shows that 1 cup of bleu cheese crumbles weighs 4.75 ounces. To cost 1 cup, multiply the cost per ounce ($0.23) times the ounces per cup (4.75):

$0.23 × 4.75 = $1.0925

One cup of bleu cheese crumbles costs a little over $1.09.

COSTING EGGS

NOTE

Formerly, a case held 12 flats, but the 6-flat case has become the norm today.

Recipes typically call for a specific number of eggs, which are usually packed in numbers divisible by 12—one dozen. A commercial flat of eggs holds 30 eggs, and a standard purchase unit is a 6-flat case, or 180 eggs.

Costing one egg requires simple division:

Y% means yield percentage ✦ AS means as served (or used) ✦ AP means as purchased ✦ AS ÷ AP = Y% ✦
AS ÷ Y% = AP ✦ AP × Y% = AS ✦ Cost per AP unit ÷ Y% = Cost per servable unit

1. Divide the cost of the purchase unit by the number of eggs it contains. If a 180-egg case costs $18, then one egg costs 10 cents:

$18 ÷ 180 = $0.10

That said, complicating the use of eggs is that they are sold in different sizes, but recipes generally call for "large" eggs. A whole large egg weighs 2 ounces and holds 1.777 ounces of shelled egg–the yolk and white. Whites constitute two-thirds (66.6 percent) of the whole shelled egg, and the yolks one-third (33.3 percent).

Some recipes call for shelled eggs, usually described as *pooled eggs*. To use pooled eggs properly, you need to know that a quart of pooled eggs equals 19.44 large eggs, meaning that if one egg costs $0.10, then a quart costs $1.944. A pound of pooled eggs equals nine large eggs, so if one egg costs $0.10, 1 pound costs $0.90.

COSTING MISCELLANEOUS DAIRY PRODUCTS

Dairy products such as individual butter pats, coffee creamers, and cheese slices are sold by the count. That is, a case of creamers, for instance, will be designated as having a certain number of creamers inside. To cost these items, then, you just divide the purchase unit cost by the number in the unit.

As an example, assume a case of creamers costs $8.95 and holds 400 creamers. (Creamer packaging is now more varied but is near 400/case.) One creamer will cost:

$8.95 ÷ 400 = $0.02237

So one creamer costs about 2.24 cents.

PURCHASING DAIRY PRODUCTS

As with the Costing Dairy Products section, we'll go through the purchasing formulas for the dairy foods category in the same order: liquids, cheeses, eggs, and miscellaneous.

PURCHASING DAIRY LIQUIDS

The formula for determining a correct volume of dairy liquid to buy is quite simple if your recipes are expressed in *volume measures*. The formula is:

AS fluid ounces needed ÷ Fluid ounces in a purchase unit
= # of purchase units

Example
Given: Your production plan calls for an aggregate of 512 fluid ounces of whole milk. Your experience tells you that you buy whole milk in gallon containers. Since 1 gallon equals 128 fluid ounces, you divide 512 by 128:

512 ÷ 128 = 4

You need 4 gallons of whole milk.

1 gal. = 4 qt. = 16 c. = 128 fl. oz. ✦ 1 qt. = 2 pt. = 4 c. = 32 fl. oz. ✦ 1 pt. = 2 c. = 16 fl. oz. ✦
1 c. = 8 fl. oz. = 16 tbsp. ✦ 1 fl. oz. = 2 tbsp. ✦ 1 tbsp. = 3 tsp. ✦ 1 lb. = 16 oz.

FORMULA   If the quantities in your recipes are expressed in weight but you buy the dairy product by volume, the procedure for converting a weight of dairy liquid to a volume is done in two stages:

Stage 1:

1. Determine the number of pints needed.

AS ounces needed ÷ Ounces per pint = # of pints needed

Stage 2:

2. Determine the number of purchase units needed.

Pints per purchase unit ÷ Pints needed = Purchase units needed

1. Convert, if necessary, any pound measures of the dairy liquid to ounces by multiplying the pounds by 16.
2. Look up the item's volume-to-weight relationship in the Dairy table using the Ounces per Pint column.
3. Divide the total weighed ounces needed by the Ounces per Pint column value. Your answer will be the number of pints needed.
4. Convert the number of pints to the purchase unit for this item (typically a quart, half gallon, or gallon) by dividing the number of pints in the purchase unit into the number of pints needed. Your answer will be the number of purchase units needed.

Example
Given: A recipe calls for 6 pounds of 2 percent milk, and you buy this milk in half gallons.

1. Convert the 6 pounds to ounces:

6 × 16 = 96

2. The Dairy Products table shows that there are 17.2 ounces of 2 percent milk in one pint.
3. Divide the ounces needed by ounces per pint.

96 oz. ÷ 17.2 oz. per pint = 5.58 pints

4. Since there are 64 fluid ounces in a half gallon and 16 ounces per pint, divide the 64 by 16 to calculate the number of pints in the purchase unit.

64 ÷ 16 = 4

5. Divide the total pints needed (5.58) by the number of pints in the purchase unit (4):

5.58 ÷ 4 = 1.395

You will need about 1.4 half gallons of 2 percent milk.

PURCHASING CHEESES

The formula you'll need to use to plan your cheese purchases has two variations.

IN THE WORKBOOK

Part II, the Workbook, has one worksheet to help you plan your purchases of dairy products:

✦ Dairy products, Purchasing Worksheet 8

Y% means yield percentage ✦ AS means as served (or used) ✦ AP means as purchased ✦ AS ÷ AP = Y% ✦
AS ÷ Y% = AP ✦ AP × Y% = AS ✦ Cost per AP unit ÷ Y% = Cost per servable unit

FORMULA 1 The first version of the formula for converting AS cups to AP weight in pounds is:

(AS cups × Ounce weight per cup) ÷ 16 = AP in pounds

Basically, all you are doing here is multiplying the ounce weight of a cup by the number of cups needed and then converting that answer (which will be a number of ounces) to pounds, by dividing the ounces needed by 16.

Example

Given: You need 2 cups of diced cheddar. The Dairy Products table shows that a cup of diced cheddar weighs 4.65 ounces. Do the math:

1. Multiply the number of cups needed (2) by the weight per cup (4.65):

2 cups × 4.65 oz. = 9.3 oz.

2. Divide 9.3 ounces by 16 to convert the ounces to pounds:

9.3 ÷ 16 = 0.58125 lb.

Thus, you need approximately 0.58 pounds of cheddar cheese.

But say, instead, that you need a half gallon of diced cheddar. Because the cheese in this form will pack down a bit in a half-gallon container, you need to add a factor of 3.5 percent to the number of cups you are going to use before proceeding. The compaction factors are:

+ 1.5 percent for a quart
+ 3.5 percent for a half gallon
+ 7 percent for a gallon

1. Multiply the 8 cups in the half gallon by 0.035:

8 × 0.035 = 0.28

2. Add the 0.28 to the 8-cup multiplier and proceed as just shown.

8.28 cups × 4.65 oz. per cup = 38.5 oz.
38.5 oz. ÷ 16 oz. = 2.406 lb.

After rounding, it appears that you will need 2.41 pounds of cheddar.

FORMULA 2 The alternate method for converting AS cups per pound to AP pounds is as follows:

AS cups ÷ Cups per pound = AP pounds

Example

Given: You need a half gallon of diced cheddar. The Dairy Products table shows that there are 3.441 individual cups of diced cheddar per pound. Factoring compaction, you will use 8.28 cups rather than 8 cups.

1. Divide the 8.28 cups you need by the number of cups per pound (3.441).

8.28 ÷ 3.441 = 2.406

1 gal. = 4 qt. = 16 c. = 128 fl. oz. ✦ 1 qt. = 2 pt. = 4 c. = 32 fl. oz. ✦ 1 pt. = 2 c. = 16 fl. oz. ✦
1 c. = 8 fl. oz. = 16 tbsp. ✦ 1 fl. oz. = 2 tbsp. ✦ 1 tbsp. = 3 tsp. ✦ 1 lb. = 16 oz.

Notice that this is the same answer as the first method: You need to buy and/or use 2.41 pounds of cheddar cheese.

PURCHASING EGGS

There are three formulas that will come in handy for planning your egg purchases.

FORMULA 1 This is the formula for converting quarts of pooled eggs to AP large eggs:

AS quarts of pooled large eggs × 19.44 = AP large eggs

Example
Given: You need 3 quarts of pooled large eggs. Formula 1 table indicates that there are 19.44 shelled large eggs per quart. Determine how many eggs to buy to get 3 quarts.

1. Multiply the quarts by 19.44:

3 × 19.44 = 58.32

Thus, you need 58.32 large eggs to obtain 3 quarts, pooled.

FORMULA 2 The second egg formula is for converting quarts of pooled eggs to AP medium eggs:

AS quarts of pooled medium eggs × 22 = AP medium eggs

Example
Given: You need 3 quarts of pooled medium eggs. Note 4 of the Dairy table shows that there are 22 pooled medium eggs per quart. Determine how many eggs to buy to get 3 quarts.

1. Multiply the number of quarts by 22:

3 × 22 = 66

Therefore, you need 66 medium eggs to obtain 3 quarts, pooled.

FORMULA 3 The third egg formula is for converting a weight of large eggs to a count:

AS pounds of large eggs × 9 = AP count

Example
Given: You need 6 pounds of pooled large eggs. Note 5 of the Dairy table states that there are 9 large shelled eggs in 1 pound.

1. Multiply the number of pounds you need by 9 to determine how many eggs to buy:

6 × 9 = 54

You need 54 large eggs.

2. There are 6 flats in a case and 30 eggs in a flat, so there are 180 eggs per case.
   ✦To convert your egg count to dozens, divide the eggs needed by 12.

◆ To convert to flats needed, divide by 30.

◆ To convert to cases, divide by 180.

PURCHASING MISCELLANEOUS DAIRY PRODUCTS

As noted in the costing section, certain dairy products come in specific, precounted packs. Presliced cheeses, individual coffee creamers, and butter pats are three such products sold this way. You buy a case that has an exact count of the product inside. To plan a purchase for this type of food, you divide the number you need by the count per case. Your answer will be the number of purchase units required to fulfill your need.

FORMULA: This is the formula for converting piece counts to AP units:

Total count needed ÷ Count per purchase unit = AP units

Example

Given: A banquet for 600 guests requires two butter pats for each. In all, you need 1,200 pats (2 times 600), and 400 pats come in one case:

1. Divide the butter pat count by the count per case.

1,200 pats needed ÷ 400 pats per case = 3 cases

Order 3 cases—or more, because mistakes happen and some of the guests will want extra butter.

Dairy Products

Item	Ounces per Cup	Cups per Pound	Ounces per Pint	Pints per Pound	Pounds per Pint
American Process, pasteurized, diced	4.94	3.239	9.880	1.62	0.62
American Process, pasteurized, melted	8.60	1.860	17.200	0.93	1.08
American Process, pasteurized, shredded	4.00	4.000	8.000	2.00	0.50
Blue, crumbled	4.75	3.368	9.500	1.68	0.59
Brie or Camembert, melted	8.47	1.889	16.940	0.94	1.06
Brie or Camembert, packed	8.67	1.845	17.340	0.92	1.08
Buttermilk, 1%	8.70	1.839	17.400	0.920	1.09
Buttermilk, 2%	8.6	1.86	17.20	0.93	1.08
Cheddar, diced	4.65	3.441	9.300	1.72	0.58
Cheddar, melted	8.60	1.860	17.200	0.93	1.08
Cheddar, shredded	4.00	4.000	8.000	2.00	0.50
Cool Whip	2.60	6.154	5.200	3.077	0.33
Cotijo, crumbled	4.20	3.810	8.400	1.905	0.53
Cottage, large curd	7.40	2.162	14.800	1.08	0.93
Cottage, small curd	7.90	2.025	15.800	1.01	0.99
Cottage Cheese, lowfat	8.15	1.963	16.300	0.982	1.02
Cottage Cheese, nonfat	8.65	1.850	17.300	0.925	1.08
Cream Cheese	8.20	1.951	16.400	0.98	1.03
Crema Mexicana	8.50	1.882	17.000	0.941	1.06
Crème Fraiche	8.15	1.963	16.300	0.982	1.02
Curds, Drained, 1/3 in. dice	4.75	3.368	9.500	1.684	0.59
Double Devon Cream	8.15	1.963	16.300	0.982	1.02
Dulce de Leche, canned	10.5	1.524	21.000	0.762	1.31
Edam, shredded	5.30	3.019	10.600	1.51	0.66
Egg Powder, sifted	3.00	5.333	6.000	2.67	0.38
Egg Substitute	8.65	1.85	17.3	0.92	1.08
Eggs, hard-cooked, chopped	6.00	2.667	12.000	1.33	0.75
Eggs, whole, shelled, pooled	8.57	1.867	17.140	0.93	1.07

Y% means yield percentage ✦ AS means as served (or used) ✦ AP means as purchased ✦ AS ÷ AP = Y% ✦
AS ÷ Y% = AP ✦ AP × Y% = AS ✦ Cost per AP unit ÷ Y% = Cost per servable unit

Dairy Products (Continued)

Item	Ounces per Cup	Cups per Pound	Ounces per Pint	Pints per Pound	Pounds per Pint
Fontina, shredded	3.80	4.211	7.600	2.11	0.48
Fromage Blanc (Bakers' Cheese)	8.90	1.798	17.800	0.899	1.11
Goat's Milk, evaporated	8.85	1.808	17.700	0.904	1.11
Gruyere, shredded	3.80	4.211	7.600	2.11	0.48
Half and Half	8.55	1.87	17.1	0.94	1.07
Half and Half, fat free	8.85	1.808	17.700	0.904	1.11
IMO–Sour Cream Substitute	8.25	1.939	16.500	0.970	1.03
Kefir, low-fat, fruit-flavored	9.10	1.758	18.200	0.879	1.14
Media Crema	8.40	1.905	16.800	0.952	1.05
Milk, 1%	8.60	1.86	17.20	0.93	1.08
Milk, 2%	8.60	1.86	17.20	0.93	1.08
Milk, whole, 4%	8.55	1.87	17.1	0.94	1.07
Milk, evaporated	8.90	1.798	17.800	0.90	1.11
Milk, powdered (from nonfat milk)	4.25	3.765	8.500	1.88	0.53
Milk, powdered (from whole milk)	4.50	3.556	9.000	1.78	0.56
Milk, sweetened condensed	10.80	1.481	21.600	0.74	1.35
Monterey Jack, diced	4.65	3.441	9.300	1.72	0.58
Monterey Jack, shredded	4.00	4.000	8.000	2.00	0.50
Mozzarella, part skim, shredded	4.00	4.000	8.000	2.00	0.50
Muenster, shredded	4.00	4.000	8.000	2.00	0.50
Non-Dairy Creamer	8.55	1.871	17.100	0.936	1.07
Non-Dairy Creamer, fat-free	8.77	1.824	17.540	0.912	1.10
Parmesan, grated, dry	3.40	4.706	6.800	2.35	0.43
Parmesan, grated, fresh	3.00	5.333	6.000	2.67	0.38
Provolone, diced	4.65	3.441	9.300	1.72	0.58
Provolone, shredded	4.00	4.000	8.000	2.00	0.50
Quark–European Bakers' Cheese	8.60	1.860	17.200	0.930	1.08
Queso Fresco, shredded	3.40	4.706	6.800	2.353	0.43

1 gal. = 4 qt. = 16 c. = 128 fl. oz. ♦ 1 qt. = 2 pt. = 4 c. = 32 fl. oz. ♦ 1 pt. = 2 c. = 16 fl. oz. ♦
1 c. = 8 fl. oz. = 16 tbsp. ♦ 1 fl. oz. = 2 tbsp. ♦ 1 tbsp. = 3 tsp. ♦ 1 lb. = 16 oz.

Dairy Products (Continued)

Item	Ounces per Cup	Cups per Pound	Ounces per Pint	Pints per Pound	Pounds per Pint
Rice "Milk" Drink	8.60	1.860	17.200	0.930	1.08
Ricotta, whole or part skim	8.68	1.843	17.360	0.92	1.09
Sour Cream	8.54	1.874	17.080	0.94	1.07
Sour Cream, fat-free	8.65	1.850	17.300	0.925	1.08
Sour Cream, Mexican, fresh	8.50	1.882	17.000	0.941	1.06
Soy "Milk"	8.65	1.850	17.300	0.925	1.08
Swiss, diced	4.94	3.239	9.880	1.62	0.62
Swiss, melted	8.60	1.860	17.200	0.93	1.08
Swiss, shredded	4.00	4.000	8.000	2.00	0.50
Whipping Cream	8.40	1.9	16.8	0.95	1.05
Whipping Cream, heavy	8.40	1.905	16.800	0.952	1.05
Yogurt, Plain, European Style	8.70	1.839	17.400	0.920	1.09
Yogurt, Sweetened, European Style	9.00	1.778	18.000	0.889	1.13
Yogurts	8.60	1.860	17.200	0.93	1.08

Notes

1. **Eggs:**

Size of Eggs	Jumbo	Extra-Large	Large	Medium	Small
Shelled Ounce Weight Each	2.3	2.05	1.777	1.55	1.30

   - Whites constitute 66.66%, yolks, 33.33% (or two-thirds white, one-third yolk).
   - Yield of 1 large egg, shelled: 1.174 ounces white and .586 ounce yolk (roughly: 1.2 and 0.6).
   - 1 dozen large eggs yields about 21 ounces pooled eggs, or 14 ounces whites and 7 ounces yolks.
   - 1 quart of pooled eggs equals 19.44 large eggs or 22 medium eggs.
   - 1 pound of pooled (shelled) eggs equals 9 large eggs (1.86 cups).

2. **Milks and Creams:**
   - Nonfat, 1%, 2% milks, and 2% buttermilk all weigh 34.4 ounces per quart.
   - Whole milk weighs 34.2 ounces per quart.
   - 1 pound of whole milk equals 15 fluid ounces, or 1.875 cups.
   - Heavy whipping cream weighs 33.6 ounces per quart.
   - Egg substitutes weigh 34.6 ounces per quart.

Y% means yield percentage ✦ AS means as served (or used) ✦ AP means as purchased ✦ AS ÷ AP = Y% ✦
AS ÷ Y% = AP ✦ AP × Y% = AS ✦ Cost per AP unit ÷ Y% = Cost per servable unit

8 BEVERAGES

everages are wonderful money-making menu items for those in the food service industry. They provide a good profit margin and require very little labor to prepare and serve. The potential profits on nonalcoholic drinks like coffee, iced tea, and soda are enormous. For instance:

- A 12-fluid-ounce serving of iced tea will cost you only about 3 cents for the tea, and you will probably sell it for $1.25 or more.
- A gallon of dispensed soda will run you about $2 to make. From a gallon you can pour eight 16-fluid-ounce sodas without even deducting cup space for the ice. If you sell these drinks for $1.25, your sales will total $10 per gallon. That's a 500 percent markup!

Of course, there are other expenses that you have to add to the total menu item cost when working with beverages. These may include:

- Condiments (sugar, creamers)
- Paper or styrofoam cups
- Cup lids
- Straws
- Stir sticks
- Napkins
- Filters

There is one table connected to the discussion in this chapter:

- Coffee, Tea, and Cocoa

COSTING BEVERAGES

This simple costing approach works equally well for dispensed sodas, frozen juice concentrates, and brewed beverages such as coffee, cocoa, and iced tea:

1. Determine the cost per fluid ounce.
2. Multiply it by the ounces poured.
3. Add the condiment and packaging costs.

IN THE WORKBOOK

Part II, the Workbook, has one worksheet to help you cost beverages:

◆ Brewed and Dispensed Beverages, Costing Worksheet 10

Voilá! You have your product cost. To demonstrate this process, we break down beverage costing into three categories: dispensed sodas, coffee, and tea.

COSTING DISPENSED SODAS

The word *dispensed* means that the beverage is mixed in a machine at the time the order is filled. Soda-dispensing machines mix syrup or concentrate with filtered water and carbon dioxide gas to make the finished drink. This is then poured into a glass or take-out cup. If the beverage is served cold, the cup or glass is at least partially filled with ice cubes.

Soda syrups are generally mixed with five parts water and are packaged in 5-gallon "bag-in-box" containers. Hence, a 5-gallon box of syrup will yield its own 5 gallons, plus 25 gallons of water, for a total yield per box of 30 gallons. Therefore, to cost a dispensed drink:

1. Divide the cost of a container of syrup by the container's yield. In this case, 5 gallons of syrup will become 30 gallons of mixed drink:

5 parts syrup + 25 parts water = 30 parts soda

Example
Given: A 5-gallon container of syrup costs $56.10 and yields 30 gallons of mixed drink. To get the cost per fluid ounce, calculate as follows:

1. Divide the cost of the syrup ($56.10) by the yield (30 gallons):

$56.10 ÷ 30 gal. = $1.87 per gal.

2. Divide the cost per gallon by 128 (1 gallon equals 128 fluid ounces):

$1.87 ÷ 128 = $0.0146

The results are as follows:

◆ 1 fluid ounce of dispensed soda costs 1.46 cents.
◆ 16 fluid ounces costs 23.4 cents, rounded.

16 × $0.0146 = $0.2337

But don't forget to add the cost of the gas and water to the syrup cost:

◆ Water costs about 2 mills per gallon, or $0.0000156 per fluid ounce (a mill is 1/10 of 1 cent): $0.002 ÷ 128 = $0.0000156
◆ A cylinder of gas costs about $16 and carbonates 250 gallons of soda. The cost for the gas to produce a gallon of mixed drink is $0.064. A fluid ounce costs 128th of that: $0.0005. Adding the water and gas costs, the cost per fluid ounce of the mixed drink is 1.5 cents, rounded.

However, you will not actually pour 16 fluid ounces into a 16-ounce cup. Why not? First, to avoid spillage, you will not pour a beverage to the very top of the cup or glass. So you need to deduct at least 1 fluid ounce. Second, the ice will displace some of the soda. How much? That depends on how much ice you put into the cup before dispensing the drink. If you fill a 16-fluid-ounce cup to the top with ice, you will be able to pour about 7 fluid ounces of soda to the brim. If the ice comes up two-thirds of the way, you'll pour about 10 fluid ounces. If you fill the cup halfway with ice, you will be able to pour a little more than 11 fluid ounces of soda—again, to the top.

Example

Given: A 16-ounce paper cup is filled two-thirds of the way up with ice. That produces a "pour" of 10 fluid ounces to the top. Here's the math:

1. Deduct 1 fluid ounce, because you are not going to fill the cup to the brim; this leaves you with a 16-fluid-ounce container holding 9 fluid ounces of dispensed soda. So, 9 times the cost per fluid ounce ($0.015) equals $0.135, or 13.5 cents.
2. Add 10 cents to cover the cost of the cup, lid, straw, and napkin.

Your total food and packaging cost is 23.5 cents. If you sell this drink for $1.25, you will make a profit of $1.015 per drink—a 532 percent markup!

COSTING COFFEE

Commercial food service operators buy coffee either in bulk, by the pound, or in packets for brewing one pot at a time.

BULK COFFEE　Let's begin with the costing process for bulk coffee:

1. Determine the cost per pound.
2. Divide that by 16 to get the cost per AP ounce.
3. Weigh the amount of coffee that you use to brew a pot (or other amount) and multiply the cost per ounce of grounds by the ounces used.
4. Divide the cost of the grounds by the number of fluid ounces brewed. This will be your cost per brewed fluid ounce.

In addition, you'll want to keep these points in mind:

✦ The standard coffeepot holds 64 fluid ounces of liquid, whereas standard coffee machines produce closer to 60, not 64, fluid ounces in a brewing cycle.
✦ Tastes in coffee have changed over the years. In the past, rather weak coffee was acceptable in the marketplace. Today, most folks want their coffee stronger and more robust. Therefore, a 60-fluid-ounce pot of coffee today requires about 1.5 ounces of fairly dark-roasted grounds to produce good flavor—and you may find your customers want it even stronger.

Example

Given: A case of coffee contains twelve 2-pound bags of grounds and costs $123.50. To get the cost per brewed fluid ounce, follow three steps:

1. Divide the case cost by the pounds in the case (12 2-pound bags equals 24 pounds):

$123.50 ÷ 24 = $5.15, rounded

2. Divide the cost per pound by 16:

$5.15 ÷ 16 = $0.3219, or 32.2 cents per AP ounce.

1 gal. = 4 qt. = 16 c. = 128 fl. oz. ✦ 1 qt. = 2 pt. = 4 c. = 32 fl. oz. ✦ 1 pt. = 2 c. = 16 fl. oz. ✦
1 c. = 8 fl. oz. = 16 tbsp. ✦ 1 fl. oz. = 2 tbsp. ✦ 1 tbsp. = 3 tsp. ✦ 1 lb. = 16 oz.

Using 1.5 ounces of grounds for a 60-fluid-ounce yield, the coffee costs:

1.5 × $0.322 = $0.483

3. Divide the coffee cost by the fluid ounces yielded:

$0.483 ÷ 60 fl. oz. = $0.00805 per brewed fl. oz.

So, one brewed fluid ounce costs 8 mills, or 0.8 cent–that is, less than a penny. A 12-fluid-ounce cup will cost you 9.6 cents:

12 × $0.008 = 9.6 cents

To determine your actual costs for brewing coffee, use this common approach:

1. Take a particular period of time and record the coffee sales made and the number of pots brewed during this period.
2. Calculate a total production cost by multiplying the cost per brewed pot by the number of pots brewed.
3. Divide this coffee production cost by the number of sales. This tells you your average cost per sale and includes the cost of all the coffee made during this period (even coffee your staff drank, coffee that was tossed out, refills, etc.).

Likewise, to cost your condiment and paper expenses for this period:

1. Take a beginning and closing inventory of these items.
2. Subtract the closing inventory from the opening inventory (plus purchases) to get the usage. Then cost each item's usage and total these expenses.
3. Divide that amount by the number of total sales to arrive at your average paper and condiment costs per sale.
4. Add this amount to the average cost per sale for the coffee itself, and you have your total average product cost per sale.

If your business is all take-out, you can refine this by separating the small, medium, and large cup sales (from your cash register tape) and cost them individually based on the fluid ounces poured for each size, then add the average sale's condiment/paper costs. This enables you to price these items accordingly.

PACKET COFFEE   Costing coffee sold in packets is pretty straightforward. You derive the cost of a packet by dividing the cost of a case of packets by the number of packets in the case. Each packet cost will represent the ideal cost of a brewed pot of coffee–*ideal* meaning that every packet was successfully used to brew a pot of coffee. But mistakes happen: Someone might forget to put the pot in the machine, or a packet might be damaged or stolen, so be mindful of these factors.

To cost iced coffee, determine your cost per poured fluid ounce and multiply that by the ounces poured per drink. Add your condiment and packaging costs to calculate your total product cost.

COSTING TEA

ICED TEA   This popular drink is a real winner for the house. It is easy to make, has a low food cost, and produces little, if any, waste. The tea bags used in commercial

Y% means yield percentage ✦ AS means as served (or used) ✦ AP means as purchased ✦ AS ÷ AP = Y% ✦
AS ÷ Y% = AP ✦ AP × Y% = AS ✦ Cost per AP unit ÷ Y% = Cost per servable unit

food service come in rather large sizes: 1 ounce each. According to the manufacturers, one tea bag produces a gallon of brewed tea. So, to cost iced tea, follow these steps:

1. Divide the cost of a case of tea bags by the number of bags in the case. This represents the food cost for 1 gallon.
2. Divide the cost per gallon by 128 to get the cost of 1 fluid ounce.
3. Multiply the cost per fluid ounce by the number of fluid ounces in a serving.

Example
Given: A case of 96 commercial tea bags costs $28.20. To determine the cost per fluid ounce:

1. Divide the case cost ($28.20) by the number of bags in the case (96):

$28.20 ÷ 96 = $0.29375, or 29.4 cents, rounded

2. Divide the cost per bag, $0.294, by 128:

$0.294 ÷ 128 = $0.0022968, or 0.23 cents per fl. oz.

This is less than a fourth of a cent!
Now assume, with refills, you pour 20 ounces of iced tea per serving:

20 fl. oz. × $0.0023 = $0.046

Thus, the total iced tea cost is 4.6 cents. Yes, this means you can serve a generous portion of iced tea for less than a nickel! Even if you, like some operators, brew your iced tea stronger, and use two tea bags per gallon—meaning your portion cost doubles to just under a dime—if you sell the drink for $1.25, you still have a substantial margin of profit: $1.15.

Bulk (loose) tea leaves are seldom used, but if you use bulk tea rather than bagged tea, brew 2 ounces of tea leaf to 1 gallon of water. Divide the 2-ounce tea-leaf cost by 128 ounces to calculate the cost per fluid ounce.

There are, however, a couple of offsetting expenses for this very profitable drink: lemon and sugar:

NOTE

The Book of Yields recommends using two tea bags per gallon of iced tea.

✦ Lemons can cost as much as 50 cents a piece or as little as 15 cents. Taking an average cost of 30 cents and cutting each lemon into 8 wedges gives you a cost per wedge of 3.75 cents.
✦ Sugar packets run about a half-cent each, and sugar substitute packets cost about a penny. Creamers may be used as well. They cost about 2 cents each.

But even factoring in these costs, iced tea remains a highly profitable menu item for restaurateurs.

HOT TEA Hot tea orders are filled using individual tea bags, so you cost these drinks by adding the cost of a tea bag to the condiment costs (sugar, cream, lemon). Tea bags vary in cost from about 5 to 12 cents each, which is obviously higher for the better-quality, handpicked varieties. Such teas are, however, served primarily in upscale restaurants, where they are most likely priced at an astronomical markup. Thus, the product cost will remain low, as a percentage of the menu price.

1 gal. = 4 qt. = 16 c. = 128 fl. oz. ✦ 1 qt. = 2 pt. = 4 c. = 32 fl. oz. ✦ 1 pt. = 2 c. = 16 fl. oz. ✦
1 c. = 8 fl. oz. = 16 tbsp. ✦ 1 fl. oz. = 2 tbsp. ✦ 1 tbsp. = 3 tsp. ✦ 1 lb. = 16 oz.

PURCHASING BEVERAGE ITEMS

We'll demonstrate five purchasing formulas in this section, each using a different beverage item.

IN THE WORKBOOK

Part II, the Workbook, has 1 worksheet to help you plan your beverage purchases:

✦ Brewed and Dispensed Beverages, Purchasing Worksheet 9

NOTE

Formula 1 is based on the yield of 1 slightly rounded cup of dark-roasted grounds yielding 1 gallon of coffee.

FORMULA 1 For the first formula, we'll learn how to convert gallons of brewed coffee to an AP bulk weight.

AS gallons × 3.2 ounces per gallon = AP ounces coffee grounds

The example explains how we arrive at this formula.

Example
Given: You need 8 gallons of brewed coffee. According to Note 1 of the Coffee, Tea, and Cocoa table, a rounded half cup of drip-grind coffee grounds weighs 1.5 ounces and yields 60 fluid ounces of fairly robust coffee. Sixty fluid ounces is 46.875 percent of a gallon. We need to find how many ounces of coffee grounds are needed for 1 gallon of coffee.

1.5 oz. ÷ .46875 = 3.2 oz.

Therefore, 3.2 ounces of coffee grounds yield 1 gallon of brewed coffee.

8 gal. × 3.2 oz./gal. = 25.6 (or 26 oz., rounded) coffee grounds

FORMULA 2 This formula is for converting gallons of brewed iced tea to an AP bulk weight:

AS gallons × 2 ounces per gallon = AP ounces bulk tea

NOTE

This formula makes strong iced tea. You can use 1 ounce in the formula for weaker tea.

Example
Given: You need 4 gallons of brewed iced tea. The Coffee, Tea, and Cocoa table shows that 2 ounces of tea leaf yields 1 gallon of strong tea. To find the ounce weight of bulk tea needed, multiply the number of gallons of brewed tea needed by 2.0 ounces:

4 gal. × 2 oz./gal. = 8 oz. bulk tea

This equates to eight each 1-ounce bags of tea leaf.

FORMULA 3 Here you'll learn how to convert gallons of hot cocoa to an AP bulk weight of cocoa powder:

AS gallons × 3.35 ounces per gallon = AP ounces cocoa powder

Example
Given: You need 2 gallons of brewed cocoa. The Coffee, Tea, and Cocoa table tells you that 1 cup of cocoa weighs 3.35 ounces and that you will need one cup of cocoa powder to make 1 gallon of brewed cocoa.

Y% means yield percentage ✦ AS means as served (or used) ✦ AP means as purchased ✦ AS ÷ AP = Y% ✦
AS ÷ Y% = AP ✦ AP × Y% = AS ✦ Cost per AP unit ÷ Y% = Cost per servable unit

1. Multiply the number of brewed gallons needed times 3.35.

2 gal. brewed cocoa × 3.35 oz./gal. = 6.7 oz. of cocoa powder

NOTE

Cocoa is often sold in a
powdered form that
includes a sweetener and
powdered dairy whitener
or milk. These powders
come in bags that are
added to a cocoa
dispensing machine. The
fluid-ounce yield of a bag
can be calculated from
the product description
on its case or invoice.

FORMULA 4 For converting gallons of brewed cocoa to packages of premixed cocoa drink, follow this formula:

AS fluid ounces brewed cocoa ÷ Fluid-ounce yield from 1 pack of premix = AP packs

Example
Given: A case of 12 bags of premixed cocoa yields 1,728 fluid ounces of brewed cocoa; 1 bag yields 144 fluid ounces (1,728 ÷ 12 = 144). You anticipate selling 54 8-fluid-ounce portions. This equals 432 fluid ounces (54 × 8 = 432). To find the number of bags you'll need:

1. Divide the AS fluid ounces (432) by the fluid-ounce yield of 1 bag (144):

432 ÷ 144 = 3

You will need three bags of premixed cocoa.

NOTE

Most drink suppliers
provide the dispensing
machines and set them
up correctly as a part of
their marketing strategy,
to make the process easy
for you.

FORMULA 5 Our final formula is for converting fluid ounces of dispensed soda to AP units:

AS fluid ounces dispensed soda ÷ Fluid-ounce yield of 1 AP unit = AP units

As described in the Costing section, dispensed sodas come in boxed bags of syrup concentrate and are mixed on site with water and gas to produce a mixed drink. The syrup-to-water ratio is generally 1 part syrup to 5 parts water, resulting in a yield of 6 parts. Hence, a 5-gallon box of syrup will yield its own 5 gallons plus 25 gallons of water, for a total yield per box of 30 gallons.

In contrast, juice concentrates often have a mixing ratio of 1 to 3 or 1 to 4. Use the ratio for your product as noted on your invoice or as stated on the container.

Example
Given: You anticipate selling 1,600 20-fluid-ounce root beer drinks over the next week. To fulfill your sales projection, follow these steps:

1. Calculate the total fluid ounces you'll serve:

1,600 drinks × 20 fl. oz. per drink = 32,000 fl. oz.

One box of syrup yields 30 gallons, which equals 3,840 fluid ounces.

2. Divide the AS fluid ounces (32,000) by the fluid-ounce yield per box (3,840):

32,000 ÷ 3,840 = 8.333 boxes

You'll need to have nine boxes on hand.

1 gal. = 4 qt. = 16 c. = 128 fl. oz. ✦ 1 qt. = 2 pt. = 4 c. = 32 fl. oz. ✦ 1 pt. = 2 c. = 16 fl. oz. ✦
1 c. = 8 fl. oz. = 16 tbsp. ✦ 1 fl. oz. = 2 tbsp. ✦ 1 tbsp. = 3 tsp. ✦ 1 lb. = 16 oz.

Coffee, Tea, and Cocoa

Item	Ounces per Cup	Cups per Pound	Tablespoons per Pound
Cocoa	3.35	4.80	76.40
Coffee Beans	2.50	6.40	102.40
Coffee	2.80	5.70	91.00
Coffee	2.00	8.00	128.00
Tea, Chamomile	0.85	18.82	301.18
Tea, Chai Blend	3.65	4.38	70.14
Tea, English Breakfast	2.40	6.67	106.67
Tea, Genmaichi	3.15	5.08	81.27
Tea, Green Sencha	2.75	5.82	93.09
Tea, Gunpowder Green	3.80	4.21	67.37
Tea, Hibuscus Flowers	2.80	5.71	91.43
Tea, Jasmine Green	3.10	5.16	82.58
Tea, Lapsang Souchong	2.20	7.27	116.36
Tea, Leaf, bulk	2.40	6.70	106.70
Tea, Leaf, Green, Japanese	2.15	7.44	119.07
Tea, Leaf, Green, Japanese, fine	3.75	4.26	68.26
Tea, Oolong	2.60	6.15	98.46
Tea, Red Rose Petals	0.66	24.24	387.88
Tea, Rooibos (Red Bush)	1.90	8.42	134.74
Tea, Rosehips, flakes	4.30	3.72	59.53
Tea, Yerba Matte	2.45	6.53	104.49

Notes

1. **Coffee:** A rounded half cup of dark-roast, drip-grind coffee grounds (1.5 ounces) yields 1 standard pot of coffee; 60 fluid ounces; 1 rounded cup (3.2 oz) of dark, drip-grind coffee yields a gallon of brewed coffee; 1 pound of dark, drip-grind coffee grounds yields 4.9 gallons of brewed coffee. Lighter roasts will yield about 3 gallons of coffee of the same strength or weaker coffee of the same volume. There are approximately 210 individual coffee beans in one AP ounce, roasted. The weight of one cup of whole roasted beans may well vary from 2.3 to 2.9 ounces depending on the size of the beans and the darkness of the roast. Larger, more lightly roasted beans weigh less than small, dark-roasted beans, by volume.

2. **Tea, Leaf and Bulk:** Three single-use tea bags equal 1 tablespoon bulk tea. So, 1 tea bag equals 1 teaspoon tea. For strong iced tea, use 2 ounces tea to 1 gallon water. Pour 1 quart boiling water over tea; steep 5 minutes; strain; add 3 quarts cold water.

3. **Cocoa:** One cup of cocoa yields 1 gallon of hot cocoa drink. Mix the cocoa with sugar. Liquefy with 1 part hot water, and extend with 3 parts hot milk.

4. **Water-to-ice-cube Yield:** 1 gallon of water yields approximately 30 cups of small to medium ice cubes.

9 | MEATS

Animal protein products (beef, pork, lamb, poultry, seafood, etc.) obviously are popular menu items. They are also expensive to buy when compared to the produce and starchy items that generally make up the balance of food offered on menus. Consequently, controlling the purchasing, storage, and production of these expensive foods and intelligently pricing them on menus is critical to a food service operation's financial success.

The discussion in this chapter makes reference to one table:

+ Meats

It lists the following information:

+ Common name for the item
+ North American Meat Processors (NAMP) number (See the note on page 105.)
+ Average as-purchased weight for the item in pounds
+ Trim loss in pounds
+ Primary yield after trimming in pounds
+ Primary yield percentage based on the AP weight
+ Number of primary usable ounces per AP pound
+ Usable trim in pounds

NOTE

Although defined as animal protein products here, seafood is given its own chapter, Chapter 10, and poultry is covered in Chapter 11.

You'll find the Meats table to be a useful guide for comparing your actual yields as well as costing your portions. Note that the trim yields reflect standard trimming practices for slightly above-average restaurants. Specifically, most fat and connective tissue have been removed in order to obtain the weight labeled as the Primary-Use Yield (fourth column in the table). The last column, Trim: Miscellaneous Use in Pounds, lists the weight of scraps, bones, or sinew that can be ground or used for sauces, brochettes, stews, or stocks.

COSTING MEATS

In this section, we'll first address procedures for costing meats according to these delineations:

+ Preportioned meats

NOTE

The North American Meat Processors (NAMP) Association is an organization that wrote the *Meat Buyers Guide*, in which standard specifications are listed for the cuts and market forms of beef, pork, veal, lamb, and poultry products sold in the United States. By using the NAMP number (the first column in the Meats table), wherever you may be in the United States, you can be certain of the cut or piece you are ordering.

IN THE WORKBOOK

Part II, the Workbook, has one worksheet to help you cost many types of meat products:

♦ Meats, Costing Worksheet 11

NOTE

Because breakfast meats are often cooked ahead, you may end up with unsold leftovers. Be sure to have other recipes that will use up these leftovers, such as breakfast gravies, bacon dressings, quiche, club sandwiches, and so on.

♦ Trimmed meats
♦ Cooked meats

The discussion continues with notes and guidelines on specific meat products: prime rib, lamb, and pork.

COSTING PREPORTIONED MEATS

When it comes to cutting meat, many operations cut their meat in-house; others order their meat products precut; and still others do some cutting in-house and order certain meat products precut. It is now possible to buy most meat menu items—beef patties, steaks, chops, and some whole roasts—already trimmed, portioned, and packed for immediate use on the cooking line. The procedure for costing these items is, therefore, a simple one-step calculation:

1. Divide the cost of the purchase unit by the number of pieces or portions it contains. Your answer will be both the AP and AS cost per item.

Many breakfast and lunch meats fall into the preportioned category, too. Bacon strips, sausage links or patties, Canadian bacon slices, and ham steaks are all sold by size. You pick the size you want for your menu, which is stated by the meat supplier as a particular number of pieces per pound (such as eight links per pound, which means each link weighs 2 ounces). You cost these products as follows:

1. Divide the cost of 1 pound by the number of pieces in a pound. Your answer will be the cost of one slice, link, or patty.
2. Multiply that cost by the number you put on a plate to get your portion cost.

COSTING TRIMMED MEATS

When you cost meats that you trim before cooking, you have to decide how to handle the cost of the trimmed-away but still usable meat. Will you include it in the cost of the primary item (steaks, chops, roasts, etc.), or will you deduct its value from the cost of the primary item? The Meats, Costing Worksheet 11, shows you how to do both.

We'll use a primary item, New York steak, to explain the costing process for trimmed meats. To start, note that the Meats table shows that a 10-pound strip loin with a 1-inch "tail" (from which New York steaks are cut) has a usable trim weight of 1 pound. We'll also assume that you do use these meaty trimmings in other recipes.

If you do not deduct the value of the trimmings from the cost of the strip loin, the cost of the steaks will include the cost of the trimmings, and the recipes that use these trimmings will show no cost for the trimmed meat. Deducting the value of the trimmings from the cost of the strip loin reduces the cost of the loin by an amount equal to the value of the trimmings. Therefore, you really should take the deduction from the primary item and apply the value of the trimmings to the recipes in which they are used. The usable trimmings value will seldom be as high as the base item value (strip loin, in this case) cost per AP pound.

To illustrate, say you are going to grind some of the trimmings into beef patties. Ground beef costs less per pound than strip loins. This is so for stew meats, bones, scraps for stocks, and standard brochette meats, too. (Your meat supplier can tell you

---

Y% means yield percentage ♦ AS means as served (or used) ♦ AP means as purchased ♦ AS ÷ AP = Y% ♦
AS ÷ Y% = AP ♦ AP × Y% = AS ♦ Cost per AP unit ÷ Y% = Cost per servable unit

what those items sell for, if you don't already know.) You can only deduct the market value of the trimmings as determined by the way you are going to use them—ground meat, stew meat, bones for stock, or whatever.

USING THE TRIM YIELD PERCENTAGE TO HELP IN COSTING Some operators sell meats by a weight that varies from order to order. For instance, a menu may offer a 6-, 8-, 10-, or 12-ounce filet mignon. In this case, the operator has to know the value of a trimmed ounce of meat in order to put a sensible (profitable) menu price on each size of steak.

Filet mignon is cut from beef tenderloin. Tenderloins are sold pretrimmed or untrimmed. The Meats table shows that one 7.5-pound whole tenderloin has a trim yield percentage of 58.7 percent and a usable trim of 1.5 pounds. Assume this tenderloin costs $54 and that the trimmings consist of 1 pound of meat with a value of $4, and a half-pound of sinew (for stocks) with no market value. To calculate the cost of one usable, trimmed ounce of filet mignon, follow this four-step process:

1. Deduct the value of the usable trim ($4) from the whole tenderloin's cost ($54):

$54 − 4 = $50

2. Multiply the AP weight of 7.5 pounds by the trim yield percentage of 58.7 percent:

7.5 lb. × 0.587 = 4.4 lb.

After trimming, you have 4.4 pounds of ready-to-cook, trimmed tenderloin.

3. Divide the adjusted AP cost of the whole tenderloin ($50) by 4.4 pounds:

$50 ÷ 4.4 = $11.36

The $11.36 is the cost of a trimmed pound of tenderloin.

4. Divide that by 16 for the cost per trimmed ounce:

$11.36 ÷ 16 = $0.71

One trimmed ounce of tenderloin costs 71 cents; a 6-ounce steak costs 6 times $0.71, or $4.26, and a 10-ounce steak costs $7.10.

COSTING USING A PORTIONS-PER-PIECE APPROACH When the trim yield percentage is not used, food service operators usually place steaks and chops on their menus based on a fixed weight—an 8-ounce sirloin steak, for instance. The muscle, or piece, from which they cut their steaks, is typically a consistent size, so after a little experience the operator knows how many steaks of a certain weight can be obtained from one larger piece. To cost these steaks or chops takes one step:

1. Divide the cost of the larger piece by the number of steaks or chops it yields. The answer is the cost per steak or chop.

The trim yield percentage here doesn't matter much. Deducting the cost of usable trim from the AP cost of the larger unit should come into play, but once that is done, just do the simple division to get your chop or steak cost.

1 gal. = 4 qt. = 16 c. = 128 fl. oz. ♦ 1 qt. = 2 pt. = 4 c. = 32 fl. oz. ♦ 1 pt. = 2 c. = 16 fl. oz. ♦
1 c. = 8 fl. oz. = 16 tbsp. ♦ 1 fl. oz. = 2 tbsp. ♦ 1 tbsp. = 3 tsp. ♦ 1 lb. = 16 oz.

Example

Given: A 10-pound New York strip loin costs $64 and has a usable trim of 1 pound and the usable trim has a value of $4.

1. Deduct the $4 from the $64: $60. Assume that you get 15 steaks from the loin.
2. Divide the adjusted cost of the loin ($60) by the number of steaks it yields (15):

$60 ÷ 15 = $4.00

Each steak costs $4.

COSTING COOKED MEATS

Costing a weight of cooked meat is a simple two-step process:

1. Determine the cost of a trimmed pound or ounce, as shown in the first example.
2. Divide the trimmed pound or ounce cost by the cooking yield percentage.

That's it. Your answer will be the cost of a trimmed and cooked weight.
   To determine your cooking yield percentage, do these calculations:

1. Weigh the meat in its *oven-ready* state (after trimming but before cooking).
2. Weigh it after it is cooked and has rested.
3. Divide the cooked weight by the raw weight. The answer is your cooking yield percentage.

Example

Given: Your oven-ready roast weighs 12 pounds. After cooking and resting, it weighs 10.2 pounds.

1. Divide the cooked weight of 10.2 pounds by the raw weight of 12 pounds.

10.2 ÷ 12 = 0.85

After multiplying 0.85 by 100 to get the percent, you have a cooking yield percentage of 85 percent.

Example

Given: You want to know the cost of 4 ounces of trimmed and cooked beef top round. The roast had an AP weight of 16 pounds, cost $51, and had 1 pound of usable trim. The usable trim has a value of $3 per pound.

1. Deduct the usable trim value ($3) from the AP cost ($51):

$51 − $3 = $48

The roast now has a value of $48.

2. The Meats table shows that a top round will trim out to 75 percent of its AP weight (16 pounds), and 75 percent of 16 pounds equals 12 pounds, so divide the roast's adjusted AP cost of $48 by the trimmed roast's weight of 12 pounds:

$48 ÷ 12 lb. = $4

Thus, 1 pound of oven-ready top round costs $4.

Y% means yield percentage ♦ AS means as served (or used) ♦ AP means as purchased ♦ AS ÷ AP = Y% ♦
AS ÷ Y% = AP ♦ AP × Y% = AS ♦ Cost per AP unit ÷ Y% = Cost per servable unit

Now, given that the cooked roast weighs 10.2 pounds, do the math.

1. Divide the cooked weight by the oven-ready weight to calculate the cooking yield percentage:

$$10.2 \div 12 = 0.85, \text{ or } 85\%$$

2. Divide the cost per trimmed pound ($4) by the cooking yield percentage (0.85):

$$\$4 \div 0.85 = \$4.70$$

In this case, 1 pound of trimmed and cooked top round costs $4.70.

3. Divide the pound cost by 16 to get the cost per ounce:

$$\$4.70 \div 16 = \$0.294, \text{ or } 29.4 \text{ cents}$$

A portion of 4 ounces of cooked top round will cost four times 29.4 cents: $1.18, rounded.

PURCHASING MEATS

We'll step through three formulas and several examples to familiarize you with methods for accurately planning your meat purchases.

IN THE WORKBOOK

Part II, the Workbook, has one worksheet to help you plan your purchases of many types of meat products:

✦ Meats, Purchasing Worksheet 10

FORMULA 1 The first formula details how to use portion yields to determine how many whole pieces to buy:

Portions needed ÷ Portions yielded per piece = AP pieces

The term *piece* or *whole piece* refers to a relatively large muscle or muscle group from which smaller cuts (portions) are made. The whole piece is ordinarily a purchase unit, such as a New York strip loin. The smaller pieces (portions) are steaks, cutlets, chops, and the like.

Use this formula when you know two things:

1. How many portions you need
2. The number of portions you usually get from a whole piece

Example

Given: You need 48 trimmed and portioned New York steaks, weighing 7 ounces each, and you know that 1 whole piece–1 New York strip loin–yields 16 steaks of 7 ounces each. Do the math:

48 ÷ 16 = 3

You see that you need three whole strip loins.

FORMULA 2 You can convert a trimmed raw weight to a raw purchase weight using this equation:

# of pounds trimmed, raw meat ÷ Trim yield percentage = AP weight

Use this formula when you want to calculate the number of pounds to purchase or use and you know the trim yield percentage for the raw, as-purchased piece of meat.

Meat Matters

This sidebar contains notes on prime rib, lamb, and pork.

Prime Rib

Notice that the prime rib in the Meats table has an NAMP number of 109. This is virtually untrimmed except for a bit of meat that is removed from under the *fat-cap*. A 109 prime rib comes with a thick layer of fat, partial backbones, rib bones, and a fair amount of sinew, some or all of which have to be trimmed off for roasting. This used to be the most popular market form of prime rib because of its relatively low cost per pound. As you can see from the table, half of the purchased weight of a 109 must be trimmed away if you want to have a boneless, oven-ready roast that is perfect for carving on a buffet line.

Today, many chefs prefer to order prime ribs that have been partially or completely trimmed. The NAMP 109D and the NAMP 112 are examples of pretrimmed prime ribs. Because these are now quite popular market forms of prime rib, the cost per usable pound has come down considerably. In fact, a 109 can actually cost *more* than an oven-ready, boneless 112! Of course, the 109 does provide the kitchen with meat trimmings, sinew, and bones, which can then be used in other recipes; but their value is not great enough to entice as many chefs into using a 109 as in the past.

Dealing with unsold cooked roasts such as prime rib has become easier for those chefs who have modern "cook-and-hold" ovens that cook at low temperatures and produce better cooking yields. Another important advantage these ovens have over other ovens is their holding capability: they can safely hold a cooked roast for a full day at a medium to medium-rare serving temperature! Leftover prime rib can be cut up and made into a *hash,* a menu item that has become rather popular for breakfast and lunch. The meat can also be cleaned and the "eye" meat used for sandwiches, salad, or sautés. The outer meat, though a bit loose, can be added to hash, soups, and salads. These leftovers, however, can be very expensive after trimming away all the fat and connective tissue. A cold, leftover, boneless prime rib, for example, will yield only about 59 percent of its cooked and chilled weight in usable meat—and that is after the trim loss and cooking loss! These meats can easily cost double the AP price per pound. The lesson is: Learn to accurately predict your sales and prepare accordingly. Overproducing is costly!

Lamb

The split lamb rack in the Meats table has had its spine and chine bones removed and then has been *frenched.* This means that the shoulder blade was also removed and the rib bones were cleaned of all meat and tissue up to the small muscle, just in front of the primary loin muscle. The top layer of fat was also removed.

Lamb racks can be sold whole (usually for two guests) or sectioned into smaller pieces. There will be at least seven ribs per rack, usually eight.

Veal

+ Veal is often sold in preportioned or precut forms: cube steaks, slices, chops, cutlets, foreshanks, hindshanks (whole or cross-cut), ground and calf's liver, as well as sweetbreads (thymus and pancreas).
+ Veal breasts, after some defatting and detissuing, trim out to around 13 ounces per AP pound. They are often braised and served as-is in some of their braising liquor.
+ Veal legs are boned, defatted, and detissued, yielding 7.1 ounces per AP pound. The various muscles are then sliced into cutlets or scaloppine. Veal leg can be roasted, but it tends to be dry.
+ Veal racks are marketed with either six or seven ribs. They can be cut into individual chops; a single chop is a typical portion.

Pork

Pork is available in scores of precut and preportioned market forms (breakfast meats were addressed earlier). Most market forms of preprocessed or precut pork products can be costed using one of the methods already described.

+ Pork shoulder (Boston butt) can be used for stews and braises and is also often used for making sausage. When used for sausage, the blade bone is removed, along with dense cartilage, but all of the remaining meat and fat find their way into the grinder. When used in moist cooking recipes, much of the fat is removed, along with the blade bone and heavy cartilage, resulting in a trim yield of 12 ounces per AP pound.
+ Spare ribs: There are 14 rib bones on each side of the pig. These ribs are sold in two forms: back ribs (NAMP 422) and spare ribs (NAMP 416). As their name implies, the back ribs (often called baby back ribs) are cut near the top of the back. A rack of back ribs must have at least eight ribs.
+ Spare ribs are of two types: regular and St. Louis-style (NAMP 416A). St. Louis-style ribs are cut just beneath the back ribs and are just ribs. Plain spare ribs are longer and may include portions of the sternum and diaphragm, as well as flank meat. A rack of spare ribs must have at least 11 ribs.

Y% means yield percentage ✦ AS means as served (or used) ✦ AP means as purchased ✦ AS ÷ AP = Y% ✦
AS ÷ Y% = AP ✦ AP × Y% = AS ✦ Cost per AP unit ÷ Y% = Cost per servable unit

Example
Given: You are prepping 48 New York strip steaks weighing 7 ounces each. Follow these steps:

1. Multiply 48 times 7 to compute the total ounces of trimmed weight needed:

48 × 7 = 336 oz.

2. Convert this to pounds by dividing the ounces by 16:

336 ÷ 16 = 21 lb.

3. The Meats table shows the yield percentage for New York strip loin is 70 percent.

21 lb. ÷ 0.70 = 30 lb.

Therefore, you need to buy or use 30 pounds of raw New York strip loin. If, then, your AP strip loin steaks weigh 10 pounds each, you need three of them.

NOTE

Convection ovens can easily shrink meat cooked to medium-rare in the center by 20 percent, resulting in a cooked yield percentage of 80 percent. In contrast, a slow-cooking oven may shrink meat cooked to medium-rare by only 9 percent, resulting in a cooked yield percentage of 91 percent.

FORMULA 3 Here's the formula for converting a trimmed and cooked weight to a raw AP weight:

AS trimmed and cooked weight ÷ (Trim yield percentage × Cooking yield percentage) = AP weight

To complete this formula, you need to know what your cooking yield percentage is for the meat in question. This percentage depends on the degree of doneness desired, combined with the shape of the meat and your oven's tendency to shrink meats as they cook. That means you must use your experience to determine this cooked yield percentage.

To execute the formula, follow three steps:

1. Calculate the total weight you need to serve or use.
2. Multiply your meat's trim yield percentage (from *The Book of Yields* or your own experience) by the cooked yield percentage. This will result in a new, combined percentage that is smaller than either of the two original percentages. It is called a *finished yield percentage*.
3. Divide the trimmed and cooked weight you need to serve by the finished yield percentage.

Your answer will be the number of pounds of raw, as-purchased meat you need to buy or cost out.

FORMULA 3a Here is the same formula restated, using the finished yield percentage in lieu of the parenthetical Formula 3:

AS trimmed and cooked weight ÷ Finished yield percentage = AP weight

Proceed to complete this formula in two steps:

1. Determine what the finished yield percentage is by multiplying your trim yield percentage by your cooking yield percentage.
2. Divide the number of pounds of trimmed and cooked meat you need by the finished yield percentage.

Again, your answer will be the number of pounds of raw, as-purchased meat you need to buy, use, or cost out.

Example

Given: You need to serve 85 portions of 7-ounce cooked, boneless prime rib. Determine the amount of trimmed, cooked meat you need to serve or use.

1. Multiply 85 by 7 ounces:

85 × 7 = 595 oz.

2. Convert this to pounds by dividing 595 by 16:

595 oz. ÷ 16 = 37.2 lb.

So, you need to serve 37.2 pounds of boneless, trimmed, and cooked prime rib.

Given: You have an NAMP 109 prime rib and want to determine the trim yield percentage. This is provided in the Meats table, which shows the 109 rib yields 50 percent: raw, boned, defatted, and detissued. Thus, the trim yield percentage is 50 percent.

Given: Now you have a 22-pound, 109 prime rib that, after trimming, weighs 11 pounds, and you want to calculate the cooking yield percentage. Assume here that your experience shows that, in your ovens, cooking a trimmed 109 prime rib weighing 11 pounds yields 9.65 pounds when slow-cooked to medium-rare.

1. Divide the cooking yield weight (9.65 pounds) by the oven–ready weight (11 pounds):

9.65 ÷ 11 = 0.877, or 87.7%

Your cooking yield percentage is 87.7 percent.

2. To calculate the finished yield percentage, multiply the trim yield percentage (0.50) by the cooking yield percentage (0.877):

0.50 × 0.877 = 0.4385, or 43.85%

3. Finally, to use the finished yield percentage to determine the necessary AP weight, divide the AS weight (37.2 pounds) by the finished yield percentage (43.85%):

37.2 lb. ÷ 0.4385 = 84.8 lb.

You need to start with 84.8 pounds of 109 prime rib in order to serve 37.2 pounds of trimmed, cooked beef. If all your 109 roasts weigh 22 pounds, you will need just under four of them on hand to produce the 37.2 pounds of cooked meat. But do not *assume* they all weigh 22 pounds; they might all weigh 20 pounds, leaving you short. The point is, weigh the raw roasts before deciding how many to cook.

Y% means yield percentage ✦ AS means as served (or used) ✦ AP means as purchased ✦ AS ÷ AP = Y% ✦ AS ÷ Y% = AP ✦ AP × Y% = AS ✦ Cost per AP unit ÷ Y% = Cost per servable unit

Meats

Item Name	NAMP Number	AP Weight in Pounds	Trim Loss in Pounds	Primary-Use Yield in Pounds	Yield Percent	Number of Usable Ounces per AP Pound	Trim: Miscellaneous Use in Pounds
Beef Ball Tip—Bottom Sirloin Butt	185B	14	3.0	11	78.6%	12.6	2.0
Beef Bones, Marrow	134	40	0	40	100%	16	0
Beef Bottom Round	170	21	4.5	16.5	78.6%	12.6	3.0
Beef Prime Rib (See note 1.)	109	20	10.0	10	50.0%	8.0	5.0
Beef Strip Loin (New York) 1 in. tail	180	10	3.0	7	70.0%	11.2	1.0
Beef Tenderloin, Pismo, defatted	189A	7	0.9	6.1	87.1%	13.9	0.4
Beef Tenderloin, whole	189	7.5	3.1	4.4	58.7%	9.4	1.5
Beef Top Round	168	16	4.0	12	75.0%	12.0	1.0
Beef Top Sirloin Butt	184	15	4.4	10.6	70.7%	11.3	1.0
Beef Tri-Tip, Bottom Sirloin Butt	185C	3	1.1	1.9	63.3%	10.1	0.3
Lamb Bones, Marrow	None	40	0	40	100%	16	0
Lamb Foreshank	210	1.05	0.00	1.05	100.0%	16.0	0.00
Lamb Leg, defatted; leg and shank bones intact	233A	10.87	3.41	7.46	68.6%	11.0	1.33
Lamb Leg, trimmed of fat and bone, imported	233A	7.5	3.70	3.8	50.7%	8.1	2.5
Lamb Leg, fully defatted, boned, shank-off	233A	10.87	5.17	5.70	52.4%	8.4	2.77
Lamb Leg, shank off, boneless; defatted, detissued	234A	5.76	0.874	4.89	84.8%	13.6	0.00
Lamb Loin, short-cut, trimmed, 2 in. tail; trimmed to loin and tender	232A	2.93	1.93	1.00	34.1%	5.4	0.71
Lamb Rack Double, trimmed french	204	7	3.0	4	57.1%	9.1	1.25
Lamb Rack, split & chined, trimmed to french	204A	3.38	1.84	1.54	45.5%	7.3	0.82
Lamb Ribs, breast bones off	209A	1.02	0.09	0.93	91.4%	14.6	0.14
Lamb Shoulder, outside, boned, detissued, defatted	207A	9.37	4.90	4.48	47.8%	7.6	2.40
Pork Leg, boned, skinned, defatted	401A	14	5.25	8.75	62.5%	10.0	3.25
Pork Leg, boned, skinned, defatted	401C	14	2.60	11.4	81.4%	13.0	0.75
Pork Loin, boneless, defatted	413	7	1.75	5.25	75.0%	12.0	0.75
Pork loin, whole, boned, defatted	412A	9	4.25	4.75	52.8%	8.4	2.75
Pork Shoulder, Boston Butt	406	8	1.50	6.5	81.3%	13.0	1.5

1 gal. = 4 qt. = 16 c. = 128 fl. oz. ♦ 1 qt. = 2 pt. = 4 c. = 32 fl. oz. ♦ 1 pt. = 2 c. = 16 fl. oz. ♦
1 c. = 8 fl. oz. = 16 tbsp. ♦ 1 fl. oz. = 2 tbsp. ♦ 1 tbsp. = 3 tsp. ♦ 1 lb. = 16 oz.

Meats (Continued)

Item Name	NAMP Number	AP Weight in Pounds	Trim Loss in Pounds	Primary-Use Yield in Pounds	Yield Percent	Number of Usable Ounces per AP Pound	Trim: Miscellaneous Use in Pounds
Pork Tenderloins	415	1	0.125	0.875	87.5%	14.0	0.1
Veal Breast	313	10	2.0	8.0	80.0%	12.8	1.5
Veal Double Rack, frenched	306	16	9.75	6.25	39.1%	6.3	7.0
Veal Leg, trimmed of fat and bone	334	35	19.5	15.5	44.3%	7.1	16.0

Notes

1. **Prime Rib (109):** 109s in the table had the cap, tail, backstrap, and all bones, plus most exterior connective tissue, removed. Low, slow cooking will reduce the servable weight another 12% at medium-rare. Thus, 1 pound of raw 109 yields 7 ounces, well-trimmed cooked meat—a 44% yield.

2. Convection ovens will increase the shrink (cooking loss) by 20 or 25 percent.

3. All lamb items are U.S. domestic unless noted as Imported.

Y% means yield percentage ✦ AS means as served (or used) ✦ AP means as purchased ✦ AS ÷ AP = Y% ✦
AS ÷ Y% = AP ✦ AP × Y% = AS ✦ Cost per AP unit ÷ Y% = Cost per servable unit

10

SEAFOOD

nlike red meats, which are aged for weeks to improve their flavor and texture, seafood has to be used soon after it is *harvested*. If allowed to age for more than a few days, fish and shellfish begin to lose weight due to moisture loss. They soon deteriorate in both texture and flavor, to the point of spoilage. Therefore, when you are dealing with seafood, two rules apply:

1. For fresh seafood, buy it just before you need it and use it fast!
2. For frozen seafood, once it has thawed, be even faster about cooking and serving it.

In this chapter, one table is referenced:

+ Seafood: In addition to being of use for costing and purchasing purposes, you'll find the notes in this table helpful for understanding the various types of fish.

Before we get into the costing and purchasing procedures for seafood, a definition of terms as used in this chapter is in order:

+ *Finfish.* As the name implies, these are fish that have fins. Examples include salmon, trout, and halibut. The Seafood table gives you the yield percentages obtained from preparing *fish fillets* from a *dressed* or *drawn* finfish. In addition, there are many new additions to the Seafood table that are described as H&G and G&G (described later in this list).
+ *Fish fillet.* A fish fillet is cut from one side of the fish and has no skin or bones. Note that many chefs have come to prefer receiving their fillets with the skin on because it better preserves the quality of the fillet. Many fish lend themselves very well to cooking with the skin on; basses, trout, salmon, breams and pike, for instance.
+ *Fish steak.* In contrast to a fillet, a steak is a crosscut of the fish. Steaks are composed of both sides of the fish and include skin and bones.
+ *Drawn fish.* This is a fish that has been eviscerated (gutted) but has its head, fins, and tail intact.
+ *Dressed fish.* This is a fish that has been gutted and has had its scales removed and the head, fins, and tail trimmed away.
+ *H&G (headed and gutted).* This is similar to a dressed fish in that the fish will have had its head removed and will have been gutted. The scales and fins will not have

been removed. Sometimes the tail and collars will have been removed, but this is not a given.

+ *G&G (gilled and gutted)*. This is a fish whose gills and guts have been removed but heads, tails, fins, and scales are intact.

In terms of cost, a dressed fish will be more expensive per AP pound than the same fish in a drawn form. Because fillets require extra processing and yield less weight from the AP fish compared to steaks, fillets are generally more expensive than steaks. Consequently, fillet portions are usually smaller than portions of fish steaks.

COSTING FINFISH PORTIONS

We'll tackle the costing procedures for finfish in the following order: fillets, steaks, and piece counts.

COSTING FILLETS

IN THE WORKBOOK

Part II, the Workbook, has one worksheet to help you cost seafood products:

+ Seafood, Costing Worksheet 12

If all your fillets are the same weight, the simplest way to cost them is to take two steps:

1. Discern the number of fillets obtained from an AP amount of fish.
2. Divide the number of fillets into the cost of the AP fish.

The answer is your average cost per fillet. If, however, your fillets vary in size, do these calculations:

1. Look up the fillet yield percentages in the Seafood table, or use your own fillet yield test results.
2. Determine the fillet cost per ounce. To do this, divide the cost of the AP fish by the number of ounces of fillets it yields.

Example

Given: A dressed salmon weighs 7 pounds and costs $29.40. To cost an ounce of fish fillet, follow three steps:

1. Determine the cost per AP pound from the invoice, or divide the total AP cost by the AP pounds:

$29.40 ÷ 7 lb. = $4.20 per AP lb.

2. The Seafood table shows that a dressed salmon yields 75 percent of its weight in fillets, so divide the AP cost per pound ($4.20) by the yield percentage (0.75):

$4.20 ÷ 0.75 = $5.60

3. The $5.60 is the AS cost per pound of your fillets, and 1 ounce is one-sixteenth of the pound cost, so divide $5.60 by 16:

$5.60 ÷ 16 = $0.35

One as-served (or as-used) ounce of salmon fillet costs 35 cents. A raw 4-ounce salmon fillet portion will be 4 times $0.35, or $1.40.

Y% means yield percentage ✦ AS means as served (or used) ✦ AP means as purchased ✦ AS ÷ AP = Y% ✦
AS ÷ Y% = AP ✦ AP × Y% = AS ✦ Cost per AP unit ÷ Y% = Cost per servable unit

COSTING STEAKS

Costing fish steaks is a simple, one-step process:

1. Divide the cost of the fish (minus the value of any fillets you cut from it) by the number of steaks it produces.

The reason you deduct the value of fillets is because you can't get all steaks from a fish. The area near the tail is too narrow to cut into steaks so it has to be cut into fillets. If, say, you cut 10 ounces of tail fillets from the salmon in the previous example, you would deduct \$3.50 (10 ounces × \$0.35 = \$3.50) from the cost of the fish (\$29.40). This leaves the remaining fish with a value of \$25.90. If you then cut 10 steaks from the remaining fish, the steaks would have an average value of \$2.59 (\$25.90 ÷ 10 = \$2.59).

COSTING PIECE COUNTS

Finfish are now commonly sold in frozen, precut portions of steaks or fillets and as whole fish, such as boned trout. Vendors offer these products in a variety of sizes. You cost these portions simply by dividing the cost of the purchase unit by the number of portions it contains. Many crustaceans and mollusks are also sold by counts per pound.

COSTING CRUSTACEANS

Crustaceans are shellfish: shrimp, lobster crab, and crawfish are popular examples.

COSTING SHRIMP

Shrimp is the most commonly served crustacean and is very often sold frozen. Frozen, shell-on, headless Black Tiger shrimp are usually packed in 4-pound blocks. Frozen Gulf White shrimp are typically marketed in 5-pound blocks. Peeled and deveined shrimp are often IQF (individually quick frozen) and packaged in 2- or 2.5-pound bags. However packaged, the number of shrimp per pound is expressed as a range, such as 21–25, rather than an exact count per pound. Therefore, to cost an individual shrimp:

1. Determine an average count per pound.
2. Divide that into the cost per pound.

Example
Given: A 4-pound, 21–25 count box of shrimp averages 22 shrimp per pound and costs \$40. Here's the math.

1. Calculate the number of shrimp in the box:

4 × 22 = 88

2. Divide the cost of the box by the number of shrimp in the box:

\$40 ÷ 88 = \$0.4545

Each shrimp will cost a little over 45 cents.

1 gal. = 4 qt. = 16 c. = 128 fl. oz. ✦ 1 qt. = 2 pt. = 4 c. = 32 fl. oz. ✦ 1 pt. = 2 c. = 16 fl. oz. ✦
1 c. = 8 fl. oz. = 16 tbsp. ✦ 1 fl. oz. = 2 tbsp. ✦ 1 tbsp. = 3 tsp. ✦ 1 lb. = 16 oz.

A pound of ordinary (green), headless shrimp will yield about 80 percent of its original weight after peeling but before cooking and about 65 percent of its original weight after both peeling and cooking. Therefore, costing peeled, raw shrimp is done by dividing the AP cost per pound by 0.80. You cost peeled and cooked shrimp by dividing the AP cost per pound by 65 percent.

COSTING LOBSTER

NOTE

Whole lobsters are often priced on menus on a daily basis because the purchase prices you will pay vary widely, even from day to day. Bad weather that makes it impossible to harvest lobsters may mean you cannot put them on your menu at all until the weather improves.

Lobsters are marketed either as frozen tails or as whole, live animals. Lobster tails are marketed by size, so costing a tail is just a matter of dividing the cost per pound by the number of tails in a pound. (Divide 16 by the ounces per tail to get the number of tails per pound.)

Live lobster prices vary with seasons and locality. A fresh Maine lobster will yield an average of 26 percent of its live weight in cooked meat. To cost this meat by the ounce:

1. Divide the AP cost per pound by its yield percentage (0.26).
2. Divide that amount by 16.

Cost whole lobsters by dividing the total cost by the pounds purchased. This gives you the cost per pound.

COSTING CRABS

Crabs come in many market forms and types. You can buy them live, whole but cooked, cooked and partially cleaned, just legs, canned, and frozen. The type of crab your menu features often depends on your locale and the time of year. How you cost the type of crab you sell depends on how you feature them on your menu:

+ If you sell the cooked meat in various recipes, do your own tests for cooked meat yields.
+ If you sell them whole, cost them by the each.

COSTING CRAWFISH

Crawfish (or crayfish) are commonly marketed as cleaned tails, sold by the pound. To cost crawfish tails:

1. Divide the cost per AP pound by 16 to get the AP cost per ounce.
2. Multiply that by the ounces in a portion or recipe.

COSTING MOLLUSKS

Mollusks include clams, oysters, scallops, mussels, conch, and snails. The first four types are *bivalves*, which means they have two opposing shells. When you buy these fresh, be sure they are alive. Their shells should be closed, or nearly so, and they should react to being tapped by closing. Live clams and oysters are sold by weight and come in a number of varieties and sizes. Treat them as you would any other item you buy as a count-per-pound. That is:

1. Count the number you bought and divide that number into the purchase price to get the cost for one.
2. Multiply that cost by the count used in your portion or recipe.

Keep in mind that if your sales of these mollusks are not brisk, you may well lose some to spoilage, as they do not live long after harvesting. Accordingly, cost the number that you actually have available to serve against the entire purchase price.

Scallops are sold already shucked and, like shrimp, are packed by size. Do a physical count per pound in order to verify that your count is what you expected. Scallops are fairly expensive, and counts can vary from stated amounts, so be watchful. Otherwise, cost them in the normal piece-count fashion.

COSTING CANNED TUNA

NOTE

It is not common practice to cost drained tuna by the cup or quart, but if you must, a cup of either type will weigh approximately 5.7 ounces, and a quart, approximately 23 ounces. If your recipe calls for one or more whole cans of tuna, use the cost per can as your recipe unit cost.

Although many fine restaurant menus feature fresh tuna, many more food service operators use canned tuna. The typical pack is a number-5 squat can, which usually holds 66 to 67 ounces of tuna, including the packing medium, either water or oil. Most operators buy the water-packed tuna.

Canned tuna is often either described as "chunk light yellowtail" or a "solid white albacore." Both types will yield nearly identical drained weights of 48 to 49 ounces per number-5 squat can. The less expensive chunk light tuna is used for making tuna fish sandwich spreads, tuna salad for luncheon plates, and tuna melts (grilled sandwiches with cheese). The more expensive solid albacore is used in recipes whose presentations feature the whole pieces of tuna. To cost either type of tuna by weight, complete these steps:

1. Divide the cost of the can by 48.6 ounces. This will give you the cost per drained ounce.
2. Multiply the cost per ounce by the number of ounces in your recipe.

PURCHASING SEAFOOD

IN THE WORKBOOK

Part II, the Workbook, has one worksheet to help you plan your purchases of seafood products:

✦ Seafood, Purchasing Worksheet 11

We'll cover two formulas and two methods that you'll find of use when you're planning your seafood purchases.

FORMULA 1 First the formula for converting trimmed fillet weights to purchase weights:

AS fillet weight in pounds ÷ Yield percentage = AP in pounds

Example

Given: You are to serve 640 ounces of swordfish loin. The Seafood table shows that a loin yields 90 percent after trimming.

1 gal. = 4 qt. = 16 c. = 128 fl. oz. ✦ 1 qt. = 2 pt. = 4 c. = 32 fl. oz. ✦ 1 pt. = 2 c. = 16 fl. oz. ✦
1 c. = 8 fl. oz. = 16 tbsp. ✦ 1 fl. oz. = 2 tbsp. ✦ 1 tbsp. = 3 tsp. ✦ 1 lb. = 16 oz.

NOTE

Swordfish portions are usually boneless "steaks" but are costed like fillets.

1. To convert the 640 ounces to pounds, divide by 16:

640 ÷ 16 = 40 lb.

Your AS amount is 40 pounds.

2. Divide the AS of 40 pounds by 90 percent (0.90):

40 ÷ 0.90 = 44.44 lb.

You need to buy approximately 44.5 pounds of swordfish loin.

FORMULA 2   The second formula shows you how to convert an as-served count to a purchase unit measure:

Pieces needed ÷ Count per AP unit measure = # of AP unit measures

Here, the AP unit measure refers to how the purchase unit is measured. This is usually pounds.

Example
Given: You are serving 88 shrimp cocktails, and each portion contains 5 shrimp. Your purchase unit is a 4-pound box, so the purchase unit measure is a pound. Also assume the shrimp used for the cocktail averages 22 per pound. Use three steps to determine how many boxes to buy:

1. Calculate the total number needed–88 portions times 5 shrimp each:

88 × 5 = 440 each

2. Divide the pieces needed (440) by the count per pound (22):

440 shrimp ÷ 22 shrimp per lb. = 20 lb. of shrimp

3. Convert the purchase unit measure to the purchase unit–a box of shrimp. You need 20 pounds of shrimp, and since there are 4 pounds per box, you need 5 boxes:

20 lb. ÷ 4 lb. per box = 5 boxes

METHOD FOR CONVERTING AP COSTS TO REFLECT CULLS

If you want to account for any culls (items that you find unusable due to spoilage or defects), use this method:

1. Subtract the cull weight or count from the AP weight or count.
2. Divide that number by the original weight or count.

The answer will be your culled yield percentage. (This is a lot like a trim yield percentage.)

Example
Given: Due to spoilage and defects, you have a loss of 10 oysters per 100 purchased. Do the math:

1. Subtract 10 from 100:

100 − 10 = 90

Y% means yield percentage ♦ AS means as served (or used) ♦ AP means as purchased ♦ AS ÷ AP = Y% ♦
AS ÷ Y% = AP ♦ AP × Y% = AS ♦ Cost per AP unit ÷ Y% = Cost per servable unit

2. Divide the culled count (90) by the AP count (100):

90 ÷ 100 = 0.90

Use this culled yield percentage of 90 percent to cost the remainder of your oysters, as follows:

1. Assume the 100 oysters cost $20. Each AP oyster, therefore, costs 20 cents:

$20 ÷ 100 = $0.20

2. Divide the AP cost per each of $0.20 by its culled yield percentage (0.90):

$0.20 ÷ 0.90 = $0.222

Your culled, usable oysters actually cost 22.2 cents each.

METHOD FOR CONVERTING PORTION WEIGHTS IN OUNCES TO AP WEIGHTS IN POUNDS

This is a practice common to nearly every purchasing process. At some point, you will be converting the total ounces of as-served food to pounds. Can you guess how? Yes, you divide the ounces by 16 to convert the ounces to pounds. To convert these AS pounds to AP units, you divide the AS pounds by the number of pounds in an AP unit. You have seen this before, but here it is again as a reminder.

Example
Given: You need to serve 320 AS ounces of sea scallops:

320 oz. ÷ 16 oz. = 20 lb.

You need 20 pounds of scallops.

If scallops come in 5-pound boxes, how many boxes do you need? Four boxes, because:

20 lb. ÷ 5 lb. per box = 4 boxes

Seafood

Item	Fillet Yield Percent*	Edible Ounces per AP Pound
Ahi Tuna, H&G, center cut	60%	9.6
Ahi Tuna, H&G, center cut, bloodline trimmed	45%	7.2
Ahi Tuna, H&G	70%	11.2
Albacore Tuna, whole fish	55%	8.8
Bass, H&G	70%	11.2
Bass, whole fish	45%	7.2
Bass, Sea, drawn	50%	8.0
Bass, Striped, drawn	60%	9.6
Catfish, drawn	45%	7.2
Cod, Atlantic, drawn	45%	7.2
Cod, Pacific, drawn	35%	5.6
Flounder, drawn	45%	7.2
Halibut, dressed	60%	9.6
Halibut, H&G	70%	11.2
Halibut, whole fish	55%	8.8
John Dory, whole fish	30%	4.8
Ling Cod, H&G	65%	10.4
Mahi Mahi, H&G	70%	11.2
Monkfish Tails	65%	10.4
Ono, Hawaiian Wahoo, H&G	65%	10.4
Opah, Hawaiian Moonfish, H&G	65%	10.4
Petrale Sole, whole fish	35%	5.6
Pompano, drawn	45%	7.2
Salmon, dressed	75%	12
Salmon, G&G	70%	11.2
Sand Dabs, whole fish	50%	8.0
Snappers, whole fish	40%	6.4

Y% means yield percentage ✦ AS means as served (or used) ✦ AP means as purchased ✦ AS ÷ AP = Y% ✦
AS ÷ Y% = AP ✦ AP × Y% = AS ✦ Cost per AP unit ÷ Y% = Cost per servable unit

Seafood (Continued)

Item	Fillet Yield Percent*	Edible Ounces per AP Pound
Spearfish, H&G	65%	10.4
Swordfish, dressed	60%	9.6
Swordfish, H&G	65%	10.4
Swordfish, H&G, center cut	60%	9.6
Swordfish, loin	90%	14.4
Tilapia, dressed	45%	7.2
Trout, drawn	50%	8.0
Tuna, loin	95%	15.2

*Fishing/harvesting methods, time, temperature, and distance in shipping all affect yields. The yield percentages listed in this table are, therefore, approximate.

Notes

1. **Finfish:** Finfish are seldom sold whole (called *round*). Most are eviscerated (gutted) and are called *drawn* fish. The edible portion yield of drawn finfish ranges from 35% to 75%. Generally, the larger the fish, the higher the yield.
   + *H&G (Headed and Gutted):* This is similar to a dressed fish in that the fish will have had its head removed and been gutted. The scales and fins will not have been removed. Sometimes the tail and collars will have been removed, but this is not a given.
   + *G&G (Gilled and Gutted):* This is a fish whose gills and guts have been removed but heads, tails, fins, and scales are intact.
      + A *dressed* fish is scaled and eviscerated, and has had its head and fins removed.
   + A *fillet* may be a whole side or a part of a side. It is boneless and often skinless.
   + A *steak* is a crosscut of the fish, and includes bones and skin.
2. **Crustaceans—Crab, Lobster, Crayfish, Shrimp:** These seafood products are commonly sold frozen by weight or a count per pound.
   + Crab yields vary according to species and handling. Fresh Dungeness crab yields 15 to 25% picked, cooked meat. Whole, cooked Dungeness crab yields 20 to 25% picked, cleaned meat. Lump, claw, and backfin crabmeat are considered the best meat and are priced accordingly. Crabmeat marked *special* is the least expensive.
   + Fresh lobster (Maine or spiny) yields between 20 and 33% picked, cooked meat. Lobsters lose weight very fast once out of water. A 1.5-pound Maine lobster, in good condition, will yield an 8- to 9-ounce tail.
   + Crayfish sized an average of 10 per pound, whole and very fresh, are about as large as is marketed. The count per pound does vary but should not exceed 15 to 18, for restaurant use. Counts up to 30 per pound are not uncommon in very casual Louisiana-style establishments. Smaller crayfish actually have a 5% larger tail meat yield than larger sizes because of the extra shell weight found with larger sizes. The percentage of tail meat to purchased weight is 15 to 20%, if very fresh.
   + Headless shrimp yield 80 to 85% peeled, deveined meat. Raw, peeled shrimp, when briefly cooked, yield 65 to 70% of their original headless weight.

1 gal. = 4 qt. = 16 c. = 128 fl. oz. ✦ 1 qt. = 2 pt. = 4 c. = 32 fl. oz. ✦ 1 pt. = 2 c. = 16 fl. oz. ✦
1 c. = 8 fl. oz. = 16 tbsp. ✦ 1 fl. oz. = 2 tbsp. ✦ 1 tbsp. = 3 tsp. ✦ 1 lb. = 16 oz.

3. Mollusks—Clams, Conch, Oysters, Mussels:

Clams	Count per Bushel	Inch Size
Littlenecks	450–600	1 to 2
Cherrystones	300–400	2 to 3
Topnecks	200–250	3 to 3.5
Chowders (average 125 to 180)	Under 200	Over 3.5

+ *Littleneck clams* are the most tender and most expensive. Chowders are the toughest and least expensive. *Surf clams* are sold processed as frozen strips or chopped in cans. Soft-shell *steamer* clams range in market size from 1.5 to 4 inches long. *Quahog clams* are harvested around 3 to 6 inches long. *Geoduck clams* grow to over 9 inches and are usually harvested at 3 pounds but grow larger and yield 50% meat. *Manila clams* measure 1.24 to 1.5 inches.

+ Conch yields about 50% of its in-shell weight. Most conch processed in the United States is actually *whelk*.

+ Blue mussels yield 25 to 55% meat, depending on feed, season, and spawning cycle. An 8-gallon bushel yields 800 to 1,000 animals. Meat yield of one bushel ranges from 10 to 30 pounds. One pound of blue mussels averages 16 mussels.

+ Green New Zealand mussels are larger and meatier than the blues, yielding 45 to 55% meat.

+ Oyster varieties are numerous and are packed according to sizes, which vary widely. For example, Bluepoint oysters are 220 to the bushel—1 gallon meat represents one bushel; Olympia oysters are 400 per bushel—1 gallon represents 500 or more.

+ *Frozen* scallops are typically packaged in 4-pound blocks and are sized as a range count per pound. U-10 (under 10 per pound) is the largest size. Sea scallops are relatively large, ranging from U-10 to about 30 per pound. Bay scallops are much smaller, with counts up to 90 per pound. Sea scallops have better flavor, appearance, and texture, and are more expensive than bay scallops.

+ *Fresh* scallops (typically sea scallops) are sold as dry or wet and are also packaged by a count (range) per pound. Dry scallops are also known as Day Boats and divers. Divers are harvested by hand in the winter months. Day Boats are often hand harvested and are available most of the year. Dry scallops will have the scent of the ocean, a sticky or tacky feel, and a slightly grayish color to them. Wet (or processed) scallops are less expensive and will have been dipped in a solution of sodium tripolyphosphate to extend their shelf life, whiten their color, and firm their texture. Wet scallops, when cooked, weep more than the dry type, which makes it more difficult to caramelize their surfaces.

Y% means yield percentage ✦ AS means as served (or used) ✦ AP means as purchased ✦ AS ÷ AP = Y% ✦ AS ÷ Y% = AP ✦ AP × Y% = AS ✦ Cost per AP unit ÷ Y% = Cost per servable unit

II | POULTRY

hicken, turkey, game hen, quail, and duckling are among the most popular types of poultry on menus today. Chicken, in particular, is tremendously profitable, as is turkey, although the latter is not as popular as chicken. This chapter will explain how to make decisions about selecting the market forms of various poultry items that are most suitable for your operation. It also addresses the options you have when assigning costs to poultry items, as well as planning your purchases.

COSTING POULTRY

IN THE WORKBOOK

Part II, the Workbook, has one worksheet to help you cost poultry products:

✦ Poultry, Costing Worksheet 13

This section covers costing procedures in this order: chicken, turkey, geese, small birds, and duckling.

One table is referenced in the discussion in this chapter:

✦ Poultry

COSTING CHICKEN

Chicken is by far the most popular type of poultry and is marketed in numerous ways. For example, you can buy a whole chicken with or without its giblets. Giblets consist of the heart, gizzard, and liver; the neck is also typically included with giblets. When sold without giblets, the bird is designated as a *WOG* ("without giblets"). Because many menus do not market every part of a bird, poultry processors "fabricate" whole birds into market forms such as breasts, half breasts, legs, thighs, and wings. Additionally, you can order these items with further refinements. Breasts can be had without skin or bones or with skin but no bones. You can even buy just the interior breast muscle, known as a *tender* or *tenderloin*. Legs and thighs are available joined, separated, or completely skinned and boned. Wings are sold whole and in pieces: the first joint is called a *drumette;* the second joint is called, simply, the *second joint*. Finally, you can buy these special market forms already breaded, seasoned, or marinated. Of course, you can buy half chickens or quarters as well.

The Poultry table lists the yields that you can obtain from a whole fryer/broiler chicken weighing nearly 59 ounces, with giblets. It also lists piece yields for three weights of turkeys. You will find the Poultry Costing Worksheet 13 of help in calculating the

NOTE

As it does for meat, the North American Meat Processors Association (NAMP) publishes a *Poultry Buyers Guide* that clearly defines poultry marketing terminology and describes various cuts and market forms of poultry items, so be sure to have that reference handy when you are costing and planning purchases of poultry.

costs for the breasts, legs, thighs, and wings obtained from whole birds. Remember, though, if you are going to use only one or two parts (breasts and wings, for instance) in your recipes, buy those particular items—that is, pieces—and be done with it.

PIECE COUNTS   When you buy just the parts (pieces) your menu calls for, costing is easy. Breasts, for instance, are usually sold as half breasts (a standard portion) and are often packaged in boxes of 24 pieces. These are available in various sizes and with or without bones or skin. You simply designate the exact size and trim you want to receive and do a *piece-count* costing, whereby you simply divide the cost of the box by 24 to get the cost per each.

COSTING PARTS OF WHOLE BIRDS   If you process whole birds into their respective parts—breasts, wings, thighs, and legs—you cost these parts by dividing the adjusted cost of the bird by the part's yield percentages. The Poultry table on chicken shows the weight yields of these parts. They add up to 67.9 percent of the original AP weight. You use this percentage to "adjust" the purchase price of the bird. For instance, if a bird costs $4.04 coming in the door, so to speak, its adjusted cost will be $5.95:

$4.04 ÷ 0.679 = $5.95

Then, when you want to calculate the cost of a certain part, say, the whole breast (both halves with skin and bones), you multiply the whole breast's yield percentage of 29.6 percent by the adjusted cost of the whole bird. If you do this with the wings, legs, and thighs, those costs will add up to the original price of the bird. This approach works as well when you first deduct the dollar value of the usable trim, the giblets, and backs from the AP cost. Simply follow two steps:

1. Subtract the value of those usable items from the AP cost per bird.
2. Divide by the total yield percentage of 67.9 percent to arrive at the adjusted cost per bird.

Example
Given: One AP chicken costs $4.04 (not deducting giblet costs). Its breasts, wings, legs, and thighs represent 67.9 percent of its original weight. Now do the math.

1. Adjust the AP cost by dividing the AP cost ($4.04) by the parts' yield percentage (0.679):

$4.04 ÷ 0.679 = $5.95

This is the adjusted cost per bird.

2. Multiply the various parts' yield percentage by the adjusted cost of $5.95. The Poultry table shows the yield for both breast halves is 29.6 percent of the AP weight, so:

$5.95 × 0.296 = $1.76

Therefore,

+ The yield for both wings is 10.7 percent of the AP weight:

$5.95 × 0.107 = $0.64

Y% means yield percentage ✦ AS means as served (or used) ✦ AP means as purchased ✦ AS ÷ AP = Y% ✦
AS ÷ Y% = AP ✦ AP × Y% = AS ✦ Cost per AP unit ÷ Y% = Cost per servable unit

+ The yield for both drumsticks is 11.4 percent of the AP weight:

$5.95 × 0.114 = $0.68

+ The yield for both thighs is 16.3 percent of the AP weight:

$5.95 × 0.163 = $0.97

When rounded, these totals add up to $4.05. Without rounding, they add up to $4.04, which equals the AP cost of the bird. If you first deduct the cost of the giblets, neck, and back from the original AP cost of the bird, the results will still add up to the lower adjusted cost of the AP bird. (The Poultry Costing Worksheet shows you how to cost these parts even further, including deducting the giblet costs first.)

COSTING TURKEY

The method just described for chicken works for costing turkey parts as well. Simply plug in the yield percentages for the turkey parts to cost the turkey's various pieces.

COSTING PARTS OF TURKEY Because of the popularity of turkey breast meat, the breasts are often sold as separate items, as are legs. Legs are typically packed whole, and you cost these by the each using the piece-count approach: Divide the cost of the purchase unit, such as a case of legs, by the number of legs in the case.

Breasts are sold with or without the skin and bones and with or without wing meat or rib meat attached. A raw, bone-in breast yields 73.6 percent of its AP weight in raw, skinless, boneless meat. To cost this meat, divide the cost per AP pound by 0.736. The same breast will yield 50 percent of its AP weight in cooked meat, so to cost the cooked meat, divide the AP cost per pound by 0.50.

Turkeys are sold as hens (females) and as toms (males). A tom is generally larger than a hen, though hens are now marketed in the 22- to 24-pound range, which is well into the market weight range for toms. As a percentage of its weight, a tom has more dark meat than a hen and a hen more light meat than a tom. The Poultry table indicates that the tom has more breast meat than a hen; but note that the tom listed in the table is bigger and more mature, resulting in a larger, more developed breast than the smaller, younger hens. The ratio of light to dark meat is 1.3 to 1 for a tom and 1.6 to 1 for a hen of equal size. Hens generally yield more usable meat per AP pound because their bones are smaller than those of toms.

COSTING COOKED TURKEY When pricing a banquet featuring cooked turkey meat, divide the cost per pound by the cooked meat yield percentage. The carving yield for a cooked 22-pound hen is 36.3 percent. If the AP cost per pound is $0.79, divide that cost by the cooked and carved yield percentage:

$0.79 per lb. ÷ 0.363 = $2.176 per lb.

+ A cooked ounce will cost one-sixteenth of the cooked pound cost:

$2.176 per lb. ÷ 16 oz./lb. = $0.136 per cooked oz.

+ A 5-ounce portion will cost you five times that, or $0.68.

You will get a 41 percent cooked meat yield from a roasted turkey if you not only carve the meat from the cooked bird but also hand-pull the remaining meat from its bones.

This increase in the yield will result in a lower cost per ounce. Because of the lower food cost, this approach to preparing turkey banquets is used by chefs who preplate their foods, rather than carve and plate them on a buffet line.

The following equations show how using a 41 percent yield will lower the food cost for the 5-ounce portion in the preceding example. Again, the AP cost per pound is $0.79.

1. Divide $0.79 by the 41 percent cooked, carved, and pulled meat yield:

$0.79 per lb. ÷ 0.41 = $1.93 per lb.
$1.93 per lb. ÷ 16 oz./lb. = $0.12 per cooked oz.

A 5-ounce portion will now cost $0.60, which is 8 cents less and translates to a reduction in cost of nearly 12 percent. How so? The savings of $0.08 divided by the original portion cost of $0.68 equals 0.1176, which is 11.76 percent.

COSTING GEESE

A young goose weighing 11 pounds will be composed of the following cuts as percentages of its AP weight:

+ Back and ribs: 21 percent
+ Breasts: 24 percent, including the bone and skin (Actual breast meat is about 12 percent.)
+ Legs and thighs: 22 percent
+ Wings: 16 percent
+ Neck, gizzard, heart: 14 percent
+ Liver: 3 percent (unless purposefully fattened for sale as foie gras)

Cost the various pieces by using the same method described for chicken or turkey pieces.

COSTING SMALL BIRDS

Quail, Cornish game hens, and squab (young pigeons) are sold whole or halved. Use the piece-count approach to cost these items.

COSTING DUCKLING

Ducklings, a rather popular poultry item, are sold whole and halved, as well as in breast halves, legs, and thighs. A standard portion is either a half duckling or a rather large half breast. Today, you can buy half duckling already cooked and with the rib bones removed.

The meat yield from a whole duckling is 32 percent. It is also 30 percent bone and 38 percent skin and fat. As percentages of its body weight, a duckling breaks down this way:

+ Breasts: 30 percent
+ Legs and thighs: 25 percent
+ Back and ribs: 25 percent
+ Neck, gizzard, heart: 5 percent
+ Liver: 3 percent (unless purposefully fattened for duck foie gras)

Cost duckling pieces just as you would chicken pieces. If a portion is a half duckling, simply divide the whole duckling's cost by 2.

PURCHASING POULTRY

IN THE WORKBOOK

Part II, the Workbook, has one worksheet to help you more accurately plan your poultry purchases:

✦ Poultry, Purchasing Worksheet 12

When you are buying whole chickens, turkeys, or other birds for the purpose of processing them into equal numbers of breasts, wings, thighs, and drumsticks, keep in mind that each bird yields two of each type of part. In order to calculate how many whole birds to order, therefore, you must add up all the part types needed and divide by 2. If you are not going to use equal numbers of a bird's parts, order just the parts you need rather than whole birds. As noted earlier, poultry processors market the various parts in different ways, so you can specify exactly the size and amount of trim you want. Except for wings, these parts can be ordered skinless and boneless. If, however, you feel it is advantageous to order whole parts and then skin and bone them yourself, the following four formulas show you how to go about it.

FORMULA 1   The formula for converting boneless, skinless half breasts to untrimmed half breasts is this:

> **AS weight breast meat ÷ Breast meat yield percentage**
> **= AP weight of whole breast halves**

Example

Given: You need 360 ounces of boneless, skinless half breasts. To determine how many ounces of untrimmed half breasts you need to get 360 ounces:

1. Obtain the yield percentage of boneless, skinless breast halves. (This is the trimmed weight divided by the untrimmed weight.) The Poultry table shows that a boneless, skinless half breast weighs 5.7 ounces, and the untrimmed half breast, 8.7 ounces. So:

5.7 ÷ 8.7 = 0.655 (65.5 percent)

2. Divide the AS weight of 360 ounces by 0.655 and you get 550 ounces. Therefore, you'll need 550 ounces, or 34.3 pounds of bone-in/skin-on half breasts.

This formula approach works the same for the legs and thighs.

FORMULA 2   Here's the formula for converting boneless, skinless turkey breast weight to whole turkey breast weight:

> **AS weight of full, boneless, skinless turkey breast ÷ Yield percentage**
> **= AP whole breast weight**

Example

Given: You need an AS amount of 312 ounces of boned, skinned turkey breast meat. Here's how to find the whole breast weight needed:

1. Divide the AS amount by the yield percentage (Y%) to determine the AP amount.
2. Divide the trimmed weight by the untrimmed weight to find the Y%. The Poultry table shows that a tom turkey breast weighs 144 ounces whole, and 106 ounces, boneless, skinless:

106 ÷ 144 = 0.7361

This is the poultry Y%.

3. Divide 312 by 0.7361 to get 423.9 ounces.

Thus, you'll need to buy 423.9 ounces of whole turkey breast to have 312 ounces to use. You will need 26.5 pounds (423.9 ÷ 16 = 26.5).

FORMULA 3   This is the formula for converting AS weight of cooked, carved turkey to AP whole turkey weight:

AS weight of cooked, carved turkey ÷ 0.363 = AP weight of raw turkey

Holiday banquets often feature roast turkey, and extensive testing shows that the best yield of cooked meat comes from a 20- to 24-pound hen, cooked in a conventional oven at 325°F to an internal thigh temperature of 165°F. After a brief rest, the cooked turkey will yield 36.3 percent of its AP weight (including neck and giblets) in carved meat. (The total yield, including meat that is hand-pulled from the carcass after carving, is 41 percent.)

If you are carving the turkeys on a buffet line, use the 36.3 percent carved meat yield factor to calculate how many pounds of raw turkey to buy. If you are going to carve and pull off all the remaining carcass meat and then reheat it for service, use the 41 percent yield formula (Formula 4).

Example (Carved Meat Only)

Given: You are going to serve turkey carved on a buffet line in 5-ounce portions of cooked meat to 150 guests. The total weight served will be 750 ounces (5 × 150 = 750). To convert the ounces to pounds, follow these steps:

1. Divide the number of ounces by 16:

750 oz. ÷ 16 oz./lb. = 46.9 lb.

2. Divide the weight needed (46.9 pounds) by the carved meat yield (0.363):

46.9 lb. ÷ 0.363 = 129.2 lb.

You'll need to order 129.2 pounds of raw turkey.

FORMULA 4   Here is the final formula is for converting cooked, carved, and pulled turkey to an AP raw weight:

**AS weight of carved and pulled turkey ÷ 0.41
= AP weight of raw turkey**

NOTE

If the meat is precarved and the extra pulled meat is added to the amount being served, use the 41 percent yield factor.

1. Divide the 46.9 pounds by 41 percent:

46.9 lb. ÷ 0.41 = 114.3 lb.

You should order 114.3 pounds of raw turkey.

It's a good idea to order a bit more than the formula indicates, however, to account for possible mistakes in production or on the serving line or to accommodate extra guests. Many chefs pad the calculated AP weight by 5 percent or more.

Y% means yield percentage ✦ AS means as served (or used) ✦ AP means as purchased ✦ AS ÷ AP = Y% ✦
AS ÷ Y% = AP ✦ AP × Y% = AS ✦ Cost per AP unit ÷ Y% = Cost per servable unit

DECIDING BETWEEN TRIMMED AND UNTRIMMED

If you are not sure whether to buy an item already trimmed, here's a simple test you can do to help you decide: Divide the cost per pound of an untrimmed food by the cost per pound of the trimmed item. If this untrimmed price percentage (the untrimmed price expressed as a percentage of the trimmed price) is greater than the food's trim yield percentage, you should buy the trimmed food. The reason is that, although a trimmed food's cost per pound will always be more than an untrimmed food's cost, you will be buying or using less of it and may be spending less on the trimmed food.

Example

Given: Whole chicken breasts cost $2.73 per pound, and boneless, skinless breasts cost $2.92 per pound.

1. To determine the trim yield percentage for breasts, divide the trimmed weight given in the Poultry table (11.4 ounces) by the whole weight (17.4 ounces):

11.4 ÷ 17.4 = 0.655

Thus, the trim yield percentage for whole to boneless, skinless breasts is 65.5 percent.

2. To calculate the percentage of the untrimmed price per pound to the trimmed price per pound, divide the whole breast cost ($2.73) by the trimmed cost ($2.93):

$2.73 ÷ $2.93 = 0.9317, or 93.2 percent, rounded

The untrimmed price percentage of 93.2 percent is larger than the trim yield percentage of 65.5 percent, meaning that the trimmed food is the better buy. How? Say you need 10 pounds of boneless, skinless breast meat. Because of the amount of trimming you would have to do, you would have to buy 15.27 pounds of whole breasts to end up with 10 pounds of cleaned breasts. Remember, the trim yield percentage means that you will only get 65.5 percent of any weight that you start with in cleaned breast meat. So, if you want to end up with 10 pounds, you have to divide the 10 pounds by 0.655 to calculate how many pounds of whole breast to start with; that is:

10 lb. ÷ 0.655 = 15.27 lb.

and:

15.27 lb. × $2.73/lb. = $41.68

In comparison, 10 pounds of skinless, boneless breasts at $2.93 per pound will cost $29.30. You are better off with the trimmed meat not only in food cost, but also in labor costs. (The Purchasing Worksheets contain a worksheet called Trimmed versus Untrimmed Prices that explains this in more detail, and includes a table you can use to help make decisions of this sort.)

Poultry

Item Name	Part Type	Ounce Weight	Percent of Original Weight	Ounce Weight of Each	Each: Percent of Original Weight
Chicken, Large Fryer					
Whole	Whole Bird	58.8	100.0%		
Clean Meat	General	28.2	48.0%		
Bones	General	21.0	35.7%		
Skin	General	7.6	12.9%		
Separable Fat	General	2.0	3.4%		
Gizzard	General			0.60	1.0%
Heart	General			0.25	0.4%
Liver	General			1.10	1.9%
Neck, skinless	General			1.70	2.9%
Neck, with skin	General			2.80	4.8%
Water, blood, and cutting loss	General			3.10	5.3%
Back	General			10.90	18.5%
Wings, whole	Wings	6.3	10.7%	3.15	5.4%
Wings, first joint (drumette)	Wings	3.0	5.1%	1.50	2.6%
Wings, second joint (middle)	Wings	2.5	4.3%	1.25	2.1%
Wings, tips	Wings	0.8	1.4%	0.40	0.7%
Breast, whole (both halves)	Breast	17.4	29.6%		
Breast, boneless, skinless	Breast	11.4	19.4%		
Breast, tenderloins, both	Breast	2.4	4.1%		
Breast Half, boneless, skinless	Breast			5.70	9.7%
Breast Half, whole, each	Breast			8.70	14.8%
Breast, tenderloins, each	Breast			1.20	2.0%
Legs, whole (drum and thigh)	Legs	16.2	27.6%		
Drumsticks, whole	Legs	6.7	11.4%		
Drumsticks, skinless	Legs	6.2	10.5%		
Drumstick Meat, detissued	Legs	3.2	5.4%		
Legs, whole, each	Legs			8.10	13.8%

Y% means yield percentage ✦ AS means as served (or used) ✦ AP means as purchased ✦ AS ÷ AP = Y% ✦
AS ÷ Y% = AP ✦ AP × Y% = AS ✦ Cost per AP unit ÷ Y% = Cost per servable unit

Poultry (Continued)

Item Name	Part Type	Ounce Weight	Percent of Original Weight	Ounce Weight of Each	Each: Percent of Original Weight
Drumstick, skinless, each	Legs			3.10	5.3%
Cleaned Meat from 1 Drumstick	Legs			1.60	2.7%
Drumstick, whole, each	Legs			3.35	5.7%
Thighs, whole	Thighs	9.6	6.3%		
Thighs, skinless	Thighs	8.1	13.8%		
Thighs, skinless, boneless	Thighs	5.9	10.0%		
Thighs, whole, each	Thighs			4.80	8.2%
Thighs, skinless, each	Thighs			4.05	6.9%
Thighs, skinless, boneless, each	Thighs			2.95	5.0%
Turkey, hen (10 pounds)					
Whole	Whole bird	160.0	100.0%		
Legs and thighs	General	47.0	29.4%		
Breast, whole	General	47.0	29.4%		
Breast, full, boneless, skinless	General	35.0	21.9%		
Back and Ribs	General	32.0	20.0%		
Wings	General	19.0	11.9%		
Gizzard	General	6.1	3.8%		
Neck	General	6.0	3.8%		
Liver	General	3.4	2.1%		
Heart	General	0.6	0.4%		
Turkey, hen (14 pounds)					
Hen (14 pounds)	Whole bird	224.0	100.0%		
Breast, whole	General	79.5	35.5%		
Breast, full, boneless, skinless	General	59.6	26.6%		
Legs and Thighs	General	57.0	25.4%		
Back and Ribs	General	46.0	20.5%		
Wings	General	25.3	11.3%		
Gizzard	General	6.3	2.8%		

Poultry (Continued)

Item Name	Part Type	Ounce Weight	Percent of Original Weight	Ounce Weight of Each	Each: Percent of Original Weight
Neck	General	5.4	2.4%		
Liver	General	3.6	1.6%		
Heart	General	0.7	0.3%		
Turkey, tom (22 pounds)					
Tom	Whole bird	352.0	100.0%		
Breast, whole	General	144.0	40.9%		
Breast, full, boneless, skinless	General	106.0	30.1%		
Legs and Thighs	General	84.0	23.9%		
Back and Ribs	General	64.8	18.4%		
Wings	General	33.4	9.5%		
Neck	General	12.0	3.4%		
Gizzard	General	6.3	1.8%		
Liver	General	4.5	1.3%		
Heart	General	1.4	0.4%		

Notes

1. **Chicken:** 1 cup of cooked chicken liver weighs 5 ounces.

   A whole raw chicken without giblets or neck will yield about 83% of its original weight when roasted.

2. **Ducklings:** Yield 30% bone, 38% skin and fat; meat yield is 32%.

Body Composition	Percent
Breasts	30%
Legs and Thighs	25%
Back and Ribs	25%
Wings	12%
Neck, Gizzard, and Heart	5%
Liver	3%
Whole 7-pound Duckling	100%

Y% means yield percentage ✦ AS means as served (or used) ✦ AP means as purchased ✦ AS ÷ AP = Y% ✦
AS ÷ Y% = AP ✦ AP × Y% = AS ✦ Cost per AP unit ÷ Y% = Cost per servable unit

The Proper Use of Cans, Scoops, Hotel Pans, and Sheet Trays in Costing

As noted where appropriate in Chapters 1 through 11 of *The Book of Yields,* accurate costing of certain items can be affected by factors other than weight and size—specifically, kitchen utensils and cans. Therefore, this chapter addresses how to properly account for such containers and utensils as cans, scoops, hotel pans, and sheet trays.

Three tables are referenced in the discussion in this chapter:

1. Can Sizes
2. Scoop or Disher Sizes
3. Sizes and Capacities of Hotel Pans

CANS

Obviously, the size of the can in which a food item is packaged will have to be factored in to any costing process. To help you with that, refer to the Can Sizes table, which lists the maximum capacities of various can sizes measured in the following ways:

+ U.S. fluid ounces
+ Milliliters
+ U.S. cups
+ Imperial (British) cups

If you are using all of the ingredients in a can and want to cost the value of one of the measures listed, divide the number of measures into the cost of one can. If your recipe calls for more than one measure, multiply the number of measures in your recipe by the cost of one measure.

Example
Given: A number-303 can of tomato paste costs $2.90. The Can Sizes table shows that one 303 can holds 16.18 fluid ounces, or 2.023 U.S. cups.

1. To get the cost per fluid ounce, divide the cost of the can ($2.90) by 16.18:

$2.90 ÷ 16.18 = $0.179 per fl. oz.

2. To cost a cup, either multiply that answer times 8 ($1.43) or divide $2.90 by the 2.023 cups that equal the capacity of the number-303 can:

$2.90 ÷ 2.023 = $1.43

SCOOPS

NOTE

If you frequently use a particular canned food, say, tomato paste (no draining), it is a good idea to actually measure the fluid ounces *and* cups that you obtain in your kitchen. The reason is that your cans may not be filled to maximum capacity and your cooks may not be gleaning every morsel of food from every can. Use the methods just described, but use your own yields to do your actual costing.

NOTE

You can use this same approach to cost ladles of food as well. Just be sure to scrape the food to the top of the ladle, when necessary.

Scoops, also called *dishers*, are handheld, metal half-rounds used to portion out fairly exact volumes of foods onto serving dishes. Every scoop has a number stamped onto the curved "blade" on the inside of the bowl. This number tells you how many scoops of that size will equal a single quart (32 fluid ounces). A number-4 scoop will hold one-fourth of a quart—that is, 8 fluid ounces.

When you know the cost of one fluid ounce of a particular food, you can cost the value of any single scoop of that food by multiplying its capacity in fluid ounces by the cost per fluid ounce. The Scoop or Disher Sizes table tells you how many fluid ounces equal one level scoop. The key word here is *level:* You have to scrape the food across the edge of the container from which you are scooping the food in order to get a level scoop.

Say that a fluid ounce of some food costs 9 cents, and that you are using a number-8 scoop to serve it. The table shows that a number-8 scoop holds 4 fluid ounces. Multiply the cost per fluid ounce (9 cents) by the fluid-ounce capacity (4) to get the cost of the level scoopful:

$0.09 × 4 = $0.36

HOTEL PANS

Hotel pans, also called *steam table pans,* are made out of stainless steel (or heatproof, food-grade plastic) in eight standard sizes with respect to their length and width. Each size comes in three depths: shallow, medium, and deep. The Sizes and Capacities of Hotel Pans table gives you all these variations for stainless-steel hotel pans. It also lists their capacities in quarts and liters in two ways: when the pans are filled to the brim and when they are filled to what is called a *nonspill capacity.*

Y% means yield percentage ✦ AS means as served (or used) ✦ AP means as purchased ✦ AS ÷ AP = Y% ✦
AS ÷ Y% = AP ✦ AP × Y% = AS ✦ Cost per AP unit ÷ Y% = Cost per servable unit

Hotel pans are used to hold a number of single portions or a mass of food that should equal a known number of portions.

1. To cost the value of a hotel pan's contents, multiply the cost per portion by the number of portions the pan contains.

2. If you know the value of the whole pan but don't know the value of a portion, divide the pan content's value (food cost) by the portions you get from it.

NOTE OF SOUP TUREENS

Soup is often held for service on a steam table or in a stand-alone soup-warmer. Probably you'll know the cost of the soup (by the fluid ounce and serving size) from your recipe development. However, soup evaporates in these warming units, and your yield may shrink after a few hours, increasing your portion costs and often causing your soup to become salty or too thick or to just taste overdone. Be sure to keep just enough soup in your tureens to ensure that the flavors stay fresh.

Example

Given: A hotel pan holds 16 portions of salmon fillet, and each fillet costs $2. Using the first approach, the cost of the entire pan will be $32:

$2 × 16 = $32

If, however, you have a hotel pan of baked lasagna worth $12, and you get 12 portions from one pan, using the second approach, the cost per portion is $1:

$12 ÷ 12 = $1

SHEET TRAYS

Many recipes are baked on, and portioned off, sheet trays. Sheet cakes and various pastry bars are examples. The Pans and Trays table identifies types of sheet trays and gives you a variety of standard portion sizes and number of portions that can be cut from a full sheet tray. Use this information to cost portions by dividing the number of portions you get from a tray into the cost of one sheet tray recipe.

1 gal. = 4 qt. = 16 c. = 128 fl. oz. ✦ 1 qt. = 2 pt. = 4 c. = 32 fl. oz. ✦ 1 pt. = 2 c. = 16 fl. oz. ✦
1 c. = 8 fl. oz. = 16 tbsp. ✦ 1 fl. oz. = 2 tbsp. ✦ 1 tbsp. = 3 tsp. ✦ 1 lb. = 16 oz.

Can Sizes

Standard U.S. Can	U.S. Fluid Ounces	Milliliters	U.S. Cups	Imperial Cups
Number 10	104.900	3102.263	13.113	10.918
Number 5	56.600	1673.862	7.075	5.891
Number 3 cylinder	49.560	1465.664	6.195	5.158
Number 2 1/2	28.550	844.324	3.569	2.972
Number 2	19.690	582.303	2.461	2.049
Number 303	16.180	478.500	2.023	1.684
Number 300	14.590	431.478	1.824	1.519
Number 211 cylinder	12.998	384.397	1.625	1.353
Number 1 picnic	10.480	309.931	1.310	1.091
8 ounce	8.320	246.052	1.040	0.866
6 ounce	5.830	172.414	0.729	0.607

Note

The fluid ounces and milliliters above specify the capacity of these cans to contain liquids. Food packers sometimes use near-standard custom-size cans that contain less volume. Read the can label for precise weight or volume data regarding its contents.

Y% means yield percentage ✦ AS means as served (or used) ✦ AP means as purchased ✦ AS ÷ AP = Y% ✦
AS ÷ Y% = AP ✦ AP × Y% = AS ✦ Cost per AP unit ÷ Y% = Cost per servable unit

Scoop or Disher Sizes

Disher Size Number	U.S. Fluid Ounces	Milliliters	Cups per Scoop	Scoops per Cup
4	8.000	236.588	1.000	1.000
5	6.400	189.271	0.800	1.250
6	5.333	157.716	0.667	1.500
8	4.000	118.294	0.500	2.000
10	3.200	94.635	0.400	2.500
12	2.666	78.843	0.333	3.001
16	2.000	59.147	0.250	4.000
20	1.600	47.318	0.200	5.000
24	1.333	39.422	0.167	6.002
30	1.066	31.525	0.133	7.505
40	0.800	23.659	0.100	10.000
60	0.533	15.763	0.067	15.009

Note

Accurate portioning with dishers requires level scraping across the top of the disher cup. The number imprinted on the blade of the scoop states how many level scoops of that size are in one 32-fluid-ounce quart.

---

1 gal. = 4 qt. = 16 c. = 128 fl. oz. ♦ 1 qt. = 2 pt. = 4 c. = 32 fl. oz. ♦ 1 pt. = 2 c. = 16 fl. oz. ♦
1 c. = 8 fl. oz. = 16 tbsp. ♦ 1 fl. oz. = 2 tbsp. ♦ 1 tbsp. = 3 tsp. ♦ 1 lb. = 16 oz.

Sizes and Capacities of Hotel Pans

Stainless Steam Table Pans, General Size	Common Name	Dimension (Inches) Width × Length × Depth	Brimful Capacity Quarts	Liters	Nonspill Capacity Quarts	Liters
Full	Full shallow	12 × 20 × 2.5	8.3	7.85	6.0	5.68
	Full medium	12 × 20 × 4	14.0	13.25	12.0	11.36
	Full deep	12 × 20 × 6	21.0	19.87	18.0	17.03
Standard Half	Half shallow	12 × 10 × 2.5	4.3	4.07	3.0	2.84
	Half medium	12 × 10 × 4	6.7	6.34	6.0	5.68
	Half deep	12 × 10 × 6	10.0	9.46	9.0	8.52
Long Half	Long half, 1 inch	6.5 × 20 × 1.25	2.1	1.99	1.5	1.42
	Long half, shallow	6.5 × 20 × 2.5	3.7	3.50	25.0	2.37
	Long half, medium	6.5 × 20 × 4	5.7	5.39	4.5	4.26
	Long half, deep	6.5 × 20 × 6	8.2	7.76	7.0	6.62
Two-Thirds	Two-thirds, 1 inch	12 × 14 × 1.25	4.0	3.79	3.0	2.84
	Two-thirds, shallow	12 × 14 × 2.5	5.6	5.30	4.5	4.26
	Two-thirds, medium	12 × 14 × 4	9.3	8.80	8.0	7.57
	Two-thirds, deep	12 × 14 × 6	14.0	13.25	12.0	11.36
Third	Third, shallow	12 × 7 × 2.5	2.6	2.46	2.0	1.89
	Third, medium	12 × 7 × 4	4.1	3.88	3.5	3.31
	Third, deep	12 × 7 × 6	6.1	5.77	5.5	5.20
Fourth	Fourth, shallow	6 × 10 × 2.5	1.8	1.70	1.4	1.32
	Fourth, medium	6 × 10 × 4	3.0	2.84	2.5	2.37
	Fourth, deep	6 × 10 × 6	4.5	4.26	3.8	3.55
Sixth	Sixth, shallow	6 × 7 × 2.5	1.2	1.14	0.9	0.85
	Sixth, medium	6 × 7 × 4	1.8	1.70	1.5	1.42
	Sixth, deep	6 × 7 × 6	2.7	2.56	1.4	1.32
Ninth	Ninth, shallow	4 × 7 × 2.5	0.6	0.57	0.5	0.47
	Ninth, medium	4 × 7 × 4	1.6	1.51	1.3	1.18

Note

Pan dimensions are rounded. For instance, a full shallow pan is actually 12.75 × 20.75 × 2.5 in. Hard plastic food pans hold between 5 and 20 percent less because of thicker wall construction. The larger the pan, the less the plastic material reduces the pan's capacity compared to stainless.

Y% means yield percentage ✦ AS means as served (or used) ✦ AP means as purchased ✦ AS ÷ AP = Y% ✦
AS ÷ Y% = AP ✦ AP × Y% = AS ✦ Cost per AP unit ÷ Y% = Cost per servable unit

Sheet Trays

Standard sheet trays (also called sheet pans, baking pans, bun pans) are of two primary sizes. A full sheet tray is 18 × 26 in. (46 × 66 cm). A half size measures 13 × 18 in. (33 × 46 cm). Commercial kitchen ovens, refrigerators, tables, racks, and so on are designed to fit the full sheet tray: 18 × 26 in. The area of 1 full sheet tray is 468 in^2 (3,036 cm^2).

Full Sheet Tray Cutting Yields

Width × Length (Inches)	Number of Cuts per Width × Length	Piece Size (Square Inches)	Number of Pieces
4.5 × 2	4 × 13	9.0	52
2.5 × 2.6	7 × 10	6.5	70
3 × 2	6 × 13	6.0	78
2.25 × 2	8 × 13	4.5	104
2 × 2	9 × 13	4.0	117

Width × Length (Centimeters)	Number of Cuts per Width × Length	Piece Size (Square Centimeters)	Number of Pieces
11.4 × 5	4 × 13	57.0	52
6.4 × 6.6	7 × 10	42.2	70
7.6 × 5	6 × 13	38.0	778
5.7 × 5	8 × 13	28.5	104
5 × 5	9 × 13	25.0	117

13 | MEASUREMENT CONVERSION

WESTERN SYSTEMS OF MEASURE

In the food service profession, the measurements of greatest concern are volume, weight, length, and temperature. There are three Western measurement systems:

1. Metric
2. American (United States)
3. British (imperial)

This chapter references two tables:

1. Metric System
2. Measurement Conversions

AMERICAN AND IMPERIAL SYSTEMS

The imperial and U.S. systems both use equivalent pounds and ounces to measure weights. This system is referred to as *avoirdupois,* a French term roughly translated as "goods of weight." Avoirdupois pounds and ounces are used to measure weight (mass), and specify that a pound equals 7,000 *grains* and is divided into 16 ounces.

Further delineations in the avoirdupois system are as follows:

+ 1 ounce equals 437.5 grains.
+ 1 gram equals 15.43236 grains (1 standard grain equals 64.79891 milligrams).

When you divide 437.5 grains in 1 ounce by 15.43236 grains in 1 gram, it equals 28.34952; thus, there are 28.35 grams per avoirdupois ounce.

However, when it comes to fluid ounces, the American and imperial systems differ: the U.S. fluid ounce of water weighs 29.573 grams, while the imperial weighs 28.413. The reason lies in history. The American colonists adopted the wine gallon measure of 231 cubic inches to measure liquids, whereas the English used both the wine gallon and an ale gallon, of 282 cubic inches. But in 1824, the English abandoned both these gallon measures in favor of a standard British imperial gallon. The imperial gallon was defined as the volume of 10 pounds of water at 62 degrees Fahrenheit, and was calculated to be 277.42 cubic inches, which is a slight overstatement. Here's the math: 1 cubic inch equals 16.387064 cubic centimeters, so:

$$16.387064 \times 277.42 = 4,546.08$$

NOTE

Of course, time is an important measurement in food service, but the system for that—fortunately—is universal and so is not covered here.

NOTE

The term *grain* in the avoirdupois system actually refers to a grain of wheat, an ancient unit of measure for weighing gold.

NOTE

Volume measures—such
as gallons—are defined
by volume (cubic)
standards. This means a
gallon is determined by
its cubic inches, not its
stated weight.

Ten pounds (avoirdupois) equals 160 ounces of 28.3495 grams per ounce: 4,535.92 grams. However, the imperial gallon was assigned a weight of 4,546.08 grams (10 grams extra). A cubic centimeter of water weighs 1 gram, and 4,546.08 divided by 160 ounces equals 28.413 grams per ounce; hence, the imperial fluid ounce exceeds the avoirdupois ounce by a slight 0.063 gram per ounce. The imperial gallon would have to be 276.6799047 cubic inches to equal 28.35 grams per fluid ounce.

The United States stayed with the 231 cubic-inch gallon, which was divided into 128 ounces:

+ 231 cubic inches times 16.387 cubic centimeters equals 3,785.4 (1 cubic centimeter of water weighs 1 gram).
+ 3,785.4 grams divided by 128 fluid ounces equals 29.573 grams per U.S. fluid ounce.

Thus, the U.S. fluid ounce is a full 1.22 grams heavier than the avoirdupois ounce. Consequently, U.S. fluid ounces, measuring spoons, and cups are about 4 percent larger than their imperial counterparts, whereas the imperial pint, quart, and gallon are about 20 percent larger than the U.S. pint, quart, and gallon because they contain more ounces.

Metric System

The third system, the metric, is far more simple and logical. It links the way distance, weight, area, and volume are measured. Here's how it works:

+ A *meter* measures length (this is the unifying measure for the entire metric system).
+ A *liter* measures liquid volume.
+ A *gram* measures mass (weight).

NOTE

By international
agreement, the liter was
assigned a mass (weight)
of 1,000 grams
(1 kilogram).

Now here's the liter–meter–gram connection:

+ A liter is defined as one-tenth of a meter, cubed. Picture a square box (a cube) that is about 4 inches long on all sides. One-tenth of a meter equals 10 centimeters (cm):

10 cm × 10 cm × 10 cm = 1,000 cu cm

So there are 1,000 cm^3 (cubic centimeters) in 1 liter.

+ The liter is, by definition, composed of 1,000 milliliters; therefore, 1 liter of water contains 1,000 milliliters, each weighing 1 gram and occupying 1 cubic centimeter exactly.
+ In summary: 1 milliliter equals 1 cubic centimeter (of water) equals 1 gram; 1 kilogram equals 1 liter of water; 1 liter contains 1,000 milliliters; and each of these weighs 1 gram (1,000 grams equals 1 kilogram).

The Metric System table summarizes all this and provides abbreviations and equivalent measures.

1 gal. = 4 qt. = 16 c. = 128 fl. oz. ✦ 1 qt. = 2 pt. = 4 c. = 32 fl. oz. ✦ 1 pt. = 2 c. = 16 fl. oz. ✦
1 c. = 8 fl. oz. = 16 tbsp. ✦ 1 fl. oz. = 2 tbsp. ✦ 1 tbsp. = 3 tsp. ✦ 1 lb. = 16 oz.

Metric System

This Unit	Measures	Abbreviation	Relates to	Equivalent U.S. Measure
Meter	Length	m	Feet, yards	39.37 in. (1.09 yd.)
Square Meter	Area	m^2	Square yard	1.1959 sq. yards
Liter	Liquid volume	L	Quart	33.8 fl. oz. (1.056 qt.)
Cubic Meter	Volume	m^3	Cubic yard	35.3 cu. ft. (1.307 cu. yd.)
Gram/Kilogram	Mass (weight)	g/kg	Ounce/pound	1 g =.035 oz./1 kg = 2.2 lb.

Metric System Prefixes (Using Liters as Sample Application)

Prefix	Meaning	Example	Abbreviation	Number Expressions
milli	One-thousandth	Milliliter	mL	1/1,000th or .001 liter
centi	One-hundredth	Centiliter	cL	1/100th or .01 liter
deci	One-tenth	Deciliter	dL	1/10th or .1 liter
The item: Liter	One, each, whole	Liter	L	1 liter
deka	Ten	Dekaliter	daL	10 liters
hecto	Hundred	Hectoliter	hL	100 liters
kilo	Thousand	Kiloliter	kL	1,000 liters

Volume

Items	Equivalent U.S. Fluid Ounces	Equivalent Milliliters	Equivalent Cubic Inches	Equivalent Measure
U.S. Fluid Ounce	1	29.57353	1.805	Equals 1.041 imperial ounce
U.S. Measuring Cup	8	236.58824	14.43	8 fl. oz. per cup
U.S. Tablespoon	0.5	14.786765	0.9023	16 tbsp. per cup
U.S. Teaspoon	0.166666	4.928921667	0.3	3 tsp. per tbsp.
U.S. Pint	16	473.17648	28.875	2 cups per pint
U.S. Quart	32	946.35296	57.75	2 pints per quart
U.S. Gallon	128	3785.41184	231	Equals .833 imperial gallon
Liter	33.814	1000	61.02374	Equals 1.056 U.S. quarts

Note

One 8-U.S.-fluid-ounce (29.573 mL) cup equals 236.6 grams; 8 ounces avoirdupois equals 226.796 grams.

Y% means yield percentage ✦ AS means as served (or used) ✦ AP means as purchased ✦ AS ÷ AP = Y% ✦
AS ÷ Y% = AP ✦ AP × Y% = AS ✦ Cost per AP unit ÷ Y% = Cost per servable unit

Volume (Continued)

Items	Equivalent U.S. Fluid Ounces	Equivalent Milliliters	Equivalent Cubic Inches	Equivalent Measure
Imperial Fluid Ounce	1	28.413	1.734	Equals .961 U.S. fl. oz.
Imperial Cup, Liquid	8	227.304	13.87	Equals .9607 U.S. cup
Imperial Tablespoon	0.5	14.20655	0.86659	16 per imperial cup
Imperial Teaspoon	0.1666666	4.73551	0.28886	
U.S. Measuring Cup	8.33	236.58824	14.43	Equals 1.04 imperial cup
U.S. Tablespoon	0.52	14.786765	0.9025	
U.S. Teaspoon	0.17	4.928921667	0.3	
Imperial Pint	20	568.26	34.677	2.5 imperial cups per pint
Imperial Quart	40	1136.52	69.354	20 imperial cups per imperial gallon
Imperial Gallon	160	4545.92	277.42	
Liter	35.19508	1000	61.02374	Equals 0.264 U.S. gallon

Measuring Spoons . . . contain the following:

Spoon Size (U.S.)	Milliliters (rounded)	Milliliters (exact)	U.S. Fl. Oz.	Imperial Fl. Oz.
Tablespoon	15	14.78680	0.5	0.520421
Teaspoon	5	4.92892	0.166667	0.173474
Half Teaspoon	2.5	2.46446	0.0833335	0.086737
Quarter Teaspoon	1.25	1.23223	0.04166675	0.0433685

Mass (Weight)

Unit of Measurement	Grams	Kilograms	Ounces (avoirdupois)	Pounds (avoirdupois)
Ounce	28.34952313	0.02835	1	0.0625
Pound	453.59237	0.45359	16	1
Gram	1	0.00100	0.03527396	0.002204623
Kilogram	1,000	1.00000	35.27396	2.204623

Temperature

In the Fahrenheit system, there are 180 degrees between the freezing and boiling points of water. In Fahrenheit, water freezes at 32 and boils at 212 (at sea level). In the Celsius (Centigrade) system, there are 100 degrees between freezing and boiling. In Celsius, water freezes at 0 and boils at 100.

To convert from one system to the other, first reduce the 180 and 100 figures to 9 and 5. The 32 is either added or subtracted within the formulas.

To convert from Celsius to Fahrenheit, multiply the Celsius value by 180/100 (use 9/5), then add 32. For example, to change 22°C to Fahrenheit: $22 \times 9 = 198$; $198/5 = 39.6$; $39.6 + 32 = 71.6°F$.

To convert Fahrenheit to Celsius, first subtract 32 from the Fahrenheit, then multiply by 5/9. For example, change 72°F to Celsius: $72 - 32 = 40$; $40 \times 5 = 200$; $200/9 = 22.2°C$.

Length

1 mile equals 5,280 feet, or 1,760 yards, or 1,609.3 meters.

1 meter equals 39.37 inches, or 3.28 feet, or 1.0936 yards.

1 yard equals 36 inches, or 3 feet, or .914 meter.

1 foot equals 12 inches, or one-third (.333) yard, or 0.3048 meter.

1 inch equals 2.54 centimeters.

Measurement Conversions

A: To convert this item	B: Into this item	B Multiply A by:	Or, to convert to:	Multiply A by:
LIQUID VOLUME				
U.S. Fluid Ounce	Milliliters	29.57353	Liters	0.02957353
U.S. Cup, Liquid	Milliliters	236.588	Liters	0.236588
U.S. Pint	Milliliters	473.1765	Liters	0.473176
U.S. Quart	Milliliters	946.3529	Liters	0.94635
U.S. Gallon	Milliliters	3785.41	Liters	3.785412
Imperial Fluid Ounce	Milliliters	28.413	Liters	0.028413
Imperial Cup, Liquid	Milliliters	227.304	Liters	0.227304
Imperial Pint	Milliliters	568.26	Liters	0.56826
Imperial Quart	Milliliters	1136.52	Liters	1.13652
Imperial Gallon	Milliliters	4546.08	Liters	4.54608
Milliliters	U.S. fluid ounce	0.033814	Imperial fluid ounce	0.0351951
Milliliters	Cup of U.S. fluid ounce	0.0042265	Cup of imperial fluid ounce	0.00439938
Milliliters	U.S. pint	0.002113376	Imperial pint	0.0017952
Milliliters	U.S. quart	0.001056688	Imperial quart	0.0008796
Milliliters	U.S. gallon	0.0002641721	Imperial gallon	0.000219961248
Liters	U.S. fluid ounce	33.814	Imperial fluid ounce	35.195
Liters	U.S. cup	4.22675	Imperial cup	4.33938
Liters	U.S. pint	2.113	Imperial pint	1.75975
Liters	U.S. quart	1.05669	Imperial quart	0.879877
Liters	U.S. gallon	0.26417	Imperial gallon	0.219969
Milliliters	Liters	0.001		
Liters	Milliliters	1000		
U.S. Fluid Ounce	Imperial fluid ounce	1.04084	Imperial cup, liquid	0.130105
U.S. Cup, Liquid	Imperial cup, liquid	1.04084	Imperial pint	0.416337
U.S. Pint	Imperial pint	0.832674	Imperial quart	0.416337
U.S. Quart	Imperial quart	0.83267	Imperial gallon	0.208169
U.S. Gallon	Imperial gallon	0.832674		

1 gal. = 4 qt. = 16 c. = 128 fl. oz. ✦ 1 qt. = 2 pt. = 4 c. = 32 fl. oz. ✦ 1 pt. = 2 c. = 16 fl. oz. ✦
1 c. = 8 fl. oz. = 16 tbsp. ✦ 1 fl. oz. = 2 tbsp. ✦ 1 tbsp. = 3 tsp. ✦ 1 lb. = 16 oz.

Measurement Conversions (Continued)

A: To convert this item	B: Into this item	B Multiply A by:	Or, to convert to:	Multiply A by:
Imperial Fluid Ounce	U.S. fluid ounce	0.96076	U.S. cup, liquid	0.120095
Imperial Cup, Liquid	U.S. cup, liquid	0.96076	U.S. pint	0.48038
Imperial Pint	U.S. pint	1.20095	U.S. quart	0.600475
Imperial Quart	U.S. quart	1.20095	U.S. gallon	0.300327
Imperial Gallon	U.S. gallon	1.20095		
U.S. SYSTEM				
U.S. Fluid Ounce	U.S. cup	0.125	U.S. pint	0.0625
U.S. Fluid Ounce	U.S. quart	0.03125	U.S. gallon	0.0078125
U.S. Cup	U.S. fluid ounce	8	U.S. pint	0.5
U.S. Cup	U.S. quart	0.25	U.S. gallon	0.0625
U.S. Pint	U.S. fluid ounce	16	U.S. cup	2
U.S. Pint	U.S. quart	0.5	U.S. gallon	0.125
U.S. Quart	U.S. fluid ounce	32	U.S. cup	4
U.S. Quart	U.S. pint	2	U.S. gallon	0.25
U.S. Gallon	U.S. fluid ounce	128	U.S. cup	16
U.S. Gallon	U.S. pint	8	U.S. quart	4
IMPERIAL SYSTEM				
Imperial Fluid Ounce	Imperial cup	0.125	Imperial pint	0.05
Imperial Fluid Ounce	Imperial quart	0.025	Imperial gallon	0.00625
Imperial Cup	Imperial fluid ounce	8	Imperial pint	0.4
Imperial Cup	Imperial quart	0.2	Imperial gallon	0.05
Imperial Pint	Imperial fluid ounce	20	Imperial cup	2.5
Imperial Pint	Imperial quart	0.5	Imperial gallon	0.125
Imperial Quart	Imperial fluid ounce	40	Imperial cup	5
Imperial Quart	Imperial pint	2	Imperial gallon	0.25
Imperial Gallon	Imperial fluid ounce	160	Imperial cup	20
Imperial Gallon	Imperial pint	8	Imperial quart	4

Y% means yield percentage ✦ AS means as served (or used) ✦ AP means as purchased ✦ AS ÷ AP = Y% ✦
AS ÷ Y% = AP ✦ AP × Y% = AS ✦ Cost per AP unit ÷ Y% = Cost per servable unit

Measurement Conversions (Continued)

A: To convert this item	B: Into this item	B Multiply A by:	Or, to convert to:	Multiply A by:
CUPS AND SPOONS				
Fluid Ounce	Tablespoons	2	Teaspoons	6
Cups	Tablespoons	16	Teaspoons	48
Teaspoons	Tablespoons	0.33333		
Tablespoons	Teaspoons	3		
Tablespoons	Cup	0.0625		
U.S. Tablespoon	Milliliters	14.78677	U.S. fluid ounces	0.5
U.S. Teaspoon	Milliliters	4.92892	U.S. fluid ounces	0.16666666
U.S. Tablespoon	Imperial Tablespoons	1.04084	Imperial fluid ounces	0.5204
U.S. Teaspoon	Imperial teaspoons	1.04084	Imperial fluid ounces	0.173474
Imperial Tablespoon	Milliliters	14.20655	Imperial fluid ounces	0.5
Imperial Teaspoon	Milliliters	4.735516	Imperial fluid ounces	0.1666666
Imperial Tablespoon	U.S. tablespoons	0.96076	U.S. fluid ounces	0.4803806
Imperial Teaspoon	U.S. teaspoons	0.96076	U.S. fluid ounces	0.1601268
U.S. Cup (Liquid) 237 mL	Imperial cup, liquid	1.04084	Imperial tablespoons	16.65346195
Imperial Cup (Liquid) 227 mL	U.S. cup, liquid	0.96076	U.S. tablespoons	15.372179107
Milliliters	U.S. tablespoons	0.067628	U.S. teaspoons	0.20288
Milliliters	Imperial tablespoons	0.07039	Imperial teaspoons	0.21117
WEIGHT (MASS)				
Ounce (avoirdupois)	Pound (avoirdupois)	0.0625		
Ounce (avoirdupois)	Gram	28.349523125		
Ounce (avoirdupois)	Kilogram	0.028349523125		
Pound (avoirdupois)	Ounce (avoirdupois)	16		
Pound (avoirdupois)	Gram	453.592		
Pound (avoirdupois)	Kilogram	0.45359237		
Kilogram	Gram	1000		
Kilogram	Ounce (avoirdupois)	35.27396		
Kilogram	Pound (avoirdupois)	2.204623		

1 gal. = 4 qt. = 16 c. = 128 fl. oz. ✦ 1 qt. = 2 pt. = 4 c. = 32 fl. oz. ✦ 1 pt. = 2 c. = 16 fl. oz. ✦
1 c. = 8 fl. oz. = 16 tbsp. ✦ 1 fl. oz. = 2 tbsp. ✦ 1 tbsp. = 3 tsp. ✦ 1 lb. = 16 oz.

Measurement Conversions (Continued)

A: To convert this item	B: Into this item	B Multiply A by:	Or, to convert to:	Multiply A by:
Gram	Kilogram	0.001		
Gram	Ounce (avoirdupois)	0.035274		
Gram	Pound (avoirdupois)	0.002204623		
LENGTH				
Inch	Feet	0.0833334	Yard	0.0277778
Inch	Centimeter	2.54	Meter	0.0254
Feet	Inch	12	Yard	0.33333
Feet	Centimeter	30.48	Meter	0.3048
Yard	Inch	36	Feet	3
Yard	Centimeter	91.44	Meter	0.9144
Centimeter	Inch	0.393701	Feet	0.03280841
Centimeter	Yard	0.0109361	Meter	0.01
Meter	Inch	39.3701	Feet	3.28084
Meter	Yard	1.09361	Centimeter	100
AREA				
Square Inch	Square centimeter	6.4516	Square meter	0.00064516
Square Inch	Square feet	0.0069444	Square yard	0.000771605
Square Feet	Square centimeter	929.0304	Square meter	0.0929034
Square Feet	Square inch	144	Square yard	0.111111
Square Yard	Square centimeter	8361.2736	Square meter	0.836128
Square Yard	Square inch	1296	Square feet	9
Square Centimeter	Square inch	0.155	Square feet	0.00107639
Square Centimeter	Square yard	0.000119599	Square meter	0.0001
Square Meter	Square inch	1550	Square feet	10.7639
Square Meter	Square yard	1.19599	Square centimeter	10000

Y% means yield percentage ♦ AS means as served (or used) ♦ AP means as purchased ♦ AS ÷ AP = Y% ♦ AS ÷ Y% = AP ♦ AP × Y% = AS ♦ Cost per AP unit ÷ Y% = Cost per servable unit

Measurement Conversions (Continued)

A: To convert this item	B: Into this item	B Multiply A by:	Or, to convert to:	Multiply A by:
LENGTH				
Inch	Centimeter	2.54	Meter	0.0254
Centimeter	Inch	0.3937	Foot	0.0328
Foot	Centimeter	30.48	Meter	0.3048
Meter	Inch	39.37008	Foot	3.28

TEMPERATURE CONVERSIONS

Celsius to Fahrenheit:

$(C \times 9/5) + 32 = F$

Multiply the Celsius temperature times 9/5 and add 32 to that answer.

Examples:

Celsius = 60   60 × 9 = 540   540/5 = 108   108 + 32 = 140   So, 60°C = 140°F.

Fahrenheit to Celsius:

$(F - 32) \times 5/9 = C$

Subtract 32 from the Fahrenheit temperature. Multiply the answer times 5/9.

Examples:

Fahrenheit = 140   140 − 32 = 108   108 × 5 = 540   540/9 = 60   So, 140°F = 60°C

Celsius = Fahrenheit equivalents: (Sample: At 0° Celsius, Fahrenheit equals 32: 0°C = 32°F)

10°C = 50°F   20°C = 68°F   30°C = 86°F   40°C = 104°F   50°C = 122°F

60°C = 140°F   70°C = 158°F   80°C = 176°F   90°C = 194°F   100°C = 212°F

1 gal. = 4 qt. = 16 c. = 128 fl. oz. ♦ 1 qt. = 2 pt. = 4 c. = 32 fl. oz. ♦ 1 pt. = 2 c. = 16 fl. oz. ♦
1 c. = 8 fl. oz. = 16 tbsp. ♦ 1 fl. oz. = 2 tbsp. ♦ 1 tbsp. = 3 tsp. ♦ 1 lb. = 16 oz.

14 | SIMPLE FORMULAS

This chapter contains 18 simple formulas you might use on a regular basis, as you do your food costing conversions and plan your purchases of the products you need to complete your recipes.

Simple Formulas

To Convert This	To This	Do This
Tablespoons per Ounce (avoirdupois)	Tablespoons per gram	Divide the number of tablespoons per ounce by 28.349. (This is answer A.)
Tablespoons per Ounce (avoirdupois)	Tablespoons per 100 grams	Multiply answer A by 100.
Tablespoons per Ounce (avoirdupois)	Tablespoons per kilogram	Multiply answer A by 1,000.
Ounces (avoirdupois) per Tablespoon	Grams per tablespoon	Multiply tablespoons by 28.349.
Grams per Tablespoon	Ounces (avoirdupois) per tablespoon	Divide grams per tablespoon by 28.349.
Ounces (avoirdupois) per Cup	Grams per liter	Multiply the ounces by 28.349, then multiply that answer by 4.2267.
Ounces (avoirdupois) per Quart	Grams per liter	Multiply the ounces by 28.349, then multiply that answer by 1.05669.
Fluid Ounces per Tablespoon	Milliliters per tablespoon	Multiply fluid ounces by 29.573.
Milliliters per Tablespoon	Fluid ounces per tablespoon	Divide milliliters per tablespoon by 29.573.
Fluid Ounces per Cup	Milliliters per liter	Multiply the ounces by 29.573, then multiply that answer by 4.2267.
Fluid Ounces per Quart	Milliliters per liter	Multiply the ounces by 29.573, then multiply that answer by 1.05669.
Cups	Liters	Multiply the number of cups by .23658.
Liter	Cups	Multiply the number of liters by 4.22675.
Cups per Pound	Cups per kilogram	Multiply the cups per pound by 2.2046.
Cups per Kilogram	Cups per pound	Divide cups per kilo by 2.2046.
Pints per Pound	Pints per kilogram	Multiply the pints per pound by 2.2046.
Quarts per Pound	Quarts per kilogram	Multiply the quarts per pound by 2.2046.
Pounds per Pint or Quart	Kilograms per pint or quart	Multiply the "pounds per" by .45359.

1 gal. = 4 qt. = 16 c. = 128 fl. oz. ✦ 1 qt. = 2 pt. = 4 c. = 32 fl. oz. ✦ 1 pt. = 2 c. = 16 fl. oz. ✦
1 c. = 8 fl. oz. = 16 tbsp. ✦ 1 fl. oz. = 2 tbsp. ✦ 1 tbsp. = 3 tsp. ✦ 1 lb. = 16 oz.

15

STANDARD PORTION SIZES

This section lists Standard Serving Sizes frequently used by food service operators when plating foods. The chart shows an average size plus a range of sizes from small to large. This list is a guide but your portion sizes may differ because of various factors, so it is to be relied on as a good starting point but is by no means rigid.

Planning a menu or a particular menu item involves deciding how big a portion of food will be on the plate. Key food and production costs are determined by the quantity you serve.

VARIANCES

Factors that cause chefs and managers to use portion sizes other than those shown below are:

The age and gender of the guests:

+ Young adults are likely to require larger portions than seniors.
+ Males tend to have bigger appetites than females.

The activity level of the guests:

+ Athletes burn more fuel than sedentary diners, so may need larger portions.
  The time lapse between meals.
+ Guests at an afternoon reception may have skipped lunch and be hungrier.
+ A cocktail reception that is followed by a full meal dictates smaller portions.
+ Social and economic influences.
+ City dwellers may eat smaller portions than their "country cousins".
+ The affluent tend to eat smaller portions than the less affluent.

Pay attention . . . to the food that is left on the plates after clearing. When you see a pattern of large amounts of uneaten leftover foods, consider using smaller portions in the future . . . and also check the quality of the food to be sure it is palatable.

Finally, knowing your market, i.e., the eating customs of your clientele is the key in determining how large your portions should be. Serve your particular market!

Basic Sizes

Menu Item	Average Measure	Low Range	High Range
SOUP, SALAD, BREAD			
Soup	6 fl. oz.	4 fl. oz.	8 fl. oz.
Soup, entrée	10 fl. oz.	8 fl. oz.	12 fl. oz.
Salad Greens	3 oz.	2 oz.	5 oz.
Salad Dressing	1.5 fl. oz.	1 fl. oz.	3 fl. oz.
Bread	4 oz.	3 oz.	6 oz.
Bread Roll, 1.5 oz. each	2 each	1 each	3 each
Butter	1.5 oz.	1 oz.	2 oz.
BEEF ENTREES			
Filet Mignon	6 oz.	4 oz.	7 oz.
New York Steak	10 oz.	8 oz.	12 oz.
Prime Rib, boneless	10 oz.	8 oz.	12 oz.
Prime Rib, Large, boneless	16 oz.	14 oz.	18 oz.
Sirloin Steak	8 oz.	6 oz.	10 oz.
Falt Iron Steak	6 oz.	5 oz.	8 oz.
Culotte Steak	7 oz.	6 oz.	8 oz.
Tri-Tip Steak	7 oz.	6 oz.	8 oz.
Tri-Tip, Roasted, sliced	5 oz.	3 oz.	6 oz.
CHICKEN ENTREES			
Breast, Boneless, Skinless	6 oz.	4 oz.	8 oz.
Breast, Skin-on	7 oz.	5 oz.	9 oz.
Wings	6 each	4 each	7 each
Quarter	1/4th whole 3 lb. fryer	1/4th	1/4th
Half	1/2 whole 3 lb. fryer	half	half
SEAFOOD ENTREES			
Fish Filets	7 oz.	4 oz.	8 oz.
Fish Steaks	8 oz.	6 oz.	9 oz.
Shrimp,16-20	5 each	5 each	7 each

1 gal. = 4 qt. = 16 c. = 128 fl. oz. ✦ 1 qt. = 2 pt. = 4 c. = 32 fl. oz. ✦ 1 pt. = 2 c. = 16 fl. oz. ✦
1 c. = 8 fl. oz. = 16 tbsp. ✦ 1 fl. oz. = 2 tbsp. ✦ 1 tbsp. = 3 tsp. ✦ 1 lb. = 16 oz.

Basic Sizes (Continued)

Menu Item	Average Measure	Low Range	High Range
Scallops, Sea	5 oz.	4 oz.	6 oz.
Trout, whole, 8 oz.	1 each	1 each	1 each
Shellfish in shells	12 oz.	10 oz.	16 oz.
PORK ENTREES			
Chop, bone-on	7 oz.	5 oz.	9 oz.
Tenderloin Medallions	4 oz.	3 oz.	5 oz.
Roast Loin, sliced	5 oz.	4 oz.	7 oz.
Pulled Pork	6 oz.	5 oz.	7 oz.
Baby Back Ribs	10 oz.	8 oz.	12 oz.
St. Louis Style Ribs	12 oz.	10 oz.	16 oz.
Ham Steak	8 oz.	6 oz.	9 oz.
VEAL			
Loin Chops	8 oz.	7 oz.	9 oz.
Rib Chops, bone in	10 oz.	9 oz.	12 oz.
Scallopini (leg)	6 oz.	4 oz.	7 oz.
Entrée Sauces	2.5 fl. oz.	2 fl. oz.	3 fl. oz.
PASTA ENTRÉE			
Cooked Pasta	10 oz.	8 oz.	12 oz.
Pasta Sauce	5 fl. oz.	4 fl. oz.	6 fl. oz.
Vegetables	4 oz.	3 oz.	5 oz.
POTATOES			
Baker, 70 or 80 Count	1 each	1 each	1 each
Red Rose, Creamers	4 oz.	3 oz.	5 oz.
Mashed	6 oz.	4 oz.	8 oz.
Scalloped	6 oz.	4 oz.	8 oz.
Rices & Grains	5 oz.	3 oz.	7 oz.
DESSERTS			
Pie, 9 inch	1/8th pie, slice	1/10th pie	1/6th pie

Y% means yield percentage ✦ AS means as served (or used) ✦ AP means as purchased ✦ AS ÷ AP = Y% ✦
AS ÷ Y% = AP ✦ AP × Y% = AS ✦ Cost per AP unit ÷ Y% = Cost per servable unit

Basic Sizes (Continued)

Menu Item	Average Measure	Low Range	High Range
Cake, Sheet	2x3" piece	2x2" piece	3x3" piece
Cake, 8 inch, round	1/10th cake, slice	1/12th slice	1/8th slice
Ice Cream	6 fl. oz.	4 fl. oz.	8 fl. oz.
Pudding, Custard	6 fl. oz.	4 fl. oz.	8 fl. oz.
Pastries	1 each, 4 oz.	1 each, 2.5 oz.	1 each 6 oz.
Cookies. 1 ounce	3 each	2 each	4 each
BEVERAGES			
Water	20 fl. oz.	12 fl. oz.	32 fl. oz.
Iced tea	20 fl. oz.	12 fl. oz.	32 fl. oz.
Coffee	16 oz.	12 fl. oz.	24 fl. oz.
Hot Tea	1 bag, 2 C water	1 bag, 1 C water	1.5 bags, 3 C water
Wine	5 fl. Oz	4.5 fl. oz.	6 fl. oz.
Beer	12 fl. oz.	10 fl. oz.	16 fl. oz.
Cocktail	1.5 fl. oz. Alcohol + mix	1.25 fl. oz. Alc.	1.75 fl. oz. Alc.
Soft Drink	20 fl oz.	12 fl. oz.	32 fl. oz.
BREAKFAST ITEMS			
Bacon Strips	3 each	2 each	4 each
Sausage Links	3 each	2 each	4 each
Sausage Patties, 3 oz.	1 each	1 each	1 each
Ham Steak	5 oz.	3 oz.	6 oz.
Eggs, Large	2 each	1 each	3 each
Hash Browns	4 oz.	2 oz.	6 oz.
Country Fried Potatoes	5 oz.	4 oz.	7 oz.
Country Gravy	4 fl. oz.	3 fl. oz.	6 fl. oz.
Biscuits	2 each	2 each	3 each
Toast	2 slices	2 slices	3 slices
English Muffin	1 each, split	1 each	1 each
Butter pats, .5 oz.	2 each	1 each	4 each

1 gal. = 4 qt. = 16 c. = 128 fl. oz. ✦ 1 qt. = 2 pt. = 4 c. = 32 fl. oz. ✦ 1 pt. = 2 c. = 16 fl. oz. ✦
1 c. = 8 fl. oz. = 16 tbsp. ✦ 1 fl. oz. = 2 tbsp. ✦ 1 tbsp. = 3 tsp. ✦ 1 lb. = 16 oz.

Basic Sizes (Continued)

Menu Item	Average Measure	Low Range	High Range
Jam/Jelly P.C.	2 each	1 each	4 each
Juice	5 fl. oz.	4 fl. oz.	8 fl. oz.
Pancake Batter	6 fl. oz.	4 fl. oz.	10 fl. oz.
LUNCH ITEMS			
Sandwich Meats, fresh	4 oz.	3 oz.	6 oz.
Sandwich Meats, cured	2 oz.	1.5 oz.	3 oz.
Hamburger patty	4 oz.	3 oz.	8 oz.
Cheese, sliced	1 oz.	1/2 oz.	2 oz.
French Fries, 1/4"	4 oz.	3 oz.	6 oz.
French Fries, shoestring	4 oz.	3 oz.	6 oz.
Steak Fries	5 oz.	4 oz.	8 oz.
Potato Salad	3.5 oz.	3 oz.	6 oz.
Cole Slaw	3 oz.	2.5 oz.	5 oz.
Garden Salad	4 oz.	3.5 oz.	5 oz.
HORS D'OEUVRE ITEMS			
Crudites (raw veggies)	2 oz.	1 oz.	3 oz.
Olives	1.5 oz.	1 oz.	2 oz.
Cheeses	2 oz.	1 oz.	2.5 oz.
Cured Meats	2 oz.	1.5 oz.	3 oz.
Shrimp, 16-20	3 each	2 each	4 each
Fresh Fruit pieces	3 oz.	2 oz.	5 oz.
Dips and Spreads	2.5 fl. oz.	2 fl. oz.	3 fl. oz.
Salsa	3 fl. oz.	2 fl. oz.	4 fl. oz.
Chips, tortilla	1 oz.	1/2 oz.	1.5 oz.
Baguette Slices	3 slices	2 slices	5 slices

Y% means yield percentage ✦ AS means as served (or used) ✦ AP means as purchased ✦ AS ÷ AP = Y% ✦
AS ÷ Y% = AP ✦ AP × Y% = AS ✦ Cost per AP unit ÷ Y% = Cost per servable unit

PART II

Part II

THE WORKBOOK

The purpose of the Workbook is to help you learn food costing and purchasing in conjunction with Part I of *The Book of Yields*. Part I contains useful food measurement facts and formulas that can make this learning process easier and faster. Part II will help you understand the reasoning behind this process and how to do the math required to accurately and efficiently cost recipes and order the right amount of food.

HOW THE WORKBOOK IS ORGANIZED

The Workbook is divided into three sections:

1. Price Lists
2. Costing Worksheets
3. Purchasing Worksheets

PRICE LISTS

The first section contains fairly comprehensive lists of foods used in the food service industry in the United States. Included on these lists are the food name, its standard wholesale package size and price, and the measures of purchase units that you would typically use to order and receive products from a wholesale vendor. These purchase unit measures are a very important part of the price list, and of the entire workbook. The sequence of foods in the price lists is the same as that in the tables in Part I. (Note: The price lists contain food items beyond those covered in Part I, such as bottled condiments, bases, and frozen foods.) The prices and worksheets that follow are also used in a set of quizzes and exercises that your instructor may assign as homework, tests, or classroom drills.

COSTING WORKSHEETS

The Costing Worksheets contain a set of cost-breakdown worksheets. The object of these worksheets is to step you through the process of costing out an ingredient's recipe unit measure and an entire recipe. Therefore, included in this section is a recipe-costing worksheet–that is, Recipe Card for Costing, number 16.

The Recipe Card worksheet (Costing Worksheet 16) follows a standard format, making it easy for you to follow which columns to multiply in order to extend an ingredient's unit cost to a total cost for that ingredient. At the bottom of the worksheet are a variety of yield measurements by which the total amount produced from the recipe can be measured. This simple format makes it possible to determine the cost(s) of any yield measure(s).

The other costing worksheets are designed to be used with specific foods or types of foods. For instance, there is a worksheet for dry herbs and spices, another for items you trim and then use by volume measures, one for poultry, another for going from a dry good bought by weight but used by volume, and many others.

Before you begin using the worksheets, it's a good idea to take some time to familiarize yourself with them. As you do, notice that each one follows the same logical approach to doing a cost breakdown. Each starts with the food item in an as-purchased (AP) amount—that is, the purchase unit. It then instructs you to get the cost of the purchase unit from the price list and enter it on the worksheet. From that point you complete the cost breakdown following the instructions on the right-hand side of the worksheet. Each line on every costing worksheet gives a precise instruction regarding where to get the information you need or how to do the math in that step.

At a certain point in the worksheets it is often necessary to "plug in" a measure from a table in Part I, in order to complete the costing process. This is usually a trim yield percentage, a weight-to-volume equivalent, or a cooking yield. This is a critical step, as it shows you exactly where, when, and how to use the tables in Part I. For instance, say your recipe calls for 5 tablespoons of dry, whole-leaf basil. The top of the Dry Herbs and Spices costing worksheet first shows you how to calculate the cost of 1 ounce of basil. From the Dry Herbs and Spices table, you find the number of tablespoons of basil in 1 ounce and write that number on the worksheet, then follow the instruction to divide the ounce cost by that number in order to get the cost per tablespoon. Then you can enter the dry herb or spice cost for that recipe unit (tablespoon) cost on any recipe card.

Here, step by step, is how to use the costing worksheets:

1. Start with a list of ingredients on a recipe card.
2. Select the appropriate worksheet for the food type and enter the food name at the top.
3. Refer to the price list for the purchase unit and price.
4. Enter the price and pack information on the worksheet.
5. Break down the food measures and costs following the step-by-step instructions on the worksheet.
6. Plug in the conversion or yield amount from the Part I tables, where necessary.
7. Complete the worksheet, at which point you will have arrived at the cost of the recipe unit measure.
8. Enter the recipe unit measure on the recipe card.
9. Complete this process for all ingredients and add up the Unit Cost column on the recipe card. This will be your total recipe cost.
10. Enter the recipe yield information you want to use on the recipe card (e.g., 20 portions, 2 gallons, 12 loaves, etc.).
11. Using simple division (as noted on the recipe card), calculate the cost per yield unit of measure.

1 gal. = 4 qt. = 16 c. = 128 fl. oz. ✦ 1 qt. = 2 pt. = 4 c. = 32 fl. oz. ✦ 1 pt. = 2 c. = 16 fl. oz. ✦
1 c. = 8 fl. oz. = 16 tbsp. ✦ 1 fl. oz. = 2 tbsp. ✦ 1 tbsp. = 3 tsp. ✦ 1 lb. = 16 oz.

The costing worksheets make it easier to use the data and formulas given in Part I. Moreover, they can really speed up the process of learning recipe costing, for two important reasons:

1. They organize the process, showing you how to logically go from a purchase unit to a recipe unit.
2. They show you how to do the math.

PURCHASING WORKSHEETS

The Purchasing Worksheets contain both worksheets and forms to help you figure out how much of a given food to buy so that you can supply all the recipes you might use for a particular banquet, special event, or period of time. In short, the worksheets show you how to convert recipe units back to purchase units.

Because the purchasing process is a little more complicated than the costing process, the Purchasing section begins with an overview that explains the procedure in detail. Briefly, during the purchasing process, take these steps:

1. Combine all the same ingredients from your recipes.
2. Convert the needed number of recipe unit measures (tablespoons, ounces, piece counts, portions, etc.) to an equivalent number of purchase unit measures (pounds, gallons, etc.).
3. Convert those measures to actual purchase unit packs—the as-purchased (AP) units, such as cases, tubs, containers, bags, and so on.

Along the way, you will be able to compare the purchase unit measure amounts that you need for a production plan against your current inventory and par stock levels. You'll finish by filling out a Food Order Form, provided as Purchasing Worksheet 20. The purchasing worksheets (like the costing worksheets) are intended to be used with specific types of foods, which are clearly identified. The formulas that enable you to convert a recipe unit back to a purchase unit are on each worksheet. (These formulas, along with examples of how to use them, are found in the purchasing sections in the chapters in Part I.)

Each purchasing conversion worksheet states the formula for that food or type of food and gives the instruction for filling in a short series of boxes that lead you to the answer. The mathematical operators ($\div$, $\times$, $-$, $+$, or $=$) are supplied between the boxes on each line. This makes it very easy to follow the formula. Here is a list of the worksheets and forms you will be using in the purchasing process, in the order you'll be using them, where CW stands for *Costing Worksheet* and PW stands for *Purchasing Worksheet*.

1. Recipe Card for Costing (CW 16)
2. Ingredient Aggregating Form (PW 14)
3. Recipe Unit Measures to Purchase Unit Measures Conversion worksheets (PW 1–13)
   3a. Purchase Unit Measures (PW 15)
4. Amounts Needed versus Par (PW 16)
   4a. Inventory Form (PW 17)
   4b. Food Weight Log (PW 18)

NOTE

You do not need prices to complete the purchasing worksheets. The purchase unit prices are only used in the final step of filling out the Food Order Form (Purchasing Worksheet 20).

NOTE

Flavor Bases (Purchasing Worksheet 13) is different from the others in that it does not rely on the yields and equivalents in Part I to complete. Part I does not address these products because their yields are specific to the brand of flavor base being used, and the yield data are always provided on the product container. The worksheet explains all this completely to enable you to determine how much to buy or cost out—just like the other conversion worksheets.

Y% means yield percentage ✦ AS means as served (or used) ✦ AP means as purchased ✦ AS ÷ AP = Y% ✦
AS ÷ Y% = AP ✦ AP × Y% = AS ✦ Cost per AP unit ÷ Y% = Cost per servable unit

5. Purchase Unit Measures to Purchase Unit Packs (PW 19)
6. Food Order Form (PW 20)

You may not need the subordinate forms (labeled "a" or "b") in all situations; they are optional. However, they do complete the process and, as such, will help you to understand the entire purchasing process more fully.

Purchasing Worksheet 21, Trimmed versus Untrimmed, addresses the problem of determining the price point at which the food cost of a pretrimmed food is lower than the cost of buying the same food in a raw, untrimmed state. A form for completing this calculation is provided at the end of that worksheet. It will help you understand the concept and will come in handy when your job requires you to choose between buying a pretrimmed and an untrimmed food.

PRICE LISTS

1
Dry Herbs and Spices

Item	Purchase Unit	Pack	Purchase Unit Cost
Allspice	Container	16 oz.	$20.74
Anise, Star	Jar	6 oz.	$19.60
Anise Seed	Container	12 oz.	$22.30
Basil, ground	Container	12 oz.	$13.50
Basil, whole leaf	Container	30 oz.	$26.03
Bay Leaf, whole	Container	8 oz.	$14.08
Bay Leaf, ground	Container	14 oz.	$21.43
Caraway Seed, whole	Container	16 oz.	$21.20
Cardamom, ground	Case	6 ea.: 16 oz. container	$236.85
Cardamom, whole	Case	6 ea.: 8 oz. container	$61.50
Cayenne, ground	Container	18 oz.	$21.20
Celery Salt	Container	30 oz.	$6.83
Celery Seed	Container	16 oz.	$9.22
Chervil, whole leaf	Container	4 oz.	$23.85
Chile Flakes, Chipotle	Box	10 lb.	$72.40
Chile Flakes, crushed	Container	12 oz.	$8.69
Chile Pods, dry—various	Pound	16 oz.	$16.75
Chile Pods, Habanero	Pound	16 oz.	$43.00
Chile Powder, Ancho	Container	160 oz.	$67.75
Chile Powder, Chipotle	Container	160 oz.	$69.90
Chile Powder, Habanero	Container	160 oz.	$170.85
Chile Powder, Red	Container	18 oz.	$8.47
Chinese 5 Spice	Container	16 oz.	$28.75
Chives, Dry	Case	12 ea.: 1 oz. cans	$38.10
Cinnamon, ground	Container	16 oz.	$22.23
Cinnamon Sticks, 4"	Container	8 oz.	$11.71
Cloves, ground	Container	16 oz.	$24.12
Cloves, whole	Container	14 oz.	$26.30

1 gal. = 4 qt. = 16 c. = 128 fl. oz. ✦ 1 qt. = 2 pt. = 4 c. = 32 fl. oz. ✦ 1 pt. = 2 c. = 16 fl. oz. ✦
1 c. = 8 fl. oz. = 16 tbsp. ✦ 1 fl. oz. = 2 tbsp. ✦ 1 tbsp. = 3 tsp. ✦ 1 lb. = 16 oz.

Dry Herbs and Spices (Continued)

Item	Purchase Unit	Pack	Purchase Unit Cost
Coriander, ground	Container	12 oz.	$9.75
Cream of Tartar	Container	25 oz.	$15.98
Cumin, ground	Container	4.5 lb.	$25.87
Curry Powder	Container	16 oz.	$10.98
Dill Weed	Container	5 oz.	$11.18
Epazote, ground	Container	12 oz.	$18.75
Fennel Seed	Container	14 oz.	$12.03
Fenugreek Seed	Container	240 oz.	$40.15
Garlic, granulated	Container	26 oz.	$10.95
Garlic, powdered	Container	21 oz.	$8.64
Garlic Salt	Container	40 oz.	$8.41
Ginger, ground	Container	16 oz.	$16.29
Gumbo Filé Powder	Case	6 ea.: 12 oz. jars	$66.08
Hibiscus Flowers	Bag	3 oz.	$11.19
Lemon Pepper	Container	28 oz.	$10.82
Mace, ground	Container	16 oz.	$39.34
Marjoram, whole leaf	Container	20 oz.	$34.40
Mustard, ground	Container	16 oz.	$6.58
Mustard Seed, whole	Case	6 ea.: 24 oz. containers	$76.15
Nutmeg, ground	Container	16 oz.	$15.93
Onion, Chopped, dehydrated	Box	3 lb.	$10.03
Onion, granulated	Container	10 oz.	$3.60
Onion, powdered	Container	20 oz.	$6.52
Oregano, ground	Container	13 oz.	$11.02
Oregano, whole leaf	Container	24 oz.	$24.01
Paprika, ground	Container	16 oz.	$5.55
Parsley Flakes	Container	10 oz.	$11.90
Pepper, Black, cracked	Container	16 oz.	$11.15

Y% means yield percentage ✦ AS means as served (or used) ✦ AP means as purchased ✦ AS ÷ AP = Y% ✦
AS ÷ Y% = AP ✦ AP × Y% = AS ✦ Cost per AP unit ÷ Y% = Cost per servable unit

Dry Herbs and Spices (Continued)

Item	Purchase Unit	Pack	Purchase Unit Cost
Pepper, Black, coarse grind	Container	16 oz.	$12.09
Pepper, Black, table grind	Container	16 oz.	$11.15
Pepper, Black, whole	Container	18 oz.	$12.68
Pepper Corns, green	Container	6 oz.	$2.52
Pepper, White, ground	Container	18 oz.	$18.53
Pickling Spice, whole	Container	13 oz.	$9.04
Poppy Seed, whole	Container	20 oz.	$8.72
Poultry Seasoning	Container	16 oz.	$22.00
Pumpkin Pie Spice Mix	Container	18 oz.	$21.60
Rosemary, ground	Container	11 oz.	$14.93
Rosemary, whole	Container	6 oz.	$9.04
Saffron, whole	Container	1 oz.	$139.35
Sage, rubbed	Container	6 oz.	$11.22
Salt, Kosher Flake	Case	12 ea.: 48 oz. boxes	$18.07
Salt, Regular	Bag	25 lb.	$5.06
Salt, Sea	Case	6 ea.: 35 oz. containers	$47.60
Salt, Sea, Red Hawaiian	Container	4 oz.	$12.67
Salt, Seasoning (Lawry's)	Case	4 ea.: 5 lb. boxes	$54.95
Sesame Seed	Container	18 oz.	$7.55
Tarragon, leaf	Container	3.5 oz.	$11.55
Thyme, ground	Container	11 oz.	$12.03
Thyme, whole leaf	Container	6 oz.	$8.49
Turmeric, ground	Container	18 oz.	$19.55
Wasabi Powder	Case	6 ea.: 14 oz.	$68.13

1 gal. = 4 qt. = 16 c. = 128 fl. oz. ✦ 1 qt. = 2 pt. = 4 c. = 32 fl. oz. ✦ 1 pt. = 2 c. = 16 fl. oz. ✦
1 c. = 8 fl. oz. = 16 tbsp. ✦ 1 fl. oz. = 2 tbsp. ✦ 1 tbsp. = 3 tsp. ✦ 1 lb. = 16 oz.

2
Fresh Herbs

Item	Purchase Unit	Pack	Purchase Unit Cost
Arugula	Box (4 lb.)	Loose	21.00
Basil	Box (1 lb.)	12 count	$12.84
Chervil	Bag	6 count	$10.68
Chives	Bag	6 oz.	$11.65
Cilantro	Bag	16 oz.	$4.28
Dill Weed	Bag	6 bunches	$12.35
Marjoram	Bag	6 bunches	$11.70
Mint	Bag	6 bunches	$12.95
Oregano	Bag	6 bunches	$11.50
Parsley, curly	Bag	6 count, 3.5 oz. ea.	$9.10
Parsley, Italian (flat leaf)	Bag	6 bunches	$9.65
Rosemary	Bag	6 bunches	$11.90
Sage	Bag	6 bunches	$11.40
Tarragon	Bag	6 oz.	$12.55
Thyme	Bunch	2 oz.	$3.76
Watercress	Bag	12 bunches	$22.40

Y% means yield percentage ✦ AS means as served (or used) ✦ AP means as purchased ✦ AS ÷ AP = Y% ✦
AS ÷ Y% = AP ✦ AP × Y% = AS ✦ Cost per AP unit ÷ Y% = Cost per servable unit

3
Vegetables

Item	Purchase Unit	Pack	Purchase Unit Cost
Alfalfa Sprouts	Bag	1 lb.	$4.05
Artichoke Hearts, quartered, marinated	Case	6 ea.: 3 kilo cans	$88.90
Artichoke Hearts, quartered	Case	6 ea.: 3 kilo cans	$76.25
Artichokes, 18 count	Case	18 ea.	Seasonal $18–$48/case
Artichokes, 36 count	Case	26 ea.	Seasonal $18–$48/case
Arugula	Box	4 lb.	$20.40
Asparagus: jumbo, standard, thin	Case	15 lb.	Seasonal $25–$45/case
Avocados, Haas	Case	48 count	Seasonal $40–$85/case
Bean Sprouts	Box	2 ea.: 5 lb. bags	$6.56
Beans, Green	Case	25 lb.	$55.20
Broccolini	Box	18 count	$32.05
Broccoli Crowns	Case	20 lb.	$24.20
Broccoli Florets	Case	4 ea.: 3 lb. bags	$27.50
Broccoli, whole	Case	30 lb: 20 bunches	$22.45
Cabbage, Green	Bag	3 ea.: 40 oz. heads	$9.95
Cabbage, Napa	Case	30 lb.	$18.90
Cabbage, Red	Bag	3 ea.: 40 oz. heads	$11.65
Carrots, Baby	Bag	20 lb.	$22.75
Carrots, table, medium	Bag	25 lb.	$14.05
Cauliflower, florets	Box	2 ea.: 3 lb. bags	$20.40
Cauliflower, whole	Bag	9 ea.: 30 oz. heads	$29.45
Celery, diced 1/2 in.	Box	4 ea.: 5 lb. bags	$35.25
Celery, whole	Bag	3 ea.: 2 lb. heads	$10.00
Chile Pepper, Serrano	Bag	10 lb.	$17.65
Chile Peppers, Anaheim	Bag	10 lb.	$20.15
Chile Peppers, Chipotle in Adobo	Case	12 ea.: 7 oz. jars	$23.65
Chile Peppers, Chipotle Morita	Bag	1 lb.	$21.55
Chile Peppers, Guajillo	Bag	1 lb.	$19.50

1 gal. = 4 qt. = 16 c. = 128 fl. oz. ✦ 1 qt. = 2 pt. = 4 c. = 32 fl. oz. ✦ 1 pt. = 2 c. = 16 fl. oz. ✦
1 c. = 8 fl. oz. = 16 tbsp. ✦ 1 fl. oz. = 2 tbsp. ✦ 1 tbsp. = 3 tsp. ✦ 1 lb. = 16 oz.

Vegetables (Continued)

Item	Purchase Unit	Pack	Purchase Unit Cost
Chile Peppers, Jalapeno	Bag	10 lb.	$21.15
Chile Peppers, Japones	Bag	1 lb.	$18.45
Chile Peppers, Pasilla/Poblano	Bag	10 lb.	$22.15
Chile Peppers, Pequin	Bag	1 lb.	$31.90
Chile, Dry Cascabel	Box	10 lb.	$85.34
Chile, Dry, Chipotle Morita	Box	10 lb.	$67.65
Chile, Dry, Guajillo	Box	10 lb	$68.65
Chile, Dry, Japones	Box	10 lb	$39.70
Chile, Dry, Pasilla	Box	25 lb.	$134.83
Chile, Dry, Pequin	Box	2 ea.: 1 lb. bags	$46.02
Cucumber	Bag	6 count: 10 oz. ea.	$5.95
Eggplant	Bag	6 count: 19 oz. ea.	$16.25
Garlic Paste	Case	12 ea.: 3.15 oz. tubes	$84.60
Garlic, chopped	Tub	5 lb.	$14.83
Garlic, peeled	Case	4 ea.: 5 lb. tubs	$47.16
Garlic, whole	Box	5 lb.	$19.40
Grape Leaves in Brine	Case	12 ea.: 16 oz. jars	$122.45
Hoyas (Corn Husks)	Bag	1.5 lb.	$35.95
Kale, Flowering	Case	24 count: 12 oz. ea.	$28.75
Kale, Green	Case	24 count: 20 oz. ea.	$17.40
Leeks	Case	12 count	$29.55
Lettuce, Green Leaf	Case	24 heads	$21.00
Lettuce, Iceberg, natural	Case	24 heads	$25.45
Lettuce, Red Leaf	Case	24 heads	$21.50
Lettuce, Romaine	Case	24 heads	$21.70
Mushrooms, Button	Box	10 lb.	$22.60
Mushrooms, Crimini	Box	10 lb.	$25.85
Mushrooms, Dried, Chanterelle	Bag	1 lb.	$65.55

Y% means yield percentage ✦ AS means as served (or used) ✦ AP means as purchased ✦ AS ÷ AP = Y% ✦
AS ÷ Y% = AP ✦ AP × Y% = AS ✦ Cost per AP unit ÷ Y% = Cost per servable unit

Vegetables (Continued)

Item	Purchase Unit	Pack	Purchase Unit Cost
Mushrooms, Dried, Morels	Box	1 lb.	$228.90
Mushrooms, medium	Box	10 lb.	$20.70
Mushrooms, Morels, dried	Box	2 ea.: 1 lb. bags	$702.67
Mushrooms, Oyster	Box	5 lb.	$25.85
Mushrooms, Oyster, dried	Box	5 lb.	$124.75
Mushrooms, Porcini, dried	Box	1 lb.	$36.02
Mushrooms, Portobello	Box	5 lb.	$24.30
Mushrooms, Shiitake	Box	5 lb.	$25.50
Mushrooms, sliced	Box	10 lb.	$20.80
Mushrooms, White, premium	Box	10 lb.	$26.95
Okra	Box	12 lb.	$12.80
Olive Tapenade	Jar	1 gallon	$69.90
Olive, Kalamata, pitted	Container	4.4 lb.	$34.56
Olives, Kalamata, in brine	Case	12 ea.: 8 oz. jars	$68.60
Onions, Cocktail	Case	12 ea.: 32 oz. jars	$34.13
Onions, Dehydrated, chopped	Box	15 lb.	$56.40
Onions, Green	Box	2 lb., 4 oz. per bunch	$5.12
Onions, Red, Jumbo	Bag	5 lb.	$9.05
Onions, Yellow, medium	Bag	50 lb.	$15.50
Peas, Snow	Bag	10 lb.	$48.10
Peas, Sugar Snap	Box	10 lb.	$50.10
Peppers, Green Bell	Box	25 lb.	$25.10
Peppers, Red Bell	Bag	25 lb.	$30.60
Peppers, Yellow Bell	Bag	5 lb.	$28.90
Potato Pearls (instant) 600 Svg/Cse	Case	12 ea.: 28 oz. bag	$62.00
Potato, Red Creamer (1.25" diam.)	Box	50 lb.	$59.75
Potato, Red, #2	Case	50 lb.	$20.55
Potato, Russet (Baker) 70 ct.	Case	50 lb.	$27.20

1 gal. = 4 qt. = 16 c. = 128 fl. oz. ✦ 1 qt. = 2 pt. = 4 c. = 32 fl. oz. ✦ 1 pt. = 2 c. = 16 fl. oz. ✦
1 c. = 8 fl. oz. = 16 tbsp. ✦ 1 fl. oz. = 2 tbsp. ✦ 1 tbsp. = 3 tsp. ✦ 1 lb. = 16 oz.

Vegetables (Continued)

Item	Purchase Unit	Pack	Purchase Unit Cost
Radishes, Red	Bag	5 lb.	$16.60
Shallots, peeled, fresh	Box	4 lb.	$13.68
Shallots, whole	Box	5 lb.	$8.50
Spinach, baby	Bag	4 lb.	$18.60
Spinach, clipped	Box	4 ea.: 2.5 lb. bags	$21.30
Spinach, untrimmed	Box	20 lb.	$26.00
Squash, Banana	Box	30 lb.	$27.60
Squash, Yellow, fancy	Box	25 lb.	$28.35
Squash, Zucchini, medium	Box	20 lb.	$20.35
Tomatillo	Case	10 lb.	$24.95
Tomato, 5 × 6, two-layer (60 ct.)	Lug	20 lb.	$25.45
Tomato, Cherry	Flat	12 pt.	$22.10
Tomato, Grape	Flat	10 lb.	$20.45
Tomato, Roma	Flat	25 lb.	$26.10

Y% means yield percentage ✦ AS means as served (or used) ✦ AP means as purchased ✦ AS ÷ AP = Y% ✦
AS ÷ Y% = AP ✦ AP × Y% = AS ✦ Cost per AP unit ÷ Y% = Cost per servable unit

4
Fruit

Item	Purchase Unit	Pack	Purchase Unit Price
Apples, Fuji, 88 count	Case	40 lb.	$34.95
Apples, Granny Smith, 88 count	Case	40 lb.	$37.60
Apples, Red Delicious, 88 count	Case	40 lb.	$26.80
Apricots, dry	Box	5 lb.	$34.90
Banana Chips	Bag	5 lb.	$21.70
Bananas, 150 count	Case	40 lb.	$28.70
Blackberries, IQF*	Box	10 lb.	$23.95
Blueberries, IQF*	Box	30 lb.	$82.70
Boysenberries, IQF*	Box	10 lb.	$26.95
Currants, Zante	Box	5 lb.	$45.85
Dates, California, pitted	Box	5 lb.	$26.10
Dates, Medjool, whole	Box	5 lb.	$62.10
Figs, Calimyrna, dried	Box	5 lb.	$46.05
Figs, Black, Mission	Box	5 lb.	$27.45
Grapefruit, Ruby	Case	40 count	$22.55
Grapes, Green, seedless	Flat	16–21 lb.	$33.35
Grapes, Red, seedless	Flat	16–21 lb.	$28.95
Kiwifruit	Flat	36 count	$17.90
Lemons, 115 count	Box	40 lb.	$20.20
Lemons, 165 count	Box	40 lb.	$24.55
Limes, 200 count size	Bag	5 lb.	$13.75
Melon, Cantaloupe, whole	Box	3 ea.	$12.85
Melon, Cantaloupe, diced, 3/4 in.	Pail	20 lb.	$53.64
Melon, Watermelon	Varies	Varies	Seasonal: Hi: $.50/lb.
Melons, Musk varieties	Varies	Varies	Seasonal: Avg: $4 ea.
Nectarines	Lug	64 count, 25 lb.	Seasonal $17.25

1 gal. = 4 qt. = 16 c. = 128 fl. oz. ✦ 1 qt. = 2 pt. = 4 c. = 32 fl. oz. ✦ 1 pt. = 2 c. = 16 fl. oz. ✦
1 c. = 8 fl. oz. = 16 tbsp. ✦ 1 fl. oz. = 2 tbsp. ✦ 1 tbsp. = 3 tsp. ✦ 1 lb. = 16 oz.

Fruit (Continued)

Item	Purchase Unit	Pack	Purchase Unit Price
Oranges, 88 count	Case	40 lb.	$22.00
Papaya, Hawaiian	Case	10 lb./9–12 count	$24.25
Peaches	Lug	64 count, 25 lb.	Seasonal: $17.75
Pears, Asian	Flat	14 count	$29.65
Pears, d'Anjou, 135 count	Case	44 lb.	$27.55
Pears, Red	Flat	20 lb.	$27.10
Pineapple	Box	8 count	$27.85
Raisins, Dark	Box	30 lb.	$48.65
Raisins, Light	Box	5 lb.	$18.40
Raspberries, IQF*	Box	10 lb.	$45.80
Strawberries	Flat	12 pt. seasonal	$18.95

*IQF: individually quick frozen

Y% means yield percentage ✦ AS means as served (or used) ✦ AP means as purchased ✦ AS ÷ AP = Y% ✦
AS ÷ Y% = AP ✦ AP × Y% = AS ✦ Cost per AP unit ÷ Y% = Cost per servable unit

5
Number-10 Cans

Item	Pack	Price
Apple Pie Filling	Case: 6 ea. #10 cans	$56.65
Applesauce, fancy	Case: 6 ea. #10 cans	$33.45
Apples, sliced in water	Case: 6 ea. #10 cans	$40.30
Apricot Halves, in juice	Case: 6 ea. #10 cans	$39.15
Apricot Preserves	Case: 6 ea. #10 cans	$65.28
Apricots, diced in light syrup	Case: 6 ea. #10 cans	$39.15
Beans, Baked, fancy	Case: 6 ea. #10 cans	$32.61
Beans, Blue Lake, fancy	Case: 6 ea. #10 cans	$26.75
Beans, Garbanzo	Case: 6 ea. #10 cans	$26.60
Beans, Green	Case: 6 ea. #10 cans	$28.35
Beans, Green, Italian	Case: 6 ea. #10 cans	$30.45
Beans, Kidney	Case: 6 ea. #10 cans	$31.05
Beans, Pinto	Case: 6 ea. #10 cans	$24.85
Beets, Diced	Case: 6 ea. #10 cans	$27.40
Beets, Julienne	Case: 6 ea. #10 cans	$29.85
Beets, Sliced	Case: 6 ea. #10 cans	$28.80
Carrots, Diced	Case: 6 ea. #10 cans	$27.90
Carrots, Sliced	Case: 6 ea. #10 cans	$26.90
Chili con Carne with Beans	Case: 6 ea. #10 cans	$62.40
Corn Niblets	Case: 6 ea. #10 cans	$29.45
Fruit Cocktail	Case: 6 ea. #10 cans	$39.40
Fruit for Salad	Case: 6 ea. #10 cans	$40.10
Hominy, White	Case: 6 ea. #10 cans	$17.95
Menudo Stew	Case: 6 ea. #10 cans	$70.10
Mushroom Pieces and Stems	Case: 6 ea. #10 cans	$47.05
Nopalitos (Cactus leaf pads)	Case: 6 ea. #10 cans	$37.80
Olives, Ripe Pitted, jumbo	Case: 6 ea. #10 cans	$69.80
Olives, Ripe Pitted, medium	Case: 6 ea. #10 cans	$67.50

1 gal. = 4 qt. = 16 c. = 128 fl. oz. ✦ 1 qt. = 2 pt. = 4 c. = 32 fl. oz. ✦ 1 pt. = 2 c. = 16 fl. oz. ✦
1 c. = 8 fl. oz. = 16 tbsp. ✦ 1 fl. oz. = 2 tbsp. ✦ 1 tbsp. = 3 tsp. ✦ 1 lb. = 16 oz.

Number-10 Cans (Continued)

Item	Pack	Price
Olives, Ripe, sliced	Case: 6 ea. #10 cans	$51.75
Olives, Ripe, wedged	Case: 6 ea. #10 cans	$59.90
Peaches, Diced in Light Syrup	Case: 6 ea. #10 cans	$34.65
Peaches, halves in juice, 30–35 count	Case: 6 ea. #10 cans	$34.40
Peaches, julienned in light syrup	Case: 6 ea. #10 cans	$36.75
Peaches, sliced in light syrup	Case: 6 ea. #10 cans	$35.85
Pear Halves, in juice	Case: 6 ea. #10 cans	$41.30
Pears, diced in light syrup	Case: 6 ea. #10 cans	$41.80
Pears, sliced in juice	Case: 6 ea. #10 cans	$45.65
Pears, sliced in syrup	Case: 6 ea. #10 cans	$38.50
Peas, Sweet	Case: 6 ea. #10 cans	$31.40
Peppers, Green Chile, diced	Case: 6 ea. #10 cans	$66.90
Peppers, Green Chile, strips	Case: 6 ea. #10 cans	$40.10
Peppers, Green Chile, whole	Case: 6 ea. #10 cans	$68.60
Peppers, Jalapeno, sliced	Case: 6 ea. #10 cans	$46.10
Peppers, Jalapeno, whole	Case: 6 ea. #10 cans	$41.90
Pineapple Chunks	Case: 6 ea. #10 cans	$41.75
Pineapple Tidbits	Case: 6 ea. #10 cans	$32.20
Pineapple, Crushed	Case: 6 ea. #10 cans	$42.05
Pineapple, sliced, 66 count	Case: 6 ea. #10 cans	$40.10
Plums, halves	Case: 6 ea. #10 cans	$36.20
Potatoes, White, whole, 120–150 count	Case: 6 ea. #10 cans	$36.50
Prunes, pitted in juice, 190–220 count	Case: 6 ea. #10 cans	$104.60
Sauerkraut	Case: 6 ea. #10 cans	$29.85
Spinach	Case: 6 ea. #10 cans	$32.90
Tomatillos, crushed	Case: 6 ea. #10 cans	$49.40
Tomato Paste, 26%	Case: 6 ea. #10 cans	$32.35
Tomato Purée	Case: 6 ea. #10 cans	$25.00

Y% means yield percentage ✦ AS means as served (or used) ✦ AP means as purchased ✦ AS ÷ AP = Y% ✦
AS ÷ Y% = AP ✦ AP × Y% = AS ✦ Cost per AP unit ÷ Y% = Cost per servable unit

Number-10 Cans (Continued)

Item	Pack	Price
Tomato Sauce	Case: 6 ea. #10 cans	$24.19
Tomatoes, crushed	Case: 6 ea. #10 cans	$21.30
Tomatoes, diced	Case: 6 ea. #10 cans	$20.25
Tomatoes, whole	Case: 6 ea. #10 cans	$25.95
Yams, cut	Case: 6 ea. #10 cans	$41.65
Yams, whole, 30–40 count	Case: 6 ea. #10 cans	$45.65

1 gal. = 4 qt. = 16 c. = 128 fl. oz. ✦ 1 qt. = 2 pt. = 4 c. = 32 fl. oz. ✦ 1 pt. = 2 c. = 16 fl. oz. ✦
1 c. = 8 fl. oz. = 16 tbsp. ✦ 1 fl. oz. = 2 tbsp. ✦ 1 tbsp. = 3 tsp. ✦ 1 lb. = 16 oz.

6
Starches

Starchy Items	Purchase Unit	Pack	Purchase Unit Price
LEGUMES, DRY			
Adzuki Beans	Box	10 lb.	$41.55
Anasazi Beans	Box	10 lb.	$38.10
Black Turtle Beans	Box	20 lb.	$27.95
Cannellini Beans, Organic	Box	10 lb.	$47.75
Cranberry Beans	Box	10 lb.	$38.60
Fava Beans	Box	10 lb.	$38.35
Flageolet Beans	Box	10 lb.	$38.50
Great Northern Beans	Box	20 lb.	$28.50
Kidney Beans	Box	20 lb.	$33.20
Lima Beans	Box	20 lb.	$32.30
Lentils, imported, fancy	Box	10 lb.	$47.25
Lentils, Standard	Box	20 lb.	$25.10
Mung Beans	Box	10 lb.	$40.10
Navy Beans	Box	10 lb.	$46.30
Red Beans, small	Box	10 lb.	$51.30
Small White Beans	Box	20 lb.	$31.95
Split Peas	Box	20 lb.	$23.20
RICE, GRAIN			
Arborio Rice, U.S. Domestic	Bag	10 lb.	$26.25
Arborio, Imported	Bag	22.2 lb.	$40.30
Barley, Pearled	Box	20 lb.	$8.47
Basmati Rice	Box	10 lb.	$25.65
Bulgur Wheat, fine	Box	10 lb.	$28.41
Cous Cous	Box	10 lb.	$18.41
Hominy Grits, quick	Case	12 ea.: 24 oz. boxes	$22.65
Long Grain Parboiled White Rice	Box	25 lb.	$28.45
Long Grain White Rice	Box	50 lb.	$39.35

Y% means yield percentage ✦ AS means as served (or used) ✦ AP means as purchased ✦ AS ÷ AP = Y% ✦
AS ÷ Y% = AP ✦ AP × Y% = AS ✦ Cost per AP unit ÷ Y% = Cost per servable unit

Starches (Continued)

Starchy Items	Purchase Unit	Pack	Purchase Unit Price
Medium Grain White Rice	Bag	50 lb.	$49.35
Oatmeal, quick	Case	12 ea.: 42 oz. boxes	$32.25
Uncle Ben's Brown Rice	Bag	25 lb.	$37.45
Uncle Ben's Converted L.G. White Rice	Bag	25 lb.	$31.35
Uncle Ben's Short-Grain Rice	Box	10 lb.	$48.00
Wild Rice, broken	Box	10 lb.	$85.75
PASTA			
Angel Hair	Case	4 ea.: 5 lb.	$24.50
Bow Ties	Case	2 ea.: 5 lb.	$18.60
Cappellini, 10-in.	Case	20 lb.	$16.10
Egg Noodles, wide	Case	2 ea.: 5 lb.	$13.70
Fettuccini, 10-in.	Box	20 lb.	$24.10
Fettuccini, 20-in.	Box	20 lb.	$24.95
Lasagna, ridged, 20-in.	Box	10 lb.	$15.90
Linguini, 10-inch	Box	20 lb.	$21.80
Macaroni, Elbow	Case	2 ea.: 10 lb.	$21.05
Manicotti	Box	2 lb.	$12.05
Orzo	Case	2 ea.: 10 lb.	$24.50
Penne, natural color	Case	2 ea.: 10 lb.	$23.95
Penne, tri-color	Case	2 ea.: 10 lb.	$27.25
Rigatoni, 2 × 2-inch	Case	2 ea.: 5 lb.	$13.25
Rotini, Garden, (tri-color)	Case	2 ea.: 10 lb.	$28.00
Shells, medium	Case	2 ea.: 10 lb.	$21.65
Shells, small	Case	2 ea.: 10 lb.	$24.40
Spaghetti (1.8 mm)	Case	2 ea.: 10 lb.	$23.00
Tortellini, Cheese-filled, frozen	Case	3 ea.: 4 lb. packs	$48.65
Tortellini-Cheese-filled, frozen, tri-color	Case	3 ea.: 4 lb. packs	$50.95
Vermicelli (1.6 mm), 10-in.	Case	2 ea.: 10 lb.	$23.75
Ziti	Case	2 ea.: 10 lb.	$21.20

1 gal. = 4 qt. = 16 c. = 128 fl. oz. ✦ 1 qt. = 2 pt. = 4 c. = 32 fl. oz. ✦ 1 pt. = 2 c. = 16 fl. oz. ✦
1 c. = 8 fl. oz. = 16 tbsp. ✦ 1 fl. oz. = 2 tbsp. ✦ 1 tbsp. = 3 tsp. ✦ 1 lb. = 16 oz.

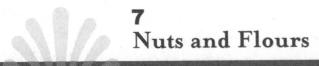

7
Nuts and Flours

Starchy Item	Purchase Unit	Pack	Purchase Unit Price
NUTS			
Almond Flour	Case	2 ea.: 5 lb. bags	$135.35
Almonds, blanched, sliced	Case	3 ea.: 2 lb. bags	$68.20
Cashews, pieces, roasted	Case	3 ea.: 2 lb. bags	$41.50
Coconut, shredded	Box	10 lb.	$20.25
Hazelnuts, whole, peeled	Box	5 lb.	$88.50
Macadamia Nuts	Box	5 lb.	$74.80
Peanut Butter	Case	6 ea.: 5 lb. cans	$58.98
Peanuts, dry-roasted	Case	3 ea.: 2 lb. bags	$19.40
Pecan Pieces	Case	3 ea.: 2 lb. bags	$69.75
Pine Nuts, shelled	Case	3 ea.: 2 lb. bags	$107.50
Pistachio Nuts, shelled	Box	3 ea.: 2 lb. bags	$81.10
Sesame Seed, Black	Container	5 lb.	$22.56
Sesame Seed, Toasted	Container	5 lb.	$27.16
Sesame Seed, White	Container	5 lb.	$22.50
Sunflower Seed Kernels, raw	Box	25 lb.	$62.70
Walnut Halves and Pieces	Case	3 ea.: 2 lb. bags	$54.15
FLOURS, GRAINS, CRUMBS			
All-Purpose Flour	Bag	50 lb.	$22.90
Big Loaf Bread Flour	Bag	50 lb.	$16.95
Bread Crumbs, plain	Case	50 lb.	$35.95
Buckwheat Groats	Bag	10 lb.	$30.40
Cake Flour	Bag	50 lb.	$22.35
Cornmeal Mix	Case	6 ea.: 5 lb. bags	$46.25
Cornmeal, Blue	Box	10 lb.	$38.85
Cornmeal, coarse	Bag	50 lb.	$20.25

Y% means yield percentage ✦ AS means as served (or used) ✦ AP means as purchased ✦ AS ÷ AP = Y% ✦
AS ÷ Y% = AP ✦ AP × Y% = AS ✦ Cost per AP unit ÷ Y% = Cost per servable unit

Nuts and Flours (Continued)

Starchy Item	Purchase Unit	Pack	Purchase Unit Price
Cornmeal, Quaker, fine	Bag	25 lb.	$22.50
Cracker Crumbs	Bag	25 lb.	$23.95
Graham Cracker Crumbs	Box	10 lb.	$22.05
High Gluten Flour	Bag	50 lb.	$21.90
Japanese Breadcrumbs	Bag	15 lb.	$20.15
Masa Harina, Corn Flour	Bag	10 lb.	$36.20
Oreo Cookie Crumbs	Bag	10 lb.	$28.65
Pastry Flour	Bag	50 lb.	$18.30
Polenta	Bag	25 lb.	$29.05
Semolina Flour, unbleached	Bag	50 lb.	$26.80
Wheatberries	Box	10 lb.	$23.25
Whole Wheat Flour	Bag	50 lb.	$21.15

1 gal. = 4 qt. = 16 c. = 128 fl. oz. ♦ 1 qt. = 2 pt. = 4 c. = 32 fl. oz. ♦ 1 pt. = 2 c. = 16 fl. oz. ♦
1 c. = 8 fl. oz. = 16 tbsp. ♦ 1 fl. oz. = 2 tbsp. ♦ 1 tbsp. = 3 tsp. ♦ 1 lb. = 16 oz.

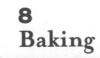

8
Baking

Item	Purchase Unit	Pack	Purchase Unit Price
SWEETENERS			
Apricot Glaze	Tub	20 lb.	$63.05
Butterscotch Topping	Case	6 ea.: #5 cans	$37.15
Caramel Topping	Case	6 ea.: #5 cans	$39.15
Chocolate Sprinkles	Case	4 ea.: 6 lb. cartons	$45.40
Confectioner's Sugar 6X	Bag	25 lb.	$18.45
Corn Syrup, Light	Case	4 ea.: 1 gallon	$42.10
Equal Packets	Case	2,000 count	$35.75
Fudge Topping	Case	6 ea.: #10 cans	$91.45
Granulated Sugar, Beet	Bag	50 lb.	$23.65
Granulated Sugar, fine, cane	Bag	50 lb.	$26.60
Honey	Case	6 ea.: 5 lb. cans	$107.20
Light Brown Sugar	Bag	50 lb.	$35.20
Pineapple Topping	Case	6 ea.: #5 cans	$44.65
Rainbow Sprinkles	Case	4 ea.: 6 lb. cartons	$40.70
Splenda Packets	Case	2,000 ea.	$38.10
Sugar Packets	Box	3,000 ea.	$23.15
Sugar Packets, Turbinado, 4.5 grams	Box	1,200 ea.	$28.45
Sweet 'n Low Packets	Case	3,000 ea.	$23.45
Syrup, assorted flavors for drinks	Case	6 ea.: 750 mL bottles	$23.75
Syrup, Pancake	Case	4 ea.: 1 gal.	$24.75
SPECIAL ITEMS			
Arrowroot	Can	20 oz.	$17.80
Baking Powder	Case	6 ea.: 5 lb. cans	$49.75
Baking Soda	Case	12 ea.: 24 oz. boxes	$19.40
Chocolate Chips, 1,000 count	Box	25 lb.	$63.65

Y% means yield percentage ✦ AS means as served (or used) ✦ AP means as purchased ✦ AS ÷ AP = Y% ✦
AS ÷ Y% = AP ✦ AP × Y% = AS ✦ Cost per AP unit ÷ Y% = Cost per servable unit

Baking (Continued)

Item	Purchase Unit	Pack	Purchase Unit Price
Chocolate Chips, Imitation, 4,000 count	Box	25 lb.	$45.75
Cocoa Powder, 22% fat	Tub	5 lb.	$25.35
Cornstarch	Case	24 ea.: 16 oz. boxes	$22.70
Cream of Tartar	Can	25 oz.	$18.02
Gelatin, plain, granulated	Case	12 ea.: 16 oz. bags	$110.60
Milk, Nonfat Dry Powder	Bag	25 lb.	$86.20
Salt, Kosher Flake	Case	12 ea.: 3 lb. boxes	$22.80
Salt, plain	Bag	50 lb.	$9.75
Spray Pan Coating	Box	6 ea.: 14 oz. cans	$24.95
Strawberry Glaze	Case	6 ea.: #10 cans	$34.90
Yeast, active, dry	Case	12 ea.: 2 lb. bags	$63.60
Yeast, SAF, instant dry	Case	20 ea.: 16 oz. bags	$49.95

1 gal. = 4 qt. = 16 c. = 128 fl. oz. ✦ 1 qt. = 2 pt. = 4 c. = 32 fl. oz. ✦ 1 pt. = 2 c. = 16 fl. oz. ✦
1 c. = 8 fl. oz. = 16 tbsp. ✦ 1 fl. oz. = 2 tbsp. ✦ 1 tbsp. = 3 tsp. ✦ 1 lb. = 16 oz.

9
Fats and Dairy

Item	Purchase Unit	Pack	Purchase Unit Price
FATS			
Butter, Pats, Foil, 61.5 per lb.	Case	4 ea.: 3.25-lb. cartons	$35.60
Butter, Reddie Pats, 90 per lb.	Case	12 lb.	$39.85
Butter, Salted, 1 lb. prints*	Case	30 lb.	$52.30
Butter, Unsalted, 1 lb. prints*	Case	30 lb.	$50.75
Butter, Whipped	Tub	2 ea.: 5 lb.	$21.90
Butter-It (for griddle frying)	Case	3 ea.: 1 gal.	$36.90
Corn Oil	Jug	35 lb.	$25.90
Cottonseed Oil	Case	4 ea. gal.	$36.40
Fry Max Liquid Shortening	Jug	35 lb.	$42.80
Margarine, 1 lb. prints*	Case	30 lb.	$38.60
Oil, Almond, roasted	Case	6 ea.: 1-liter bottles	$113.90
Oil, Hazelnut	Case	1 liter	$21.90
Oil, Grapeseed	Case	1 liter	$13.05
Oil, Avocado	Case	6 ea.: 1-liter bottles	$109.05
Oil, Toasted Sesame	Case	6 ea.: 1-liter bottles	$98.00
Oil, Black Truffle	Bottle	8 fl. oz.	$95.70
Oil, White Truffle	Bottle	8 fl. oz.	$108.35
Oil, Walnut	Case	6 ea.: 1-liter bottles	$83.35
Olive Oil, Extra Virgin Italian	Case	3 ea.: 1 gal,	$87.60
Olive Oil, Pomace, Italian	Case	3 ea.: 1 gal,	$62.15
Olive Oil, Pure	Case	3 ea.: 1 gal,	$86.45
Pan Coating, spray aerosol	Case	6 ea.: 14 oz. cans	$21.53
Peanut Oil	Jug	35 lb.	$64.20
Shortening, all-purpose, solid	Box	50 lb.	$57.15
Shortening, cake	Box	50 lb.	$64.65

Y% means yield percentage ◆ AS means as served (or used) ◆ AP means as purchased ◆ AS ÷ AP = Y% ◆
AS ÷ Y% = AP ◆ AP × Y% = AS ◆ Cost per AP unit ÷ Y% = Cost per servable unit

Fats and Dairy (Continued)

Item	Purchase Unit	Pack	Purchase Unit Price
Shortening, Liquid, premium	Jug	35 lb.	$57.35
Shortening, Liquid, standard	Jug	35 lb.	$30.20
Whipped Butter	Box	2 ea.: 5 lb. pails	$29.75
DAIRY			
Asiago, whole	Wheel	12 lb.	$64.32
Blue Cheese	Wheel	6 lb.	$22.45
Blue Cheese, crumbles	Case	4 ea.: 5 lb. bags	$73.55
Brie Cheese (60% fat)	Wheel	1 kilo	$14.60
Cheddar Cheese, Mild	Block	10 lb.	$27.25
Cheddar Cheese, Sharp	Pound	1 lb.	$5.40
Cheese Slices, Swiss or American	Case	4 ea.: 120 slices ea.	$57.05
Cotija Cheese	Pound	1 lb.	$3.62
Cottage Cheese, Small Curd, 2%	Box	2 ea.: 5 lb. tubs	$14.35
Cream Cheese	Case	4 ea.: 3 lb. blocks	$26.40
Cream, Heavy 34–36% fat	Half gallon	half gallon	$5.94
Creamer, Nondairy	Case	12 ea.: quarts	$17.25
Creamers (half-and-half), PCs**	Case	390 ea.: 3/8 oz.	$10.82
Creamers, all flavors, PCs**	Case	288 ea.	$18.40
Creamers, nondairy, individual PCs**	Case	400 ea.	$7.50
Creamers, nondairy, powdered 2.8g	Case	2,000 ea.	$35.57
Eggs, whole in shell, large	Case	15 dozen	$25.90
Feta Cheese	Case	2 ea.: 8 lb. tubs	$66.65
Goat Cheese	Box	2 kilos	$36.70
Gorgonzola	Wheel	7 lb.	$31.28
Gouda Cheese	Pound	1 lb.	$4.99
Gruyère Cheese	Pound	1 lb.	$7.81
Half-and-Half	Quart	1 qt.	$1.62
Margarine, solid, all veg.	Case	30 1 lb. prints	$22.60

1 gal. = 4 qt. = 16 c. = 128 fl. oz. ✦ 1 qt. = 2 pt. = 4 c. = 32 fl. oz. ✦ 1 pt. = 2 c. = 16 fl. oz. ✦
1 c. = 8 fl. oz. = 16 tbsp. ✦ 1 fl. oz. = 2 tbsp. ✦ 1 tbsp. = 3 tsp. ✦ 1 lb. = 16 oz.

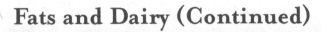

Fats and Dairy (Continued)

Item	Purchase Unit	Pack	Purchase Unit Price
Mayonnaise, heavy duty, whole egg	Case	4 ea.: 1 gal.	$33.35
Mayonnaise, whole egg	Pail	30 lb.	$28.60
Milk, 2 percent	Gallon	1 gal.	$3.90
Milk, condensed, sweetened	Case	24 ea.: 14 oz. cans	$36.14
Milk, evaporated	Case	48 ea.: 12 oz. cans	$54.10
Milk, Nonfat, dry granules	Bag	25 lb.	$50.85
Milk, whole, 4 percent	Gallon	1 gal.	$6.85
Monterey Jack, Natural	Case	2 ea.: 5 lb. blocks	$26.90
Mozzarella Cheese, fresh	Container	2 ea.: 3 lb. pieces	$28.30
Mozzarella Cheese, natural	Pound	1 lb.	$1.95
Parmesan Cheese, fresh, whole	Pound	1 lb.	$5.60
Pizza Cheese, 80/10/10	Case	6 ea.: 5 lb. bags	$62.45
Provolone	Pound	1 lb.	$2.15
Ricotta	Case	4 ea.: 5 lb. tubs	$33.55
Romano Cheese	Pound	1 lb.	$5.95
Sour Cream	Box	2 ea.: 5 lb. tubs	$10.60
Swiss Cheese, natural	Pound	1 lb.	$3.86
Yogurt, plain	Case	6 ea.: 32 oz. cartons	$19.60

*1-lb. print (of butter): 1-lb. brick (of butter)

**PC: portion control

Y% means yield percentage ♦ AS means as served (or used) ♦ AP means as purchased ♦ AS ÷ AP = Y% ♦
AS ÷ Y% = AP ♦ AP × Y% = AS ♦ Cost per AP unit ÷ Y% = Cost per servable unit

10
Condiments

Item	Purchase Unit	Pack (Oz.-Fl. Oz.)	Purchase Unit Price
A-1 Sauce	Case	24 ea.: 5 fl. oz. bottles	$58.60
Achiote Paste	Can	2.2 lb.	$45.45
Adobo Sauce	Case	4 ea.: 1 gal.	$193.41
Artichoke Hearts, Marinated (Cara Mia)	Case	6 ea.: half gal. (80 ct.)	$94.95
Bar-B-Que Sauce, Cattlemans	Case	4 ea.: gal.	$56.50
Base, Au Jus (1 lb. yields 4 gallons 1:4)	Case	6 ea.: 1 lb. jars	$47.70
Base, Beef (1 lb. yields 5 gallons 1:5)	Case	4 ea.: 5 lb. tubs	$145.70
Base, Chicken, 1:5	Case	3 ea.: 4 lb. tubs	$88.65
Base, Clam, 1:5	Case	6 ea.: 1 lb. jars	$52.90
Base, Ham, 1:4	Case	6 ea.: 1 lb. jars	$48.45
Base, Vegetable Stock, 1:4	Case	6 ea.: 1 lb. jars	$36.90
Capers, Non Pareil	Case	6 ea.: 32 oz. jars	$47.55
Chili Sauce	Case	6 ea.: #10 cans	$23.60
Cranberry Sauce, jellied	Case	6 ea.: #10 cans	$49.90
Cranberry Sauce, whole	Case	6 ea.: #10 cans	$54.10
Curry Paste	Case	6 ea.: 9 oz. jars	$36.19
Dressing: French	Case	4 ea.: gal.	$47.90
Dressing: Bleu Cheese	Case	4 ea.: gal.	$73.00
Dressing: Catalina	Case	4 ea.: gal.	$42.75
Dressing: Creamy Caesar	Case	4 ea.: gal.	$61.25
Dressing: Italian (Oil and Vinegar)	Case	4 ea.: gal.	$35.95
Dressing: Ranch	Case	4 ea.: gal.	$46.95
Dressing: Ranch Packets (Yield: 36 gal.)	Case	18 envelopes	$32.50
Dressing: Thousand Island	Case	4 ea.: gal.	$46.85
Enchilada Sauce	Case	6 ea.: #10 cans	$38.70
Hoisin Sauce	Case	6 ea.: 5 lb. cans	$27.25
Horseradish, prepared	Case	12 ea.: 32 oz. jars	$38.95
Horseradish, prepared	Case	4 ea.: gal.	$52.30

1 gal. = 4 qt. = 16 c. = 128 fl. oz. ✦ 1 qt. = 2 pt. = 4 c. = 32 fl. oz. ✦ 1 pt. = 2 c. = 16 fl. oz. ✦
1 c. = 8 fl. oz. = 16 tbsp. ✦ 1 fl. oz. = 2 tbsp. ✦ 1 tbsp. = 3 tsp. ✦ 1 lb. = 16 oz.

Condiments (Continued)

Item	Purchase Unit	Pack (Oz.-Fl. Oz.)	Purchase Unit Price
Hot Sauce, Cholula	Case	12 ea.: 5 fl. oz. bottles	$26.08
Jelly PCs, assorted fruit flavors (0.5 oz.)	Case	400 ea.	$26.85
Ketchup, 33 percent	Case	6 ea.: #10 cans	$27.25
Kitchen Bouquet	Bottle	1 qt.	$7.69
Knorr Swiss Demi Glace Base (33 gal.)	Case	4 ea.: 2 lb. cans	$64.15
Lea & Perrin's Worcestershire	Case	24 ea.: 5 fl. oz. bottles	$42.10
Marinara Sauce	Case	6 ea.: #10 cans	$27.60
Marinara Sauce, Delux	Case	6 ea.: #10 cans	$50.90
Mayonnaise, heavy duty, whole egg	Pail	30 lb.	$33.30
Mayonnaise, whole egg	Pail	30 lb.	$28.68
Mustard, Brown, Gulden's	Case	4 ea.: gal.	$30.45
Mustard, Dijon	Can	1 ea.: 9 lb. cans	$22.49
Mustard, prepared, plain	Case	4 ea.: gal.	$21.55
Mustard, whole grain	Case	6 ea.: 17.6 oz. crock	$64.50
Nacho Cheese Sauce (576 fl. oz.)	Case	6 ea.: #10 cans	$51.50
Pesto Sauce	Case	3 ea.: 30 oz. bottles	$47.20
Pickle Relish, sweet	Case	4 ea.: gal.	$33.07
Pizza Sauce	Case	6 ea.: #10 cans	$23.07
Ponzu Sauce	Case	6 ea.: half gal.	$99.43
Salsa, Picante	Case	4 ea.: gal.	$46.55
Seaweed, Green Dried Nori	Box	12 ea.: 50 count	$136.31
Soy Sauce	Case	4 ea.: gal.	$43.60
Sriracha Hot Sauce	Case	12 ea.: 28 oz.	$37.67
Steak Sauce, Heinz	Case	24 ea.: 5 fl. oz. bottles	$46.90
Sun-Dried Tomato Pesto	Case	3 ea.: 30 oz. jars	$51.85
Sun-Dried Tomato Halves in Olive Oil	Case	12 ea.: 32 oz. jars	$114.20
Sun-Dried Tomatoes, julienned	Case	2 ea.: 5 lb. bags	$142.63
Tahini (Sesame) Paste	Case	12 ea.: 16 oz. cans	$102.10

Y% means yield percentage ✦ AS means as served (or used) ✦ AP means as purchased ✦ AS ÷ AP = Y% ✦
AS ÷ Y% = AP ✦ AP × Y% = AS ✦ Cost per AP unit ÷ Y% = Cost per servable unit

Condiments (Continued)

Item	Purchase Unit	Pack (Oz.-Fl. Oz.)	Purchase Unit Price
Tamarind Purée, frozen	Case	6 ea.: 30 oz.	$144.72
Teriyaki Sauce	Case	4 ea.: gal.	$45.40
Tabasco Sauce	Case	12 ea.: 5 fl. oz. bottles	$34.89
Vinegar, Balsamic	Case	12 ea.: 16.75 oz. bottles	$46.80
Vinegar, Cider, 50 grain	Case	4 ea.: gal.	$22.80
Vinegar, Japanese Rice Wine, seasoned	Case	4 ea.: gal.	$127.50
Vinegar, Raspberry	Case	12 ea.: 16.75 fl. oz. bottles	$34.65
Vinegar, Red Wine, 50 grain	Case	4 ea.: gal.	$18.35
Vinegar, White Distilled, 50 grain	Case	4 ea.: gal.	$12.25
Vinegar, White Wine, Tarragon, 50 grain	Case	4 ea.: gal.	$19.60
Vinegar, Wine-based Imported, 70 grain	Case	6 ea.: 500-mL bottles	$42.15
Worcestershire Sauce	Case	4 ea.: gal.	$29.10

1 gal. = 4 qt. = 16 c. = 128 fl. oz. ✦ 1 qt. = 2 pt. = 4 c. = 32 fl. oz. ✦ 1 pt. = 2 c. = 16 fl. oz. ✦
1 c. = 8 fl. oz. = 16 tbsp. ✦ 1 fl. oz. = 2 tbsp. ✦ 1 tbsp. = 3 tsp. ✦ 1 lb. = 16 oz.

11
Beverages

Item	Purchase Unit	Pack	Purchase Unit Cost
Apple Juice, concentrate (5:1)	Case	6 ea.: 64 fl. oz. cans	$133.35
Clam Juice	Case	12 ea.: 46 fl. oz. cans	$31.70
Clamato Juice	Case	12 ea.: 16 fl. oz. cans	$23.30
Cocoa Mix—Carnation (1728 fl. oz. yield)	Case	12 ea.: 1.5 lb. bags	$75.40
Coffee Grounds, 2 oz. packs	Case	192 envelopes	$106.10
Coffee Grounds, Arabica	Case	12 ea.: 2 lb. bags	$123.50
Coffee Grounds, dark roast	Case	6 ea.: 5 lb. cans	$209.00
Coffee Grounds, decaf	Case	19 ea.: 8.75 oz. bags	$80.55
Cranberry Juice, concentrate (4:1)	Case	6 ea.: 64 fl. oz. cans	$143.75
Cranberry Juice, Ocean Spray	Case	12 ea.: 46 fl. oz. cans	$37.80
Fountain Syrups (5:1 Mix)	Box	5 gal.	$62.75
Grapefruit Juice	Case	12 ea.: 32 fl. oz. cans	$38.65
Iced Tea	Case	4 boxes: 24 ea. 1 oz. bags	$26.80
Lemonade, concentrate (6:1)	Case	12 ea.: 32 fl. oz. cans	$45.75
Orange Juice, concentrate (4:1)	Case	12 ea.: 32 fl. oz. cans	$47.85
Pineapple Juice	Case	12 ea.: 46 fl. oz. cans	$27.90
Prune Juice	Case	12 ea.: 46 fl. oz. cans	$46.35
Sanka Brand Decaf Grounds	Case	128 ea.: 1.25 oz. bags	$83.50
Tea Bags, Bigelow (individual) Constant Comment	Case	6 boxes: 28 bags in ea.	$18.30
Tea Bags, Chamomile	Case	6 boxes: 28 bags	$18.60
Tea Bags, Green, Tips, China	Case	6 boxes, 24 count	$22.84
Tea Bags, Lipton (individual)	Case	10 boxes: 100 bags in ea.	$40.30
Tomato Juice	Case	12 ea.: 46 fl. oz. cans	$17.30
Tropical Fruit Juice, concentrate (3:1)	Case	6 ea.: 64 fl. oz. cans	$63.05
V-8 Juice	Case	12 ea.: 46 fl. oz. cans	$30.45
PAPER PRODUCTS FOR BEVERAGES			
Cup, foam, 12 oz.	Case	24 sleeves: 25 count	$43.15

Y% means yield percentage ♦ AS means as served (or used) ♦ AP means as purchased ♦ AS ÷ AP = Y% ♦
AS ÷ Y% = AP ♦ AP × Y% = AS ♦ Cost per AP unit ÷ Y% = Cost per servable unit

Beverages (Continued)

Item	Purchase Unit	Pack	Purchase Unit Cost
Cup, foam, 16 oz.	Case	10 sleeves: 100 count	$54.35
Cup, foam, 20 oz.	Case	24 sleeves: 25 count	$59.85
Cup, foam, 8 oz.	Case	40 sleeves: 25 count	$21.65
Cup, paper, hot, 16 oz.	Case	1,000 count	$93.35
Cup, paper, cold, poly, 32 oz.	Case	600 count	$170.15
Cup, paper, hot, 12 oz.	Case	1,000 count	$95.70
Filters, Coffee (60 oz. pot)	Case	2 packs: 500 filters in ea.	$9.55
Filters, Iced Tea	Case	2 packs: 250 filters in ea.	$13.35
Lid for 12, 16, or 20 oz. hot cup	Case	10 sleeves: 100 count	$41.55
Lid, 32-oz. cold cup	Case	8 sleeves: 120 count	$44.50
Lid, dome, 12, 16 oz. black, hot cup	Case	10 sleeves: 100 count	$78.95
Straws, plastic, wrapped	Case	24 boxes: 500 count	$78.50
BEVERAGES WITH ALCOHOL			
Absolute Vodka	Each	1 liter	$22.00
Amaretto di Saronno	Each	1 liter	$20.55
Bacardi 151 Rum	Each	1 liter	$16.56
Bacardi Light Rum	Each	1 liter	$18.33
Bailey's Irish Cream	Each	1 liter	$20.40
Beefeater's Gin	Each	1 liter	$20.83
Beer, Domestic U.S.	Case	24 ea.: 12 fl. oz. bottles	$9.95
Beer, Imported (Prices can vary!)	Case	24 ea.: 12 fl. oz. bottles	$22.00
Boxed Wine (bag in box)	Box	5 liters	$9.49
Canadian Club	Each	1 liter	$17.67
Champagne Ordinaire	Each	750 mL	$8.99
Clan MacGregor Scotch	Each	1 liter	$6.58
Cointreau	Each	750 mL	$29.72
Couvosier VS Cognac	Each	1 liter	$33.44
Crème de Cacao, White or Dark	Each	1 liter	$9.95

1 gal. = 4 qt. = 16 c. = 128 fl. oz. ✦ 1 qt. = 2 pt. = 4 c. = 32 fl. oz. ✦ 1 pt. = 2 c. = 16 fl. oz. ✦
1 c. = 8 fl. oz. = 16 tbsp. ✦ 1 fl. oz. = 2 tbsp. ✦ 1 tbsp. = 3 tsp. ✦ 1 lb. = 16 oz.

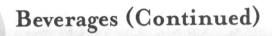

Beverages (Continued)

Item	Purchase Unit	Pack	Purchase Unit Cost
Crème de Cassis	Each	1 liter	$9.83
Crème de Menthe, White or Green	Each	1 liter	$9.84
Cuervo Gold Tequila	Each	1 liter	$14.85
Cutty Sark Scotch	Each	1 liter	$22.67
Dry Sack Sherry	Each	750 mL	$11.67
Frangelico	Each	750 mL	$17.31
Galliano	Each	750 mL	$23.29
Glenfiddich Single Malt Scotch	Each	1 liter	$33.90
Grand Marnier	Each	1.75 liter	$55.50
Harvey's Bristol Cream	Each	750 mL	$12.84
Jack Daniel's Sour Mash	Each	1 liter	$20.50
Jim Beam Bourbon	Each	1 liter	$12.13
Johnnie Walker Red (Scotch)	Each	1 liter	$24.00
Kahlua	Each	1 liter	$19.58
Korbel Brandy	Each	1 liter	$11.09
Meyers Rum	Each	1 liter	$18.50
Old Bushmill's Irish Whiskey	Each	1 liter	$19.33
Old Crow Bourbon	Each	1 liter	$8.33
Ouzo	Each	1 liter	$15.25
Peppermint Schnapps	Each	1 liter	$9.20
Pernod	Each	750 mL	$17.90
Port	Each	750 mL	$12.99
Sake	Each	750 mL	$5.25
Southern Comfort	Each	1 liter	$15.33
Tia Maria	Each	1 liter	$25.00
Vermouth, Dry	Each	750 mL	$7.55

Y% means yield percentage ✦ AS means as served (or used) ✦ AP means as purchased ✦ AS ÷ AP = Y% ✦
AS ÷ Y% = AP ✦ AP × Y% = AS ✦ Cost per AP unit ÷ Y% = Cost per servable unit

12
Meats

Item	Purchase Unit	Pack	Purchase Unit Cost
BEEF			
Back Ribs	Case	60 lb. 6–8" ea.	$53.61
Ball Tip, Bottom Sirloin Butt 185B	Pound	15 lb.	$2.56
Bones, Femur (for Stocks)	Case	25 lb.	$68.75
Brisket, Deckle Off	Case	50 lb.	$124.00
Corned Beef, fat round 15%	Pound	1 lb.	$4.20
Corned Beef, sliced	Box	12 zip-bags 8 oz. ea.	$30.95
Franks, All Beef, 6 in., 8 per lb.	Case	10 lb.	$43.95
Franks, All Beef, 8 in., 4 per lb.	Case	10 lb.	$32.95
Ground Beef Patties, 80/20	Case	30 ea.: 5 1/3 oz. patties	$19.70
Ground Beef Patties, 75/25	Case	40 ea.: 4 oz. patties	$19.63
Ground Beef, 80/20	Case	4 ea.: 5 lb. bags	$37.47
Ground Beef, Angus, 80/20	Case	20 lb.	$42.20
Inside Top Round (NAMP 168)	Piece	23 lb.	$43.24
Liver, Preportioned Steaks	Box	40 ea.: 4 oz. slices	$18.50
New York Striploin (180) 1 × 1	Piece	13 lb.	$75.27
New York Striploin (180A) 1 × 1	Piece	13 lb.	$59.54
Oxtails, cut (frozen)	Case	15 lb.	$79.58
Pastrami, flat round, 15%	Pound	1 lb.	$3.97
Pastrami, sliced	Case	12 zip-bags 8 oz. ea.	$30.95
Prime Rib (109) 23 lb. avg. Choice	Pound	1 lb.	$5.51
Prime Rib (109) 23 lb. avg. Select	Pound	1 lb.	$4.69
Prime Rib (112A) 13 lb.	Pound	1 lb.	$7.07
Prime Rib (112A) Angus, 13 lb. avg.	Pound	1 lb.	$8.64
Prime Rib (112A) Select	Pound	1 lb.	$5.78
Short Loin (for T-bones) (174) 0 × 1	Pound	1 lb.	$8.38
Sirloin Butt (184)	Case	3 ea.: 13 lb. pieces	$146.64
Sirloin Butt, Cap-Off (NAMP 184B)	Pound	1 lb.	$4.65

1 gal. = 4 qt. = 16 c. = 128 fl. oz. ✦ 1 qt. = 2 pt. = 4 c. = 32 fl. oz. ✦ 1 pt. = 2 c. = 16 fl. oz. ✦
1 c. = 8 fl. oz. = 16 tbsp. ✦ 1 fl. oz. = 2 tbsp. ✦ 1 tbsp. = 3 tsp. ✦ 1 lb. = 16 oz.

Meats (Continued)

Item	Purchase Unit	Pack	Purchase Unit Cost
Stew Meat	Box	2 ea.: 5 lb. bags	$34.42
Tender Tips	Pound	1 lb.	$7.65
Tenderloin Butt (defatted, 191A)	Piece	2 lb.	$21.50
Tenderloin, defatted (189A) choice	Piece	5 lb.	$62.80
Tenderloin, defatted (189A) select	Piece	5 lb.	$53.82
Tenderloin, Whole (189), fat-on	Piece	7 lb.	$58.66
Top Round, split, tied, 1" fat (169)	Case	2 ea.: 9 lb. pieces	$56.33
Tri-Tip (1/2 in. fat), (NAMP 185C)	Case	30 lb.	$79.50
Tri Tip, peeled (NAMP 185D)	Pound	1 lb.	$4.78
VEAL			
Bones, Knuckle, cut	Case	50 lb.	$189.00
Chop, Frenched, 12 oz. ea. (1306E)	Case	16 chops, 12 oz. ea.	$240.00
Eye of Round, Provimi	Piece	6 ea., 1.5–2 lb.	$141.60
Ground Veal	Pound	1 lb.	$4.74
Top Round, Select (NAMP 349A)	Pound	1 lb.	$12.20
LAMB			
Chops (NAMP 1204B)	Pound	1 lb.	$7.82
Ground Lamb	Pound	1 lb.	$3.12
Leg, boned, rolled, tied (234)	Box	8 pieces/26 lb.	$136.30
Leg, whole (NAMP 233A)	Piece	6 lb.	$28.94
Loin, bone-in, 2 in. trim	Box	4 ea., 6 lb. average	$139.18
Rack, Frenched (NAMP 204C)	Pound	1 lb.	$8.36
Shanks (NAMP 210), 1 lb. ea.	Pound	1 lb.	$3.97
Stew Meat	Pound	1 lb.	$3.81
Top Round	Pound	1 lb.	$6.89
PORK			
Back Ribs (NAMP 422)	Pound	1 lb.	$4.46
Bacon, 18/22 Strips per lb.	Case	15 lb.	$41.45

Y% means yield percentage ✦ AS means as served (or used) ✦ AP means as purchased ✦ AS ÷ AP = Y% ✦
AS ÷ Y% = AP ✦ AP × Y% = AS ✦ Cost per AP unit ÷ Y% = Cost per servable unit

Meats (Continued)

Item	Purchase Unit	Pack	Purchase Unit Cost
Bacon, Ends and Pieces	Case	15 lb.	$17.75
Boston Butt (NAMP 406 Shoulder)	Pound	1 lb.	$1.38
Canadian Bacon	Piece	1 lb.	$4.45
Chop, 1 in. (10 oz. chops)	Pound	1 lb.	$7.41
Chorizo Links	Pound	1 lb.	$238
Franks, Pork & Beef, 6 in., 6 per lb.	Case	10 lb.	$26.25
Ham Hocks	Pound	1 lb.	$1.49
Ham Shanks	Pound	1 lb.	$1.89
Ham Steaks	Pound	1 lb.	$3.44
Ham, Boneless, water added	Piece	15 lb.	$37.95
Ham, Buffet Carving, boneless	Case	2 ea.: 12 lb. pieces	$77.76
Ham, Boneless, Cure 81	Each	8 lb.	$33.92
Ham, Prosciutto, Di Parma	Pound	1 lb.	$10.69
Ham, Prosciutto, Boneless, Hormel	Piece	7 lb.	$47.11
Ham, Serrano, Boneless	Piece	18 lb.	$299.28
Leg, B.R.T.* (NAMP 402B)	Pound	1 lb.	$2.68
Leg, whole (NAMP 401A)	Pound	1 lb.	$2.15
Loin, boneless (NAMP 413)	Pound	1 lb.	$3.29
Loin, whole (NAMP 410)	Pound	1 lb.	$2.59
NY Hot Italian Links	Pound	1 lb.	$2.96
Pork Meat for Stewing	Pound	1 lb.	$1.99
Salt Pork	Pound	1 lb.	$1.79
Sausage Links, 1 oz. ea.	Pound	1 lb.	$2.45
Sausage, Bulk	Box	10 lb.	$23.25
Spare Ribs (NAMP 416)	Pound	1 lb.	$2.17
Tenderloin (NAMP 415)	Pound	1 lb.	$4.41
DELI MEATS			
Bologna	Pound	1 lb.	$2.88

1 gal. = 4 qt. = 16 c. = 128 fl. oz. ✦ 1 qt. = 2 pt. = 4 c. = 32 fl. oz. ✦ 1 pt. = 2 c. = 16 fl. oz. ✦
1 c. = 8 fl. oz. = 16 tbsp. ✦ 1 fl. oz. = 2 tbsp. ✦ 1 tbsp. = 3 tsp. ✦ 1 lb. = 16 oz.

Meats (Continued)

Item	Purchase Unit	Pack	Purchase Unit Cost
Canned Ham	Can	5 lb.	$7.95
Cooked Corned Beef	Pound	1 lb.	$3.39
Cooked Top Round	Pound	1 lb.	$3.39
Coppa, mild and hot	Pound	1 lb.	$6.22
Corned Beef Bottom Round, raw	Pound	1 lb.	$2.24
Corned Beef Brisket, uncooked	Pound	1 lb.	$1.89
Danish Ham	Pound	1 lb.	$2.59
Dry Salami	Pound	1 lb.	$4.59
Mortadella	Pound	1 lb.	$3.12
Olive Loaf	Pound	1 lb.	$2.69
Pepperoni	Pound	1 lb.	$2.93
Prosciutto, domestic	Pound	1 lb.	$9.50
Prosciutto de Parma	Pound	1 lb.	$10.69
Smoked Pork Loin	Pound	1 lb.	$2.49
Smoked Turkey Breast	Pound	1 lb.	$2.95
Tavern Ham, flat	Pound	1 lb.	$1.89
Toscano Salami	Pound	1 lb.	$4.67
Turkey Ham or Pastrami	Pound	1 lb.	$2.57
White Turkey Roll	Pound	1 lb.	$1.59

*B.R.T.: boned, rolled, tied

Y% means yield percentage ✦ AS means as served (or used) ✦ AP means as purchased ✦ AS ÷ AP = Y% ✦
AS ÷ Y% = AP ✦ AP × Y% = AS ✦ Cost per AP unit ÷ Y% = Cost per servable unit

13
Poultry

Item	Purchase Unit	Pack	Purchase Unit Cost
CHICKEN FRYERS			
Backs and Necks	Pound	1 lb.	$0.46
Breast, skin on, boneless 5 oz.	Case	24 ea.	$21.15
Breast, skinless, boneless 4 oz.	Case	48 ea.	$33.05
Breast, skinless, boneless 5 oz.	Case	48 ea.	$42.50
Breast, skinless, boneless 6 oz.	Case	24 ea.	$28.35
Breast, skinless, boneless 7 oz.	Case	24 ea.	$31.25
Gizzards, frozen	Case	6 ea.: 5 lb. bags	$28.95
IQF* All 8 Pieces	Case	27 lb./96 pieces	$59.40
IQF* Drumsticks/2.6 oz. ea.	Case	15.5 lb./96 pieces	$45.35
IQF* Half Breasts/6.5 oz. ea.	Case	19 lb./48 pieces	$53.30
IQF* Halves/17 oz. ea.	Case	24.5 lb./24 pieces	$46.60
IQF* Quarters/8.75 oz. ea.	Case	30 lb./60 pieces	$58.05
IQF* Thighs/3.5 oz. ea.	Case	40 lb.	$57.90
IQF* Whole Legs/6.3 oz. ea.	Case	18.9 lb./48 pieces	$33.25
IQF* Wing Drumettes	Case	15 lb./200–240 pc.	$29.75
Liver	Case	4 ea.: 5 lb. tubs	$30.75
Meat, Leg, cooked, pulled	Bag	10 lb.	$36.90
Tenderloins, frozen, bulk	Case	4 ea.: 5 lb. blocks	$123.00
Thighs, boneless 6 oz.	Case	24 ea.	$22.40
White Meat, cooked & pulled	Case	10 lb.	$49.80
Whole Fryers (2.75 lb. ea.) WOG	Case	38.5 lb./14 birds	$42.05
TURKEY			
Breast, bone in with ribs	Pound	1 lb.	$2.14
Breast, boneless	Pound	1 lb.	$3.13
Breast, cooked and smoked, bone in	Pound	1 lb.	$4.63
Dark Meat, boneless, skinless	Pound	1 lb.	$1.29
Drumstick	Pound	1 lb.	$0.69

1 gal. = 4 qt. = 16 c. = 128 fl. oz. ✦ 1 qt. = 2 pt. = 4 c. = 32 fl. oz. ✦ 1 pt. = 2 c. = 16 fl. oz. ✦
1 c. = 8 fl. oz. = 16 tbsp. ✦ 1 fl. oz. = 2 tbsp. ✦ 1 tbsp. = 3 tsp. ✦ 1 lb. = 16 oz.

Poultry (Continued)

Item	Purchase Unit	Pack	Purchase Unit Cost
Ground, 5% fat	Pound	1 lb.	$1.49
Links, "Gourmet Flavors," 4 per lb.	Pound	1 lb.	$2.95
Tenderloins	Pound	1 lb.	$2.85
Thighs	Pound	1 lb.	$0.91
Turkey Ham, Tavern Loaf	Box	2 ea.: 7 lb. loaves	$32.06
Whole Hens 18 lb.	Pound	1 lb.	$1.23
Whole Toms 30 lb.	Pound	1 lb.	$1.26
Whole, Petite 9 lb.	Pound	1 lb.	$1.44
Game Hens	Case	24 ea.: 9 oz. halves	$44.20

* IQF: individually quick frozen

Y% means yield percentage ✦ AS means as served (or used) ✦ AP means as purchased ✦ AS ÷ AP = Y% ✦
AS ÷ Y% = AP ✦ AP × Y% = AS ✦ Cost per AP unit ÷ Y% = Cost per servable unit

14
Seafood

Item	Purchase Unit	Pack	Purchase Unit Cost
FROZEN or CANNED (unless marked fresh)			
Bass, Striped Filet, Farm-raised, fresh	Box	10 lb.	$122.90
Bass, Whole, Chilean, headed, gutted, fresh	Each	15 lb.	$182.99
Catfish, 4-oz. filets, IQF*	Case	15 lb.	$68.30
Clams, chopped, surf	Case	4 blocks: 5 lb. ea.	$73.60
Clams, whole in shell	Box	10 ea.: 1 lb. bags	$37.35
Clams, Sea, canned	Case	12 ea.: 51 fl. oz. cans	$118.65
Cod, 5 oz. fillets, IQF*	Case	10 lb.	$57.30
Crab Legs, Snow crab, IQF*	Case	10 lb.	$90.15
Crabmeat, imitation	Case	6 ea.: 5 lb. boxes	$84.89
Crabmeat, snow, 65% body/35% leg	Box	5 lb.	$53.83
Halibut Steaks, 4 oz., IQF*	Case	10 lb.	$103.50
Halibut Steaks, 6 oz., IQF*	Case	10 lb.	$110.55
Halibut Steaks, 8 oz., IQF*	Case	10 lb.	$141.45
Halibut, H&G, 10–20 lb. each, fresh	Each	15 lb.	$105.89
Lobster Tail, Australian, 8–10 oz.	Box	10 lb.	$297.00
Lobster Tail, Canadian, 5–6 oz.	Box	10 lb.	$239.00
Lobster Tail, warm water, 10–12 oz.	Case	4 ea.: 10 lb. boxes	$792.00
Lobster Tail, warm water, 7–8 oz.	Case	4 ea.: 10 lb. boxes	$817.68
Mahi Mahi Filet, skin-on, 3–6 lb. ea., fresh	Carton	20 lb.	$149.98
Mahi Mahi, 8 oz. filets, IQF*	Case	10 lb.	$60.45
Monkfish Tail, fresh	Carton	10 lb.	$96.79
Mussels, cooked	Case	5 ea.: 2 lb. bags	$29.80
Ono Filet, skin-on, fresh	Carton	10 lb.	$103.99
Opah Filet, Hawaiian	Carton	20 lb.	$211.98
Salmon Fillets, Coho, IQF* 8 oz.	Case	10 lb.	$72.65
Salmon Fillets, skinless, IQF* 6 oz.	Case	10 lb.	$61.79
Salmon filets, skinless, IQF* 8 oz.	Case	10 lb.	$66.11

1 gal. = 4 qt. = 16 c. = 128 fl. oz. ✦ 1 qt. = 2 pt. = 4 c. = 32 fl. oz. ✦ 1 pt. = 2 c. = 16 fl. oz. ✦
1 c. = 8 fl. oz. = 16 tbsp. ✦ 1 fl. oz. = 2 tbsp. ✦ 1 tbsp. = 3 tsp. ✦ 1 lb. = 16 oz.

Seafood (Continued)

Item	Purchase Unit	Pack	Purchase Unit Cost
Salmon, Side, smoked, Norway	Side	2.5 lb.	$85.70
Salmon, Atlantic, whole, fresh	Each	12 lb.	$55.93
Scallops, 20–30 count	Case	2 ea.: 5 lb. boxes	$93.65
Scallops, Bay, 80–120 count	Case	2 ea.: 5 lb. boxes	$48.50
Scallops, under 10 count, fresh	Box	8 lb.	$107.90
Shrimp, Bay, 150–250 (cooked)	Box	2 bags: 5 lb. ea.	$53.15
Shrimp, Bay, 250–350 (cooked)	Case	6 bags: 5 lb. ea.	$115.66
Shrimp, Tiger 21/25 (cooked)	Case	4 boxes: 2.5 lb. ea.	$92.22
Shrimp, Tiger 21/25 (raw)	Case	6 boxes: 4 lb. ea.	$110.95
Shrimp, Tiger 16/20 (raw)	Case	6 boxes: 4 lb. ea.	$136.00
Smoked Salmon, domestic U.S.	Side	2.5 lb.	$29.38
Smoked Salmon, Norwegian	Filleted side	5 lb.	$168.60
Smoked Salmon, Scottish	Filleted side	1 lb.	$85.95
Snapper, 6–8 oz. fillets, IQF*	Case	10 lb.	$62.90
Sole ("Dover") 5 oz. fillets, IQF*	Case	10 lb.	$45.45
Sole, Petrale, fillet, fresh	Carton	0 lb.	$94.90
Sole, Petrale, fillet, IQF*	Case	10 lb.	$58.90
Swordfish Loin, skin-on, fresh	Carton	10 lb.	$96.99
Swordfish Steaks, 8 oz. IQF*	Case	10 lb.	$88.10
Trout, boned, 8 oz.	Case	6 ea.: 5 lb. boxes	$132.30
Trout, boneless, butterfly, 6 oz.	Case	2 ea.: 5 lb. boxes	$68.30
Tuna Steaks, IQF*, 5 oz.	Case	10 lb.	$58.42
Tuna, Ahi #1, fillet, medium, fresh	Carton	20 lb.	$310.55
Tuna, Ahi #2, loin, Yellowfin, fresh	Carton	20 lb.	$198.49
Tuna, Canned, chunk light in water	Case	6 cans: 66.5 oz. ea.	$45.79
Tuna, Canned, Albacore in water	Case	6 cans: 66.5 oz. ea.	$103.30

*IQF: individually quick frozen

Y% means yield percentage ✦ AS means as served (or used) ✦ AP means as purchased ✦ AS ÷ AP = Y% ✦
AS ÷ Y% = AP ✦ AP × Y% = AS ✦ Cost per AP unit ÷ Y% = Cost per servable unit

COSTING
WORKSHEETS

Guide to Using the Costing Worksheets

Worksheet Number	Worksheet Title	Use
	Guide to Selecting a Worksheet	Use to find the worksheet you need.
1	Weights to Volumes	Use for costing flour, meal, bran, crumbs; nuts and seeds; sweeteners; special baking items; dairy products; and fats and oils.
2	Trimmed or Cooked Foods	Use to cost vegetables and fruit; rice, grains, cereals, and dry legumes.
3	Piece Counts	Use to cost vegetables and fruit; some crustaceans and mollusks, and some poultry.
4	Volume (Fluid Ounce) Items	Use to cost condiments, some sweeteners, bottled items, packaged beverages, and fats and oils.
5	Dry Herbs and Spices	Use to cost dry herbs and spices.
6	Fresh Herbs	Use to cost fresh herbs.
7	Canned Goods	Use to cost foods packaged in number-10 cans.
8	Pastas	Use to cost pastas.
9	Eggs	Use to cost eggs.
10	Brewed and Dispensed Beverages	Use to cost coffee, tea, and dispensed drinks.
11	Meats	Use to cost meats: beef, veal, pork, and lamb.
12	Seafood	Use to cost finfish, some crustaceans, and mollusks.
13	Poultry	Use to cost poultry: chicken, turkey, and other birds.
14	Rendered, Reduced, and Clarified Items	Use to cost clarified butter, rendered fats, and other similar products.
15	Flavor Bases: Stocks, Sauces, and Others	Use to cost stock and sauce bases.
16	Recipe Card for Costing	Use to determine recipe costs and yields.

Measurement Conversion and Costing Worksheet

1

Weights to Volumes

Item Name: _____ (Given)

As-Purchased (AP) Unit: _____ (Package Type: Bag, Box, etc.)

Cost of the AP Unit: $ _____ (From Invoice or Price List)

Fill in the next two lines if the AP package is measured in pounds. Skip to "Ounce Measures" below if the item is sold in ounces.

Pounds per AP Unit: _____ (Invoice or Package Weight)

Cost per Pound: $ _____ (AP unit cost ÷ AP pounds)

OUNCE MEASURES

Ounces per AP Unit: _____ (Package Weight or

AP pounds × 16)

Cost per AP Ounce: $ _____ (AP unit cost ÷ Ounces per unit)

Ounces per Cup: _____ (From Part I)

Cost per Cup: $ _____ (Ounces per cup × Cost per ounce)

(For a pint cost, multiply the cup cost by 2; for a quart, multiply by 4 and add 1.5 percent for compaction; for a half-gallon, multiply by 8 and add 3.5 percent for compaction; for a gallon, multiply by 16 and add 7 percent for compaction. Do not add compaction factors for liquids, fats, oils, or condiments.)

Pint Cost: $ _____ Quart Cost: $ _____ Gallon Cost: $ _____

Cost per Tablespoon: $ _____ (Cost per cup ÷ 16)

Cost per Teaspoon: $ _____ (Tablespoon cost ÷ 3)

NOTES:

Measurement Conversion and Costing Worksheet

2 | Trimmed or Cooked Foods

Processed Recipe Item Name: _____ (Given)

Raw Item Name: _____ (Given)

Raw Purchase Unit (AP): _____ (Package Description)

Cost per Raw AP Unit: $ _____ (Invoice or Price List Amount)

Pounds per Raw AP Unit: _____ (Pounds in AP Unit)

and/or

Ounces per Raw AP Unit: _____ (Ounces in AP unit or

AP pounds × 16)

Cost per Raw AP Pound: $ _____ (AP unit cost ÷ AP pounds)

and/or

Cost per Raw Ounce: $ _____ (AP unit cost ÷ Ounces in unit, or

Cost per AP pound ÷ 16)

Yield Percentage: (Decimal) or % _____ (From Part I)

Cost per Processed Pound: $ _____ (AP pound cost ÷ Yield %)

Cost per Processed Ounce: $ _____ (Raw ounce cost ÷ Yield %, or

Processed pound cost ÷ 16)

Continue if the trimmed or cooked item is also measured by volume (cups, pints, spoons).

Processed Ounces per Cup: _____ (Cooked or Trimmed Weight per Cup

from Part I)

Cost per Processed Cup: $ _____ (Processed ounces per cup

× Processed ounce cost)

Cost per Processed Tablespoon: $ _____ (Cost per processed cup ÷ 16)

Pint Cost: (Cup cost × 2): $ _____

Quart Cost: (Cup cost × 4) + 1.5%: $ _____

Half Gallon Cost: (Cup cost × 8) + 3.5%: $ _____

Gallon Cost: (Cup Cost × 16) + 7%: $ _____

(Note: To account for possible compaction of produce cut into small bits, when using these larger units add 1.5 percent to a quart cost, 3.5 percent to a 2-quart volume cost, and 7 percent to a full-gallon measure cost.)

Measurement Conversion and Costing Worksheet

3

Piece Counts

Name: Recipe Item Description: _____ (Given)

Raw Item Name: _____ (Given)

As-Purchased (AP) Unit: _____ (Package Type or Measure)

Cost of AP Unit: $ _____ (From Invoice or Price List)

Total Raw Count in AP Unit: _____ (AP Pack Count)

Cost of Each, Raw: $ _____ (AP cost ÷ Total count)

Usable (Culled) Count: _____ (From Part I)

Yield Percentage: (Decimal) or % _____ (From Part I, or Culled count ÷ Raw count)

Cost of Each Culled: $ _____ (AP cost ÷ Culled count, or Cost of each raw ÷ Yield %)

NOTES:

Measurement Conversion and Costing Worksheet

4 | Volume (Fluid Ounce) Items

Item Name: _____ (Given)

As-Purchased (AP) Unit: _____ (From Invoice or Price List)

Containers in AP Unit: _____ (From Invoice or Price List)

Cost of One Container: $ _____ (AP unit cost ÷ Number of containers)

(To convert milliliters to fluid ounces, divide the milliliters in the container by 29.574.)

Fluid Ounces in One Container: _____ (From Invoice or Container Label)

Cost per Fluid Ounce: $ _____ (Container cost × Fluid ounces in 1)

Cost per Cup: $ _____ (8 × Fluid-ounce cost)

Cost per Pint: $ _____ (2 × Cup cost)

Cost per Quart: $ _____ (4 × Cup cost or 2 × Pint cost)

Cost per Gallon: $ _____ (16 × Cup cost or 4 × Quart cost)

For "Wet" Items Measured by Weight

Cost per Container: $ _____ (From Above)

Total Ounces in Container: _____ (From Invoice or Label)

Cost per Ounce: $ _____ (Container cost ÷ Total ounces)

Ounce Weight per Cup: _____ (From Part I)

Cost per Cup: $ _____ (Ounce cost × Ounces per cup)

(For a pint cost, multiply the cup cost by 2; for a quart, multiply by 4; for a gallon, multiply by 16.)

Pint Cost $ _____ Quart Cost $ _____ Gallon Cost $ _____

NOTES:

Measurement Conversion and Costing Worksheet

5

Dry Herbs and Spices

Item Name: _____ (Given)

As-purchased (AP) Unit: _____ (Package Type or measure)

Cost of AP Unit: $ _____ (From invoice or price list)

Total Ounces in AP Unit: _____ (Ounces in AP container)

Cost per AP Ounce: $ _____ (AP unit cost ÷ Total ounces)

ITEMS USED BY WEIGHT-TO-VOLUME

Cup Cost

Ounces per Cup: _____ (From Part I)

Cost per Cup: $ _____ (Ounce cost × Ounces per cup)

Spoon Costs

Tablespoons per Ounce: _____ (From Part I)

Cost per Tablespoon: $ _____ (Cost per ounce ÷ Tablespoons per ounce,
or Cup cost ÷ 16)

Cost per teaspoon: $ _____ (Cost per tablespoon ÷ 3)

ITEMS USED BY COUNT

Number per Ounce

Count per Ounce: _____ (Number each per ounce from Part I)

Cost per Each: $ _____ (Ounce cost ÷ Count per ounce)

Number per Tablespoon:

Count per Tablespoon: _____ (From Part I)

Cost per Tablespoon: $ _____ (From above)

Cost per Each: $ _____ (Cost per tablespoon 4 Count per
tablespoon)

Measurement Conversion and Costing Worksheet

6 | Fresh Herbs

Item Name: _____ (Given)

As-purchased Unit: _____ (Pack type or measure)

Cost per AP Unit: $ _____ (From invoice or price list)

Number of Bunches per AP Unit: _____ (Number of bunches in AP unit)

Cost per Bunch: $ _____ (AP unit cost ÷ Number of bunches in unit)

Ounces per Bunch: _____ (From Part I, or Total AP unit weight ÷ Number of bunches)

Cost per AP Ounce: $ _____ (Cost per AP bunch ÷ Ounces per bunch)

Number of Garnish Leaves per AP Ounce: _____ (Your count, or from Part I)

Cost per Garnish Leaf: $ _____ (Cost per ounce ÷ Number of leaves per ounce)

Tablespoons of Chopped Leaf per AP Ounce: _____ (From Part I data, or use method in note 8 at bottom of Fresh Herbs table)

Cost per Chopped Tablespoon: $ _____ (Cost per AP ounce ÷ Tablespoons per AP ounce)

Cost per Chopped Cup: $ _____ (Cost per chopped tablespoon 3 16)

NOTES:

Measurement Conversion and Costing Worksheet

7 | Canned Goods

DRAINED WEIGHTS

Use with the USDA list of Minimum Drained Weights.

Number-10 Can Item Name: _____ (Given)

As-Purchased Unit: _____ (Invoice package)

AP Unit Cost: $ _____ (From invoice or price list)

Number of Cans in AP Unit: _____ (From invoice or price list)

Cost per Can: $ _____ (AP unit cost ÷ Number of cans)

Minimum Drained Ounce Weight: _____ (From Part I USDA list)

Cost per drained ounce: $ _____ (Can cost ÷ drained ounces per can)

Note: *To cost an undrained weight of canned food, and to cost a cup, quart, or half gallon of either a drained or undrained canned product, use the Canned Food Weight-to-Volume table in Part I.*

UNDRAINED WEIGHTS AND VOLUMES

Number-10 Can Item Name: _____ (Given)

As-Purchased Unit: _____ (Invoice package)

AP Unit Cost: $ _____ (From invoice or price list)

Number of Cans in AP Unit: _____ (From invoice or price list)

Cost per Can: $ _____ (AP unit cost ÷ Number of cans)

Actual Ounce Weight per Can: _____ (From volumes table)

Actual Cost per Ounce: $ _____ (Can cost ÷ Actual ounces per can)

Cost per Cup: $ _____ (Ounces per cup × Actual cost per ounce)

Cost per Quart: $_____ (Ounces per quart × Actual cost per ounce)

Cost per Half Gallon: $ _____ (Ounces per half gallon × Actual cost per ounce)

DRAINED WEIGHTS AND VOLUMES

Use the Canned Foods Weight-to-Volume table in Part I for the measurement data.

Number-10 Can Item Name: _____ (Given)

As-Purchased Unit: _____ (Invoice package)

AP Unit Cost: $ _____ (From invoice or price list)

Number of Cans in AP Unit: _____ (From invoice or price list)

Cost per Can: $ _____ (AP unit cost ÷ Number of cans)

Drained Ounces per Can: _____ (From weight-to-volumes table in Part I)

Drained Cost per Ounce: $ _____ (Can cost ÷ Drained ounce per can)

Cost per Drained Cup: $ _____ (Ounce per cup × Drained cost per ounce)

Cost per Drained Quart: $ _____ (Ounce per quart × Drained cost per ounce)

Cost per Drained Half Gallon: $ _____ (Ounce per half gallon × Drained cost per ounce)

Miscellaneous Canned or Bottled Produce Items

DRAINED WEIGHTS

Item Name: _____ (Given)

As-Purchased Unit: _____ (Invoice package)

AP Unit Cost: $ _____ (From invoice or price list)

Number of Containers in AP Unit: _____ (From invoice or price list)

Cost per Container: $ _____ (AP unit cost ÷ Containers in AP unit)

Drained Ounces: _____ (From part I)

Cost per Drained Ounce: $ _____ (Container cost ÷ drained ounces)

PIECE COUNTS

Item Name: _____ (Given)

Cost per Container: $ _____ (From Above)

Piece Count in AP Unit: _____ (From Part 1)

Cost per Piece: _____ (Container Cost ÷ Piece count)

DRAINED VOLUMES

Item Name: _____ (Given)

Cost per Drained Ounce: $ _____ (From above)

Drained Ounces per Cup: _____ (From part 1)

Cost per Cup: $_____ (Cost per Drained ounce × Ounces per cup)

Measurement Conversion and Costing Worksheet

8 | Pastas

Name: Pasta Type: _____ (Given)

As-Purchased Unit: _____ (Package type from invoice)

Cost per AP Unit: $ _____ (From invoice or price list)

Pounds in AP Unit: _____ (From invoice or price list)

Cost per Raw AP Pound: $ _____ (AP unit cost ÷ Pounds in unit)

Cost per Raw AP Ounce: $ _____ (AP pound cost ÷ 16)

RAW WEIGHT TO COOKED WEIGHT COSTING

Cost per Cooked Pound (Dry Pasta): $ _____ (Raw pound cost ÷ 2.5 yield factor from Part I)

Cost per Cooked Pound (Fresh Pasta): $ _____ Raw cost ÷ 2.0 yield factor from Part I

DRY WEIGHT TO DRY VOLUME COSTING

Pasta Name: _____ (Given)

Ounce Weight per Cup: _____ (From Part I)

Ounce Weight per Quart: _____ (From Part I)

Cost per Raw Cup: $ _____ (Raw ounce cost, above, × Raw ounces per cup for pasta type from Part I)

Cost per Raw Quart: $ _____ (Raw ounce cost, above, × Raw ounces per quart for pasta type from Part I)

(**Note:** Raw weight to cooked weight or to dry volume conversions are fairly predictable, whereas volume-to-volume outcomes are less precise. To determine a volume yield and then cost that volume of cooked pasta based on a raw volume, conduct your own cooked-volume yields test. Outcomes vary according to the degree of doneness desired and, more importantly, the shape of the raw pasta.)

NOTES:

Measurement Conversion and Costing Worksheet

9 | Eggs

Egg Size: _____ (Given or from invoice)

As-Purchased Unit: _____ (From invoice: case, 36-pack, etc.)

Purchase Unit Cost: $ _____ (From invoice or price list)

AP Subunit: _____ (Flat, 36-pack, carton of 12, etc.)

Number of Subunits in AP Unit: _____ (From invoice or AP unit pack)

Cost per Subunit: $ _____ (AP unit cost ÷ Number of subunits in

AP unit)

Number of Eggs in 1 Subunit: _____ (From invoice, pack, or physical count)

Cost of 1 Egg: $ _____ (Subunit cost ÷ Number eggs in 1 subunit)

Note: If you know how many eggs are in the entire AP unit, you can determine the cost of 1 egg rather quickly: Simply divide the AP unit cost by the total egg count.

LARGE EGGS

Cost of 1 Quart of Large Shelled (Pooled) Eggs

According to Part I, there are 19.44 large shelled eggs per quart, so use this formula:

$ Cost of 1 large egg × 19.44 = $ Cost per quart

Thus, cost per quart:

Cost of 1 egg $ _____ × 19.44 = $ _____ Cost per quart of large shelled eggs

Cost of 1 Pound of Large Shelled (Pooled) Eggs

According to Part I, there are 9 large shelled eggs per pound, so use this formula:

$ Cost of 1 large egg × 9 = $ Cost per pound

Thus, cost per pound:

Cost of 1 egg $ _____ × 9 = $ _____ Cost of 1 pound of large shelled eggs

NOTES:

Measurement Conversion and Costing Worksheet

10 | Brewed and Dispensed Beverages

COFFEE (PREPORTIONED PACKAGING)

One package brews a predetermined amount of coffee.

As-Purchased Unit: _____ (Case, carton, etc., from invoice)

Cost per AP Unit: $ _____ (From invoice or price list)

Number of Packages in As-Purchased Unit: _____ (From invoice or AP unit)

Cost per Package: $ _____ (AP unit cost ÷ Number of packages)

Yield in Fluid Ounces per Package: _____ (Manufacturer's yield instruction, or your brewing results)

Cost per Brewed Fluid Ounce: $ _____ (Package cost ÷ Fluid ounce yield)

COFFEE (BULKLOOSE GROUNDS)

As-Purchased Unit: _____ (Case, carton, etc., from invoice)

Cost per AP Unit: $ _____ (From invoice)

Total Pounds in AP Unit: _____ (Invoice, or computed from pack)

Cost per Pound: $ _____ (AP unit cost ÷ Total pounds)

Cost per Ounce: $ _____ (Pound cost ÷ 16)

Fluid Ounce Yield of 1 Ounce Grounds: _____ (Your yield test result; or from Part I, 1.5 ounces yields 60 fluid ounces, or 1 ounce yields 40 fluid ounces)

Cost per Brewed Fluid Ounce: $ _____ (Ounce cost ÷ Fluid ounce yield)

Cost per Brewed 6-Ounce Cup: $ _____ (Brewed fluid ounce cost × 6)

Yield of 1 Pound Grounds: _____ (5 Gallons, from Part I, or 16 × Your 1-ounce yield test)

ICED TEA

As-Purchased Unit: _____ (From invoice)

Cost of AP Unit: $ _____ (From Invoice)

Total Ounces in AP Unit: _____ (From pack or invoice)

Cost per Ounce of Tea Leaf: $ _____ (AP unit cost ÷ Total ounces)

Fluid Ounce Yield of 1-Ounce Tea Leaf: _____ (From Part I: 64, or use your own yield test results)

Cost of 1 Brewed Fluid Ounce: $ _____ (Fluid ounce yield ÷ Ounce cost)

DISPENSED DRINKS

As-Purchased Unit: _____ (Product description)

Cost of AP Unit: $ _____ (From invoice)

Fluid Ounces in AP Unit: _____ (Calculate from invoice:
Number of quarts $\times$ 32, or
Number of gallons $\times$ 128)

Mix Ratio

   Syrup to water: _____ parts syrup to _____ parts water (From package instructions)

Fluid ounce yield after mixing: _____

(Multiply fluid ounce in AP unit times parts water. Add this to fluid ounces in AP unit.)

Cost per mixed fluid ounce: $ _____

Divide cost of AP unit by the mixed fluid ounce yield. Add the CO_2 and water costs of $0.0006 per fluid ounce below.

Final cost per mixed fluid ounce: $ _____

(Cost per mixed fluid ounce plus $0.0006)

Measurement Conversion and Costing Worksheet

11

Meats

There are two ways to cost trimmed meats:

+ Method A: This method *does not* deduct the value of the trimmings (usable or not) from the cost of the trimmed piece.

+ Method B: This method *does* deduct the value of the usable trim from the cost of the trimmed piece.

RAW MEAT TO TRIMMED PIECE: METHOD A

With this method, all of the value of any usable trim (sinew, bones, ground meat, stew meat, brochette meat, etc.) obtained from the trimming remains with the primary piece. This results in the trimmed piece being relatively more expensive but assigns a zero value to the trimmings. This method is quicker but is used only when the trim from the primary piece is not really put to use—that is, it has no other salable (menu) or cooking use in your operation, not even for stocks or employee meals.

When the value of the usable trim is not deducted from the AP cost, use this process.

Prepared Meat Item Name: _____ (Given)

Base Meat Name: _____ (Original meat item)

Base Meat NAMP Number: _____ (NAMP guide or invoice)

As-Purchased (AP) Piece Weight in Pounds: _____ (Invoice amount or weigh out*)

Cost per AP Pound: $ _____ (From invoice or price list)

A: Total Cost of Raw AP Piece: $ _____ (AP pounds × Cost per pound, or Invoice amount)

Trimmed Weight (Pounds): _____ (Weigh out or use yield % from Part I × AP weight)

Trimmed Yield Percentage: (Decimal) _____ or _____ % (Trimmed pounds ÷ AP pounds, or use Part I %)

Cost per Pound of Trimmed Piece: $ _____ (AP pound cost ÷ Trim % or AP cost ÷ Trimmed pounds)

If loose blood was in the meat package, include the blood weight in your initial AP weight. Cutting loss, loose blood, and unusable trim weights plus usable trim weight and the trimmed piece weight should equal the AP weight.

RAW MEAT TO TRIMMED PIECE: METHOD B

This method is used when the usable trim is put to use in your operation in lieu of having to order the trimmed items separately. (You might also order these trimmed items, such as extra bones or brochette meat; but the point is that these trimmings are going to be used and have a usable value.) After completing your normal trimming of the meat item, add up the value of the trimmings and deduct their assigned value from your cost of the entire piece, as purchased. The cost values assigned to your usable trim items are what you would pay had you bought them.

USABLE TRIM DEDUCTIONS

Item	Pounds	Market Price per Pound	Total Value
Bones and Sinew		$	$
Ground Meat			
Stew Meat			
Brochette Meat			
		TOTAL:	$

Here is how to plug in the usable trim total value to the worksheet:

Prepared Meat Item Name: _____ (Given)

Base Meat Name: _____ (Original Meat Item)

Base Meat NAMP Number: _____ (NAMP Guide or Invoice)

As-Purchased (AP) Piece Weight in Pounds _____ (Invoice Amount or Weigh Out)

Cost per AP Pound: $ _____ (From Invoice or Price List)

Total Cost of Raw AP Piece: $ _____ (From invoice, or AP pounds × Pound cost)

Minus Value of Usable Trim: $ _____ (Enter Total Trim Deductions)

B: Cost of Trimmed Piece: $ _____ (AP cost – Trim value)

Trimmed Weight (Pounds): _____ (Weigh out, or use yield % from Part I × AP weight)

Cost per Pound of Trimmed Piece: $ _____ (Trimmed piece cost ÷ Trimmed weight in pounds)

COOKED MEAT BY WEIGHT

This section can be used by itself if you buy ready-to-cook meats (pretrimmed). It can also be used to complete the costing of a trimmed piece from above.

Meat Item: _____ (Given, or from Above)

Cost of Raw, Trimmed Piece: $ _____ (Invoice, or from Above, A or B)

Pound Weight of Raw, Trimmed Piece: _____ (From Above, Invoice, or Weigh Out)

Cost per Pound Raw, Trimmed: $ _____ (Cost of whole raw, trimmed piece ÷ Pound weight of trimmed piece)

Pound Weight of Cooked Piece: _____ (Weight after cooking and resting)

Cooked Yield Percentage: (Decimal) _____ or _____% (Cooked weight ÷ Raw trimmed weight)

Cost per Pound of Cooked Piece: $ _____ (Cost of raw trimmed piece ÷ Cooked pounds, or raw pound cost ÷ Cooked yield %)

Cost per Ounce of Cooked Piece: $ _____ (Cooked pound cost ÷ 16)

PORTION COST

Use this section when known portions are obtained from a single piece (item).

Name of Portioned Item: _____ (Given, e.g., 7-ounce steak)

Name of AP Piece: _____ (Given, or invoice name)

Cost of Raw AP Piece: $ _____ (From above)

Number of Servable Portions from Piece: _____ (Your estimate or count)

Cost per Servable Portion: $ _____ (Cost per AP piece ÷ Portions per piece)

NOTES:

Measurement Conversion and Costing Worksheet

12 | Seafood

FINFISH: DRESSED FISH AND FILLETS

A *dressed* fish has its intestines, scales, head, tail, and fins removed. Here, the word *fillet* refers to a whole side, after boning and skinning. Fillet portions are dealt with in the next section.

Processed Item Name: _____ (Given, e.g., Salmon Fillet)

Raw Item Name: _____ (Given, e.g., Dressed Salmon)

As-Purchased Unit: _____ (Package Description)

As-Purchased Unit Cost: $ _____ (From Invoice or Price List)

Pounds in AP Unit: _____ (From invoice or weighout)

Net Pounds after Filleting: _____ Actual weight, or yield % from Part I × Original AP lbs.)

Yield Percentage: (Decimal) _____ or _____ % (From Part I, or Net weight ÷ Purchased weight)

Cost per Filleted Pound: $ _____ (AP pound cost ÷ Yield %)

Cost per Filleted Ounce: $ _____ (Fillet pound cost ÷ 16)

Number of Ounces per Filleted Portion: _____ (Recipe specification)

Cost per Filleted Portion: $ _____ (Fillet ounce cost × Ounce per portion)

SEAFOOD BOUGHT BY COUNT PER POUND

Item Name: _____ (Given)

As-Purchased Unit: _____ (From invoice, or given)

Cost of AP Unit: $ _____ (From invoice or price list)

Pounds in AP Unit: _____ (Count, or from invoice)

Cost per AP Pound: $ _____ (Cost of AP unit ÷ Number of pounds in AP unit)

Average Count per Pound: _____ (Actual count, or Middle of count range on invoice)

Cost of Each: $ _____ (Pound cost ÷ Per pound count)

Measurement Conversion and Costing Worksheet

13 | Poultry

BASIC POULTRY COSTING WORKSHEET (A)

Use this first section of the worksheet if your poultry has no giblets or you want to include the cost of giblets in your costing. Use the sections that follow for costing individual poultry pieces.

Name of Poultry Item: _____ (Given)

Size or Type of Bird: _____ (Given or from invoice)

As-Purchased Unit: _____ (Given or from invoice)

Total AP Unit Cost: $ _____ (From invoice or price list)

Pound Weight of AP Unit: _____ (From invoice or weigh out)

Cost per AP Pound: $ _____ (AP unit cost ÷ AP pounds)

Number of Birds in AP Unit: _____ (Count or from invoice)

Actual Average Weight per Bird: _____ (Total AP weight ÷ Total number of birds)

Cost per Bird: $ _____ (AP unit cost ÷ Bird count)

Cost per AP Ounce: $ _____ (AP pound cost ÷ 16)

Note: *Fresh poultry, especially chickens, are often packed in ice for shipping. Be sure you clean off the ice and briefly drain the wet chickens before weighing. Compare their drained weight to the invoice weight.*

Whole poultry is sold with giblets (heart, gizzard, neck, and/or liver) or without giblets (called WOG). If you do not use the giblets, buy poultry WOG, because the total cost is usually less than that for whole birds with giblets. If you do use the giblets, then you should deduct the total value of the giblets from the as-purchased unit cost before proceeding with further costing. The giblet values are the market prices for the respective items. The usable giblet costs would then be added to the recipes in which they are used.

Use the Usable Giblet Deductions form below to determine the value of the usable giblets.

USABLE GIBLET DEDUCTIONS*

Item	Pounds	Market Price per Pound	Total Value
Necks		$	$
Gizzards			
Hearts			
Livers			
Backs			
		TOTAL:	$

*Remove, separate, and weigh each giblet type.

WORKSHEET SHOWING DEDUCTION OF GIBLET COSTS (B)

Name of Poultry Item: _____ (Given)

Size or Type of Bird: _____ (Given or from invoice)

As-Purchased Unit: _____ (Given or from invoice)

Total AP Unit Cost: $ _____ (From invoice or price list)

Pound Weight of As-Purchased Unit: _____ (From invoice or weigh out)

Cost per AP Pound: $ _____ (AP unit cost ÷ AP pounds)

Cost per AP Ounce: $ _____ (AP pound cost ÷ 16)

Usable Giblets Value: $ _____ (From giblet value box, above)

AP Unit Cost Less Giblet Value: $ _____ (AP unit cost − Giblet value.
This is the adjusted cost of AP unit.)

Net Weight (Pounds) of Poultry, WOG: _____ (Weight after removing giblets)

Total Cost per Pound, WOG: $ _____ (Adjusted cost ÷ Net pounds)

Total Cost per Ounce, WOG: $ _____ (WOG pound cost ÷ 16)

Cost per Individual WOG Bird: $ _____ (Adjusted cost ÷ Total number of birds)

CHICKEN, LARGE FRYERS: PARTS

If you do not deduct the value of the giblets and are simply assigning the cost of the whole bird to the breasts, wings, legs, and thighs, divide the average cost of one AP whole bird by 67.9 percent to get the new adjusted cost. (The 67.9 percent is the combined yield of the breasts, wings, legs, and thighs from the AP bird.) If you do deduct the dollar value of the giblets, first subtract that amount from the original AP cost per bird before calculating the adjusted cost. To cost each part, multiply its yield percentage by the adjusted cost. To cost the total cleaned meat, just enter the AP bird's original cost.

Original Cost of one AP Bird

$_____ Divided by 0.679 Adjusted cost: $ _____

PARTS: LARGE FRYER WITH OR WITHOUT GIBLETS

Cost of Whole Large Fryer: $ _____ (Given or from above, A or B)

Total Clean Meat: $ _____ (Enter the AP cost of 1 whole bird)

Wings, Both: $ _____ (% of original weight × Adjusted cost from Part I: 10.7% × Adjusted cost)

Wings, Each: $ _____ (% of original weight × Adjusted cost from Part I: 5.4% × Adjusted cost)

Wing, First Section, Each: $ _____ (% of original weight × Adjusted cost from Part I: 2.6% × Adjusted cost)

Wing, Second Section, Each: $ _____ (% of original weight × Adjusted cost from Part I: 2.1% × Adjusted cost)

Breast, Whole, Both Halves: $ _____ (% of original weight × Adjusted cost from Part I: 29.6% × Adjusted cost)

Breast, Whole/Half, Each: $ _____ (% of original weight × Adjusted cost from Part I: 14.8% × Adjusted cost)

Leg and Thigh, Whole, Both: $ _____ (% of original weight × Adjusted cost from Part I: 27.6% × Adjusted cost)

Drumsticks, Whole, Both: $ _____ (% of original weight × Adjusted cost from Part I: 11.4% × Adjusted cost)

Leg Meat, Both: $ _____ (% of original weight × Adjusted cost from Part I: 5.4% × Adjusted cost)

Thighs, Whole, Both: $ _____ (% of original weight × Adjusted cost from Part I: 16.3% × Adjusted cost)

Thigh Meat, Both: $ _____ (% of original weight × Adjusted cost from Part I: 10% × Adjusted cost)

PARTS: LARGE FRYERS WITHOUT GIBLETS

The chicken yields and percentages listed in Part I are based on a whole fryer with giblets. If you buy fryers without giblets, you have to determine the percentage of the whole fryer's weight that your respective fryer parts represent.

Here is how to figure out the cost of each type of fryer part from scratch:

1. Enter the average cost of a whole fryer (given, or from worksheets or your invoice).
2. Add up the total ounce weight of all the fryers in your sample test group and enter that weight below.
3. Cut your sample birds into their parts (breasts, legs, etc.). Weigh each total set of the same parts and put the answer in column B. (Put their part or bird section name in column A.)
4. Divide each set's weight by the total weight of all the birds in your sample. The answer is the yield percentage for that type of part. Write that percentage in column C.
5. Multiply the yield percentage in column C by the cost of one whole fryer. Put this answer in column D. This answer will show the cost value of two wings, two breasts, etc. (This assumes that each of your sample birds has two wings, breast halves, legs, and thighs.)
6. Divide column D by 2. Put this answer in column E. That will be the cost of one part. Use this form to weigh single backs, too. Just skip column D and put your first costing answer in column E.

Note: *Percentages may not add up to 100 percent due to cutting losses of bird bits, blood, and water. Cutting losses of 3 to 5 percent of the original weight are common.*

Here is the form to fill out to determine the yield percentages and to calculate your costs: (Fill in average costs from known values or from worksheets above.)

Average Cost of One Whole Fryer: $ _____   Cost per Pound: $ _____

Total Ounce Weight of All Whole Fryers in Sample: _____   Ounce Cost: $ _____

A	B	C	D	E
Bird Section (Part Name)	Ounce Weight: Set	Percent of Whole	Cost of 2 Parts	Cost of 1 Part
			$	$

POULTRY, GENERAL

The preceding worksheet for a large chicken fryer without giblets works for any bird: turkey, duckling, goose, and so on. Here is another version of that worksheet, omitting references to fryers. These are the steps to follow to figure out the cost of each type of bird part from scratch:

1. Enter the average costs of a whole bird on the following form (given, or from worksheets or your invoice).

2. Add up the total ounce weight of all the birds in your sample test group and enter that weight on the following form.

3. Cut your sample birds into their parts (breasts, legs, etc.). Weigh each total set of the same parts and put the answer in column B. (Put their part or bird section name in column A.)

4. Divide each set's weight by the total weight of all the birds in your sample. The answer is the yield percentage for that type of part. Write that percentage in column C.

5. Multiply the yield percentage in column C by the cost of one whole bird. Put this answer in column D. This answer will show the cost value of two wings, two breasts, and so on. (This assumes that each of your sample birds has two wings, breast halves, legs, and thighs.)

6. Divide column D by 2. Put this answer in column E. That will be the cost of one part. Use this form to weigh single backs. Just skip column D and put your first costing answer in column E.

Note: *Percentages may not add up to 100 percent due to cutting losses of bird bits, blood, and water. Cutting losses of 3 to 5 percent of the original are common.*

Here is the form to fill out to determine the yield percentages and calculate your costs.

Bird Type and Description: _____

Average Cost of One Whole Bird: $ _____   Cost per pound $ _____

Total Ounce Weight of all Whole Birds in Sample: _____   Cost per ounce: $ _____

A	B	C	D	E
Bird Section (Part Name)	Ounce Weight: Set	Percent of Whole	Cost of 2 Parts	Cost of 1 Part
			$	$

Measurement Conversion and Costing Worksheet

14 | Rendered, Reduced, and Clarified Items

Name of Rendered Item: _____ (Clarified butter, duck fat, bacon fat, etc.)

Base Item Name: _____ (Food being rendered, e.g., whole butter, whole duck fat)

As-Purchased Unit: _____ (Given, or from invoice)

Cost of AP Unit: $ _____ (Given, from invoice, or comparable vendor price. May be a price per pound.*)

Pounds per AP Unit: _____ (Given, or from invoice)

Cost per AP Pound: $ _____ (AP unit cost ÷ AP pounds)

Ounce Yield per AP Pound: _____ (From Part I or your measure)

Ounce Cost: $ _____ (AP pound cost ÷ Ounce yield per pound)

Fluid Ounce Cost: $ _____ (AP unit cost ÷ Total fluid ounce yield)

The clarified butter yield of 75 percent as stated in Part I is a *weighed* yield. One pound of whole butter yields 12 weighed ounces of clear butterfat. However, the fluid ounce yield is greater because butterfat is lighter than whole butter. One pound of whole butter will yield 12.864 *fluid ounces* of clarified butter, which is 80.4 percent of the original 2-cup volume that 1 pound of whole butter equals.

+ To cost a fluid ounce of clarified butter, divide the cost of 1 pound of raw butter by 12.864. Fluid ounce cost: $ (AP pound cost ÷ 12.864)

+ To cost a cup of clarified butter, multiply the fluid ounce cost by 8. Cup cost: $

+ To cost a pint of clarified butter, double the cup cost. Pint cost: $

+ To cost a quart of clarified butter, multiply the cup cost by 4. Quart cost: $

+ To cost a gallon of clarified butter, multiply the cup cost by 16. Gallon cost: $

It may be difficult to assign an as-purchased cost per pound to some fats. This happens when you render fats trimmed out of ducks, geese, or pork, for instance. In these cases, assign an AP cost per pound that you would have had to pay had you purchased these items from a vendor. Your meat vendor or a local butcher can give you those prices.

Measurement Conversion and Costing Worksheet

15 | Flavor Bases: Stocks, Sauces, and Others

Item Name: _____ (Given)

As-Purchased Unit: _____ (From invoice or price list)

Cost of AP Unit: $ _____ (From invoice or price list)

If the AP unit is a single container, proceed here. If the AP unit contains subunits or smaller containers, skip to the Subunits Breakdown, next.

Total Pounds in AP Unit: _____ (From package description)

Cost per Pound: $ _____ (AP unit cost ÷ Total pounds)

Cost per Ounce AP Base: $ _____ (AP pound cost ÷ 16)

Fluid Ounce Yield of 1 Pound: _____ (Recipe on package)

Cost of 1 Prepared Fluid Ounce: $ _____ (Pound cost × Fluid ounce yield per pound)

Cost per Cup: $ _____ (Fluid ounce cost × 8)

Cost per Pint: $ _____ (Fluid ounce cost × 16)

Cost per Quart: $ _____ (Fluid ounce cost × 32)

Cost per Gallon: $ _____ (Fluid ounce cost × 128)

SUBUNITS BREAKDOWN

If the AP unit contains smaller (sub-) units such as boxes, jars, or cans, determine the cost per subunit and then proceed with the cost breakdown to determine the cost per prepared fluid ounce.

Number of Subunits in AP Unit: _____ (From invoice or package)

Cost per Subunit: $ _____ (AP unit cost ÷ Number of subunits)

Fluid Ounce Yield of 1 Subunit: _____ (From label or package recipe)

Cost of 1 Prepared Fluid Ounce: $ _____ (Subunit cost ÷ Subunit fluid ounce yield)

Cost per Cup: $ _____ (Fluid ounce cost × 8)

Cost per Pint: $ _____ (Fluid ounce cost × 16)

Cost per Quart: $ _____ (Fluid ounce cost × 32)

Cost per Gallon: $ _____ (Fluid ounce cost × 128)

Costing Worksheet

16

Recipe Card for Costing

Recipe Name: _____ Recipe Number: _____

To calculate Total Cost per Item in column E: Multiply column A by column D. Column F is for Volume Equivalents.

A	B	C	D	E	F
Amount	Recipe Unit	Item	Recipe Unit Cost	Total Cost per Item	Ounce Weight (Optional)
			$	$	
		Total Ounce Weight			
		Total Cost of Recipe		$	

Total Recipe Cost $ _____

YIELD COSTING

Formula

Total recipe cost ÷ Number yielded

	Yield Types	Number Yielded	Cost of One Yield Type
A	Fluid ounces		$
B	Cups		
C	Quarts		
D	Gallons		
E	Liters		
F	Ounces by weight		
G	Pounds		
H	Kilos		
I	Portions		
J	Pieces		
K	Containers		
L	Servings per Container	Just fill in #:	
M	Total servings (Yield # of K times L)		

Recipe Name: _____ Recipe Number: _____

Recipe Method or Procedure

1. Follow a practical sequence.

2. Identify the tools and equipment used.

3. List initial preparations first. Be complete but brief.

4. State prep and cooking times, plus all temperatures.

5. Include holding, storing, and plating instructions.

PURCHASING WORKSHEETS

Guide to Using the Purchasing Worksheets

Worksheet Number	Worksheet or Form Name	Use
	Purchasing Worksheet List	Use to find the purchasing worksheet you need.
	Purchasing Process Overview	Introduces the purchasing process.
1	Dry Herbs and Spices	Use to plan purchases of dry herbs and spices.
2	Fresh Herbs	Use to plan purchases of fresh herbs.
3	Produce	Use to plan purchases of fresh and canned vegetables and fruit.
4	Starchy Items	Use to plan purchases of legumes, rice, grains, cereals, and pastas.
5	Baking Products	Use to plan purchases of nuts and seeds, flour, meal, bran, crumbs, sweeteners, and special items.
6	Fats, Oils, Condiments	Use to plan purchases of fats, oils, and some condiments.
7	Bottled Liquids	Use to plan purchases of fluids in general, wines, spirits, and some condiments.
8	Dairy Products	Use to plan purchases of cheeses, eggs, milk, cream, yogurt, etc.
9	Brewed and Dispensed Beverages	Use to plan purchases of coffee, tea, cocoa, Beverages and soda.
10	Meats	Use to plan purchases of beef, veal, pork, and lamb.
11	Seafood	Use to plan purchases of finfish, some crustaceans, and mollusks.
12	Poultry	Use to plan purchases of chicken, turkey, and other fowl.
13	Flavor Bases	Use to plan purchases of bases for stocks, sauces, and soups.
14	Ingredient Aggregating Form	Use to combine same recipe ingredients.

15	Purchase Unit Measure Aggregating Form	Use to combine conversion answers from other purchasing worksheets.
16	Amounts Needed versus Par	Use to record needed purchase measures and compare to inventory and pars.
17	Inventory Form (Optional)	Use to count current inventory.
18	Food Weight Log (Optional)	Use to record variations in food weights of same item over time to get an average.
19	Purchase Unit Measures to Purchase Unit Packs	Use to convert purchase unit measures needed to purchase unit packs.
20	Food Order Form	Use as food ordering form.
21	Trimmed versus Untrimmed Prices	Use to decide whether a pretrimmed food is a better buy.

Overview

The purchasing process described here uses the information from Part I and the following set of worksheets to help you determine how much food to buy or cost out, based on any amount of food you plan to prepare.

There are two kinds of documents in the purchasing worksheets set:

1. Recipe unit to purchase unit conversion worksheets

2. Forms you'll use to manage the purchasing process and order food

Each conversion worksheet is used for a particular type of food: produce, canned goods, meats, poultry, and so on. To use them, you begin with the recipe unit amount of food you need to serve or use. As you fill in the worksheet, you will convert your recipe unit measures to purchase unit measures. The purchasing process and order forms are used to convert your purchase unit measures (like pounds, heads, pieces, etc.) into purchase unit packs such as cases, bags, and so on. Using these forms, you then compare your current inventory (and par inventory needs) against the needed purchase unit packs, and, ultimately, make a food order with a vendor(s).

In short, these forms will help you to figure out how much food to buy to meet a food production plan and maintain par levels of inventory.

Here is a summary of the steps to take in order to do just that:

1. Assemble the recipes needed for the production plan.

2. Combine all the identical ingredients in your recipes and total how much you need of each ingredient.

3. Use the individual purchasing worksheets to convert your ingredients from recipe unit measures (like cups, ounces, trimmed produce, cooked pasta, steaks, etc.) back to purchase unit measures (like pounds, ounces, pieces, or counts).

4. Take a physical inventory to compare how much of these items you have on hand.

5. Compare your plan's food needs to your current inventory and par inventory levels. This tells you how much to order to produce your plan and maintain your minimum inventory levels after the production plan's foods have been used up.

6. Convert the purchase unit measures of the foods you need back to their equivalent purchase unit packs (cases, boxes, etc.) in order to execute your plan and maintain your minimum par inventory levels.

7. Order the food amounts you need.

Here are more detailed instructions for completing a purchasing procedure:

Step 1. Gather your recipes.

Step 2. Go through the recipes and add up all the total recipe unit measure amounts for each identical ingredient. For the event or period of time for which you are making up your production plan, figure out how many times you will need to make each recipe in order to serve the total number of customers expected. For instance, if a recipe serves 60 but you expect 600 guests, you need to multiply your ingredient measures by 10.

Record your totals on a scratch pad or use the Ingredient Aggregating Form (Purchasing Worksheet 14). This form will help you record the amounts needed for ingredients that are used in more than one recipe. For instance, you may use medium onions in five recipes. This form helps you combine all needs for each item on one page. You will total each food's needs by the type of recipe unit measure.

NOTE

The Purchasing worksheet section begins with a guide to the rest of the worksheets, to help you find the worksheet (numbered 1 to 21) most useful for the foods or activity you are dealing with at the time.

Step 3. Use the various purchasing conversion worksheets to convert your ingredients' recipe unit measures back to purchase unit measures. In this regard, note the following:

+ *Recipe unit measures* are often small measures such as tablespoons, cups, pints, steaks, fluid ounces, or ounces.

+ *Purchase unit measures* are usually bigger: pounds, gallons, heads, pieces, and so on. (These measures are often used to count inventory, by the way.)

+ A *purchase unit pack* is an even bigger unit: a case, box, bag, and so on. These are usually called *as-purchased units* or *purchase units;* a purchase unit pack will contain a specific number of purchase unit measures. For instance a bag (the pack) of onions may weigh 50 pounds. So in this case, a pound is the purchase unit measure and a bag is the purchase unit pack. It's fairly common for the pack to state how many purchase unit measures it contains. For instance, the bag of onions would be called a 50-pound bag, rather than just a "bag." It makes things clearer for everyone.

The purchasing conversion worksheets are organized by food types: fresh herbs, vegetables, canned goods, starchy items, and so on. (They are categorized like the food tables in Part I, to make it easier to find any food and its conversion equivalents or yield percentages.)

On each purchasing worksheet there are conversion formulas to use, with specific ways of measuring that type of food. Select the formula that converts your recipe units back to a purchase unit measure. Each formula is followed by a series of boxes called *tables* to fill in. When you do so, you complete the conversion formula.

Complete your conversions going from the recipe unit measures to the purchase unit measures. The instructions for making these conversions are on each worksheet, and the forms indicate what to add, subtract, divide, or multiply, step by step.

You may have to make more than one conversion for the same food. For instance, if one recipe calls for a whole onion, while another calls for 2 cups of chopped onion, you will use the Produce conversion worksheet (Worksheet 3) for both ways of measuring the onion. In this case, you may find the Purchase

Unit Measure form, Worksheet 15, of some help. It provides a place to record and *combine* all the recipe unit measures-to-purchase unit measure conversions for the same food. Now record your purchase-unit-measure conversion–*answers* for each food on the Amount Needed versus Par worksheet (Worksheet 16). Write the food names in column A and the purchase unit measure *amounts* in column D.

Step 4. Take and record the inventory. This involves physically counting the quantity of the needed food items you have on hand. Count the inventory by the number of purchase unit measures. (By the way, counting inventory by purchase unit packs is also a fairly common practice. Inventory lists often contain a mix of purchase unit measures and purchase unit packs. For instance, you might count onions by the pound or by the number of 50-pound bags on hand. If you have 25 pounds of onions on hand, you could enter that amount in your inventory count as either 25 pounds or as half of a 50-pound bag.)

If you are taking a full inventory of all the foods in your kitchen, consider using the Inventory sheet first and then transfer your totals to Purchasing Worksheet 16, Amounts Needed versus Par, columns B and C. If you are taking an inventory of only the items you currently need for your production plan, you can enter your inventory totals directly into columns B and C of the Amounts Needed versus Par worksheet.

Step 5. Compare your minimum par levels (the amount of food that you want to always have on hand) to the amounts needed. On the Amounts Needed versus Par worksheet, subtract column D from column B. (You are subtracting the number of purchase unit measures that you need for your production plan from the number of purchase unit measures in your current inventory.) Record this answer in column E. This is the amount that you will still have in inventory after using the food needed for your production plan.

Note: If column E is zero, this means your current inventory is exactly equal to the amount you need for your production plan. If column E is less than zero, you don't have enough food on hand to meet your plan. You must order enough food to get column E to zero or higher. How much higher? It depends on your minimum par level for the food in question. Fill in your minimum par inventory level for each food in column F. Again, this amount should be stated in the same unit of measure as the others: the purchase unit measure.

Subtract the amount in column E from your minimum par level in column F. Enter this difference in column G. This is the amount of food you need to order to make your plan and maintain your minimum par level. If the number in column G is equal to or bigger than your minimum par level in column F, you do not have to order this food. You will have enough to make your production plan and still maintain your minimum par.

If you do not have a minimum par for this food, the amount in column E states how much you will still have in inventory after your production plan needs are met. If it is zero, your plan will wipe out your inventory. If it is less than zero, you will have to order the amount in column E to just make your plan—but you should order more or you will still be out of that food as soon as you produce your plan.

If you have no minimum par, use column G to record the amount in column E that is less than zero. This is the amount you need to buy in order to simply produce your plan. If the food in question is one you normally use in your operation, you should buy even more. Often, you don't have much choice in the matter. Say you are short 10 pounds of an item. That item may only be sold in purchase unit packs of 20 pounds. Therefore, you will have to order 20 pounds just to obtain the 10 pounds you need.

Step 6. Convert your purchase unit measures to purchase unit packs. The purchase unit packs are found in the accompanying Price Lists at the beginning of the Workbook. If your food item is not listed there, refer to a vendor's invoice or contact a vendor to determine that food's price and pack.

Use the Purchase Unit Measures to Purchase Unit Pack worksheet (Worksheet 19) to convert the numbers in column G on the Amounts Needed versus Par worksheet (Worksheet 16) to the amounts you need stated in purchase unit packs. (There is an example for rice already filled in on the worksheet to help you see how this goes.) In this step, you are dividing the number of purchase unit measures you need by the number of purchase unit measures contained in one purchase unit pack. Obviously, the units of measure have to be *identical*. For instance, you have to use pounds as a purchase unit measure if your purchase unit pack is a 20-pound box or a 40-pound case.

This step is usually pretty simple. Answers from the purchasing worksheets are often measured in pounds and ounces. Converting a need for 10 or 30 pounds of rice to a number of 20-pound boxes (a purchase unit pack for rice) is pretty straightforward. You divide the number of pounds you need by the number of pounds in the purchase unit pack. Assume, for example, that rice is sold in 20-pound boxes. For 10 pounds, you would divide 10 by 20, to get 0.5, which equals a half box. For 30 pounds, then, the answer is 1.5 boxes.

That said, be aware that purchase unit packs for some foods can vary regarding how much a unit weighs. Many produce items—fresh herbs, for instance—are often sold by the bunch and vary in weight from week to week or even in the same delivery. If you are sold these items by the bunch or count rather than by a weight, you will need to monitor the relative weights of these food items and order a count using an average weight. Why? The purchasing formulas for fresh produce often result in an answer expressed as a weight, because some of these foods (such as fresh herbs or bunches of radishes or heads of cauliflower) differ in the size of their as-purchased weight from one delivery to the next. Therefore, you need to ask your vendor for current weights of the items in question when doing your ordering. However, your salesperson may not know what the weights in question are, so you need to keep your own records of average weights for items of this type.

You can use the Food Weight Log (Worksheet 18) to keep these records. (Instructions for doing this are included with the log.) You would then enter your average weight of the item from your log in column E of the Purchase Unit Measures to Purchase Unit Packs worksheet to help you determine how many purchase unit packs (or, as-purchased units) of this item you'll need. Clear instructions for completing step 6 are printed on the Purchase Unit Measures to Purchase Unit Packs worksheet. Filling it in tells you exactly how many purchase unit packs you need to order. From there, you will go to the last purchasing worksheet, the Food Order Form, on which you will round off the number of purchase unit packs needed to arrive at a practical order.

Step 7. Record the final food order. Use the Food Order Form to write up the number of purchase unit packs you need to order. These, as you know by now, are typically called as-purchased units or, more commonly, AP units. Use the Price List, price quotes from your vendor(s), or earlier invoices to fill in the cost of one purchase unit. (The instructions on the Food Order Form tell you how to complete the item costing and totaling of your order.) Note that you will have to round off many of the AP unit amounts because you usually have to order whole cases, cartons, or boxes. So, despite the fact that you may need only 30 pounds of an item, you will have to buy 40 pounds if that item is sold only in 20-pound boxes, or 50 pounds if it only comes in 50-pound containers.

NOTE

It is often possible to order broken cases of foods, but if you do, the cost per pound or per count goes up. Fresh produce or canned goods may sometimes be ordered this way. Your supplier will advise you if a case cannot be broken down. If you do order an amount that is a *partial pack*—a broken case— expect to pay a premium for the amount you do buy.

SUMMARY

Many chefs learn to do much of this work on the fly. However, when a special event comes up, or you are planning for a new food service operation, or you are just starting out as a chef, it's a good idea to follow these steps carefully before attempting to fly through them. It does get easier with practice, and it will make a difference in your profits.

Here is a list of the forms you will be using in the purchasing process, from start to finish.

1. Recipe cards (Costing Worksheet 16)
2. Ingredient Aggregating Form

3. Recipe Unit Measures to Purchase Unit Measures conversion worksheets

   3a. Purchase Unit Measures aggregating form

4. Amounts Needed versus Par worksheet

   4a. Inventory Aggregating Form

   4b. Food Weight Log

5. Purchase Unit Measures to Purchase Unit Packs

6. Food Order Form

You may not need the subordinate forms (labeled "a" or "b") in all situations; they are optional. However, they do make the process complete and will help you explore the entire purchasing process more fully.

Purchasing Worksheet
1

Dry Herbs and Spices

Converting Tablespoons to Ounces

FORMULA: AS # of tablespoons ÷ # of tablespoons per ounce = AP ounces

Divide the total number of tablespoons needed by the number of tablespoons per ounce from Part I. The answer (AP in ounces) will be the number of ounces of dry herb or spice you need to buy or cost out.

Name of Item	Tablespoons Needed	÷	Tablespoons per Ounce	=	AP in Ounces
		÷		=	
		÷		=	
		÷		=	
		÷		=	
		÷		=	
		÷		=	
		÷		=	
		÷		=	

Converting Cups to Ounces

FORMULA: AS # of cups × Ounces per cup = AP ounces

Multiply the total cups needed by the ounces per cup from Part I. The answer (AP in ounces) will be the number of ounces of dry herb to buy or cost out.

Name of Item	Cups Needed	×	Ounce per Cup	=	AP in Ounces
		×		=	
		×		=	
		×		=	
		×		=	
		×		=	
		×		=	
		×		=	
		×		=	
		×		=	
		×		=	

Converting Piece Counts to Ounces

FORMULA: Count needed ÷ Count per ounce = AP ounce

Divide the total count of items needed by the number of that item per ounce from Part I. The answer will be the equivalent number of ounces needed.

Name of Item	Count Needed	÷	Count per Ounce	=	AP in Ounces
		÷		=	
		÷		=	
		÷		=	
		÷		=	
		÷		=	
		÷		=	
		÷		=	
		÷		=	
		÷		=	
		÷		=	
		÷		=	
		÷		=	
		÷		=	
		÷		=	
		÷		=	
		÷		=	
		÷		=	
		÷		=	
		÷		=	
		÷		=	
		÷		=	
		÷		=	
		÷		=	
		÷		=	

Converting Count per Tablespoon to Number of Tablespoons

FORMULA (Step 1): Count needed ÷ Count per tablespoon = Number of tablespoons needed

Converting Number of Tablespoons Needed to Ounces

FORMULA (Step 2): Tablespoons needed ÷ Tablespoons per ounce = AP ounces

1. Divide the count needed by the count per tablespoon from Part I. The answer will be the number of tablespoons needed.

2. To convert the number of tablespoons needed to ounces, divide the tablespoons needed by the tablespoons per ounce from Part I. This answer is the as-purchased amount of dry herb or spice you need to buy or cost out.

Step 1 Table

Name of Item	Count Needed	÷	Count per Tablespoon	=	Tablespoons Needed
		÷		=	
		÷		=	
		÷		=	
		÷		=	
		÷		=	
		÷		=	

Step 2 Table

Name of Item	Tablespoons Needed	÷	Tablespoons per Ounce	=	AP in Ounces
		÷		=	
		÷		=	
		÷		=	
		÷		=	
		÷		=	
		÷		=	

Purchasing Worksheet

2

Fresh Herbs

Determining Ounces to Buy Based on the Number of Garnish Leaves Needed

FORMULA 1: Leaves needed ÷ Leaves per AP ounce = AP ounces

Divide the number of leaves needed by the number of garnish leaves per as-purchased ounce from Part I. The answer (AP in ounces) will be the equivalent number of ounces of fresh herb you need to buy or cost out.

Name of Herb	Number of Leaves Needed	÷	Number of Leaves per AP Ounce	=	AP in Ounces
		÷		=	
		÷		=	
		÷		=	
		÷		=	
		÷		=	
		÷		=	
		÷		=	

Determining Ounces to Buy Based on Number of Tablespoons of Chopped Leaf Needed

FORMULA 2: Chopped tablespoons needed ÷ Chopped tablespoons per AP ounce = AP ounces

Divide the number of chopped tablespoons needed by the number of tablespoons of chopped leaf per purchased ounce from Part I. The answer (AP in ounces) will be the equivalent number of ounces of fresh herb you need to buy or cost out.

Name of Herb	Number of Chopped Tablespoons Needed	÷	Number of Tablespoons Chopped Leaf per AP Ounce	=	AP in Ounces
		÷		=	
		÷		=	
		÷		=	
		÷		=	
		÷		=	
		÷		=	
		÷		=	

Determining Ounces to Buy Based on the Number of Cups of Chopped Leaf Needed

FORMULA 3: (Chopped cups needed × 16) ÷ Chopped tablespoons per AP ounce = AP ounce

Multiply the number of cups of chopped leaf you need by 16; divide that answer by the number of tablespoons of chopped leaf per purchased ounce from Part I. The answer (AP in ounces) will be the equivalent number of ounces of fresh herb you need to buy or cost out.

Name of Herb	Number of Chopped Cups Needed	× 16 =	# of Tbsp. Chopped Leaf Needed	÷	Number of Tablespoons Chopped Leaf per AP Ounce	=	AP in Ounces
		× 16 =		÷		=	
		× 16 =		÷		=	
		× 16 =		÷		=	
		× 16 =		÷		=	
		× 16 =		÷		=	
		× 16 =		÷		=	
		× 16 =		÷		=	
		× 16 =		÷		=	
		× 16 =		÷		=	
		× 16 =		÷		=	
		× 16 =		÷		=	
		× 16 =		÷		=	
		× 16 =		÷		=	
		× 16 =		÷		=	
		× 16 =		÷		=	
		× 16 =		÷		=	
		× 16 =		÷		=	
		× 16 =		÷		=	
		× 16 =		÷		=	

Converting a Stemless Weight to an As-Purchased Weight

FORMULA 4: Stemless weight needed ÷ Weight yield percentage = AP weight

Divide the number of ounces of stemless herb needed by its weight yield percentage for stemless leaf per bunch (from Part I). Your answer will be the number of as-purchased ounces you need to buy or cost out.

Name of Herb	Stemless Ounces Needed	÷	Weight Yield Percentage	=	AP in Ounces
		÷		=	
		÷		=	
		÷		=	
		÷		=	
		÷		=	
		÷		=	
		÷		=	
		÷		=	
		÷		=	
		÷		=	
		÷		=	
		÷		=	
		÷		=	
		÷		=	
		÷		=	
		÷		=	
		÷		=	
		÷		=	
		÷		=	
		÷		=	
		÷		=	

Purchasing Worksheet

3

Produce

Converting a Trimmed Produce Item Weight to a Raw As-Purchased Weight

FORMULA 1: Amount needed in trimmed ounces ÷ Yield % = Raw AP weight in ounces

Divide the number of ounces needed after trimming by that food's yield percentage found in Part I. The answer (raw AP weight in ounces) will be the number of ounces of fresh, untrimmed produce you need to buy or cost out.

Name of Herb	Trimmed Ounces Needed	÷	Yield Percentage	=	Raw AP Ounces
		÷		=	
		÷		=	
		÷		=	
		÷		=	
		÷		=	
		÷		=	
		÷		=	
		÷		=	
		÷		=	
		÷		=	
		÷		=	
		÷		=	
		÷		=	
		÷		=	
		÷		=	
		÷		=	
		÷		=	
		÷		=	
		÷		=	
		÷		=	
		÷		=	
		÷		=	
		÷		=	

Converting As-Served Cups of Trimmed, Cut Produce to a Raw AP Weight

FORMULA 2: (AS cups needed × Trimmed, cleaned ounce weight per cup ÷ Trimmed ounces needed) ÷ Yield % of base item = AP in ounces

Multiply the needed number of cups of the trimmed and cut produce item by the ounce weight per cup. Divide this answer by the trim yield percentage of the same item. (Get the trimmed weight per cup and the yield percentages from Part I.) The answer is the ounce weight you need to buy or cost out. Divide that by 16 to arrive at an AP pound equivalent.

Name of Herb	Number of Cups Needed	×	Ounces per Cup	=	Yield %	=	AP Ounces	÷ 16	= AP Pounds
		×		=		=		÷ 16	=
		×		=		=		÷ 16	=
		×		=		=		÷ 16	=
		×		=		=		÷ 16	=
		×		=		=		÷ 16	=
		×		=		=		÷ 16	=
		×		=		=		÷ 16	=
		×		=		=		÷ 16	=
		×		=		=		÷ 16	=
		×		=		=		÷ 16	=

NOTE ON COMPACTION

Add 3 percent to your answers when dealing with 6- to 8-cup amounts, and 7 percent when dealing with 16-cup (gallon) amounts. This will reflect the compaction of foods in these larger vessels.

Converting Cups of the Trimmed, Cut item to a Purchase Unit Other than a Weight

FORMULA 3: AS cups of the trimmed, cleaned, and cut item ÷ Cups of the trimmed, cleaned, and cut item per purchase unit = AP purchase units

Divide the needed number of cups of the trimmed and cut item by the number of cups that are obtained from a single purchase unit of the raw item. (Locate this in the right-hand column of the Part I Produce table.) The answer will be the number of purchase units you need to buy or cost out.

Item Name	Number of AS Cups Needed of Item	÷	Number of Cups of Cut Item from 1 AP Unit	=	Number of AP Units
		÷		=	
		÷		=	
		÷		=	
		÷		=	
		÷		=	
		÷		=	
		÷		=	
		÷		=	
		÷		=	

Converting a Piece Count Needed to a Purchase Unit

FORMULA 4: AS pieces ÷ Trimmed count per AP unit = AP units

Divide the number of pieces (leaves, stalks, each, etc.) needed by the count yield per AP unit stated in Part I. The answer will be the number of purchase units needed, either in weight or other AP unit measure.

Name of Item	Number of Pieces Needed	÷	Number of Pieces per AP Unit	=	Number of AP Units
		÷		=	
		÷		=	
		÷		=	
		÷		=	
		÷		=	
		÷		=	

Converting Drained Ounces to Number-10 Cans Needed

FORMULA FOR DRAINED CANNED GOODS:

AS ounces needed ÷ Drained ounce weight per can = AP # of cans

Divide the ounces needed by the USDA minimum drained weight in ounces per can from Part I. The answer will be the number of number-10 cans you need to buy or cost out.

Item Name	Drained Ounces Needed	÷	Minimum Drained Ounces per Number-10 Can	=	Number of AP Number-10 Cans
		÷		=	
		÷		=	
		÷		=	
		÷		=	
		÷		=	
		÷		=	
		÷		=	
		÷		=	
		÷		=	
		÷		=	
		÷		=	
		÷		=	
		÷		=	
		÷		=	
		÷		=	
		÷		=	
		÷		=	
		÷		=	
		÷		=	
		÷		=	
		÷		=	
		÷		=	

Converting Undrained Ounces to Number-10 Cans Needed

FORMULA FOR UNDRAINED CANNED GOODS:

AS ounces needed ÷ Total ounces (actual) per can = AP # of cans

Divide the undrained ounces needed by the total ounces per can (locate on the Canned Food Weight-to-Volume table in Part I). The answer will be the amount of number-10 cans you need to buy or cost out.

Item Name	Undrained Ounces Needed	÷	Total Ounces per Number-10 Can	=	AP Number-10 Cans Needed
		÷		=	
		÷		=	
		÷		=	
		÷		=	
		÷		=	
		÷		=	
		÷		=	
		÷		=	
		÷		=	
		÷		=	
		÷		=	
		÷		=	
		÷		=	
		÷		=	
		÷		=	
		÷		=	
		÷		=	
		÷		=	
		÷		=	
		÷		=	
		÷		=	
		÷		=	

Converting a Volume of Canned Food to Number-10 Cans Needed

FORMULA FOR VOLUMES OF DRAINED OR UNDRAINED CANNED GOODS:

(AS volumes needed × Ounces per volume measure) ÷ Net or drained ounces per can = AP # of cans

First, multiply the number of ounces per cup, quart, or half gallon (from the Canned Foods Weight-to-Volume table in Part I) by the number of cups, quarts, or half gallons needed. Second, divide the answer by the net or drained ounces per number-10 can from the same table. Your answer will be the amount of number-10 cans needed to buy or cost out.

Step 1 Table: Multiply the number of cups, quarts, or half gallons by its ounce weight to get the total ounces needed.

Item Name	Measure: Cup, Quart, Half Gallon	Number of Measures Needed	×	Ounces per Measure	=	Total Ounces Needed
			×		=	
			×		=	
			×		=	
			×		=	
			×		=	
			×		=	
			×		=	

Step 2 Table: Divide the total ounces needed by the net or drained ounces per can (from the Canned Foods Weight-to-Volume table). Your answer will be the number of cans to buy or cost out.

Item Name	Total Ounces Needed (Step 1 Answer)	÷	Net Drained Ounces per Can	=	Number of AP Cans Needed
		÷		=	
		÷		=	
		÷		=	
		÷		=	
		÷		=	
		÷		=	
		÷		=	

Miscellaneous Canned or Bottled Produce Items

FORMULA FOR CONVERTING DRAINED OUNCES NEEDED TO AP CONTAINERS:

Drained ounces needed ÷ Drained ounces per AP container = AP containers

Divide the drained ounces needed by the drained ounces per AP container from Part 1. The answer will be the number of purchase units to buy, use, or cost.

Item Name	Drained Ounces Needed	÷	Drained Ounces per Container	=	# AP Containers

FORMULA FOR USING YIELD PERCENTAGES TO COMPUTE AP CONTAINERS NEEDED:

(Drained ounces needed ÷ Yield % = Ounces needed) ÷ AP ounces per container = AP containers

Divide the number of drained ounces needed by the drained yield percentage from Part 1. Divide that answer by the AP ounces per AP container. The answer will be the number of containers to buy, use, or cost.

Item Name	Drained Ounces Needed	÷	Yield %	=	AP Ounces needed	÷	AP ounces per container	=	AP Containers

FORMULA FOR CONVERTING A PIECE COUNT TO AP CONTAINERS:

Count needed ÷ Count per AP container = AP containers needed

Divide the total count needed by the number of pieces in one container (from Part 1). The answer will be the number of purchase units to buy, use, or cost.

Item Name	Count Needed	÷	Count per AP Container	=	# AP Containers

Purchasing Worksheet

4

Starchy Items

Starchy items discussed here include legumes, rices, grains, cereals, and pastas. All formulas here use any of the corresponding tables in Part I.

Converting a Cooked Weight to a Raw AP Weight

FORMULA 1: AS cooked pounds ÷ Cooked pounds yield of 1 raw pound = AP weight

Divide the number of cooked pounds you need by the number of cooked pounds that 1 raw pound will yield (from Part I). Your answer will be the number of raw pounds you need to buy or cost out.

Item Name	Number of Cooked Pounds Needed	÷	Number of Cooked Pounds Yielded from 1 Pound Raw	=	Raw AP Pounds
		÷		=	
		÷		=	
		÷		=	
		÷		=	
		÷		=	
		÷		=	

FORMULA 1a: Alternate method using the yield percentage factor:

Cooked pounds needed ÷ Cooking yield percentage = Raw AP pounds

Divide the number of pounds of the cooked item needed (the as-served amount) by the cooking yield percentage. (Locate this percentage in the right-hand column in the Part I Legumes table or Rice, Grains, Cereals table labeled "Raw to Cooked Weight Increase Percentage." When using this figure, remember to move the decimal figure two places to the left; for example, 291% becomes 2.91.)

Item Name	Number of Cooked Pounds Needed	÷	Cooked Yield Percentage	=	Raw AP Pounds
		÷		=	
		÷		=	
		÷		=	
		÷		=	
		÷		=	
		÷		=	

NOTE

Using the percentage method is a bit more accurate because there is less rounding involved. For example, you will use 2.91 instead of 2.9 as a formula factor.

Converting Cooked Cups Needed to a Raw AP Weight

FORMULA 2: Cooked cups needed ÷ Cooked cups yielded from 1 pound raw = AP pounds

Divide the number of cups of the cooked item you need (the as-served amount) by the number of cooked cups that 1 pound raw will yield (from Part I). The answer will be the number of raw pounds you need to buy or cost out.

Item Name	Number of Cooked Cups Needed (AS Cups)	÷	Number Cooked Cups Yielded from 1 Pound Raw	=	Raw AP Pounds
		÷		=	
		÷		=	
		÷		=	
		÷		=	
		÷		=	
		÷		=	

Converting Cups of Cold Cereal or Raw Starch Needed to As-Purchased Pounds

FORMULA 3: Cups of raw starch or cold cereal item needed ÷ Cups per pound = AP pounds

This formula can be used to calculate how many pounds of raw rice or other grain or cereal you need for a recipe that calls for that food in raw cups, or for a meal calling for a specific number of cups of cold, uncooked cereal.

Divide the number of cups needed of the raw or uncooked item by the number of cups per pound (raw) from Part I. Your answer will be the equivalent number of raw pounds to buy or cost out.

Item Name	Number of Raw Cups Needed (AS Cups)	÷	Number of Cups per Raw Pound	=	AP in Pounds
		÷		=	
		÷		=	
		÷		=	
		÷		=	
		÷		=	
		÷		=	

Pasta Purchasing Formulas

FORMULA 1: Dry pasta: AS cooked pounds ÷ 2.5 = AP pounds

FORMULA 2: Fresh pasta: AS cooked pounds ÷ 2.0 = AP pounds

Both formulas use the same format: You divide the number of pounds of cooked pasta you need, the as-served weight, by a specific conversion factor.

+ The conversion factor for dry pasta is 2.5 (1 pound dry pasta yields 2.5 pounds cooked).

+ The conversion factor for fresh pasta is 2.0 (1 pound fresh pasta yields 2 pounds cooked).

Item Name	As-Served Pounds Needed	Dry Pasta ÷ 2.5	or	Fresh Pasta ÷ 2.0	=	AP Pounds
		÷ 2.5	or	÷ 2.0	=	
		÷ 2.5	or	÷ 2.0	=	
		÷ 2.5	or	÷ 2.0	=	
		÷ 2.5	or	÷ 2.0	=	
		÷ 2.5	or	÷ 2.0	=	
		÷ 2.5	or	÷ 2.0	=	
		÷ 2.5	or	÷ 2.0	=	
		÷ 2.5	or	÷ 2.0	=	
		÷ 2.5	or	÷ 2.0	=	

NOTE

You can use different conversion factors if your pasta products and cooking methods result in bigger or smaller cooked yields. It is not uncommon for cooks to obtain 3 pounds of cooked pasta from every pound of dry pasta. Results vary. Just substitute your conversion factors for the 2.5 and/or 2.0 used here.

Purchasing Worksheet

5

Baking Items

Baking items discussed here include nuts and seeds, flour, meal, brans and crumbs, sweeteners, and other special items. All formulas here use any of the corresponding tables in Part I.

Converting Cups to Pounds

FORMULA 1: (As-served or used cups × Ounces per cup) ÷ 16 = AP pounds

First multiply the number of cups needed by the ounce weight of 1 cup (ounces per cup from Part I). Divide that answer by 16 to convert the ounces to pounds. This final answer will be the number of pounds you need to buy or cost out.

Item Name	Number of Cups Needed	×	Ounces per Cup	=	Total AP Ounces Needed	÷ 16	=	AP in Pounds
		×		=		÷ 16	=	
		×		=		÷ 16	=	
		×		=		÷ 16	=	
		×		=		÷ 16	=	
		×		=		÷ 16	=	
		×		=		÷ 16	=	
		×		=		÷ 16	=	
		×		=		÷ 16	=	
		×		=		÷ 16	=	
		×		=		÷ 16	=	
		×		=		÷ 16	=	
		×		=		÷ 16	=	
		×		=		÷ 16	=	
		×		=		÷ 16	=	
		×		=		÷ 16	=	
		×		=		÷ 16	=	
		×		=		÷ 16	=	
		×		=		÷ 16	=	
		×		=		÷ 16	=	

Converting Tablespoons to AP Ounces

FORMULA 2a: (Ounces per cup ÷ 16) × Tablespoons needed = AP in ounces

Converting Tablespoons from AP Ounces to AP Pounds

FORMULA 2b: AP in ounces ÷ 16 = AP in pounds

Divide the number of ounces per cup (as stated in Part I) by 16. Multiply this answer, which is actually the ounce weight per tablespoon, by the number of tablespoons needed. Your answer will be the number of ounces you need to buy or cost out. To convert ounces to pounds, divide the number of ounces by 16.

Item Name	Ounces per Cup	÷ 16	=	Ounces per Tablespoon	×	Number of Tablespoons Needed	=	AP in Ounces	÷ 16	AP in Pounds
		÷ 16	=		×		=		÷ 16	
		÷ 16	=		×		=		÷ 16	
		÷ 16	=		×		=		÷ 16	
		÷ 16	=		×		=		÷ 16	
		÷ 16	=		×		=		÷ 16	
		÷ 16	=		×		=		÷ 16	
		÷ 16	=		×		=		÷ 16	

Converting As-Served (or As-Used) Pints to Pounds

FORMULA 3: AS pints × Pounds per pint = AP pounds

Multiply the number of pints you need by the number of pounds per pint from Part I. Your answer is the number of pounds you need to buy or cost out.

Item Name	Number Pints Needed	×	Pounds per Pint	=	AP in Pounds
		×		=	
		×		=	
		×		=	
		×		=	
		×		=	
		×		=	
		×		=	

Converting As-Served (or As-Used) Quarts to Pounds

FORMULA 4: [AS quarts × (2 × Pounds per pint) ÷ 1.5%] = AP pounds

First multiply the number of pounds per pint (from Part I) times 2. Why? Because there are 2 pints per quart; this step converts the pint weight to a quart weight. But, remember, compaction of 1.5 percent occurs at a quart volume, so add 1.5 percent to the calculated quart weight. Now multiply the number of quarts you need by that answer—the compacted quart weight. The final answer is the number of pounds you need to buy or cost out. (See following note.)

Item Name	Pounds per Pint	× 2	=	Pounds per Quart	Pounds per Quart × 1.5%	Total Last Two Columns	×	Number of Quarts Needed	=	AP in Pounds
		× 2	=				×		=	
		× 2	=				×		=	
		× 2	=				×		=	
		× 2	=				×		=	
		× 2	=				×		=	
		× 2	=				×		=	
		× 2	=				×		=	
		× 2	=				×		=	
		× 2	=				×		=	
		× 2	=				×		=	
		× 2	=				×		=	
		× 2	=				×		=	
		× 2	=				×		=	
		× 2	=				×		=	
		× 2	=				×		=	
		× 2	=				×		=	
		× 2	=				×		=	
		× 2	=				×		=	
		× 2	=				×		=	
		× 2	=				×		=	

Converting As-Served (or As-Used) Gallons to Pounds

FORMULA 5: [AS gallons × (8 × Pounds per pint) + 7%] = AP pounds

First multiply the number of pounds per pint (from Part I) by 8, because there are 8 pints per gallon; this step converts the pint weight to a gallon weight. But, remember, compaction of about 7 percent occurs with a gallon volume, so add 7 percent to the computed gallon weight. Now multiply the number of gallons you need by that answer—the compacted gallon weight. The final answer is the number of pounds you need to buy or cost out. (See following note.)

Item Name	Pounds per Pint	× 8	=	Pounds per Gallon	Pounds per Gallon × 7%	Total: Add Last Two Columns	×	Number of Gallons Needed	=	AP in Pounds
		× 8	=				×		=	
		× 8	=				×		=	
		× 8	=				×		=	
		× 8	=				×		=	
		× 8	=				×		=	
		× 8	=				×		=	
		× 8	=				×		=	
		× 8	=				×		=	
		× 8	=				×		=	

NOTE

It is not necessary to add the compaction factors to the last two formulas when dealing with foods that do not compact, such as liquids or very dense foods like packed brown sugar. Use the compaction factors when dealing with powdery or loose foods such as flours, powdered sugar, and ground or milled foods.

Purchasing Worksheet

6

Fats, Oils, and Condiments

Fats and Oils: Converting Clarified Butter Weights to Whole Butter Weights

FORMULA 1: AS ounce weight of clarified butter ÷ 0.75 = AP ounce weight, whole butter

Divide the number of weighed ounces of clarified butter needed by its conversion factor of 75 percent (from Part I). The answer will be the number of ounces of raw, whole butter you need to buy or cost out. To convert this answer to pounds, divide it by 16.

Clarified Butter Fat	Ounces Needed	÷	.75	=	AP in Ounces, Whole Butter	÷ 16	=	AP Pounds, Whole Butter
		÷	.75	=		÷ 16	=	
		÷	.75	=		÷ 16	=	
		÷	.75	=		÷ 16	=	
		÷	.75	=		÷ 16	=	
		÷	.75	=		÷ 16	=	
		÷	.75	=		÷ 16	=	
		÷	.75	=		÷ 16	=	

Fats and Oils: Converting Clarified Butter Volumes to Whole Butter Weights

FORMULA 2: AS fluid ounces of clarified butter ÷ 0.804 = AP ounce weight, whole butter

Divide the number of fluid ounces of clarified butter needed by its conversion factor of 80.4 percent. The answer will be the number of ounces of raw, whole butter you need to buy or cost out. To convert this answer to pounds, divide it by 16.

Clarified Butter Fat	Fluid Ounces Needed	÷	.804	=	AP in Ounces, Whole Butter	÷ 16	=	AP Pounds, Whole Butter
		÷	.804	=		÷ 16	=	
		÷	.804	=		÷ 16	=	
		÷	.804	=		÷ 16	=	
		÷	.804	=		÷ 16	=	
		÷	.804	=		÷ 16	=	
		÷	.804	=		÷ 16	=	
		÷	.804	=		÷ 16	=	

Fats and Oils: Converting AS Cups of Fat to AP Pounds of Fat

FORMULA 3: Cups needed ÷ Cups per pound = AP in pounds of fat

Divide the number of cups of fat you need by the number of cups per pound stated for that fat in Part I. The answer will be the number of pounds of as-purchased fat you need to buy or cost out.

Item Name	Number of Cups Needed	÷	Cups per Pound	=	AP in Pounds
		÷		=	
		÷		=	
		÷		=	
		÷		=	
		÷		=	
		÷		=	
		÷		=	
		÷		=	

Condiments: Converting AS Tablespoons to AP Ounces

FORMULA 1: AS tablespoons needed × Ounce weight of 1 tablespoon = AP ounces

Multiply the number of tablespoons needed by the ounce weight of 1 tablespoon, as stated in Part I, Condiments table. The answer will be the number of as-purchased ounces you need to buy or cost out. (These ounces are ounces by weight, not fluid ounces.)

Item Name	Number of Tablespoons Needed	×	Ounce Weight of 1 Tablespoon	=	AP in Ounces
		×		=	
		×		=	
		×		=	
		×		=	
		×		=	
		×		=	
		×		=	
		×		=	

Condiments: Converting As-Served Cups to As-Purchased Ounces

FORMULA 2: AS cups × Ounce weight of 1 cup = AP ounces

Multiply the number of cups needed times the ounce weight of 1 cup (from Part I). The answer will be the number of ounces you need to buy or cost out. Divide that answer by 16 to convert ounces to pounds.

Item Name	Number of Cups Needed	×	Ounce Weight of 1 Cup	÷	AP in Ounces	÷ 16 =	AP in Pounds
		×		=		÷ 16 =	
		×		=		÷ 16 =	
		×		=		÷ 16 =	
		×		=		÷ 16 =	
		×		=		÷ 16 =	
		×		=		÷ 16 =	
		×		=		÷ 16 =	
		×		=		÷ 16 =	
		×		=		÷ 16 =	
		×		=		÷ 16 =	
		×		=		÷ 16 =	
		×		=		÷ 16 =	
		×		=		÷ 16 =	
		×		=		÷ 16 =	
		×		=		÷ 16 =	
		×		=		÷ 16 =	
		×		=		÷ 16 =	
		×		=		÷ 16 =	
		×		=		÷ 16 =	
		×		=		÷ 16 =	
		×		=		÷ 16 =	
		×		=		÷ 16 =	

Purchasing Worksheet

7

Bottled Liquids

Converting U.S. Fluid Ounces to Bottles or Other Containers

FORMULA: U.S. fluid ounces needed ÷ Fluid ounces per container = AP containers

If the container is measured in liters or milliliters, and your recipe calls for U.S. fluid ounces, convert the number of milliliters to U.S. fluid ounces by dividing the number of milliliters in the container by 29.5735. First, convert milliliters to U.S. fluid ounces.

Item Name	Number of Milliliters in Container	÷	29.5735	=	U.S. Fluid Ounces
		÷		=	
		÷		=	
		÷		=	
		÷		=	
		÷		=	
		÷		=	
		÷		=	

Now, divide the number of fluid ounces needed by the number of fluid ounces contained in one container. Your answer will be the number of bottles or containers you need to buy or cost out. Locate the number of fluid ounces per wine or spirit bottle type or size in the Liquids table in Part I. Locate the number of fluid ounces for condiments on the container itself or on the Price List.

Item Name (Wine, Spirit, Sauce, etc.)	Container Name or Size	Fluid Ounces Needed	÷	U.S. Fluid Ounces per Container	=	Number of AP Containers
			÷		=	
			÷		=	
			÷		=	
			÷		=	
			÷		=	
			÷		=	
			÷		=	
			÷		=	
			÷		=	
			÷		=	

Purchasing Worksheet

8

Dairy Products

The dairy products category includes cheeses, eggs, milk products, and yogurt.

Purchasing Dairy Liquids

When your as-served (or as-used) recipe measurements are expressed as volumes, such as a quart or half gallon, and you purchase these items (milks, creams, yogurts) by volume, follow this formula:

AS fluid ounces needed ÷ Fluid ounces in a purchase unit = Purchase units

First convert all your recipe unit measures to fluid ounces. Then:

1. Enter the dairy liquid's name in the first column.

2. Add all of the fluid ounces in your recipes and enter that amount in column two.

3. Enter the fluid ounces contained in one purchase unit in the fourth column.

4. Divide the total fluid ounces needed by the number of fluid ounces in one purchase unit.

5. Enter your answer in the last column.

Item Name	Total Fluid Ounces	÷	Fluid Ounces in Purchase Unit	=	# of Purchase Units
		÷		=	
		÷		=	
		÷		=	
		÷		=	
		÷		=	
		÷		=	
		÷		=	
		÷		=	
		÷		=	
		÷		=	
		÷		=	
		÷		=	
		÷		=	
		÷		=	

If your recipes call for weights of dairy liquids (baking recipes typically do call for weights rather than volumes), follow this two-step procedure to convert dairy liquid weights to volumes.

Step 1: Converting weights needed to equivalent pints.

1. Enter the item's name in column 1.

2. Convert all the pounds needed to ounces and enter the result in column 2.

3. Look up the ounces per pint in the Dairy Items table and enter that number in column 4.

4. Divide the total ounces needed by the ounces per pint, and enter the answer in column 6.

Item Name	Total Ounces Needed	÷	Ounces per Pint	=	Number Pints Needed
		÷		=	
		÷		=	
		÷		=	
		÷		=	
		÷		=	
		÷		=	

Step 2: Converting pints needed to purchase units.

1. Enter the item's name in column 1.

2. Enter the total pints needed from Step 1 in column 2.

3. Enter the number of pints contained in your purchase unit in column 4.

4. Divide the total pints needed by the number of pints in a purchase unit and enter your answer in column 6.

Item Name	# Pints Needed	÷	# Pints in Purchase Unit	=	Purchase Units Needed
		÷		=	
		÷		=	
		÷		=	
		÷		=	
		÷		=	
		÷		=	

Converting As-Served (or As-Used) Cups to As-Purchased Pounds

There are two methods to make this conversion:

1. Multiply the number of cups you need by the weight per cup from Part I.
2. Divide the number of cups you need by the number of cups per pound for that item (from Part I).

Both methods produce the same answer: the weight of the as-purchased item you need to buy or cost out.

If your needs are expressed in quarts, half gallons, or gallons, first convert them to cups by multiplying:

+ Number of quarts you need by 4, then add 1.5 percent for compaction.
+ Number of half gallons you need by 8, then add 3.5 percent for compaction.
+ Number of gallons you need by 16, then add 7 percent for compaction.

NOTE

No compaction factor is needed for dense, soft, or wet items such as yogurt and sour cream. Use compaction factors for shredded or crumbled items.

FORMULA 1: (AS cups × Ounces per cup) ÷ 16 = AP pounds

Multiply the number of cups you need times the ounce weight per cup, from Part I. That answer will be in ounces. To convert to pounds, simply divide it by 16.

Item Name	Number of AS Cups Needed	×	Ounce Weight per Cup	=	AP in Ounces	÷ 16 =	AP in Pounds
		×		=		÷ 16 =	
		×		=		÷ 16 =	
		×		=		÷ 16 =	
		×		=		÷ 16 =	
		×		=		÷ 16 =	
		×		=		÷ 16 =	
		×		=		÷ 16 =	
		×		=		÷ 16 =	
		×		=		÷ 16 =	
		×		=		÷ 16 =	
		×		=		÷ 16 =	
		×		=		÷ 16 =	

FORMULA 2: AS cups ÷ Cups per pound = AP pounds

Divide the number of cups needed by the number of cups per pound, from Part I. That answer will be in pounds. (When converting from quarts, half gallons, or gallons, add the compaction factors given above to the number of AS cups needed.)

Item Name	Number of AS Cups Needed	÷	Number of Cups per Pound	=	AP in Pounds
		÷		=	
		÷		=	
		÷		=	
		÷		=	
		÷		=	
		÷		=	
		÷		=	
		÷		=	

Eggs: Converting Quarts of Pooled Eggs to an AP Count of Whole Large Eggs

FORMULA 1: Quarts needed of pooled large eggs × 19.44 = AP count of large eggs

Multiply the number of quarts of shelled (pooled) large eggs you need times 19.44 (the number of large shelled eggs contained in 1 quart, as stated in Part I). The answer will be the count of large eggs you need to buy or cost out. To convert this number to dozens, divide it by 12. (To convert it to flats, divide it by 30.)

Number of Quarts of Large Eggs Needed	× 19.44 =	AP Count Each	÷ 12 =	AP Count in Dozens	Or ÷ 30 =	AP Count in Flats
	× 19.44 =		÷ 12 =		Or ÷ 30 =	
	× 19.44 =		÷ 12 =		Or ÷ 30 =	
	× 19.44 =		÷ 12 =		Or ÷ 30 =	
	× 19.44 =		÷ 12 =		Or ÷ 30 =	
	× 19.44 =		÷ 12 =		Or ÷ 30 =	
	× 19.44 =		÷ 12 =		Or ÷ 30 =	
	× 19.44 =		÷ 12 =		Or ÷ 30 =	
	× 19.44 =		÷ 12 =		Or ÷ 30 =	

Eggs: Converting Quarts of Pooled Eggs to an AP Count of Whole Medium Eggs

FORMULA 2: Quarts needed of pooled medium eggs × 22 = AP count of medium eggs

Multiply the number of quarts of shelled medium eggs you need by 22 (the number of medium shelled eggs contained in 1 quart, as stated in Part I). The answer will be the count of medium eggs you need to buy or cost out. To convert this number to dozens, divide it by 12. (To convert it to flats, divide it by 30.)

Number of Quarts of Large Eggs Needed	× 22 =	AP Count Each	÷ 12 =	AP Count in Dozens	Or ÷ 30 =	AP Count in Flats
	× 22 =		÷ 12 =		Or ÷ 30 =	
	× 22 =		÷ 12 =		Or ÷ 30 =	
	× 22 =		÷ 12 =		Or ÷ 30 =	
	× 22 =		÷ 12 =		Or ÷ 30 =	
	× 22 =		÷ 12 =		Or ÷ 30 =	
	× 22 =		÷ 12 =		Or ÷ 30 =	

Eggs: Converting a Weight of Large Eggs to an AP Count

FORMULA 3: Pounds of large eggs needed × 9 = AP count

Multiply the number of pounds of large eggs needed by 9 (the number of shelled large eggs per pound from Part I). The answer will be the count, or number, of large shelled eggs you need to buy or cost out. To convert this number to dozens, divide it by 12. (To convert it to flats, divide it by 30.)

Number of Quarts of Large Eggs Needed	× 9 =	AP Count Each	÷ 12 =	AP Count in Dozens	Or ÷ 30 =	AP Count in Flats
	× 9 =		÷ 12 =		Or ÷ 30 =	
	× 9 =		÷ 12 =		Or ÷ 30 =	
	× 9 =		÷ 12 =		Or ÷ 30 =	
	× 9 =		÷ 12 =		Or ÷ 30 =	
	× 9 =		÷ 12 =		Or ÷ 30 =	
	× 9 =		÷ 12 =		Or ÷ 30 =	

NOTE

There are 180 eggs in a case. One case equals 15 dozen eggs, or 6 flats. To convert dozens to a number of cases, divide the number of dozens needed by 15. To convert flats to cases, divide the number of flats you need by 6.

Miscellaneous Dairy: Converting a Count Needed to a Purchase Unit Count

FORMULA: Count needed ÷ Count per purchase unit = Purchase units required

Determine how many individual pieces are needed. Divide this number by the number of pieces that come in a purchase unit. This is specified on the purchase unit or invoice. The answer will be the number of purchase units required.

Item Name	Total Count Needed	÷	Count per Purchase Unit	=	Purchase Units Required
		÷		=	
		÷		=	
		÷		=	
		÷		=	
		÷		=	
		÷		=	
		÷		=	
		÷		=	
		÷		=	
		÷		=	
		÷		=	
		÷		=	
		÷		=	
		÷		=	
		÷		=	
		÷		=	
		÷		=	
		÷		=	
		÷		=	
		÷		=	

Purchasing Worksheet

9 | Brewed and Dispensed Beverages

Converting Brewed Coffee Needs to an As-Purchased Weight of Grounds

FORMULA 1: AS gallons × 3.25 = AP grounds in ounces

Part I shows that a standard 60-fluid-ounce pot of brewed coffee requires 1.5 ounces of coffee grounds. Therefore, a full gallon requires slightly more than twice that amount, or 3.25 ounces per gallon. So, to determine the number of ounces of coffee grounds you'll need to make any number of as-served gallons of brewed coffee, you multiply the number of gallons you need times 3.25. The answer will be the number of ounces of grounds you need to buy or cost out. (If you want a stronger coffee, increase the 3.25 to a higher amount—3.75 ounces of grounds per gallon, for instance, yields a stronger coffee.)

Number of Gallons Needed	Regular Strength	Or Extra-Strong	=	AP in Ounces	÷ 16 =	AP in Pounds
	× 3.25	× 3.75	=		÷ 16 =	
	× 3.25	× 3.75	=		÷ 16 =	
	× 3.25	× 3.75	=		÷ 16 =	
	× 3.25	× 3.75	=		÷ 16 =	

Converting Brewed Iced Tea Needs to an AP Weight of Tea Leaf

FORMULA 2: AS gallons × 2 = AP tea leaf in ounces

Part I states that you need 2 ounces of tea leaves to brew 1 gallon of tea, strong enough to be suitable for iced tea. You can use less, and some tea companies suggest using less, but your iced tea may be weak if you do so, particularly after some of the ice melts in the glass. So, to determine how much tea leaf you will need to make any number of as-served gallons of brewed tea, you multiply the number of gallons of tea you want (before adding the ice) by 2. The answer will be the number of ounces of tea leaf you will need to buy or cost out. Remember, when estimating the total number of gallons needed, the ice in a glass will reduce its capacity by at least 25 percent, and you will not fill a glass to the rim; therefore, a 16-ounce glass may only hold 10 ounces of actual brewed tea. (This is roughly 60 percent of the capacity of the glass.)

Number of Gallons Needed	× 2 =	AP in Ounces	÷ 16 =	AP in Pounds
	× 2 =		÷ 16 =	
	× 2 =		÷ 16 =	
	× 2 =		÷ 16 =	
	× 2 =		÷ 16 =	

Converting Brewed Hot Cocoa Needs to an AP Weight of Cocoa Powder

FORMULA 3: AS gallons needed × 3.35 = AP ounces of cocoa powder

Part I states that 1 cup of cocoa powder weighing 3.35 ounces is needed to brew 1 gallon of cocoa. So, multiply the number of gallons you need times 3.35. The answer will be the number of ounces of cocoa powder you need to buy or cost out.

Number of Gallons Needed	× 3.35 =	AP in Ounces	÷ 16 =	AP in Pounds
	× 3.35 =		÷ 16 =	
	× 3.35 =		÷ 16 =	
	× 3.35 =		÷ 16 =	
	× 3.35 =		÷ 16 =	
	× 3.35 =		÷ 16 =	
	× 3.35 =		÷ 16 =	

Converting Dispensed Soda Needs to AP Number of Syrup Boxes

FORMULA 4: Fluid ounces of soda needed × 3,840 = # of syrup boxes

A 5-gallon box of soda syrup will yield 3,840 fluid ounces of dispensed soda. To calculate how many boxes of syrup to order or have on hand, multiply the number of drinks needed by the number of fluid ounces of soda in each drink. Then divide the total fluid ounces needed by the fluid-ounce yield of one box of syrup (3,840). The answer will be the number of boxes of syrup to buy or cost.

Number of Gallons Needed	×	Fluid Ounces per Drink	=	Total Fluid Ounces	÷	3,840	=	Number of AP Syrup Boxes (5 Gallons Each)
	×		=		÷		=	
	×		=		÷		=	
	×		=		÷		=	
	×		=		÷		=	
	×		=		÷		=	
	×		=		÷		=	
	×		=		÷		=	
	×		=		÷		=	
	×		=		÷		=	

Purchasing Worksheet

10

Meat

Converting Portions per Piece to Whole As-Purchased Pieces

FORMULA 1: Total portion count needed ÷ Portion count per piece = Number of pieces, AP

Divide the total number of portions needed by the number of portions you get from 1 whole piece. The number of portions you get from 1 piece is dictated primarily by the size of the portion in question. The formula answer will be the number of whole pieces (whole tenderloins, sirloins, strip loins, prime ribs, etc.) you need to buy or cost out.

Name of Basic Piece	Portion Name and Size	Number of Portions Needed	÷	Number of Portions per Piece	=	AP in Whole Pieces
			÷		=	
			÷		=	
			÷		=	
			÷		=	
			÷		=	
			÷		=	
			÷		=	
			÷		=	
			÷		=	

Converting a Trimmed Raw Weight to an Untrimmed Raw Purchase Weight

FORMULA 2: Number of pounds of trimmed meat ÷ Yield percentage = AP in pounds

Divide the number of pounds of raw meat you will need after trimming by its yield percentage, from Part I. The answer will be the number of pounds of raw, untrimmed meat you need to buy or cost out.

Name of Meat Item	Number of Raw Pounds Needed, Trimmed	÷	Yield %	=	AP in Pounds
		÷		=	
		÷		=	
		÷		=	
		÷		=	
		÷		=	
		÷		=	
		÷		=	
		÷		=	

Converting a Trimmed and Cooked Weight to a Raw As-Purchased Weight

FORMULA 3: AS trimmed and cooked weight ÷ (Trim yield % × Cooked yield %) = AP weight

To complete this formula, you need to know what your cooked yield percentage is for the meat in question. This percentage depends on the degree of doneness desired, combined with the shape of the meat and your oven's tendency to shrink meats as they cook. Therefore, you must determine this percentage yourself by experience. (For example: Convection ovens can easily shrink meat that is cooked to medium rare in the center by 20 percent, resulting in a cooked yield percentage of 80 percent. In contrast, a slow-cooking oven may shrink meat cooked to medium rare by only 9 percent, resulting in a cooked yield percentage of 91 percent.)

To complete the formula:

1. Multiply your trim yield percentage (from Part I or based on your experience) by the cooked yield percentage. This will result in a new, combined percentage that is smaller than either of the two original percentages. It is called a *finished yield percentage*.

2. Divide the trimmed and cooked weight you need to serve by the finished yield percentage.

The answer will be the number of pounds of raw, as-purchased meat you need to buy or cost out.

Step 1 Table

Meat Item Name	Trim Yield %	×	Cooked Yield %	=	Finished Yield Percentage
		×		=	
		×		=	
		×		=	
		×		=	

Step 2 Table

Meat Item Name	Number of Pounds Needed, Cooked and Trimmed	÷	Finished Yield Percentage	=	AP in Pounds
		÷		=	
		÷		=	
		÷		=	
		÷		=	
		÷		=	

Purchasing Worksheet

11

Seafood

Finfish: Converting a Trimmed Fillet Weight to a Particular Market Form's Weight

FORMULA 1: AS pounds ÷ Fillet yield percentage = AP pounds

Divide the number of pounds of raw, trimmed fillet you need by its yield percentage, from Part I. The answer will be the number of pounds of fish you need to buy or cost out. Part I indicates what market form the fish in question is.

Name of Fish	Number of Pounds of Trimmed Fillet Needed	÷	Fillet Yield Percentage	=	AP in Pounds
		÷		=	
		÷		=	
		÷		=	
		÷		=	

Seafood Items Bought by Count

FORMULA 2: Items needed ÷ Count per AP unit measure = AP in purchase unit measures

Divide the total count needed by the number of items per purchase unit measure. Typically, a purchase unit measure will be 1 pound, but it may be another pack that weighs something other than a pound. To be clear, fill in the name of the purchase unit measure in the form below. The final answer will be the number of purchase unit measures you need to buy or cost out. This measure may not, however, be the actual pack (or purchase unit) you have to order. For instance, shrimp is often categorized by count per pound but is sold in 4-pound boxes rather than by individual pounds. See the shrimp example in the form.

Item Name	Purchase Unit Measure	Count Needed	÷	Count per Purchase Unit Measure	=	AP in Purchase Unit Measures
Shrimp, 16–20 ct.	4 lb. box	144	÷	72 per box	=	2
			÷		=	
			÷		=	
			÷		=	

NOTE

It is common practice among seafood processors to list a *range count* such as 16–20, rather than an exact number of items per purchase unit or purchase unit measure. In these situations, you need to decide on the specific number to use in order to make the purchasing formula work. Many food service professionals use a mid-range number (such as 18 in the example just given). It is up to you to decide. At some point, you should do exact counts to determine the true average counts for the items you buy by count.

Purchasing Worksheet

12

Poultry

CHICKEN

Food service professionals today often order their chicken already sized and cut up, for a very good reason: Modern poultry processors are very efficient and can sell individually cut and sized chicken parts at prices below what it would cost an independent food service operator to process from whole chickens (when the operator's labor costs are added to the base cost of the chicken). Another reason is that it is unusual for modern menus to feature all parts of the chicken: breasts, wings, thighs, and legs; typically only breasts and wings are found on today's menus. Consequently, few operators buy whole chickens anymore. They normally order a specific count of a particular size of chicken breast, and further specify it to be boneless and/or skinless.

Those operators who do order whole breasts process them in house, serve them boneless and skinless, and use the bones and skins in their stocks. They may also feature these "as-is" breasts on their menus as whole or "whole-halves." Wings are sold by size and may be whole or sectioned into drumettes (the first joint) and the second joint. Wing tips are often sold by themselves for use in stocks.

Certainly, operators do offer half- or quarter-chickens as menu items, but there is little need to perform purchasing formula calculations for those items, as they are sold by specific size and count per case and are offered on menus in much the same form without further cutting.

That said, some operators do order whole drumsticks and thighs and remove the bones and skins in house. They use the bones and skins for stocks and put the cleaned meat into dishes on their menus. When these dark meats are cleaned in house, the operator usually does so in order to obtain leg and thigh meat that has less sinew or cartilage than is usually found in "factory-bought" dark meat. However, this is a very laborious, and therefore not very cost-efficient process.

The poultry formulas in this worksheet will enable you to determine the relationship between whole chicken parts and the same parts trimmed (boneless/skinless).

Chicken: Converting Boneless, Skinless Pieces to Untrimmed, As-Purchased Pieces

FORMULA 1: Ounces of boneless, skinless pieces needed ÷ Yield percentage = AP in ounces

Here you add up the total ounce weight of the boneless/skinless pieces needed, then determine the yield percentage for the boneless/skinless pieces by dividing the trimmed weight by the untrimmed weight, from Part I.

For example, to compute this percentage for half breasts:

1. Go to Part I to find that the untrimmed weight is 8.7 ounces and the trimmed weight is 5.7 ounces, so:

$$5.7 \div 8.7 = 0.655 \text{ (or 65.5\%)}$$

The yield percentage for half breasts is 65.5 percent.

2. Divide the total number of ounces needed by the yield percentage. The answer will be the number of untrimmed ounces you need to buy or cost out.

Step 1 Table

Name of Trimmed Part Needed	Trimmed Ounce Weight of One Part	÷	Untrimmed Ounce Weight of One Part	=	Yield Percentage
		÷		=	
		÷		=	
		÷		=	
		÷		=	
		÷		=	

Step 2 Table

Name of Trimmed Part Needed	Total Trimmed Ounces Needed	÷	Yield Percentage	=	AP in Untrimmed Ounces
		÷		=	
		÷		=	
		÷		=	
		÷		=	
		÷		=	

TURKEY

A bone-on, skin-on turkey breast yields 73.6 percent of its original weight when boned and skinned. To convert a weight of raw, boneless, skinless breast meat to a weight of whole turkey breast(s), divide the as-served weight by 0.736.

Converting Boneless Skinless Turkey Breasts to Whole Turkey Breasts

FORMULA 2: AS or as-used pounds ÷ 0.736 = AP pounds whole turkey breast

As Served or As-Used Pounds	÷	.736	=	AP Pounds Whole Breasts
	÷	.736	=	
	÷	.736	=	
	÷	.736	=	
	÷	.736	=	
	÷	.736	=	
	÷	.736	=	
	÷	.736	=	
	÷	.736	=	
	÷	.736	=	
	÷	.736	=	
	÷	.736	=	
	÷	.736	=	
	÷	.736	=	
	÷	.736	=	
	÷	.736	=	
	÷	.736	=	
	÷	.736	=	
	÷	.736	=	
	÷	.736	=	

FORMULA 3: AS pounds ÷ (Trim yield % × Cooking yield %) = AP pounds

To calculate the weight of AP whole breasts from a needed weight of boneless, skinless cooked meat, follow this process:

1. Multiply your cooking yield percentage by the trim yield percentage.
2. Divide the weight you need to serve by the product of the two yield percentages. The answer will be the raw, AP weight of whole turkey breasts to order.

Your cooking yield percentage has to be calculated in your own kitchen, by dividing your cooked breast weight by the oven-ready breast weight.

Cooked Pounds	÷	Oven-Ready Weight	=	Cooking Yield Percentage
	÷		=	
	÷		=	
	÷		=	
	÷		=	
	÷		=	
	÷		=	
	÷		=	

To complete the formula, multiply the trim yield percentage (73.6 percent) by the cooking yield percentage and put the answer in the Cooked/Trimmed Yield Percentage column. Divide the number of pounds you need to serve by this combined percentage.

AS Pounds Trimmed and Cooked	÷	Cooked/Trimmed Yield Percentage (Finished Yield Percentage)	=	AP Pounds Whole Raw Turkey Breast
	÷		=	
	÷		=	
	÷		=	
	÷		=	
	÷		=	
	÷		=	
	÷		=	
	÷		=	

Converting Cooked and Carved Whole Turkey to AP Whole Turkey

FORMULA 4: AS pounds of cooked, carved turkey ÷ 0.363 = AP pounds whole turkey

On average, whole turkey, with giblets, will yield 36.3 percent in *carved*, cooked meat. To calculate the number of pounds of raw turkey to buy or cost out, divide the number of pounds of cooked, carved meat needed by 36.3 percent.

AS Pounds Cooked and Carved Meat	÷	.363	=	AP Pounds, with Giblets
	÷		=	
	÷		=	
	÷		=	
	÷		=	
	÷		=	
	÷		=	

Converting Cooked, Carved, and Pulled Turkey to AP Whole Turkey

FORMULA 5: AS pounds of cooked, carved, and *pulled* turkey ÷ 0.41 = AP pounds whole turkey

Whole turkeys, with giblets, yield additional weight of usable meat after carving. This meat has to be hand-pulled from the carcass. The pulled meat increases the total yield of cooked meat to 41 percent of the AP weight of the turkey. To calculate the number of pounds of raw turkey to buy or cost out, divide the number of pounds of cooked, carved, and pulled meat needed by 41 percent.

AS Pounds Cooked, Carved, Pulled Meat	÷	.41	=	AP Pounds, with Giblets
	÷		=	
	÷		=	
	÷		=	
	÷		=	
	÷		=	
	÷		=	

Purchasing Worksheet

13

Flavor Bases

Part I of *The Book of Yields* does not list flavor bases (chicken stock, beef stock, chocolate mousse, etc.), but you can use this worksheet to help you to convert a volume of food produced from a base back to the amount of the paste or powdered base you would need to buy or cost out.

The volume that a container of base will produce is always stated on the container. For instance, a 1-pound jar of chicken stock base will typically produce 5 gallons of finished stock.

To make this type of conversion, divide the number of fluid measures of the finished food you need by the number of the same fluid measure that the as-purchased weight of the base produces.

For instance, say you need 1 gallon of a finished stock made from a base. If 1 gallon equals 128 fluid ounces, and a pound of the base will produce 5 gallons, it will produce 640 fluid ounces. You divide the number of fluid ounces you need (128) by the number of fluid ounces produced by the 1-pound jar (640). Of course, you could also divide 1 gallon by the 5 gallons that one jar produces. Either way, you will get the same answer of 0.20:

$$128 \div 640 = 0.20 \quad \text{or} \quad 1 \div 5 = 0.20$$

The answer, 0.20 (or 20 percent) is the amount of the 1-pound jar you would need to use to make the 1 gallon of finished base. The following table illustrates this example: You need 1 gallon of finished stock. Your base comes in a 1-pound jar and yields 5 gallons. You will need 20 percent, or one-fifth, of one jar.

A Item Name	B Recipe Unit Volume Measures	C AP Unit (Jar, Can, Pound, etc.)	D Number of Recipe Unit Measures Needed	E ÷	F Number of Recipe Unit Measures Yielded by 1 AP Unit	G =	H Number of AP Units Needed (Jar, Can Pound, etc.)
Base Example	Fluid Ounce	1-Pound Jar	128	÷	640	=	0.20
				÷		=	
				÷		=	
				÷		=	

Note the following:

+ Column B states the type of measure you are working with in your recipe.
+ Column D states the number of these recipe unit measures you need.
+ Column C states the as-purchased unit of the base.
+ Column F states how many recipe unit measures are produced by using all of a single as-purchased unit—in this case, the entire 1-pound jar.

Purchasing Worksheet

14

Ingredient Aggregating Form

You will use this form to add up various amounts needed of the same food ingredient. Here's how:

1. Read all the recipes for an event or time period and record (in sequence) each recipe unit measure for the same ingredient.

2. Add up the amounts for each kind of measure (tablespoon, cup, ounce, pound, each, etc.) for each ingredient.

3. Combine the total number of each type of measure needed for the same ingredient and enter those numbers on their respective rows in the right-hand column of the form.

Item Name	Recipe Name	Recipe Unit Measure Type (Tablespoon, Cup, Ounce, Each, etc.)	Number of Measures	Total Number and Name of Each Measure Type Needed

Ingredient Aggregating Form

Item Name	Recipe Name	Recipe Unit Measure Type (Tablespoon, Cup, Ounce, Each, etc.)	Number of Measures	Total Number and Name of Each Measure Type Needed

Use the totals from this form as the recipe unit measure amounts needed in the various purchasing conversion worksheets. (PW 1-13)

Purchasing Worksheet

15 | Purchase Unit Measures Aggregating Form

This form is a tool you can use on an as-needed basis to record and combine your purchase unit measure conversion answers for the same food. For example, assume you have a number of recipes that call for an onion, but each measures the onion in a different way (whole, by the trimmed ounce, by the cup, chopped, etc.). In this case, you will have to convert each of those recipe unit measures to a single purchase unit measure, such as a pound. Here's how:

1. Complete the conversion for each recipe ingredient using the appropriate purchasing conversion worksheet. (Each conversion worksheet has a set of formula boxes, called tables, for each way that type of food is measured. Use the formula tables you need to calculate the equivalent purchase unit measure needed based on the recipe unit measures needed.)

2. List all your conversion answers for the same food, one after the other on this form. Then add them up to get a single total purchase unit measure.

3. In Purchasing Worksheet 16, Amounts Needed versus Par, write that total in column D and the name of the food item in column A.

Item Name	Purchase Unit Measure	Number of Measures Needed	Total Number of Purchase Unit Measures Needed

Purchasing Worksheet

16

Amounts Needed versus Par

You'll find the instructions for filling out this worksheet in the Purchasing Worksheets Overview, Steps 4, 5, and 6.

A Item Name	B Current Inventory Count (Amount on Hand)	C Inventory Count in Purchase Unit Measures (Pound, Gallon, Each, Piece, etc.)	D Current Need for Plan in Purchase Unit Measures		E Amount Remaining on Hand after Filling Current Need (B — D)	F Minimum Par Amount (Operation's Minimum Par for Item)	G Minimum Order to Return to Par or Make Plan (F — E)
Rice	50	pounds	— 30	=	20	40 lb.	20 lb.
			—	=			
			—	=			
			—	=			
			—	=			
			—	=			
			—	=			
			—	=			
			—	=			
			—	=			
			—	=			
			—	=			
			—	=			
			—	=			
			—	=			
			—	=			
			—	=			
			—	=			
			—	=			
			—	=			
			—	=			
			—	=			
			—	=			

Purchasing Worksheet

17

Inventory Form

To use this form, multiply the count on hand by the cost per unit of measure to calculate the extension.

Location: Date:

Item Name	Unit of Measure	Count on Hand	×	Cost per Unit of Measure	=	Extension
			×	$	=	$
			×	$	=	$
			×	$	=	$
			×	$	=	$
			×	$	=	$
			×	$	=	$
			×	$	=	$
			×	$	=	$
			×	$	=	$
			×	$	=	$
			×	$	=	$
			×	$	=	$
			×	$	=	$
			×	$	=	$
			×	$	=	$
			×	$	=	$
			×	$	=	$
			×	$	=	$
			×	$	=	$
			×	$	=	$
			×	$	=	$
			×	$	=	$
			×	$	=	$
			×	$	=	$
			×	$	=	$

Inventory Form

Location: Date:

Item Name	Unit of Measure	Count on Hand	×	Cost per Unit of Measure	=	Extension
			×	$	=	$
			×	$	=	$
			×	$	=	$
			×	$	=	$
			×	$	=	$
			×	$	=	$
			×	$	=	$
			×	$	=	$
			×	$	=	$
			×	$	=	$
			×	$	=	$
			×	$	=	$
			×	$	=	$
			×	$	=	$
			×	$	=	$
			×	$	=	$
			×	$	=	$
			×	$	=	$
			×	$	=	$
			×	$	=	$
			×	$	=	$
			×	$	=	$
			×	$	=	$
TOTAL This page				+	=	$

(Use on Final Page of Inventory)   Extension Totals of All Pages: $ _____

Purchasing Worksheet

18

Food Weight Log

You can use this log to record foods whose weights differ over the course of time per purchase unit, such as a bunch of fresh herbs or celery, heads of broccoli, cauliflower, cabbage, and the like.

Here are the instructions for using the form:

1. Reserve at least six rows for each food item.

2. Enter the item's purchase unit (bunch, piece, etc.).

3. Weigh each item as it is received, and record its average weight. For instance, for six bunches of parsley weighing a total of 27 ounces, divide 27 by 6 to get the average weight of 4.5 ounces per bunch.

4. Enter the date you log in each entry. This will give you seasonal variances.

5. In the last column, add up the averages for that item and divide the total by the number of entries to determine total running-average weight.

Item	Purchase Unit	Average Weight	Date	Running-Average Weight

Food Weight Log

Item	Purchase Unit	Average Weight	Date	Running-Average Weight

Purchasing Worksheet

19 | Purchase Unit Measures to Purchase Unit Packs

To use this worksheet to convert purchase unit measures to purchase unit packs, follow these steps:

1. Fill in columns A, B, and C from Worksheet 16, Amounts Needed versus Par.

2. Fill in the purchase unit pack measures from the Price List or your vendors' invoices.

3. Divide column B by column E. The answer is the exact equivalent number of purchase unit packs you need.

4. Record the answer from column F on the Food Order Form. There, round up the amount, if necessary.

A Item Name	B Amount Needed in Purchase Unit Measures	C Purchase Unit Measure (Ounce, Pound, Quart, Each, etc.)	D Purchase Unit Pack (Container, Flat, Bag, Case, Box, etc.)	E Number of Purchase Unit Measures in One Purchase Unit Pack	F Purchase Units Needed: Purchase Unit Measures Needed Divided by Purchase Unit Measures in One Purchase Pack (Column B divided by Column E)

Purchasing Worksheet

20

Food Order Form

You will use this form to round off and record your answers from Purchasing Worksheet 19, Purchase Unit Measures to Purchase Unit Packs.

To use this form properly, follow these steps:

1. In column A, enter the number of purchase units (purchase unit packs) to order.

2. In column B, enter the type of purchase unit—jar, case, head, pound, each, and so on.

3. In column C, enter the food item name. Be clear, specific, and brief.

4. In column D, enter the amount you pay for one purchase unit.

5. In column F, multiply column A times column D and enter your answer here.

6. In column E, enter the name of your vendor for this item. (This step is optional.)

If desired, you can use a separate page for each vendor.

NOTE

Purchase unit costs can be obtained from the Price List, previous invoices, or your vendors' price sheets.

A Amount	B AP Unit	C Item Name	D AP Unit Cost	E Total: (A × D = E)	F Vendor
			$	$	
			$	$	
			$	$	
			$	$	
			$	$	
			$	$	
			$	$	
			$	$	
			$	$	
			$	$	
			$	$	
			$	$	
			$	$	
			$	$	
		Total This Page		$	

Total Order (All Pages): $ _____

Purchasing Worksheet

21

Trimmed versus Untrimmed Prices

Many food distributors offer foods in both a raw, untrimmed form and as a trimmed item. For instance, chicken breasts can be purchased with the skin and bones on, as boneless breasts, or as boneless-and-skinless breasts. Similarly, broccoli can be bought in whole heads, as broccoli crowns (with much of the stalks removed), or as broccoli florets (just the heads, cut into small pieces).

The more your supplier trims or otherwise prepares these foods for you, the higher will be the price per unit for the pre-prepared (trimmed) food as compared to the price per unit of the untrimmed food. Because you will have to buy more of the untrimmed food in order to end up with the trimmed amount needed, you will buy greater quantities of the untrimmed food. For instance, you will need to buy about 25 pounds of raw carrots to end up with 20 pounds of trimmed carrots. The question that a chef must answer is: Should I buy 20 pounds of trimmed carrots or 25 pounds, untrimmed?

When you are deciding whether to buy trimmed or untrimmed food, and are mainly basing your decision on the price differences between the two, how do you figure the point at which the trimmed food is, if ever, less expensive than the untrimmed food? The guiding formulas that answer this question follow.

When the untrimmed price percentage (UPP) is greater than the trim yield percentage (TYP), the trimmed food has a lower food cost. When the UPP is less than TYP, the untrimmed food has a lower food cost. Here's a fuller explanation of what these formulas mean:

+ UPP is the percentage the untrimmed price is of the trimmed price. You get it by dividing the untrimmed price per unit by the trimmed price per unit. For example, if an untrimmed price per pound is 45 cents, and the trimmed price is 65 cents, you divide 45 by 65 to get 69.2 percent, the UPP. The first formula says that when the UPP is greater than the TYP, the trimmed food has a lower food cost.

+ TYP is the yield percentage you get when you trim a food; it represents what's left for use after peeling, coring, and so on. Part I is full of trim yield percentages, so you should be familiar with them by now. The second formula says that when the UPP is less than the TYP, the untrimmed food has a lower food cost.

Example

Given: You You have a food item that you trim in order to use, say carrots. You normally peel these carrots and trim off their ends before adding them to recipes. Part I shows that medium-sized carrots have a trim yield of 81.3 percent. That means that after trimming 10 pounds of carrots you will get 8.13 pounds of trimmed carrots to use in recipes. Now a supplier tells you that it has trimmed-and-peeled carrots for 65 cents per pound, or raw and untrimmed carrots for 45 cents a pound. Which should you buy? Do the math.

NOTE

The worksheet at the end of this section will help you to quickly determine whether the UPP is greater or less than the TYP.

Calculate the UPP: Divide the 45-cents price for the raw food by the 65-cents price for the trimmed food.

$.45 ÷ $.65 = 0.692

The UPP is 69.2 percent.

Notice that this is less than the trim yield percentage of 81.3 percent; therefore, the total cost of the raw carrots you need should be less than the cost of the trimmed carrots. To prove this, now assume you need to use 20 pounds of trimmed carrots. Note that you'll need to buy more than 20 pounds of untrimmed carrots to end up with 20 pounds of trimmed carrots. This is where you'll use the most fundamental purchasing formula from Part I to determine how much raw food to buy, based on the need for a trimmed amount. The formula is:

As-served amount ÷ Yield percentage = As-purchased amount

or:

AS ÷ Y% = AP

You divide the number of pounds you need in your recipe as-served by the carrots' trim yield percentage (of 81.3 percent). The answer is the number of pounds of as-purchased, raw, untrimmed carrots you need to buy. In this case, the as-served amount is 20 pounds and the trim yield is 81.3 percent. So, plugging these figures into the purchasing formula, AS ÷ Y% = AP, you get:

20 lb. ÷ 0.813 = 24.6 lb.

You need to buy 24.6 pounds of raw carrots to end up with 20 pounds, trimmed. And the untrimmed carrots cost 45 cents per pound, so your cost for untrimmed carrots is:

$.45 × 24.6 = $11.07

The cost of the trimmed and peeled carrots is 65 cents per pound, which means you only have to buy 20 pounds, since they are already trimmed. Therefore:

20 lb. × $.65 = $13.00

The trimmed carrots will cost you $13.00, so by buying the untrimmed carrots, you would save the difference between $13.00 and $11.07 ($1.93). In this case, the UPP for carrots was 62.9 percent, which is less than the 81.3 percent TYP. This verifies the guiding formula "when UPP is less than TYP, the untrimmed food has a lower food cost."

Let's take another look at the same scenario but with the situation reversed. That is, assume the UPP is greater than the TYP. In this case, we'll say the price per pound for the trimmed carrots is 50 cents and that the cost of the untrimmed carrots is the same as in the previous example, 45 cents per pound. Therefore, the new UPP would be 90 percent. Remember, the UPP is found by dividing the untrimmed unit cost by the trimmed unit cost:

45 ÷ 50 = 0.90

The TYP for raw carrots does not change; it is still 81.3 percent, which is less than the UPP of 90 percent. So, in this case, the trimmed food should prove to be less costly than the untrimmed food. Does it? Yes. And here is why: If you multiply the new price per pound for the trimmed carrots—50 cents—by the 20 pounds needed, you get a total cost for the trimmed carrots of $10.00 (20 pounds × 0.50 = $10.00). Since the cost of the untrimmed carrots stays the same at $11.07, the cost of the trimmed food is lower than that of the untrimmed food.

Other Considerations

Going back to the first scenario, the cost of the trimmed carrots was $1.93 higher than the cost of the untrimmed carrots. Now let's consider what would be the cost of peeling the 24.6 pounds of carrots. Peeling nearly 25 pounds of carrots is no small job and will probably cost you more in labor than $1.93. Remember, though, that labor-saving costs have to add up to become *real;* that is, when you actually don't pay for the time it takes to peel the carrots. If your cook is not going to be taken off the clock, then you are still paying that half-hour's wage—you just move that cook to another task. Labor savings truly kick in when you cut someone's hours or eliminate a position altogether. Still, buying pre-prepared items can mean real savings when they enable you to prepare a menu with fewer cooks and in less time than by using fresh, untrimmed foods—*scratch ingredients.*

Of course, there are other reasons to buy pre-prepared items. Sometimes the cooking skills needed to make certain dishes are not available in certain labor markets. Also, many menu items that used to be made on-site—baking items, for instance—are now bought in a nearly finished state. So-called proof-and-bake breads and rolls, cheesecakes, pie fillings, and others come to mind. In many cases, these products not only eliminate the need for special skills, but also save time, equipment, energy, and space, and may reduce your inventory and the number of vendors you have to manage.

Nevertheless, deciding whether to use these pre-prepared *convenience items* can be complex, extending beyond purely economic considerations. Your chef may object to using them for many subjective as well as marketing reasons. Convenience items are seldom found in high-end restaurants. (These restaurants do, of course, charge higher menu prices to cover their higher labor and operating costs.) Most restaurants today use a combination of scratch ingredients and convenience items, including precut or trimmed fresh vegetables and meats. Using some pre-prepared items enables a kitchen with limited space and staff to produce a greater variety of menu items than would be possible if they had to use all scratch ingredients.

Other times, these items are used simply because it makes sense to do so. If you serve only a boneless, skinless 5-ounce chicken breast and you have no need for the chicken bones and skins, then it makes sense to consider buying the breasts already cut to size and trimmed the way you want them.

Using the Trimmed versus Untrimmed Pricing Worksheet

By using this worksheet, you can easily determine whether the UPP (Untrimmed Price Percentage) is greater or less than the food's TYP (Trim Yield Percentage). Remember, the UPP is the unit price of the untrimmed food divided by the unit price of the trimmed food. Thus:

+ If column F (UPP) is greater than column G (TYP), the trimmed food has a lower cost.
+ If column G is greater than column F, the untrimmed food has a lower cost. Take these steps to fill out the form:

1. In column A, write in the food item name.
2. In column B, enter the price of the untrimmed item's purchase unit measure (usually per pound).
3. In column D, enter the price of the trimmed item's purchase unit measure (usually per pound).
4. In column F, divide column B by column D. Enter the answer in column F.
5. In column G, enter the trim yield percentage for the food item, from Part I.
6. In column H, note which form of the food, trimmed or untrimmed, has a lower food cost. Enter a "T" if the trimmed food has a lower food cost and a "U" if the untrimmed food has a lower food cost. Remember:

+ If column F (UPP) is greater than column G (TYP), the trimmed food has a lower cost.
+ If column G is greater than column F, the untrimmed food has a lower cost.

A Item Name	B Untrimmed Unit Price	C ÷	D Trimmed Unit Price	E =	F Untrimmed Price %	G Trim Yield %	H Lower Food Cost: Trimmed or Untrimmed
		÷		=			
		÷		=			
		÷		=			
		÷		=			
		÷		=			
		÷		=			
		÷		=			
		÷		=			
		÷		=			
		÷		=			